The Allergy
BIBLE

Understanding • Diagnosing • Treating
Allergies and intolerances

The Allergy BIBLE

LINDA GAMLIN

CONSULTANT: **PROFESSOR JONATHAN BROSTOFF**

QUADRILLE

Editorial Director: Jane O'Shea

Creative Director: Mary Evans

Art Director: Helen Lewis

Project Editor: Hilary Mandleberg

Art Editor: Sue Storey

Production: Julie Hadingham

Picture Research: Nadine Bazar

Picture Assistant: Sarah Airey

First published in 2001 by Quadrille Publishing Limited
Alhambra House
27–31 Charing Cross Road
London WC2H 0LS

British Library Cataloguing-in-Publication Data
A catalogue record for this book is available from the
British Library.

ISBN 1 902757 54 8

Printed and bound in Italy by
Arnoldo Mondadori Spa, Verona

contents

Chapter 1
what is allergy?

Words matter, particularly in medicine. Using the same words to mean different things is a major difficulty for patients when discussing allergies with a doctor. Unfortunately, few patients realise this, and doctors are frequently too busy to explain what they themselves mean. The result can be a great deal of misunderstanding, confusion and mutual irritation.

Unclear meanings can also create problems if you start exploring other treatment options. The word 'allergy' is like one of those cats that eat at six different houses in the neighbourhood: everyone feels as if they own it exclusively. A conventional allergist will understand one thing by 'allergy', while a more unorthodox doctor may have a broader definition, and a herbalist or naturopath may be using the word in a completely different way again.

This is an absolute jungle for the medically unqualified, and it can be an expensive jungle if you are looking around for an answer to your health problems. With the help of this book, you should be able to make sense of all this, and understand the seemingly contradictory advice on offer.

The word **allergy** was coined in 1906 when it was used to mean altered reactivity – any change in the way the body responds to the environment, whether immunity to a disease already encountered, or a sudden fit of sneezing from pollen. Immunity to disease was soon shunted off into a separate category

altogether, leaving allergy with a narrower meaning: *any adverse reaction to substances that are normally harmless* – definition 1. In this book, that meaning is covered by the word **sensitivity**.

One group of American doctors, who later became known as clinical ecologists, stuck with this definition. Their broad view of allergy is still found among some other doctors today, generally those whose approach to medicine is fairly unorthodox. It is a concept of allergy that is also shared by most practitioners of alternative or complementary therapists.

The rift between the clinical ecologists and mainstream medicine came in the 1920s when the definition of allergy used by conventional doctors was narrowed further to mean *reactions to harmless items where the immune system is definitely involved* – definition 2. The term **immune sensitivity** is used in this book to convey that meaning.

In the 1960s, conventional allergists narrowed the definition of allergy again. It was an exciting time because the antibody known as IgE (sometimes called the allergy antibody – see box on p. 12) had just been discovered. The new, tighter meaning of allergy was *reactions to harmless items where IgE is involved* – definition 3.

If asked to define allergy, most doctors would give the second of these definitions. (Although they might prefer not to think about the fact that this definition, applied logically, includes coeliac disease – see p. 70.)

However, when they talk of 'a tendency to allergy', 'allergy treatment' or 'the allergy epidemic', doctors are generally using the third definition, and just mean IgE-mediated allergy. They may not be conscious of the fact that they are switching from one definition to another. This is not an ideal situation but, generally speaking, it does not create too many problems.

This book deals with 'allergy' in the very broadest sense of the word – all kinds of sensitivity. However – and this is purely for the purposes of clarity – where the word **allergy** is used in the text it always means **IgE-mediated allergy** (definition 3).

Other immune-mediated problems are called **non-IgE immune sensitivity** in this book.

Finally, any reaction where the immune system has no proven central role is called an **intolerance**. (As for other technical words, if you want to find the full definition, look in the index and turn to the page number shown in bold type.)

If you are reading widely on this topic, you may come across sensitivity used either according to definition 1 above, or as a synonym for intolerance. You may also encounter the word **hypersensitivity**. This is actually a precise medical term (see p. 18), but be warned that some writers use 'hypersensitivity' very loosely to mean just 'sensitivity' (definition 1).

Remember that medical politics and economics are powerful forces in all this debate over meanings. Words are quite often redefined by medical interest groups (such as professional associations) with the clear intention of staking out territory and claiming sole access to medical truth. What is at stake, ultimately, is the right of different doctors to treat patients with certain conditions – and the right of patients to choose for themselves. To add to the longstanding battle over 'allergy', there are now rival claims about the meaning of intolerance (see p. 74) which have distinctly political overtones.

When you talk with doctors, using the most appropriate terms will help enormously. Talking to a mainstream doctor about 'food allergy' when the symptoms suggest food intolerance, for example, is very likely to cause annoyance. This not unreasonable because IgE-mediated food allergy, unlike food intolerance, is a disease that can very suddenly kill an otherwise healthy person. Using the term 'food allergy' for a headache or mild bowel symptoms is, doctors feel, trivialising a potentially fatal condition.

The important thing is to get along well and communicate clearly with doctors, not to get into a battle about what words mean (in that sense, words *don't* matter – they are just labels). Avoid using the word 'allergy' unless you are sure it fits in with your doctor's perception of what is wrong. Just describing how you react – the actual symptoms – is usually the best approach. If you need a general word for your condition, 'sensitive' is usually a much more diplomatic choice than 'allergic'.

Allergies and inheritance
WHY IT RUNS IN FAMILIES

'My father had asthma as a child, and his sister had it too. In fact she died from it. My mother has never had any allergies, but one of her brothers had terrible hayfever all his life. Out of us four, only my brother Peter is completely allergy-free. I had bad eczema when I was small, as did my sister. So when our son developed eczema, and then asthma, and an allergy to house-dust mite which made his nose run all the time, I wasn't entirely surprised.' What Janey is describing is a good example of an **atopic family** – one where classical allergies, of one kind or another, affect several family members. The members of such a family are called **atopics**.

Atopics have an underlying tendency to allergy which, with luck, may never be expressed. But if they are unlucky, the tendency will lead to allergies, which can settle on the skin (atopic eczema), the nose (hayfever or perennial allergic rhinitis), the airways (asthma) or the mouth and digestive tract (food allergy). These diseases, which recur down the generations in atopic families like Janey's, are known as the **classical allergic diseases.**

The atopic tendency is coded into our DNA – in the genes that are passed from parent to child. There are also other genes that make asthma more likely to develop, and these can work in concert with the allergy-promoting genes to produce asthma in a child. And there are probably genes for dry skin, which contribute to atopic eczema.

Genes alone are not enough, however. Environment (which means, in medical terms, *everything* external that affects an individual, including diseases, diet, air, allergens such as dust mite or pollen, and even medical treatment) also plays a large part in promoting allergic reactions. In other words, genes and the external world interact to produce allergic disease. What happens in the months and years immediately after birth seems to be a crucial element.

This helps to explain why allergies are on the increase even though we are, genetically speaking, not so different from our grandparents or great-grandparents. It is also a cause for optimism, since it means we can largely reverse the trend in coming generations. All we have to do is adjust the environment, especially for newborns and young children. Luckily, most of the problem factors are ones over which we have personal control, such as smoking by parents, diet, infant feeding, hygiene (*less* is better), antibiotic treatment, house design and furnishings (see pp. 11–12).

As unique as a fingerprint

Generally speaking, inherited traits such as height or skin colour are governed, not by a single gene with a large effect, but by a great many genes each with a small effect. The many small effects add up to produce the final outcome. Atopy is probably inherited in a similar way, which would explain why some people have a very strong tendency to allergies (they have lots of the wrong genes) while other people have only a mild tendency (they have just a few).

Current estimates hold that at least twenty different genes are involved in determining atopy. This means that no two atopic individuals are going to be quite the same, because each will have a different combination of the possible variants on these twenty genes. In the words of Dr Vincent Beltrani, of Columbia University, New York, 'it is not surprising that, as a result of all the possible genetic combinations and permutations, each atopic individual possesses a unique "allergic fingerprint" and that not all atopic individuals have identical findings'.

Multi-gene inheritance has another important effect, in terms of predicting who will develop allergies. The genetic risks from the two parents add up, so if both parents have allergies themselves or come from atopic families, the risks of the child developing allergies are much higher than if only one parent is atopic. The actual figures are uncertain because the results vary considerably from one study to another. If one parent is atopic, the risk can range from 20% to 58%, whereas if both parents are atopic, the risk ranges from 50% to 80% or even more.

Note that these are just *risks* – there are no certainties here because the actual mix of genes that a child receives is a selection – half of the mother's genes and half of the father's. There's no saying which half a child gets, because this is a random selection process, similar to the shuffling and dealing of playing cards. Luck plays a big part.

Naturally enough, both atopic parents and their doctors have asked whether there is any test that could assess the number of pro-allergy genes in a newborn and so predict the chances of allergy developing in particular children. That would allow more stringent anti-allergy measures (see pp. 238–47) to be taken for the children most at risk.

Various tests have been tried, and one does work, to a limited extent. It involves measuring the level of the allergy antibody, IgE, in a blood sample taken from the umbilical cord just after birth. Very high levels of IgE give some indication of the chances of allergies developing later, but the accuracy of the prediction is, unfortunately, not that good when the test is carried out in atopic families. The test doesn't reveal much more than is already known – that the baby has atopic parents.

This same test, when carried out on newborns who are *not* from atopic families, sometimes gives a much more useful and accurate result. In one study, 75% of those babies with high levels of cord-blood IgE developed allergies a few years later, compared to only 6% of those with low levels. Unfortunately, the test does not always give such impressive results, and some disappointing studies have led doctors to conclude that it is not worthwhile as a standard test for all newborns.

This finding of high IgE in children from non-atopic families highlights an important point: pro-allergy genes are everywhere. A lot of healthy people have them, but at levels which do not cause any symptoms – yet. This explains why, with the allergy epidemic, many new allergy sufferers are coming from families never affected by allergy before. As our lifestyle becomes more pro-allergy, a baby needs fewer of the pro-allergy genes to grow into an allergic individual.

Other forms of sensitivity

The multi-gene inheritance of classical allergy is very different from the inheritance of diseases such as primary lactase deficiency (see p. 79) where there is a single gene that is at fault. Generally, speaking, all **metabolic abnormalities** (see box on p. 75) are inherited in this straightforward way, so they are an all-or-nothing affair: one child in the family gets the defective gene while another does not. No environmental triggers are needed to activate the defect.

In the case of food intolerance, if minor metabolic abnormalities play a part, as they may do for some sufferers, then there could be inheritance of the defect, but this will not necessarily lead to symptoms unless other intolerance-promoting factors (such as disturbed gut flora) are present. Those who suffer from both food intolerance and chemical intolerance (also called chemical sensitivity) are the most likely to have metabolic abnormalities, and it is interesting that such problems do sometimes affect several members of the same family. (Doctors who are sceptical about such diseases will dismiss this as simply 'learned illness behaviour' among family members, a theory that is difficult to test without a lot of expensive research.)

Inheritance plays a part in several other forms of sensitivity. It is very important, for example, in coeliac disease and dermatitis herpetiformis (see p. 70), which both stem from the same genetic feature. They are only expressed when wheat is eaten but the timing is important here – introducing wheat into a child's diet later, rather than during the first year of life, seems less likely to provoke the disease. When coeliac disease comes on in adult life, as it sometimes does, it suggests that some other environmental trigger was needed, in addition to eating wheat, to start off the disease process.

A mast cell, magnified about 10,000 times. The black granules contain histamine.

How does allergy begin?

'At the beginning, I thought I just had a cold. I kept sneezing and coughing, and my nose was dripping. It got better at the weekend, and I thought – that's good, it's gone – but then on the Monday evening it started up again. The next thing I knew, I kept getting breathless. I'd been at the sawmill a month when it began. We were cutting planks of red cedar all day, and the dust was bad, it's true. But I didn't know that saw-dust could cause you allergies. We were given dust masks, but they made you too hot. No one wore them. I found out later, from the doctor, that some men could work years at it before they got allergic to the dust, but with me it was just a month.'

Like many people with work-related allergy, Dan can actually pinpoint the time he became sensi-tised – when he began making IgE antibodies against the red cedar dust allergen. For allergies that are not caused by workplace allergens, this is rarely possible. The moment when symptoms begin may be obvious, but that is often long after sensitisation (making IgE to the allergen) first occurred. Long-term studies of children show that they may start giving positive skin-prick tests to pollens (a sign that they are making IgE to those pollens) while they are toddlers, but not develop hayfever until ten years later.

The basics of immunity

The **immune system** defends the body against infections and cancerous cells. One of its key jobs, before going on the offensive, is to recognise the difference between:
- self and non-self (e.g. the cells lining the lung, and bacteria trying to infect the lung)
- safe-non-self (e.g. a sandwich) and dangerous-non-self (e.g. *Salmonella* bacteria in the sandwich).

Through mis-regulation the immune system can cause:
- **allergies** (perceiving safe-non-self, such as pollen, as dangerous-non-self)
- **autoimmune diseases** (perceiving self as non-self).

The immune system consists of dozens of different kinds of cells (the **immune cells**) and a number of different **antibodies** – specialised 'guided missiles' (see box on p. 15) which are produced by certain immune cells.

There is also a huge array of **messenger chemicals**, which send general instructions (e.g. 'calm down!', 'go for it!' or 'exterminate!') from one type of cell to another.

Immune cells are self-contained units, many of them mobile and dispersed throughout the body. They travel around in the blood, and can move out of the blood vessels and into the surrounding tissues (skin, lung, nose, etc.).

These different components – immune cells, antibodies and messenger chemicals – interact in very complex ways. When an **immune reaction** occurs – i.e. the immune system recognises something, or mounts an attack on something – numerous different players are involved. All the reactions described in this book are very simplified versions of what actually happens.

Research shows that the first two years of life is the most vulnerable time as regards sensitisation to allergens. Very often, sensitisation occurs in the first few months, and sometimes even before birth.

Why is a young infant so easily sensitised? The answer lies not with the baby, but with the pregnant mother-to-be, whose immune system has to over-rule its natural inclination to attack anything that is non-self. Potentially, a woman's immune system could reject a foetus in just the same way that heart transplants are rejected. To prevent attacks on the foetus, the immune system is re-tuned during pregnancy, with one aspect of immunity – the part that's most keen to attack a foreign body – being damped down.

This aspect of immunity is coordinated by cells known as T-helper-1 cells, or Th1 cells for short. To protect the foetus, these Th1 cells are asked to ease up during pregnancy. Meanwhile, since immune protection is still needed, their colleagues, called T-helper-2 cells or Th2 cells, become more active.

The classical allergic diseases

These four pages are concerned only with the classical allergic diseases, that is:

hayfever (an allergy to pollen)

perennial allergic rhinitis (a nasal allergy to a year-round allergen such as house-dust mite)

asthma where this includes an allergic reaction

atopic eczema (see p. 42)

urticaria (nettle rash) where this is allergic in origin, and the accompanying **angioedema** (swelling due to fluid escaping from tiny blood vessels into the surrounding area; it is sometimes called 'water retention')

anaphylaxis (a violent allergic reaction to food, insect stings, penicillin, latex, etc.)

food allergy (in most cases, an immediate and marked reaction to food, with symptoms in the mouth; there may also be anaphylaxis).

Running the immune system

T-helper cells are, in a way, mis-named, because they do not help at all – they just give orders.

These are the supervisors of the immune reactions, telling other immune cells either to lie low or to get busy. Where Th1 and Th2 cells differ is in the types of immune cells they send into action. Among those who get their go-ahead from Th1 cells are immune cells that attack directly, without producing antibodies – these are the ones that reject transplants and could, if given free rein, reject a foetus or retard its growth.

The Th2 cells, on the other hand, have among their preferred troops the immune cells that produce IgE antibodies – the allergy-causing anti-bodies. So one effect of protecting the foetus from rejection is to push the immune system towards a greater tendency to allergy.

This shift of emphasis occurs in the mother's immune system, but it carries over into the immune system of the foetus because they are sharing the same blood supply, and the blood contains the messenger substances which fine-tune the immune system. Immediately after birth, the baby's immune system is still following the same pattern, continuing to upregulate Th2 cells and downregulate Th1 cells. This is a crucial factor in setting the stage for allergic sensitisation.

Ideally, the world that the baby encounters just after birth should nudge the immune system in the opposite direction and get it operating in a non-allergic way. But the world in which we live is far from ideal in this regard.

For one thing, it is much too clean. As far as the immune system is concerned, 'ideal' would mean encountering quite a bit of dirt, such as garden soil, in the early stages of life. The soil contains harmless bacteria which do not cause any symptoms, but do tweak the immune system towards Th1 cells and away from Th2 cells. Bacterial products in household dust may do the same thing (see p. 21).

A long period of consuming nothing but breast milk would also suit the baby's immune system rather better than being fed on cow's milk formula or being suddenly weaned onto a number of highly allergenic foods, such as egg, wheat, soy (ubiquitous

What is an allergic reaction?

The basic cause of classical allergy is an immune reaction involving mast **cells** and **IgE antibodies**.

Mast cells are plentiful in the lining of the nose, the airways, and the digestive tract. They have counterparts in the blood, called **basophils**.

Seen under the microscope, both mast cells and basophils look very granular inside. The granules are tiny storage compartments, containing stockpiles of messenger chemicals, notably **histamine**.

Histamine causes several different reactions:

- contraction of muscle around the airways. This reduces the diameter of the airway, producing an asthma attack.
- widening of blood vessels
- increased leakiness of the smallest blood vessels, allowing fluid and immune cells to escape into the surrounding area – for example, the skin or airway lining
- as a result of these two above effects, local swelling (called oedema or angioedema) and irritation – in the skin this is experienced as urticaria, or nettle rash, in the nose it causes blockage, itching and sneezing
- if sufficient histamine is released into the blood, a drastic fall in blood pressure, due to widespread opening of blood vessels, and leakage of fluid into the tissues; this occurs in anaphylaxis (see p. 58).

Histamine is released when mast cells are activated, a process called **degranulation** because the cells discharge their storage granules.

Mast cells release other substances at the same time, some of which attract more immune cells to the area, causing more inflammation. They help to produce a 'Late Phase Reaction' which occurs after the initial allergic reaction has died down, and lasts about 24 hours (see p. 13). Once activated, mast cells also start making messenger chemicals called **leukotrienes** which are highly inflammatory.

What causes a mast cell to degranulate? The answer is found on the surface of the cells, where the allergy antibody, IgE, sits. One end of the IgE molecule is bound to the mast cell, and the other end can bind to the allergen concerned. In someone allergic to egg, for example, egg allergen will bind, with great specificity, to egg-specific IgE antibody.

For the receptors to pass a message to the mast cell there have to be two IgE antibodies specific for the same allergen on the mast cell – and the allergen has to bind to both these IgE molecules, cross-linking them. This is the 'go' signal for the mast cell to degranulate.

in processed foods), fish or peanuts, before it can handle them. Not taking antibiotics before two years of age would also help (although it might, of course, be very bad for the baby in other ways). Exactly why is not yet fully understood (see p. 247).

An ideal world for the immune system would also lack the by-products of cigarette smoking, whether in the blood of a pregnant woman or in the air that a baby breathes – both seem to promote the allergic tendency. In addition, the perfect world would lack central heating, fitted carpets, draught-proofing and thick upholstery. A house like this is heaven for house-dust mites but not for innocent young immune systems.

The problem with house-dust mites – apart from the fact that they breed like wildfire, and hole-up in mattresses, armchairs and soft toys – is that they produce a highly allergenic protein in their droppings. This protein interferes with the membranes of cells, making them less stable. It irritates various immune cells, including mast cells (see box), and can even make mast cells degranulate, as if there were a true allergic reaction happening.

Once mast cells have done this, they release messenger substances that arouse the immune system and make a genuine allergic reaction – beginning with the production of IgE to the dust-mite allergen – much more likely. In other words, dust-mite allergen is an *agent provocateur*, an aggressive substance that actually provokes the immune system into reacting allergically.

Until recently it was widely assumed that allergens were just inoffensive, passive substances which the immune system happened to take objection to, in a distinctly unreasonable way. The new discoveries about dust-mite allergen raise the question: could other allergens be more aggressive than previously thought? Certainly the peanut allergen, or other substances found in peanuts, seems to destabilise cell membranes, which may explain why this powerful allergen so easily sensitises young children.

The role of genes

Faced with this non-ideal world, many children pull through without developing allergies, but others do not. This is where genes come in, making one child more susceptible to our allergy-promoting lifestyle and another child less so. Exactly how the genes make this difference is still not fully understood, but there are at least twenty genes involved (see p. 9), and it is clearly going to be a complex story. The overall effect of these genes is a greater tendency to make IgE, combined with mast cells and basophils (see box on p. 12) that are distinctly trigger-happy – much more eager to degranulate than in healthy individuals.

Given all the mayhem caused by mast cells and IgE, why does the body produce them at all? They cause a lot of damage to allergy sufferers and do little apparent good, at least for people in the Western world. The value of the mast-cell-IgE-reaction, for most of us, is historical – it wages war against large-bodied parasites such as tapeworms and schistosomes. (They are large by comparison with bacteria and viruses, and not easily tackled by other immune cells.) These unpleasant invaders have largely been eliminated in the developed world but are still rife in other countries. For millions of years such parasites were an inevitable part of human life, and this bit of our evolutionary past survives in our immune system.

The complexity of allergic reactions

'Each time the pollen season came around, I would start to get these pains, especially in my knees. I asked my doctor about it but she just looked at me rather oddly and said "take a paracetamol". I couldn't be sure it was linked to my hayfever, but the pains always came on just after the sneezing started. One year, it was all worse than usual, and I felt very tired too. My face was all puffy and I could feel that something was seriously amiss. That, as I now know, was because my kidneys were being affected. It was years before the doctor would refer me to an allergist, and I actually got an explanation for all this. I think for a long time my doctor thought I was making it up, or just imagining the pain in my knees.'

Karen suffers from a rare complication of hayfever involving an overload of pollen antigens and antibodies in the blood. Very large numbers of both are involved, and are bound to each other in dense tangled masses called immune complexes. Because these are carried around in the blood they are known as **circulating immune complexes**. They may be too large to be cleared quickly by the normal junk-munching systems that keep the blood clean.

Like a river choked with fallen leaves, which deposits some of the debris on its banks as it flows past, the blood inevitably

The other antibodies

Other than IgE, four main types of antibody exist – IgA, IgD, IgG and IgM. Although some of these antibodies help fight bacterial and viral diseases, they lack IgE's ability to tackle certain large parasites. These other antibodies do not generally bind to mast cells, and therefore do not cause IgE-style allergy. But they can be involved in various other sensitivity reactions – it is IgG antibodies that are active in coeliac disease for example, and IgA in dermatitis herpetiformis. And any kind of antibody can participate in circulating immune complexes, causing multiple symptoms (see below).

leaves behind some of the circulating immune complexes. They mostly become deposited in the tiny blood vessels called capillaries, particularly those in the skin, the kidneys and the joints. Inflammation (see p. 140) here can cause a range of symptoms.

This problem is known to doctors either as **serum sickness** or as **Type III hypersensitivity**. It is a well-known feature of several infections and of some autoimmune diseases.

Unfortunately, the potential for Type III hypersensitivity in allergies such as hayfever is much less well known among doctors, as Karen discovered. As well as affecting hayfever sufferers, Type III hypersensitivity can also be a complication of reactions to penicillin and certain other allergic reactions, such as insect-sting allergy.

When a reaction occurs to snake anti-venom – and it only occurs in an individual who has received snake anti-venom before – this too is Type III hypersensitivity. The snake anti-venom is cultured in horses, and the snake-bitten human who has received the snake anti-venom previously mounts a massive immune reaction *to the horse proteins* when snake anti-venom is injected for a second time. Large and numerous circulating immune complexes are formed, and although IgE is not involved, a very severe anaphylactoid reaction (see box on p. 59) follows.

Circulating immune complexes do not affect most allergy sufferers. But there are other immune responses that follow on from the initial allergic response in *everyone* with allergies – they are generally summed up as the '**Late Phase Reaction**'. This reaction starts 4–12 hours after the exposure to the allergen, and lasts about a day. It involves a number of different immune cells (including eosinophils – p. 19) and an even more varied array of messenger chemicals, making everything very complicated for medical researchers to investigate. When allergic symptoms become entrenched and difficult to treat, the Late Phase Reaction is usually implicated. But it has not been given much attention by doctors until recently, because the details are so complex and so poorly understood.

Cross-reactions in allergy

For the rabbi's doctor, discussing the results of the allergy tests with his patient, it was an embarrassing moment. An allergy is not inborn, it is an acquired reaction – a response by the immune system to a substance it has already encountered at least once. So, in theory, nobody can be allergic to a food they have never eaten.

Naturally enough, the rabbi had never eaten shellfish – like pork, it is a forbidden food in Judaism. But the nurse carrying out the skin-prick tests was unaware of this, and she had been told to test for all the common food allergens, so shrimp allergen was included. The test came up positive.

Fortunately, the rabbi had also been tested for inhaled allergens and had given a very strong positive reaction to house-dust mite. The likely explanation was clear: the rabbi had formed antibodies to a muscle protein of house-dust mite called tropomyosin, which is also found in shrimps and prawns. His antibodies against house-dust mite had cross-reacted with shrimp tropomyosin.

This does not mean that everyone who is allergic to house-dust mite will also react to shrimp. Firstly they must have made antibodies to tropomyosin, rather than some other dust-mite antigen. Secondly, the antibodies must be recognising a particular feature of dust-mite tropomyosin that closely resembles (chemically speaking) a particular feature of shrimp tropomyosin.

The important point about antibodies is that, on the one hand, they achieve results by being specific for their antigen (see box on p. 15), but on the other hand, they do make mistakes. In the case of allergies, this is sometimes an added problem for patients but is rarely life threatening. More seriously, there are other conditions, like coeliac disease, where cross-reactions initiate attacks on the body's own components, causing severe symptoms.

Antibodies make mistakes because they recognise antigens by homing in on tiny chemical markers, not by looking at the antigen as a whole (see box on p. 15). Although this is a nuisance for

Antigens and allergens

An **antigen** is anything which elicits an **antibody** reaction. Each antibody is specific for a particular antigen.

When they tend to cause allergies (by provoking IgE antibodies rather than other kinds of antibody – see box on p. 13) these antigens are called **allergens**. Something such as grass pollen is both an antigen (because it elicits an antibody reaction) and an allergen (because it often elicits IgE antibodies in those who are allergy-prone).

allergy sufferers, it can be a bonus in fighting diseases. For example, when viruses (such as those that cause influenza) revamp their outer coat proteins to evade the immune system, the chances are that some antibodies will still recognise them because a few of the original chemical markers persist.

Understanding cross-reactions

Many cross-reactions are between related species, and this makes sense in biological terms. The tropomyosin story is a good example – not only is tropomyosin found in dust mite and shrimps, but it also occurs in other crustacean shellfish, such as crabs and lobsters, in molluscan shellfish such as clams and oysters, and in insects. If one goes back over 300 million years, all these animals were just a twinkle in the eye of some primeval invertebrate, the common ancestor of them all.

Tropomyosin is one of those triumphs of the evolutionary process – a protein that reached near-perfection hundreds of millions of years ago, in the long-vanished ancestral species, and remains so good at its job that it has only been tinkered with by natural selection since then, never radically altered. In other words, because it works so well, it has been 'conserved' by the various animal groups descended from the shared ancestor. Although there are some differences between the tropomyosins from different descendants, the similarities are considerable.

Relatedness counts here. Shrimps and prawns are pretty closely related, as anyone can see by looking at them. Their tropomyosins are extremely similar, as are many other allergens. You're unlikely to be allergic to prawn but not shrimp. The more distant the relationship, the more differences accumulate in the antigens, so a cross-reaction between dust mite and shrimp is far less likely (the rabbi was unlucky).

Another conserved protein, parvalbumin, explains why people who are allergic to one type of fish are usually allergic to all kinds of fish (in spite of the fact that fish belong to several different families which are only distantly related). Those allergic to hen's eggs will probably be allergic to the eggs of all birds, because the primary allergens (e.g. ovalbumin) are so similar.

These conserved proteins produce cross-reactions across huge gulfs, in terms of zoological and botanical relationships. Far more easily understood are the cross-reactions between close cousins, such as dust mite and storage mites, wheat and rye, pine pollen and pine nuts, or ragweed and sunflower (both members of the daisy family).

Relatedness can be useful in explaining cross-reactions, but often fails when it comes to predicting them. Some related species do not show as many cross-reactions as one might expect. Peanuts are legumes, and highly allergenic. One would expect some peanut-allergic individuals to be allergic to other members of the legume family, such as peas, beans, carob and soy. In fact, although some patients give positive skin-prick tests, very few show actual symptoms when they eat these foods. Where symptoms do occur, they tend to be mild.

Paradoxically, those who are allergic to peanuts very often develop an allergy to tree nuts, and this usually spans several different kinds of tree nuts – yet botanically all these are very distant relatives. No tree nut is a legume and while walnuts and pecans belong to one plant family, almonds belong to another, hazelnuts to another, cashews to a fourth, and Brazils to a fifth different plant family. Here relatedness seems irrelevant, and it is shared lifestyle (surviving as a nut-producing plant) that is crucial.

A nut is just an over-sized seed that has to survive being buried in the soil – either by the plant itself (in the case of peanuts) or by a nut-eating animal such as a squirrel. All nuts must resist rotting in the soil until the following spring, and therefore contain powerful bactericidal and fungicidal compounds. Some of these may have chemical similarities that cause cross-reactions.

These functional 'lifestyle' allergens of nuts may be even more widely shared, with many seeds having something similar: recent research shows potentially cross-reacting allergens in wheat, rye, hazelnuts, sesame and poppy. It is interesting that many of those developing new allergies to sesame or poppy are already allergic to wheat and nuts.

A few cross-reactions seem to defy any explanation, such as that between house-dust mite and kiwi fruit – this appears to be just a case of chemical coincidence. Other cross-reactions can appear equally bizarre but actually have a biological basis, notably that between latex (as used in medical gloves) and various fruits and vegetables, principally chestnut, banana, avocado and kiwi fruit. This cross-reaction is due to a shared enzyme called a chitinase that protects plants against insect pests. Latex, of course, comes from the sap of the rubber tree: the tree needs such insect-protection and its sap is richly laced with chitinase.

How antibodies work – and why they make errors

Antibodies are catapult-shaped, with two **antigen binding sites** at the ends of the two arms. The other end of the antibody molecule – the handle of the catapult – is free to bind to cell receptors.

When an antibody binds to its antigen there is a 'chemical handshake': a very specific recognition event involving one of the antigen binding sites and a particular small site on the antigen molecule called the **epitope**. The two lock together. Different antibodies may recognise different epitopes.

The antibody is recognising its antigen, but it is as if we recognised other people by homing in on one small part of them, choosing a different feature for each person, whatever is most distinctive about them – the quirky right eyebrow, the hook in the nose, or the mole on the cheek. The antibody does not 'look at' the whole antigen molecule, but simply recognises a characteristic cluster of chemical features at the epitope.

Cross-reactions can occur so readily because an antigen molecule only has to resemble another molecule in one or two small areas (the epitopes) for a mistake to occur.

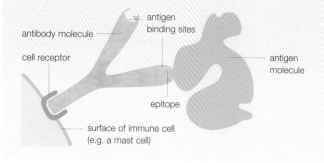

Breaking the mould

NEW DISCOVERIES ABOUT ALLERGY AND SENSITIVITY

'When I first arrived in Charlottesville in 1982, the senior allergist said "I've got to warn you that here in Virginia we have patients who have very severe fungal infection of their feet, and they also have urticaria. If you treat their feet, their urticaria gets better."' Professor Tom Platts-Mills of the University of Virginia in Charlottesville is recalling how his innovative studies of fungal infections and allergy began. That surprising observation about athlete's foot (a fungal infection) and urticaria (nettle rash) was made by his predecessor, Professor John Guerrant.

'I followed his advice,' Platts-Mills continues, 'and found he was right. Then I started noticing asthmatics in our allergy clinic who also had fungal infections of their feet. They were mostly men with severe adult-onset asthma. We gave them skin-prick tests with the fungus *Trichophyton* and these were positive – showing they had an allergic reaction to it. So we tried treating them with anti-fungal drugs and the asthma got much better.'

This discovery is not an isolated instance. Research over the last decade or so has revealed that allergic reactions to long-standing infections (**chronic infection** is the medical term) are far more common than anyone expected. Infections by fungi are frequent offenders.

An infection becomes chronic because, although the immune system tries to rout the infectious agent, it never succeeds. Making IgE may be part of that futile defensive effort. Once the immune system starts making IgE against the allergens produced by the infectious microbe, new symptoms may begin, or existing allergic symptoms may get much worse. The link between the infection and the allergy is far from obvious, however. Both the allergens and the IgE can be carried in the

Fungal infections

'Fungus' means everything from an edible mushroom or a huge bracket fungus to the specks of mould on stale bread or a shower curtain. Fungal infections are caused, not by mushroom-like fungi, but by inconspicuous mould-like forms, or by yeasts (which are single-celled fungi).

Once they are flourishing, some fungal infections may be seen as whitish or creamy-coloured patches. But at an earlier stage, the fungi are so small that they cannot be seen without a microscope. They spread as invisibly as bacteria or viruses.

Some infectious fungi can exist in two different forms – a mycelial form (long thin strands, as in a mould) or a yeast form (single cells).

bloodstream, so the symptoms may be somewhere else in the body, far away from the site of infection.

If the symptoms of the infection itself are relatively mild, they may not receive medical attention. Infection-plus-allergy often explains severe long-term allergic problems for which no cause could previously be found. This is the kind of case that gets labelled as 'intrinsic' or 'endogenous', because all the allergy tests have proved negative. Most patients in this category have had years of simply being treated with steroids (often at high doses) to suppress the symptoms.

Sometimes the infection-plus-allergy is part of a larger picture, with other allergens or irritants also contributing to the symptoms, but with no stunning improvements when they are avoided because the allergic stimulus from the infection remains.

The links between allergy and fungal infections – all those that have been discovered so far – are described below. In such cases, anti-fungal drugs, taken by mouth, usually in capsule form, could be of value. However, they must be taken for an adequate length of time, normally several months.

Bear in mind that, with the possible exception of chronic sinusitis, an allergic reaction to fungal infection is a relatively uncommon cause of symptoms. It is important that, with the help of your doctor, you start with the more likely suspects such as airborne or contact allergens. These are described in detail, for each allergic disease, in the relevant sections of Chapter 2.

Asthma

See pp. 36–41 for the common causes and usual treatment of asthma.

Trichophyton – the fungus that causes athlete's foot – can provoke allergic re-actions that contribute to asthma, as already described. This fungus may also infect other parts of the body. *Trichophyton* diseases have names that begin with *tinea* (athlete's foot, for example, is *tinea pedis*). Other terms you may come across are intertrigo (an itchy rash which develops in skin folds) and onychomycosis (also called 'ringworm of the nails' or *tinea unguinum*). The research on the link with asthma was published in a respected medical journal, *The Lancet*, but has been widely ignored, so if you

think you have this problem, you may have to be quite persistent with your doctor. Very thorough treatment with anti-fungal drugs (those which you swallow in capsule form) is required.

Chronic urticaria

See pp. 54–7 for the many possible causes of chronic urticaria.

Trichophyton infections in any part of the body (see above) can provoke allergies, producing chronic urticaria.

A great variety of other infections, including fungal, viral and chronic bacterial infections, can be the root of the problem in chronic urticaria (see p. 51). However, this may not be an allergic reaction. It could be a direct effect of the infection, provoking the immune system in such a way that it triggers mast cells (see box on p. 12) directly, without IgE.

Chronic sinusitis

See pp. 30–35 for the causes and treatment of chronic sinusitis.

Long-standing (chronic) sinusitis may be due to a fungal infection with a subsequent allergy. This is now called **allergic fungal sinusitis**. Some doctors believe that a sensitivity reaction to fungal infection (not necessarily an allergic reaction) could account for 96% of chronic sinusitis. However this is widely disputed (see pp. 32–3).

Atopic eczema (atopic dermatitis)

See pp. 42–9 for the causes and treatment of atopic eczema.

The *Trichophyton* fungus can infect eczematous skin, though this is far less common than infection by *Staphylococcus aureus* (see p. 18). Among patients infected by it, there can be an allergic reaction to *Trichophyton* which then makes the eczema worse.

There can also be an IgE reaction to a yeast, *Pityrosporum ovale*, in atopic eczema. This yeast is a commensal – i.e. a natural, and normally harmless, inhabitant of healthy skin. The inflammation of eczema makes the immune system far more tetchy so that it reacts allergically to this yeast, an innocent bystander which it normally disregards.

Fungi in the lungs

One form of infection-plus-allergy has been well recognised for many years – **allergic bronchopulmonary aspergillosis**, often shortened to **aspergillosis**.

The problem starts with the fungus *Aspergillus fumigatus*, a ubiquitous mould that is found in special abundance in damp straw, compost heaps, bird cages and any decomposing material. Its spores are everywhere, and most immune systems quickly defeat them, but in some people, especially those with asthma, the spores begin to grow in the lungs. The fungus is found in the lung mucus, but does not actually invade the lungs. However, an allergic reation then occurs to the fungus.

This disease often goes together with asthma, or can be mistaken for asthma. There are three clues that point to aspergillosis:

- rubbery plugs of phlegm, either golden-brown or green in colour
- fever whenever the asthma is severe
- worsening symptoms despite treatment.

Allergic bronchopulmonary aspergillosis is treated with steroids to control the allergic reaction, and physiotherapy to clear the mucus from the lungs.

Anti-fungal drugs have not proved very effective in the past. There are some newer anti-fungal drugs that may well be more useful, such as itraconazole and terbinafine. These are not widely used for aspergillosis at present, except in patients who also have cystic fibrosis or an immune deficiency. Because there has been no large-scale trial of these drugs, they are not usually given to people who simply have aspergillosis. However, they are sometimes prescribed for people who are unable to take steroids, or are not responding to steroid treatment. Anti-fungal drugs may become more widely used in the next few years, so it is worth discussing the possibility of this treatment with your doctor.

Candida (see box on p. 83) can also provoke an allergic reaction in eczematous skin. This is a more complex story, because while *Candida* is a commensal in the gut, it does not normally live on the skin. However, it may flourish in the disturbed skin of eczema patients. Those with atopic eczema may also develop an allergic reaction to toxins from *Staphylococcus aureus*, a bacterium that often infects skin which is already inflamed by eczema and damaged by scratching. Antibiotics are needed to treat the infection (see p. 49).

A medical earthquake

The recent discoveries about infection-plus-allergy have not posed any serious challenge to conventional thinking about allergy, because a disease of just this kind – aspergillosis (see box) – was already well known. A far more fundamental shake-up of traditional ideas about allergy and sensitivity has been necessitated by new research into atopic eczema. It is little short of an earthquake in the basic concepts of allergy and sensitivity.

To understand the extent of this earthquake, you need to know about the time-honoured system for classifying hypersensitivity reactions, which recognises four distinct types:

- **Type I hypersensitivity** – the IgE-mediated allergies (see box on p. 12) such as hayfever.
- **Type II hypersensitivity** – irrelevant to allergy, these antibody reactions mainly occur after transplant surgery, if the transplanted organ is rejected.
- **Type III hypersensitivity** – caused by a massive overload of antibodies and antigen in the blood. It is a feature of certain infections and autoimmune diseases, and can also occur in allergic reactions, though this is rare (see p. 13).
- **Type IV hypersensitivity** – the odd man out, because antibodies are not involved, or are not of central importance. Immune cells that can launch a direct attack are the movers and shakers here. These attacking-cells are sensitised for a particular antigen, such as dust mite or lanolin. Type IV hypersensitivity is a very slow reaction. Generally speaking, 48 hours pass, after an encounter with the offending substance, before the symptoms appear. The most common form of Type IV hypersensitivity is contact dermatitis (see p. 54).

Mystery has always surrounded atopic eczema. Although it crops up in the same atopic families that suffer from hayfever and asthma, and high levels of IgE in the bloodstream are typical of the disease, the actual role played by allergies in causing the symptoms is far from obvious.

The results of skin-prick tests – the standard test for an IgE-mediated reaction – are puzzling. Patients tend to give a lot of positive results, many of which don't mean much – the substances concerned do not provoke actual symptoms. On the other hand, skin-prick tests are often negative for substances that clearly do cause symptoms in challenge tests. Many children who regularly get eczema when they drink cow's milk, for example, give a negative skin-prick test to milk. This conundrum has puzzled allergists for decades.

New discoveries about eczema do not entirely solve the puzzle, but they do go some way towards an answer, by revealing an immune response that cuts across the traditional categories. The most surprising fact is that even where skin-prick tests are positive and milk-specific IgE is involved in milk-induced eczema, this is not necessarily a standard IgE-mediated allergy.

While IgE antibodies may be involved, they are not necessarily teamed up with mast cells, their usual partners in crime (see box on p. 12). Instead, the IgE molecules are attached to special skin cells called Langerhans cells and dendritic cells. These have the role of picking up the antigen and showing or 'presenting' it to attacking-cells in the skin (a task called **antigen presentation** which is the 'go' signal that starts off all immune reactions).

The involvement of these attacking-cells, which are sensitised for a particular antigen, was a big surprise when first discovered. It makes this resemble a Type IV hypersensitivity reaction (see p. 18) rather than a Type I.

IgE is not essential here, it seems – some patients do not have IgE for the substance that triggers their atopic eczema – but when Langerhans cells and dendritic cells are associated with IgE they do become far more zealous. This excitement is communicated to the attacking-cells, which mount a more powerful attack.

It looks as if what really matters in atopic eczema is the presence of antigen-specific attacking-cells in the skin, plus the heightened activity of the Langerhans cells and dendritic cells. If the individual has IgE for the antigen, it can play a part, but it is not essential.

In other words, this reaction cuts across two different categories of immune response – Type I and Type IV. (However, the kind of antigens that provoke the reaction are typical of IgE-mediated allergy, rather than the kind of antigens that provoke contact dermatitis.) This has been exploited in a new and more sensitive set of diagnostic tests for food-induced atopic eczema (see p. 69).

Why atopic eczema is a feature of atopic families is the crucial question that remains unanswered. One factor may be that high levels of IgE in the bloodstream (not IgE for a particular allergen, but total IgE) make the whole immune system more excitable and prone to over-react. The next few years will no doubt solve this part of the puzzle too.

Peace-keepers or aggressors?

'It is bad enough having a child on an ultra-strict diet – Tim can't have even a trace of cow's milk or else he becomes violently ill. What makes it worse is when people – teachers, for example – ask what's wrong. I take a deep breath and say "eosinophilic oesophagitis" then watch their eyes roll in disbelief.'

Tim's disease is caused by a particular type of immune cell called an **eosinophil**. In the right circumstances, eosinophils can be valuable – like IgE and mast cells, they are geared to destroying parasitic worms (see p. 13). They produce some very toxic substances to kill these invaders, and it is the toxins that cause serious symptoms for Tim and others like him.

Any disease with 'eosinophilic' in the name involves vast numbers of eosinophils converging on some unfortunate part of the body. The stimulus that attracts them often remains unknown but once there, the toxins they generate cause inflammation (see p. 140) of a particularly violent kind.

It is only in recent years that doctors have begun to distinguish between patients such as Tim and children with classical food allergy, and to understand the cause of Tim's symptoms. Several different forms of eosinophilic food sensitivity are now recognised (see p. 72). The exact relationship with IgE-mediated allergy remains a puzzle, because some sufferers make IgE to the culprit food but others do not.

That is not all – the eosinophil is finally coming out of the shadows and being recognised as an important agent in classical allergic diseases as well.

The fact that eosinophils appeared during the aftermath of an allergic reaction had long been known, but their role was misunderstood. What confused researchers was that eosinophils can break down histamine, the substance that kick-starts allergic symptoms (see box on p. 12). This ability gave eosinophils the appearance of peace-keeping troops, coming in at the close of battle to restore order. In fact, eosinophils are major aggressors – they do a whole lot of other things besides breaking down histamine, most of them pro-inflammatory. They can release toxins, just as they do in eosinophilic diseases (see above), and they attract other inflammatory cells into the area. In short, eosinophils play a big part in keeping allergic reactions going once the initial burst of activity is over. This 'Late Phase Reaction' is enormously important (see p. 13).

Why are allergies on the increase?

'I can't think of *any* of our friends where there isn't at least one member of the family with asthma, and often it's both children,' says Dee Gill, a university lecturer from Melbourne, and herself asthmatic. Australia is one of the countries worst affected by the allergy epidemic. 'If you go to a primary school sports day, you'll see the teachers going along the line of kids, saying, "Have you taken your asthma medication?" It's so much a part of everyday life now.'

The word 'epidemic' is now being freely used, even by the most conservative of medical scientists, to describe the increase in rates of allergy. All the classical allergic diseases seem to be on the increase, including:

- **atopic eczema** – in the US, up from 3% of children in the 1960s to 10% in the 1990s ; in Britain, more than 16% of 12–14-year-olds are now affected;
- **hayfever** – extremely rare in the 1930s (see p. 26) , affecting 3% of children in 1964, and now seen in 18% of 12–14-year-olds in many parts of the world;
- **asthma** – the figures for children in one Scottish city are: 4% in 1964, 10% in 1989, nearly 20% in 1994;
- **peanut allergy** seems also to be increasing, but there are no hard figures.

To the question 'why?' there is no simple answer – the causes are many and various. But one thing is abundantly clear: this is a disease of modern, Westernised society. Travel to rural Africa or

Are other immune diseases increasing?

These two pages deal solely with the classical allergic diseases (see box on p. 11). Many doctors have the impression that eosinophilic disorders (see p. 72) are also becoming more common, and some think that there are more cases of adult-onset coeliac disease than previously.

Asia, among people living a simple subsistence lifestyle, and you will find little or no sign of allergic diseases. There are no words in their languages for asthma or hayfever, because these are virtually unknown.

As soon as these people become more affluent, and change their lifestyle, allergic diseases appear, and the number of cases steadily rises over the years. Sometimes this coincides with a move to the towns, but it can also occur when people stay right where they are – as in Taiwan, where allergies rose dramatically with increasing affluence and a more Westernised way of life.

In the case of asthma, everyone is keen to blame air pollution, particularly traffic pollution. But a look at the research shows the link to be largely a myth. Certainly, polluted air can trigger off attacks in someone who already has asthma – but the effect is not huge, and this is not the same as causing asthma to develop in the first place. And while growing up in polluted air can increase the chances of children developing asthma, it makes only a small difference, one that simply cannot account for the massive asthma epidemic. The hollowness of the pollution argument is spectacularly evident when you consider rural New Zealand, where asthma rates are among the highest in the world, yet there are no factories, and sheep heavily outnumber motor cars.

Allergy to house-dust mites has also received a lot of publicity, and it does play an important part. Our warm, draught-free and thickly carpeted homes allow these tiny creatures to breed with abandon (see p. 114) and many people with perennial rhinitis, asthma or atopic eczema have an allergy to dust mites. Recent research shows that dust mites play a far larger role than anyone previously suspected: the dust-mite allergen actually provokes immune cells (see p. 12), and once an allergy to dust mite has begun, other allergies become more likely.

But blaming house-dust mite as the supreme cause of the allergy/asthma epidemic (as some do) is as mistaken as blaming pollution. The proof in this case comes from the highlands of New Mexico where dust mites cannot survive because the air is much too dry. Allergies, including asthma, are just as common as elsewhere in the Western world.

Spoiling the immune system

Thanks to discoveries made during the past decade, we are now beginning to understand what has made the younger generations – those born since the early 1960s – so much more susceptible to allergies. The new data reveal that the way you bring up a child's immune system matters as much as the way you bring up the child itself. You can 'spoil' an immune system all too easily, by protecting it from life's natural challenges and obstacles.

As a small child, I ate a spoonful of soil. My mother was horrified (she was still telling the story twenty years later) but research now shows that she should not have been. Exposure to certain bacteria in the soil, known as mycobacteria, is probably just the kind of education that a young immune system needs. These bacteria cause no ill-health, no symptoms at all, but they are thought to have an effect on the immune system, pushing it away from allergic reactions (see p. 11).

Children playing outdoors have probably always eaten soil, either intentionally or by accident – licking a grubby finger. Country people used to say, philosophically, 'You eat a bushel of dirt before you die', and they were probably right. Indeed, you may well *need* to eat a bit of dirt before you can live happily in an allergen-packed world. Now researchers are trying to make a vaccine using soil bacteria from Africa, to simulate this effect (see p. 169).

A study from the University of Bristol shows that children who wash their hands more than five times and have two baths a day are almost twice as likely to get asthma as children who wash their hands less than three times a day and have a bath every other day. The grubbier children are probably being protected from asthma by acquiring minor infections, with few or no symptoms. These infections could include both soil bacteria and germs that are spread from one child to another.

Other research reveals that children with older brothers and sisters are less likely to suffer from certain allergic diseases than only children or firstborn children. This seems to be due to the spread of infectious diseases, because mixing with lots of other children in a nursery produces more infections but also gives protection against allergy. Studies from the former East Germany, where sending children to day nurseries at an early age was once the norm, demonstrate that if children from small families went to nursery aged 6–11 months they were substantially less allergy-prone than if they went later. The allergy risk was highest for only children who did not go to nursery until they were over 2 years.

Researchers in Colorado have recently tackled this subject from a different angle completely, analysing house-dust for the levels of bacterial endotoxins – substances which are produced by many bacteria and which have a powerful effect on the immune system. If the house-dust contained high levels of endotoxins, babies brought up in that house were less likely to give positive skin-prick tests to common allergens such as cats, milk or house-dust mite. The babies from very clean houses, with low levels of endotoxin in the dust, were the ones with allergic reactions. (Fortunately, it is possible to have a dusty house with very little house-dust mite – see p. 115.)

The **hygiene hypothesis**, as it is known, could also explain the strange history of hayfever. For the first century of its existence, hayfever was a disease of the urban upper classes, only gradually working its way down to the poor and to rural communities: this fits in well with the gradual spread of more hygienic ways of life. In most parts of the developed world today, it shows no class distinctions, but recent investigations have found a lower rate of hayfever among children raised on a farm with animals compared to children living in the same villages without farm animals.

In addition to greater hygiene, the following aspects of modern living appear to promote an allergic tendency in children:
- smoking by the mother during pregnancy and after, which may boost IgE levels;
- exposure to a virus called Respiratory Synctial Virus (RSV) during infancy, which provokes an IgE-reaction (see p. 37);
- breathing nitrogen dioxide from gas cookers, and formaldehyde from various household sources (see p. 129); the poor ventilation of many modern houses, and the far greater time spent indoors aggravates the problem by increasing exposure to these irritants, and to allergens such as house-dust mite and moulds;
- taking antibiotics, especially penicillin, during the first two years of life (see p. 247);
- bottle-feeding and/or abrupt and early weaning onto a variety of foods.

All this knowledge about the allergy epidemic allows parents to reduce the risk of allergies developing in their own children, as described on pp. 238–49.

Age and allergy
DOES EVERYONE GROW OUT OF IT?

If you have a child with allergies, sooner or later some friend or relative will tell you not to worry because your child 'will probably grow out of it'. Your doctor may well say the same thing. But what does this mean? Do all children shake off their allergic symptoms as they get older? If the symptoms go, is the underlying disease completely cured? And why treat allergies if they disappear of their own accord? The truth is that the relationship between allergy and age is incredibly complex, and doctors only understand a tiny part of it. The best anyone can offer is a broad overview of how allergies change with age, with few explanations of the underlying mechanisms, and absolutely no predictions of what the future holds for any particular allergy sufferer.

It is certainly true that the classical allergic diseases, such as atopic eczema, hayfever and childhood asthma (see box on p. 11), frequently disappear as children grow up. Babies tend to shrug off food allergy and eczema by the time they are toddling, and a fair number of asthmatic children lose their symptoms before they are ten years old, while others do so in their teens or early twenties.

Unfortunately, the disappearance of symptoms does not mean that the underlying disease has necessarily disappeared, particularly in the case of asthma. Quite a few young adults find themselves wheezy and breathless again in their late twenties or thirties, especially if they take up smoking. One study of children who wheezed before the age of seven found that:

• 25% lost their asthma for a time – anything between two years and twenty-five years – only to get it back again by their early thirties. Some recovered and relapsed more than once.

• Over 70% shook off asthma and were still symptom-free by their early thirties when the study ended.

• Only 2% remained asthmatic throughout.

Realistically, anyone who has ever been asthmatic should regard themselves as 'at risk' indefinitely and never be careless with their health – don't smoke, keep away from smoky bars and clubs, eat a good diet with plenty of fruit and vegetables (see p. 206) and avoid activities that involve an asthma risk, such as strenuous exercise in cold air.

Workplaces with high exposure to allergens, such as sawmills, bakeries or laboratories using animals (see pp. 133–4) are not recommended for those with a history of allergy. Anyone who has ever had eczema should also take care with cosmetics and soaps, choosing the gentlest brands. They should also protect their hands (see p. 57) and avoid hairdressing or bricklaying as an occupation, or anything else where skin irritation is likely.

Moving on

Growing out of classical allergies seems to be a consequence of the child's immune system changing and maturing as it grows. This same process, unfortunately, can also substitute one allergic disease for another.

'When Alex developed eczema as a baby I hoped that she'd grow out of it in time. Well she did, gradually, and by the time she was five it seemed to have cleared up, but then she started having a snuffly nose that never really went away. A year or so later, she began wheezing whenever she got a cold, and this has now developed into asthma.' The pattern described by Alex's mother Jenny will be familiar to many parents, who watch their children slowly work their way through all the allergies in the medical textbooks. Doctors call it the **atopic march** or **allergic march**.

Fortunately, even this type of allergic pattern can have a positive outcome eventually. Many such children become allergy-free in time, and develop into healthy adults.

In the meantime, there are several itchy, wheezy or sneezy years to get through, and since childhood is a time to be enjoyed, not endured, treatments that alleviate the symptoms of allergies are generally welcomed. Being energetic, healthy, 'normal' and able to join in with sports and other activities is particularly important for a child's social development and self-confidence.

Treating the symptoms also prevents any long-term and irreversible damage, such as the thickening and loss of elasticity that occurs in the airways of children with untreated asthma.

At the same time as treating the symptoms, it makes sense to maximise the chance of the child growing out of the allergy. Parents can tip the odds in the right direction by providing an environment that reduces the chance of new allergies developing. A detailed action programme is described on pp. 248–9.

Allergies that begin in adult life

What about those people who develop classical allergic diseases for the first time as adults – or even in old age? Will they too 'grow out of it' with the passing years?

Only a minority of people develop such allergies for the first time as adults, although the numbers seem to be increasing. The older you are when your allergies begin, the less likely you are to ever throw them off. On the positive side, they are unlikely to get a great deal worse than they are at the outset, especially if you take care of yourself and keep the air at home as unpolluted and allergen-free as possible (see pp. 114–31).

In the case of asthma that develops in adulthood, there may not be an allergic reaction involved. Whereas allergies play a part in asthma for 80–90% of children, the figure is thought to be lower for adults. Nevertheless, it is well worth investigating the possible role of allergens, because avoiding them is one of the most effective treatments.

The outlook for food intolerance

Food intolerance causes a wide variety of symptoms, from baby colic to migraine. A full list is given on p. 76. Although far less is understood about food intolerance than about true allergies, there is much more certainty about the future for affected individuals. With rare exceptions, people find that the problem clears up as long as they totally avoid their problem food for a year or two. After this period of strict avoidance, they can eat the food again in moderation but should never forget that the problem can return. Eating the culprit food very regularly will turn the clock back and all the original symptoms will return. This change for the worse may be irreversible for people with severe reactions such as rheumatoid arthritis.

Safety first

Anyone who suffers the life-threatening allergic reaction known as anaphylactic shock (see p. 58) is probably going to have this for the rest of their days. Some children do become tolerant of food allergens in time (allergies to milk, eggs or soy may well disappear, whereas fish or peanut allergy is probably going to be permanent) but before concluding that there is no longer any risk, some extremely careful and cautious testing should take place. Talk to your doctor about how to proceed. Skin-prick tests may be helpful, but there must be resuscitation equipment close to hand as anaphylaxis can occur. Never give the child any of the food to eat, until you (or, preferably, the doctor) have first tested it in other, less risky, ways. For example, you can smear a little on the face to see if there is any reaction. If there is none within 24 hours, put a tiny amount on the outer lip and watch again.

If both these tests produce absolutely no reaction then a very small amount of the food can be eaten as a test: this should be done under medical supervision. The amount can be slowly increased with successive tests, until it seems certain that no reaction will occur even with a normal portion.

Chapter 2
the diseases

In medical terms, this chapter covers a lot of ground. First there are the **classical allergic diseases** (see box on p. 11) such as hayfever and immediate food allergy, which are caused by the allergy antibody, IgE (see box on p. 12). Then there is **non-IgE immune sensitivity**, a category which includes a number of quite different diseases, caused in a great variety of ways. They also vary in severity – there are serious lifelong problems such as coeliac disease and minor short-lived problems such as contact dermatitis from garden plants.

Finally (pp. 74–85) the chapter looks at diseases where the immune system seems not to be involved, or plays only a minor role: the **intolerance** reactions to food and synthetic chemicals. These are diverse and rather mysterious in origin. They would not be described as 'allergies' by most doctors, though they often are by complementary therapists (see p. 6).

These categories are not nearly as neat and tidy as they might sound. Some problems refuse to fit anywhere, such as atopic eczema caused by food. A percentage of children with this problem have IgE to the food concerned, while others do not – so where does it belong?

If you were expecting an answer to that question, you will be disappointed. Nor, quite often, are there any certain and honest answers to questions such as 'Has my baby really got asthma?' or 'Can you be sure it's irritable bowel syndrome?' There are no answers to such questions because most diseases do not exist in neat compartments, and the words we use to describe them really denote rather abstract concepts.

This does not mean that the terms used to describe diseases are invalid – doctors and medical researchers invent them to try and make sense of a complex, confusing and largely foggy reality. They also argue over them, split them, unite them and redefine them. There is a constant desire to get the medical picture of that foggy reality more precise and accurate (although medical politics gets involved too – see p. 7 – which is unfortunate).

Over time, thanks to huge amounts of research effort, things gradually get clearer. You'll no longer hear a doctor talk about 'rheumatism' or 'arthritis', because it was long since realised that these categories were useless – they included a number of diverse diseases. And while doctors might say 'food poisoning' or 'heart attack' or 'skin cancer' to a patient, they use much narrower and more precise terms when talking among themselves, and when ordering tests or prescribing treatment. Each of these categories has been split into several well-defined sub-categories.

Ideally, this process of splitting continues until each disease category has a set of well-defined symptoms (this set is known as a **syndrome**), plus a few simple and definitive diagnostic tests. This will probably depend on the cause of the disease (the **mechanism** in medical jargon) being clearly understood. Once the

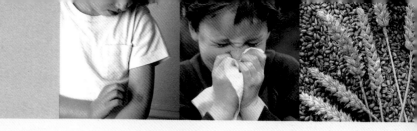

mechanism is clear, then a disease category is a truly satisfactory tool for diagnosis and treatment.

Of the disease categories mentioned in this book only a few, such as coeliac disease and hayfever, have reached that happy state. The majority are still somewhat arbitrary and debatable.

Some disease terms describe a set of symptoms with no clear underlying cause, for example, 'irritable bowel syndrome'. Others describe a well-defined response by the body, that can be caused in many different ways – an end-point that can be reached by various routes. This is true of 'asthma' or 'urticaria'.

A third type describes a much less well-defined cluster of symptoms. Idiopathic food intolerance, chemical intolerance and yeast overgrowth all come into this category. A few doctors don't even see some of these clusters as real diseases because the symptoms involved are so vague and so widely encountered. Some of the arguments used to dismiss idiopathic food intolerance are dissected on pp. 74–7. A key point made against these diseases is that the symptoms they produce are non-specific – common symptoms such as headache, fatigue and diarrhoea, which can arise in a great variety of ways. Ever since Pasteur and the germ theory, medicine has been based on the idea of each disease having *specific* symptoms and *specific* causes, and it has roared ahead on the basis of this assumption. This is the prevailing paradigm of modern medicine, and like all

paradigms it blinds people to facts that don't fit. Evidence is accumulating that there are diseases which have multiple, non-specific and variable symptoms. Chronic Fatigue Syndrome (CFS – see box on p. 85) is one of these, and its recent transformation from a doubtful diagnosis to a reputable disease recognised by conventional medicine, suggests that the paradigm might be starting to crack.

To sum up, the business of identifying and naming diseases is a complex and uncertain process, in which the concept of most diseases is only ever that – a *concept*, subject to change and refinement. This does not make it worthless – quite the opposite. These concepts are the best we can do at the present time, and accurate diagnosis is the key to getting the best treatment available now.

As regards both diagnosis and treatment, this book covers a very wide spectrum of medical opinion, from the entirely orthodox to the frankly whacky. I have tried to give an objective view of these different opinions and approaches, using the evidence currently available, in the hope that it will help readers to improve their health while wasting as little as possible of their time or money. In using this information, you should always try to work closely with your doctor (see p. 96), respecting the depth and breadth of knowledge that conventional medicine has to offer.

Hayfever

Foxtail grasses release their pollen – a potential source of hayfever symptoms.

'I gradually recognised that it was not an ordinary cold and that the symptoms were much worse on the golf course or even during a nice day rowing on Loch Lomond.' Dr John Morrison Smith, then a medical student, began suffering from hayfever in the late 1930s. 'At first I did not know what I had, and neither did any other doctor I encountered in the next two or three years...'

All the classical allergic diseases (see box on p. 11) seem to be increasing, but none has exploded quite so dramatically as hayfever. The physicians of Ancient Greece described asthma and food allergy, and the Romans recorded allergy to horses, but there were no reports of hayfever. The only account – and it is a doubtful one – comes from Persia in AD 925. Two hundred years ago, hayfever was unknown – and careful research by medical historians has shown that this was not a case of it simply being ignored, or misinterpreted as a cold.

The first case was reported in 1819, but even in the 1930s it was so rare that a succession of Scottish doctors and medical students were baffled by Dr Morrison Smith's symptoms. Today everyone knows what hayfever is, since huge numbers of people sneeze and snuffle their way through the pollen season. There are no certain explanations for this meteoric rise, but greater hygiene (see p. 21) may be an important factor.

Symptoms of hayfever

The common symptoms of hayfever are well known:
- itchiness of the nose, mouth, throat and eyes – often the first sign
- a streaming and/or blocked nose
- frequent sneezing
- red, watery eyes (very rarely, hayfever affects the eyes only, with no symptoms in the nose).

Less commonly, there may be:
- dryness of the throat if the nasal blockage results in constant breathing through the mouth
- no sense of smell due to a blocked nose (but nasal polyps can also cause this – see p. 30)
- a feverish sweaty feeling (but the body temperature is usually normal)
- swelling and inflammation of the eyelids, sometimes leading to blistering and ulceration: *there is a risk of blindness if this is not treated promptly*
- recurrent sinusitis (see p. 30)
- earache, a stuffy feeling in the ears, or 'glue ear' (see p. 29)
- itching in the ears.

Some sufferers also experience:
- Oral Allergy Syndrome (an itchy tingling mouth) from certain fruits, nuts and vegetables (see box on p. 63)
- a skin rash from pollen falling on the skin (direct contact with the leaves of the offending plants, or with droplets of moisture from them – as when mowing a lawn or using a strimmer – may also produce a rash).

Even more rarely there can be:
- stomach upsets or even colitis (inflammation of the bowel) possibly due to pollen swallowed with food or in the saliva
- irritation in the vagina
- migraine
- kidney inflammation (nephritis), leading to puffiness of the face and hands, and possibly other symptoms
- joint pains.

The last two are probably caused by pollen allergens bound to their antibodies and carried in the blood (see p. 13).

Diagnosis

The standard diagnostic tool here is the skin-prick test (see p. 91). In diagnosing hayfever there are three separate questions:

1 Is it actually hayfever?

2 Which pollen or pollens are responsible?

3 Are there allergens other than pollen also involved?

Don't be surprised if none of these questions are asked. In most countries, if you have hayfever-like symptoms during the pollen season (i.e. when most hayfever sufferers have symptoms), the doctor will conclude that you have hayfever – and that will be the end of that.

If hayfever seems plausible to you, and you respond to drug treatment, or manage well on pollen avoidance (see p. 126), then there is probably no reason to go further. Should you want a more thorough investigation, you will need to be persistent. These are good reasons for requesting a full diagnosis:

- Your symptoms are worse in the pollen season, but they never really go away, suggesting that you may be allergic to year-round allergens, such as house-dust mite or moulds, as well. It is worth knowing which ones, so that you can avoid them. If you live in an area that is always warm (such as California or Southern Australia) it may be that your culprit pollen is in the air all year round – even so, knowing which pollen it is can help with avoidance. Around the Mediterranean, the pollen from cypresses can keep hayfever going through the winter (or cause symptoms in winter only).
- Your symptoms are sometimes worse when they should be better, and vice versa. If you are consistently worse indoors with the windows closed this could indicate that a seasonal indoor allergen is the culprit – mould spores or cockroach perhaps (cockroach is often seasonal in regions with cold winters – see p. 118).
- Your symptoms begin before the pollen season begins, or go on long afterwards. Or the severity of your symptoms does not match the daily pollen count for your suspect pollen. In Britain, the mould *Cladosporium herbarum* produces spores in June, roughly coinciding with the grass-pollen season. Allergy to this mould can easily be mistaken for grass-pollen allergy. You would need skin-prick tests for both *Cladosporium* and grasses.

- You are much worse near home than elsewhere. It could just be a garden plant or tree. As one California resident observed, 'The worst offender was an olive tree on our front lawn. It's been removed.'
- You want to plan holidays free from the culprit pollen. Moving house – especially to a region with different vegetation – can be a spur to finding out exactly what your allergens are.

If you are going for a full diagnosis make sure it is done correctly. Don't accept testing with 'mixed tree and shrub pollens' for example, or 'weed pollens'. The result tells you very little. Ask for tests with specific pollens.

Treatment

Too many people allow hayfever to spoil the summer months because they are anxious about taking drugs, or feel that it is nobler to suffer. This book is not in any way complacent about the dangers from drugs (see Chapter 5), but when it comes to hayfever there really is very little cause for concern. The risks with drugs used for hayfever are absolutely minimal, and it is such a waste to miss out on the best time of year.

Most hayfever responds very well to treatment with antihistamines (see p. 138). If they make you sleepy, persist for a while, because this side-effect often wears off – or ask for one of the new non-sedating forms. The sleepiness is annoying, but it is only a minor side-effect, and not an indication of the drug causing any serious harm.

Cromoglycate drops (for the eyes or nose) do not work for everyone, but if they work for you, go for them. These are absolutely the safest of the anti-allergy drugs. Steroid drops for the nose (see p. 144) are also recommended. The dose of steroid involved is small, and very little gets into the bloodstream, so there is no risk of serious side-effects. If you suffer stinging, burning or dryness, it might be due to preservatives in the drops, not the drug itself (see p. 33). Steroid drops for the eyes should be used cautiously (see p. 144). Don't use over-the-counter decongestant drops for more than three days (see p. 29).

Immunotherapy is standard treatment for hayfever in many countries, but in Britain you will have a struggle to get it (see pp. 164–8). Some hayfever sufferers feel they do well with homeopathy (see p. 216) or acupuncture (see p. 214).

Pollen asthma

Some people with hayfever also have pollen asthma. Their asthma is worse in the pollen season but it usually persists all year round (either because there are other allergens or irritants involved, or just because the inflammation of the airways is self-perpetuating) whereas hayfever itself clears up. Treating the hayfever fully with antihistamines helps considerably with the asthma symptoms.

A blocked or runny nose
THAT LASTS ALL YEAR

'Everyone has heard of hayfever, but it's news to most people that you can have this sort of problem all year round,' complains Elizabeth. 'Before we got the treatment sorted out, Benny was "the kid with the constant cold", and I did notice other mothers looking less than enchanted at the prospect of his coming over to play.'

Benny suffers from allergic reactions to house-dust mites and cats which cause hayfever-style symptoms (see p. 26) all year round. This condition doesn't even have a common name – the medical one is **perennial allergic rhinitis** – yet it is one of the most common allergic diseases.

Any **airborne allergen** that is found in the air all year round can cause perennial allergic rhinitis:

- House-dust mite is the number one suspect in most parts of the world. Particles from other insects, such as midges and mosquitoes outdoors, and cockroaches, house flies, bloodworms (used for fish food) or carpet beetles indoors, can also cause nasal allergies.
- Mould spores can be the problem: they are found both indoors and out.
- In some regions, certain types of pollen are airborne all year round (see p. 27).
- All pets other than fish produce allergenic particles (even snakes).
- Allergens encountered at work (see p. 133) can also produce symptoms in the nose. *This is a warning sign you should not ignore* – it often means that occupational asthma is on its way (see p. 132).

Occasionally, the offending substance is being eaten not inhaled. This is less common, so you should investigate inhaled allergens first, before trying an elimination diet (see p. 29).

Skin-prick tests (see p. 91) will help to identify any airborne allergens that are responsible, but where food is the culprit, skin-prick tests are often negative (see p. 69)

Triad and NARES

Diagnosis of perennial allergic rhinitis is complicated by the fact that there are two other conditions – called **triad** and **NARES** – which produce similar symptoms and involve the immune system but are not, strictly speaking, allergies.

Triad is so called because it involves three distinct symptoms:

- perennial rhinitis
- polyps in the nose – little fleshy growths that can kill your sense of smell
- asthma.

People with triad tend to collect all three symptoms gradually, in no fixed order, over a period of years or even decades. Many are sensitive to aspirin and related drugs, and almost everyone with triad develops this sensitivity eventually.

Aspirin sensitivity can come on very suddenly and produces a reaction akin to anaphylaxis (see p. 101). This can be fatal, so it is probably best to avoid all aspirin-like drugs if you have triad, *even though you have not reacted to aspirin in the past*. Aspirin-like drugs are found in painkillers, arthritis drugs and cold remedies – check with a pharmacist before you buy (see p. 151).

If you have asthma, think twice about operations on the nose to remove polyps – they can make the asthma much worse.

The initial letters of Non-Allergic Rhinitis with Eosinophilia have been stretched a bit to get NARES. (This is a medical joke –the Latin word *nares* means nostrils.) The problem is caused by eosinophils (see p. 19), which flock into the nose and cause severe inflammation. Some people with NARES go on to develop triad.

Collateral damage

Having the nose swamped with mucus can lead to knock-on problems in the ears, sinuses and airways.

If the tube that leads from the ear to the nose (the Eustachian tube) becomes blocked, then fluid cannot drain away from the middle ear. This is called secretory otitis media, or **glue ear** – it dulls the hearing and causes an unpleasant 'popping' sensation. The ears may also feel blocked and itchy, but if children have had this problem since they were tiny they may not complain because they assume that's just the way ears are supposed to feel. Deafness is often the first sign anyone notices.

Sinusitis is another possible complication, because fluid from the sinuses should also drain into the nasal cavity. With the ouflow blocked, mucus builds up in the sinuses and can become infected by bacteria (see p. 30).

Post-nasal drip can also occur with perennial allergic rhinitis. The over-abundant mucus runs down the back of the nose, into the throat and then the airways. This produces a persistent phlegmy cough, which may occasionally be mistaken for asthma.

When the rhinitis is treated effectively, all these problems should sort themselves out, although additional treatment is usually necessary in the case of persistent sinusitis (see p. 33).

Treatment

Where an allergen such as house-dust mite or mould spores has been identified as the source of problem, eradicating it from your house (see Chapter 4) will make a huge difference, and may avoid the need for drugs. If the allergen is unavoidable, immunotherapy (see pp. 164–8) or some alternative form of desensitisation (see pp. 210–13) could be very helpful.

Where drugs are needed, nose drops are best. They get the drugs right to the target so doses are minimal, which means very few side effects. The drugs used are:

- cromoglycate to prevent the allergic reaction before it starts (see p. 148)
- antihistamines to block the allergic reaction before it produces inflammation (see p. 138)
- steroids to calm down inflammation (see p. 144).

Steroid nose drops are also useful for NARES and triad. If you are taking steroid drops continuously, your doctor should check the membranes inside your nose every six months. Make sure you put the drops in correctly, especially if you have polyps (see p. 144).

If you suffer stinging, burning or dryness, it might be due to preservatives in the drops, not the drug itself (see box on p. 33), so talk to your doctor about a different formulation.

Don't use over-the-counter decongestant drops: they do nothing to treat the allergy or inflammation, and are little more than a 'chemical crowbar' to open up the nose. Your nose gets addicted to them in a few days, and when you stop using them you get 'rebound congestion' – absolute and total blockage. It does wear off eventually, but is unpleasant meanwhile. If you are suffering this problem at this very moment, *don't* put more decongestant drops in – your nose needs to go 'cold turkey' to recover, not have its addiction fed!

If none of the anti-allergy drugs work, but decongestant drops do, then you probably have a non-allergic disease called **vasomotor rhinitis**. The symptoms are very similar to allergic rhinitis, but without the sneezing and itching. See your doctor again, because there is an effective treatment using anti-cholinergic drugs (see box on p. 156). Acupuncture (see below) can also be helpful.

An elimination diet (see p. 194) will diagnose any food reactions. It works wonders for some people with severe and unexplained perennial rhinitis, including people with such a flood of mucus that they can scarcely work or live normally. You should certainly give this diagnostic diet a try if there are clues that suggest food is the culprit (see p. 69) or if no airborne allergen can be identified. Yeast – found in bread, beer and B-vitamin tablets – is quite often the culprit in rhinitis, but it could be any food.

Acupuncture is worth trying, to reduce the blockage in the nose and stem the flow of mucus, because the autonomic nervous system (see box on p. 235) plays some part in the symptoms of allergic rhinitis (and is the sole cause of the symptoms for those with vasomotor rhinitis). For those with severe sinusitis, osteopathy can be good for draining mucus from the sinuses.

Very occasionally, psychological or emotional reactions play a part in perennial allergic rhinitis, with symptoms getting significantly worse during stressful events. One possible manifestation of this is **post-coital rhinitis**, where sex brings on rhinitis (and sometimes asthma as well). In such cases, psychotherapy should be considered. (But check you are not just allergic to the dust mites in your bed first...)

A nose by any other name...
Rhinitis means inflammation (-itis) of the nose (rhin-). The same Greek word gives us rhinoceros – 'nose-horn'.

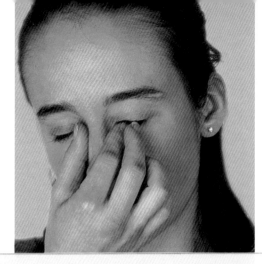

Sinusitis

Sinus cavities are something that most people just don't know they have. It's only when they start to hurt that you find out where they are. 'There is this terrible throbbing pain above and around my eyes, and in my cheeks. It's the most unpleasant feeling, but it's hard to describe to anyone who hasn't felt it,' says Gina, who suffers from chronic sinusitis (long-term inflammation of the sinus cavities). There are no figures, but chronic sinusitis seems to be increasingly common.

A sinus cavity has no function, it is just empty space without which our skulls would be much heavier. In other words, these airy spaces seem to have evolved simply to help us feel more 'light-headed'. If you have sinusitis, unfortunately, you feel just the opposite. 'I had sinusitis for years,' says Dr Wellington S. Tichenor, a New York allergist who now specialises in treating chronic sinusitis. 'I kept working but felt like I wanted to die.'

Sinus cavities are lined with a membrane which is essentially similar to that lining the nose. It contains immune cells and can produce mucus when necessary. Most of the time it doesn't need to produce much, because relatively few microbes or foreign particles get into the sinus cavities.

Any mucus that is produced should escape from the sinus cavities through narrow drainage channels, called ostia, leading to the nose. Unfortunately, the ostia are very narrow – the diameter of a pin-head – and U-shaped, making them prone to blockage. And that is not the only problem. These drainage channels are situated at the top rather than the bottom of the main sinus cavities – this arrangement was fine for our ancestors who walked on all fours, and therefore did not have to fight gravity when clearing their sinuses. Sadly for

us, natural selection has not got around to reorganising things yet. It would be a completely hopeless arrangement if not for the tiny hairs known as cilia, which lie like a carpet across the membranes lining the sinus cavities. The cilia beat rhythmically, 18 times a second, to waft the mucus upwards to the top of the sinus cavity.

This is a far-from-perfect system, and it is hardly surprising that it sometimes goes wrong. Chronic sinusitis can begin in at least three different ways:

- The sinus membranes become inflamed due to an allergic reaction – see p. 28 for likely airborne allergens.
- The drainage channels from the sinus cavities become blocked due to events in the nose (infection or allergy) or due to the growth of **polyps** (non-cancerous jelly-like lumps that can block the drainage channels). When mucus cannot drain away, it stagnates in the sinus cavities encouraging infection by bacteria or fungi. These infections cause inflammation.
- A bout of acute sinusitis (see box), due to bacterial infection, never really goes away and the persistent infection causes long-term inflammation. Note that this is unlikely: it is rare for acute sinusitis not to clear up.

Whether the problem begins through allergy or blockage or infection, once it has begun a vicious circle can be set up all too easily. Mucus output increases when there is inflammation, blocking the drainage channels even more, so the sinus cavities become clogged up and increasingly uncomfortable. More mucus pooling in the sinus cavities perpetuates any existing infections and fosters new ones.

All this infection results in more severe inflammation, causing the membranes which line the sinus cavities to swell up. Inflammation also makes polyp growth more likely. The cilia may be lost or severely depleted, and the mucus gets thicker. All this means yet more blockage. To cap it all, there can be allergic reactions to some of the microbes involved (see right), fuelling the inflammation further.

The body's own attempts to clear the sinuses are defeated, and the problem is also very resistant to medical treatment. This may make depressing reading, if you have chronic sinusitis, but don't despair. Understanding the complexities of the problem is a large part of the battle. Chronic sinusitis is not invincible, if you have a good doctor to help you – that means a doctor who also understands these complexities.

The symptoms of sinusitis are:
- pain and a sense of swelling or unpleasant fullness around the cheeks, or over and between the eyes
- earache or headache; pain around the teeth
- reduction in the senses of smell and taste
- sore throat
- coughing, particularly at night
- post-nasal drip (mucus from the back of the nose running into the throat and airways)
- bad-smelling breath
- feverishness
- for some people, severe fatigue, poor concentration and even (but very rarely) psychiatric symptoms
- irritability, especially in children.

Note that any of these symptoms can be caused in other ways, and even if you have several of them, you may not necessarily have sinusitis. On the other hand, sinusitis can go unrecognised – to some people it may seem like nothing more than a lingering cold.

Acute or chronic?

In medical terms, 'acute' means short-lived, while 'chronic' means long-lasting.

Acute sinusitis – a short, sharp dose of it, lasting less than 3–4 weeks – usually follows on from a cold. Colds are caused by viruses, but a bacterial infection can follow, and it is the bacteria that move into the sinus cavities and cause trouble. Some people are far more susceptible than others and have an attack of sinusitis after every cold.

Chronic sinusitis means symptoms lasting more than 3 months, according to some authorities, but the time point is a little arbitrary. This article deals with chronic sinusitis.

If your sinusitis has been going on for between 4 weeks and 3 months you will obviously be asking 'Is this acute or chronic?' At this point, no one can say, but you would certainly be wise to seek some expert medical treatment now, on the basis that it could be the start of chronic sinusitis. Tackling chronic sinusitis before the problem becomes entrenched and complex is a good plan.

Allergy and chronic sinusitis

Chronic sinusitis is not necessarily an allergic disease, but it can be connected with allergies (or other forms of immune sensitivity) in various ways:
- Allergic reactions can occur in the sinuses, usually in conjunction with allergic reactions in the nose.
- Even if the allergic reaction does not affect the sinuses directly, allergic reactions in the nose can block the drainage channels from the sinuses, causing an accumulation of mucus there. This may lead to sinus infections.
- Once sinusitis has begun, infectious fungi (moulds) in the sinuses may provoke allergic reactions, or other forms of immune sensitivity. This allergy to 'the enemy within' fuels more inflammation and more mucus production. Right now, **allergic fungal sinusitis** (as it is known) is a source of heated debate – see p. 32. Allergic reactions to some of the bacteria that are present may also occur.
- Chronic sinusitis – however caused – can contribute to asthma. Research on children with both sinusitis and asthma found that 80% no longer needed asthma drugs once their sinusitis had been treated, and 85% no longer wheezed. The link may be due to post-nasal drip, increased mouth-breathing, or to a nerve-connection between the sinuses and the airways (the sinobronchial reflex) which can stimulate airway inflammation. Alternatively, the sinusitis may simply fire up the immune system with messenger chemicals in the bloodstream, resulting in more powerful responses throughout the body.
- Chronic sinusitis can also be the root cause of long-standing nettle rash (chronic urticaria), and treating the sinusitis can result in a prompt and remarkable clearance of the skin symptoms.
- Some people who have chronic sinusitis are sensitive to aspirin (see box on p. 28) – a sensitivity which is also linked with asthma, nasal polyps, rhinitis and chronic urticaria. Avoiding aspirin and all other aspirin-like drugs (see p. 151) may substantially improve the sinusitis.

Diagnosis

Because so many different factors can play a part in chronic sinusitis, diagnosis should, ideally, consider the problem from several different angles:

- The sinuses are viewed using X-rays and CT scans (computed tomographic scans – they use X-rays but give a much more precise picture). These reveal how badly swollen the sinus membranes are, which sinus cavities are blocked, and how much mucus has collected in the sinuses.
- Endoscopy (see p. 92) may be used to look inside the sinus cavities. Polyps are best located by this method.
- Where allergies seem to be part of the picture, the doctor may employ skin-prick tests (see p. 91) to identify allergies to airborne allergens (from house-dust mites, moulds, pets, pollen, cockroaches, etc.)
- Laboratory tests on samples taken from your sinus cavities will be used to show which bacteria and/or fungi have set up home there. There may also be a hunt for the immune cells known as eosinophils (see p. 19) or the typical debris which they generate. The presence of large numbers of eosinophils is one indication of allergic fungal sinusitis (see below).
- Skin testing with fungi (moulds) found growing in the sinus cavities may also be tried if allergic fungal sinusitis is suspected.
- In severe cases, there may be tests of immune function, to see whether this is depressed in any way.
- Children may be tested for an inherited disorder affecting the cilia, or for cystic fibrosis – mild forms may escape detection, and can produce both chronic sinusitis and wheezing.

The enemy within

The biggest controversy in sinusitis research at the moment concerns **allergic fungal sinusitis**. The orthodox view of this condition is that:

- It affects a small minority of chronic sinusitis patients – fewer than 10%.
- There is a true IgE-mediated allergic reaction to the fungus (mould) growing in the sinus cavities. This allergic reaction is detectable with a skin-prick test (see p. 91). Immune cells known as eosinophils (see p. 19) are also key players in the inflammatory reaction to the fungi, but it is an IgE-response to the fungi that draws the eosinophils into the sinuses.
- There is clear evidence of fungal infection in the membranes of the sinus cavities.
- There may also be 'fungus balls' – a solid mass of fungus inside the sinus cavity. Or there may be 'allergic mucin', a dark sticky mucus containing fragments of the fungus.

A rare complication

In rare cases, the fungi involved in allergic fungal sinusitis can be invasive, spreading from the sinuses to the surrounding bone. This problem needs prompt and thorough treatment with anti-fungal drugs.

In 1996, researchers at the Mayo Clinic in Rochester, Minnesota, USA, caused a rumpus by claiming to have identified a different form of allergic fungal sinusitis which is overlooked by standard diagnostic techniques, and which affects 96% of patients with chronic sinusitis.

This is a staggering figure – 96% means, in effect, that they are claiming to have found the fundamental cause of virtually all chronic sinusitis. 'Up to now, the cause of chronic sinusitis has not been known. Our studies indicate that, in fact, fungus is the likely cause of nearly all of these problems,' states Dr David Sherris, one of the researchers.

According to the Mayo Clinic team:

- The fungi (moulds) are growing in the mucus of the sinus cavities, not generally in the membrane itself. They are not detected by normal diagnostic methods which tend to ignore the mucus. A special method of collecting the mucus is required to detect the fungi.
- The immune reaction to the fungi is not usually an IgE-mediated reaction, so skin-prick tests are often negative.
- Finding evidence of unusual numbers of eosinophils is adequate for diagnosis of allergic fungal sinusitis because the eosinophils are the prime movers in this sensitivity reaction to the fungi, as in several other diseases (see p. 19).

'We can now begin to treat the cause of the problem instead of the symptoms,' says Dr Eugene Kern, head of the research team. There is a lot of scepticism about these claims among other sinusitis specialists, and so far no new treatment for chronic sinusitis has emerged.

The Mayo Clinic researchers say that they are in the process of developing a drug treatment, but that it will take several more years before it is generally available. Existing anti-fungal drugs (taken in capsule form) could not work on this particular form of allergic fungal sinusitis (if it exists) because the drug does not get into the mucus. Any new treatment would probably involve inserting an anti-fungal drug directly into the sinus cavities, which is far from easy.

All we can do for now is wait and see what emerges from the ongoing research. The current treatment for allergic fungal sinusitis involves all the usual methods (see right) with special emphasis on steroids to calm the inflammation, plus anti-fungal drugs where fungal infection is detectable in the membrane. In some countries, immunotherapy is also used to reduce the immune reaction to the fungus, but this is difficult to obtain in Britain (see p. 164).

Clearing moulds from your home may help (see p. 34). So may reducing the humidity in the house (see p. 119), as humid conditions seem to be linked with allergic fungal sinusitis .

Treatment

Sinusitis can be very hard to treat, particularly if it has been going on for a long time. You need a really committed attitude if treatment is to be successful.

All these treatments should be given at the same time:

1 Antibiotics for two to three weeks minimum (it takes this long because the antibiotic has such trouble getting into the sinus cavities – if you are offered a shorter course, this suggests that the doctor does not have enough expertise with chronic sinusitis, so you might be better off with someone else). It must be the right antibiotic – commonly used ones such as penicillin, tetracycline and erythromycin are unlikely to work because the bacteria are usually resistant to them.

2 Steroid drops in the nose to combat the inflammation. It is important to put these in correctly, so that they have maximum effect (see p. 144) especially if you have polyps.

3 Irrigating the nose and sinus cavities daily with sterile salt water (saline). Your doctor will show you how to do this.

4 Tablets that reduce the congestion in the nose.

5 Nose drops that reduce congestion, but for three days only (see p. 29).

6 Steam inhalations to loosen the mucus. There are special steam vaporisers on sale (ask at a pharmacy), but you can just inhale steam from a bowl of boiling water, with a towel over your head to keep the steam in. Adding eucalyptus oil to the water may help. For a quick-and-easy version, warm up a damp flannel in the microwave and place it over your nose. Some doctors recommend having a steam vaporiser beside the bed at night, when nasal blockage is most likely to occur, but if you have allergies to house-dust mite or moulds, this is not a good idea in the long term, as a damp bedroom will favour both (and could encourage allergic fungal sinusitis).

7 A drug called guaifenesin which thins the mucus is used in some countries but rarely in Britain. Alpha-methyl-cysteine is another drug that breaks up mucus. It is mainly used in chronic bronchitis but some doctors also find it valuable in chronic sinusitis . If steam inhalations didn't work – suggesting

that the mucus is too solid to be shifted – these drugs may be worth trying.

8 Anti-fungal drugs (taken by mouth) if allergic fungal sinusitis is suspected. Sometimes these have a dramatic effect on chronic sinusitis that has previously resisted treatment.

You may also be given other drugs, such as steroid tablets. The new anti-leukotriene drugs (see p. 149) are also being tried, with some success. As well as being taken by mouth, they can be applied directly to the nose in an irrigation fluid, and may be helpful for those with nasal polyps.

Problems with nose drops

Nasal drops and washes contain preservatives and other non-drug ingredients. Some of these may act as irritants – or the pH (acidity or alkalinity) of the preparation might cause problems. If you experience burning or irritation after inserting drops or irrigating the sinuses, ask your doctor or pharmacist about trying a different preparation.

Antibiotic resistance

Bacteria are becoming resistant to the effects of antibiotics: it is probably the biggest headache facing modern medicine.

This is emerging as a particular problem in chronic sinusitis because many patients have been dosed very regularly with antibiotics. Although most of the bacteria have been killed each time, the fact that the sinus cavity is so clogged up with mucus, and so badly accessed by the blood-stream anyway, means there is always some nook or cranny where a few bacteria survive because they have not been exposed to the full lethal dose of the antibiotic. As you might expect, these survivors tend to be the 'tough ones' – those bacteria that are not just well hidden but also the least sensitive to the antibiotic.

Repeat this process many times, with frequent courses of antibiotics (separated by intervals during which the hard-to-kill bacteria multiply in numbers) and what happens? Eventually you breed a race of bacteria that are completely resistant to one or more of the antibiotics taken.

If you ever get to this point with your sinusitis, treatment is going to be extremely difficult. That's why it is so important to treat infections really thoroughly, and get rid of them completely. Expert medical help is essential for this treatment campaign.

Too many people with chronic sinusitis are careless about taking their antibiotics regularly, or feel ambivalent about them and stop the course before it's complete, or don't see the doctor again when the tablets are used up. This is courting disaster.

Don't start antibiotic treatment for chronic sinusitis until you are sure you can see it through. If you have doubts about taking antibiotics, try all the other treatments and self-help measures first. They may be sufficient, especially if you find you have an allergy underlying the chronic sinusitis and can tackle this successfully.

Should there be no improvement, you could then go on to the antibiotic programme: delaying this treatment for a few months will do no harm. What is hazardous is starting the antibiotic programme and then stopping, or not taking the drugs consistently.

Antihistamines may be prescribed to treat any allergic reactions, but some specialists feel that they can also aggravate the problems. In their experience, antihistamines dry out the mucus so that it sticks to the walls of the sinus cavities, rather than being ushered out by the cilia. Drying out the mucus may make you feel better initially, by reducing the pressure inside the sinus cavities, but it makes matters worse in the long run.

Anti-cholinergic drugs (see p. 156) are sometimes prescribed for chronic sinusitis, but they too can dry up the mucus and should be used cautiously.

After three weeks, if the sinusitis has not improved substantially, a different antibiotic is given. If there are any bacteria resistant to the first antibiotic infesting your sinus cavities, the new antibiotic is intended to kill them off.

Should you still have sinusitis after another three weeks, you will be given yet another antibiotic. Changing the antibiotic, and taking prolonged courses, is the best way of exterminating the bacteria completely, which prevents the development of antibiotic-resistant bacteria (see box).

It is crucial that you always see the doctor promptly at the end of each course, so that there is no gap between the courses – do not give the bacteria any opportunity to build up their numbers again. The last antibiotic treatment should continue for at least a week after symptoms clear up.

Dealing with allergic reactions is also important:

- If you cannot get allergy tests, try to work out for yourself if an allergen is playing a part. Ask yourself if there were any changes in your life before the sinusitis began, such as getting a new pet, moving house, increased exposure to moulds or house-dust mite, or starting a new job with exposure to allergens. When thinking about this, remember that allergies to newly encountered allergens do not develop immediately - it may take up to two years. Try avoiding the allergen concerned and seeing if you improve.
- Should you discover that an allergen is at the root of the problem, but have difficulty reducing your exposure to the offending item, try to obtain immunotherapy (see p. 164) or another form of desensitisation treatment (see p. 210).
- If you suspect allergic fungal sinusitis (see p. 32), it is well worth eliminating any mould growth in your home (see p. 120). One research study showed that the moulds growing in a patient's sinus cavities were often the same as those growing in the patient's house. It is possible that, by inhaling the mould spores from moulds in their houses, sinusitis sufferers are continually reinfecting their sinuses.

Various other self-help measures can be valuable during this medical treatment:

- Reduce your exposure to cigarette smoke (including other people's) to an absolute minimum. Cigarette smoke acts as an irritant to the nose and sinuses, but, more importantly, it paralyses the cilia, preventing them from shifting mucus out of the sinus cavities.
- Avoid breathing other irritants, especially ozone (see p. 130). Think about the chemicals you use both at work and at home – could any of these be irritants that are aggravating your sinusitis?
- Don't drink too much alcohol – it dries out the sinus membranes and makes matters worse.
- Drink plenty of water, to keep your mucus from becoming too dry and therefore hard to shift.
- Try to breathe through your nose as much as possible. The amount of oxygen in your sinus cavities drops drastically if you breathe through your mouth, and the low oxygen level probably fosters the growth of certain bacteria. Devices, such as nose clips, that help keep the nose open at night may be worth trying.
- Spicy food can help to clear nasal and sinus congestion, so try eating chilli or hot curry regularly.
- Some people find that garlic helps – either eaten or sniffed.
- If you suspect that your sinusitis might be related to food sensitivity (see p. 68) consider trying an elimination diet to identify the culprit food.
- Observe your reactions immediately after eating – some foods, such as yeast and red wine, can cause an immediate swelling of the nasal membranes in certain people. So can sulphite food additives. Avoid such items if you are affected.
- Treating gastro-oesophageal reflux (acid regurgitation from the stomach after meals) can improve sinusitis.
- See an osteopath. By gently manipulating parts of your face, a good osteopath may be able to improve the drainage from the sinus cavities.
- Some patients experience good effects from acupuncture although there are no observable changes on CT scans. Other alternative therapies, such as homeopathy or Chinese herbal medicines, have not been investigated scientifically, but some patients report good results.

Prolonged courses of antibiotics destroy many of the beneficial bacteria in the intestine, and may cause long-term bowel problems. It makes sense to take a bacterial replacer (see p. 205).

Surgery for sinusitis

Chronic sinusitis sufferers may be offered surgery to remove polyps, or to correct anatomical problems such as a deviated septum (the central division of the nose).

These operations can be very useful, but if you have asthma, try all other options first, because surgery to the nose can sometimes make asthma much worse.

Surgery on the sinus cavities themselves is also a possibility, when sinusitis does not respond to medical treatment. The operation enlarges the natural drainage channels, so that mucus drains away more easily. This rarely cures chronic sinusitis completely, but it usually makes it much easier to manage. Once the drainage channels are larger, antibiotics can be put directly into the sinus cavities, for example, avoiding the need for antibiotic tablets.

Don't agree to surgery unless other forms of treatment, such as allergen avoidance or immunotherapy, have been tried to the full. Patients for whom surgery seemed to be the only answer have sometimes found they did not need an operation once their allergies were treated.

If you decide on having an operation, make sure your surgeon has a proven track-record with *this type* of surgery. Don't be afraid to ask searching questions about how many operations of this kind the surgeon has done, how many he or she carries out per year, and the complication rates (how often things go wrong). It's a delicate job, and you want a real expert.

Asthma

Tom works for the Post Office, sorting mail on a night shift. 'After work, I come out of the sorting office – it's about five or six in the morning, and really cold – and when I suddenly hit the cold air, I feel as if I just can't breathe. My chest clamps up like anything, so much that it hurts. Then, when I get in the car and put the heater on, it's fine again.'

What Tom is describing is **bronchospasm**, the key event in asthma – a sudden, but reversible, tightening of the bands of muscle that surround the airways. The narrowed airways stop air from leaving the lungs at the normal speed, which means the lungs are still half-full when it's time for the next in-breath. Taking more air into half-full lungs produces pain and tightness in the chest, as the lungs become over-inflated. (This can be alarming, because it can seem like pain from the heart, but it is just the rib joints and chest muscles hurting as they become stretched.)

Insufficient oxygen reaches the bloodstream because there is so much stale air in the lungs, so the asthmatic also feels breathless. Meanwhile, the air being forced through the narrowed airways makes a whistling sound called **wheezing**.

Those are the common symptoms of asthma, but there are others:

• Coughing, rather than wheezing, is the main symptom for some people (see box on p. 40).
• Sometimes there is vomiting during an asthma attack, especially in children, because the overexpanded lungs put a great deal of pressure on the stomach.
• A few asthmatics suffer narrowing in the trachea (the upper part of the windpipe) rather than in the airways lower down, and therefore feel as if they are being strangled.

Bronchospasm is just the endpoint of the disease process in asthma, a process which begins with **inflammation of the airways**. Although the airway muscles relax when an asthma attack is over, and you therefore feel much better, the underlying inflammation of the airways remains.

Airway inflammation may be caused, or partially caused, by allergy. Among asthmatic children, allergies are detected in 80–90%.

Inflammation makes the lining of the airways swell up, which itself narrows the airways a little. The inflamed airway lining often makes more **mucus** than usual, in an effort to protect itself (this is basically a healthy response – mucus works like a sponge mopping up irritating dust particles so that they can be ejected by coughing – but it's excessive in asthma). This mucus can clog up the airways even more. Finally, the inflamed airways send nerve impulses direct to the airway muscles telling them to contract

Mucus alert

Asthmatic mucus is white or clear, and sometimes frothy. Greenish or yellowish mucus suggests an infection and should be reported to your doctor.

In severe cases of asthma, a lump of mucus can completely block an airway, leading part of the lung to collapse. It is vital to clear mucus from the lungs, and a physiotherapist can help with this.

What causes asthma?

This question can be answered at three different levels:

1 What makes someone predisposed to asthma?
2 What starts asthma off – in other words, what starts the inflammation process in the airways?
3 What triggers asthma attacks?

What makes someone predisposed to asthma?

The predisposition to asthma is partly inherited (see p. 8) and partly a matter of lifestyle: a poor diet makes asthma more likely (see p. 206), as does too much cleanliness (see p. 21).

What starts asthma off?

The predisposition to asthma sets the stage, but it does not, in itself, start the inflammation of the airways. That is often begun by an allergic reaction to something in the air – such as house-dust mite or pet allergens.

Alternatively, the initiating factor could be a viral infection, especially a kind known as Respiratory Syncytial Virus or RSV – there are epidemics of RSV every two or three years. Those predisposed to asthma may make an abnormal kind of immune response to chest infections caused by viruses, a response that shifts the balance of the immune system towards Th2 cells – see p. 11 – and allergy-type reactions.

A heavy dose of certain irritants, such as chlorine, or the substances used in spray-painting cars, can also initiate asthma; this mainly occurs in a workplace setting, causing **occupational asthma** (see p. 132).

What triggers asthma attacks?

Once the inflammation of the airways has begun, the airways are 'twitchy' – oversensitive – and the airway muscles contract at the smallest provocation. Irritants in the air, such as tobacco smoke, can then trigger an attack, as can a great variety of other things – from cold air or the scent of hyacinths, to thunderstorms, laughter or anxiety – see p. 39 for a full list. Exposure to the allergens that started the inflammation will also trigger an asthma attack, as will a virus (viral) infection such as a cold or flu.

For many asthmatics, the breathing pattern is disturbed by the asthma attacks, and may remain abnormal between attacks. **Hyperventilation** or 'over-breathing' can begin quite easily for asthmatics, and then adds to the overall problems. It may be difficult to tell if you hyperventilate or not, because your habitual pattern of breathing will seem normal to you, but there may be tell-tale symptoms such as dizziness, tingling of the hands and feet, numbness and muscle cramps. For a full list of symptoms see p. 227

Mind power

The muscle of the airways is the kind of muscle over which we have no conscious control, like that of the heart. It is known as **involuntary muscle**, whereas muscles in the arms and legs, which contract or relax when we tell them to, are called **voluntary muscles**. Studies with biofeedback have shown that asthmatics may, with training, gain some degree of control over these involuntary muscles. Experienced yoga practitioners are able to influence various involuntary muscles, including those in the airways.

There are also various ways in which the mind, or a person's social and emotional situation, can make asthma worse (see p. 234) but the damaging idea that it is an entirely 'psychological' disease is now discounted.

Allergens and irritants

Understanding the difference between allergens and irritants is important for asthmatics. Allergens are specific – either pollen is an allergen for you or it isn't, depending on how your immune system reacts to it. They are also a basic cause of asthma – they start it off.

Irritants, on the other hand, are non-specific: they affect every asthmatic if sufficiently concentrated, causing bronchospasm by aggravating the airway lining. And, at the levels usually encountered, they only cause trouble because the inflammation of the airways has already occurred. Irritants include cigarette smoke, other smoke and some industrial fumes, ozone (see p. 130), sulphur dioxide (given off by some foods and drinks – see box on p. 207), fly spray, air freshener or other aerosols.

Diagnosis

There are four separate aspects to diagnosis:

1 Is this really asthma or something else entirely?

2 Is it combined with other diseases, and how are they affecting the asthma?

3 What is the basic cause of the inflammation in the airways, and can this be avoided?

4 What sort of factors trigger the asthma attacks?

You may not get this full diagnostic programme, but you can probably help in finding answers to some of the questions.

Is this really asthma or something else entirely?

There are no tests that can diagnose asthma with complete certainty, but the average case of adult asthma is pretty easy to spot, and the same is true for children over five. It is also true, however, that some patients now described as asthmatic would have been given a different diagnosis (e.g. wheezy bronchitis) 30 years ago. To some extent, this is because asthma was under-diagnosed in the past: doctors were hesitant about giving a diagnosis of asthma, because of the supposed overtones of psychosomatic disease. Sweeping away that stigma has been of immense value, but certain patients (especially young children) may now get diagnosed as asthmatic without sufficient evidence. However, there are also many instances of asthma being missed.

These are two tests that should be carried out before you are given a diagnosis of asthma:

1 Peak flow is the top speed of the outgoing air from your lungs, usually measured with a simple portable machine called a peak-flow meter. Because of the narrowed airways, asthmatics have a lower peak flow than normal.

2 The **reversibility test** depends on measuring peak flow before and after inhaling a beta-2 reliever drug which relaxes the airway muscles (see p. 152). If the drug improves peak flow by more than 15%, this strongly suggests asthma.

Asthma may be difficult to diagnose in certain situations:

• In babies, who often wheeze, especially when they have colds or chest infections. This generally clears up later and does not automatically develop into asthma. There is great controversy about whether wheezy babies should be labelled 'asthmatic' or not, and how bad the wheezing should be before they are given asthma drugs. Views on this vary, so you may want to see a different doctor for a second opinion. For older children who wheeze only when they get chest infections, most doctors feel it is valuable to use asthma drugs – such treatment does not 'turn wheezing into asthma'

as is sometimes claimed. (There are several things you can do to minimise the chance of early wheezing turning into asthma later – see pp. 244–9.)

• When the main symptom is coughing (see box on p. 40).

• When asthma occurs only at night. In some asthmatics, even intensive testing reveals no abnormality in the airways during the day. The only way to diagnose the condition is to use a peak-flow meter at home, morning and evening.

• When there is a sudden one-off asthma attack in response to a powerful allergen load. This sometimes happens to hayfever sufferers at the height of the pollen season (especially during thunderstorms). Some doctors will want to start asthma drugs immediately, but it may be better to get the hayfever well controlled with antihistamines and see what happens. Often there are no further asthma attacks.

Then there are conditions that can be mistaken for asthma:

• In children, an inhaled object – such as a nut or part of a toy – becoming stuck in the airways. In babies it can also be inhalation of milk droplets; if so, the 'asthma' comes on mainly after feeding.

• Post-nasal drip (see p. 29)

• Heiner's Syndrome – (see p. 72)

• Bronchiolitis: a viral infection (generally caused by RSV – see p. 37) which affects the small airways (the bronchioles) of babies and toddlers. Unlike asthma, it usually produces fever.

• Gastro-oesophageal reflux (GER), or the rising of food from the stomach into the oesophagus. (This is commonly called heartburn, after its most typical symptom, but you can suffer from GER *without* having heartburn.) GER can aggravate existing asthma, and it can also be an asthma mimic. Babies, children and adults can all suffer from this problem. There will usually be clues such as symptoms that come on at night after a late supper, or whenever lying down.

• Hyperventilation (see p. 227) in non-asthmatics can be mis-diagnosed as asthma if it causes breathlessness.

• Aspergillosis (see box on p. 18).

• Problems with the vocal cords. Habitually contracting the vocal cords on the in-breath makes a loud wheezing sound and can cause breathlessness. This problem can mimic asthma, but it also affects those who really are asthmatic. The cause is usually psychological.

• Low-level carbon monoxide poisoning, generally from gas fires, which can cause breathlessness and fatigue.

• Bronchiectasis: stretching and damage to the airways caused by diseases caught in childhood, such as pneumonia or whooping cough. This causes lifelong breathlessness.

Is it combined with other diseases, and how are they affecting the asthma?

Any allergic problems in the nose will contribute to asthmatic symptoms in the lungs, because there are nerve-connections between the two. Long-term sinusitis can also make matters worse. Optimum treatment for the nasal and sinus symptoms (see pp. 28–35) will help considerably with the asthma.

One unlikely source of asthmatic symptoms has only recently been recognised: allergies can develop to the fungi causing athlete's foot, or other diseases (see pp. 16–17).

GER can contribute substantially to asthma, as described on p. 38. Your doctor can advise on treatment.

For older people, especially veteran smokers, asthma may be part of a larger picture of inflammation and damage to the air sacs of the lung (emphysema) and/or to the airways (bronchitis). This mosaic of problems is known as chronic obstructive pulmonary disease (COPD). It may be difficult to tell if there is asthma present, or how much it is contributing to the overall problem. Since many patients with COPD are helped by asthma drugs, and trying out the drugs does no harm, doctors often prescribe them just to see what happens.

What is the basic cause of airway inflammation?

Skin-prick tests are usually needed here, to check for allergic reactions. It may be difficult to get these in Britain, where there is a shortage of allergists (see p. 89).

Simple detective work may pinpoint allergens without the need for tests. The likely suspects are all airborne allergens – see p. 28. Remember that the reaction does not generally start as soon as exposure to the allergen begins: there is a time-lag. So a new dog or cat, or an allergen encountered at work, may cause no trouble for the first year or two.

Some irritants can also be a basic cause of asthma, but only if encountered in high doses, which usually occurs in the workplace (see box on p. 132).

In all cases, removing the allergen or irritant from the airways should be a top priority. The sooner you can end the exposure, the more likely you are to shake off the asthma, rather than have it for ever. Once the inflammation of the airways is firmly established, it just fuels itself – so act quickly.

In a minority of cases, **food sensitivity** is the initiating cause of asthma. The reaction to food is delayed, so the link will not be obvious. Skin-prick tests for the culprit food are usually negative, so an elimination diet (see p. 194) is needed to diagnose this problem and identify the food concerned. Those most likely to benefit are brittle asthmatics (those most severely affected) – as many as 60% have a food sensitivity. There are various other clues that food could be a factor (see p. 69).

When asthma begins in adulthood, there may be no clear initiating cause – it is just a question of long-term damage and irritation to the airways. But there can be allergens playing a part, so it is worth investigating this possibility.

What sort of factors trigger the asthma attacks?

Most asthmatics will recognise one or more of these as triggers:

- cold or dry air
- strong smells including perfume and fragrant flowers
- irritants in the air (such as cigarette smoke and other indoor pollutants, traffic fumes, industrial pollutants); indoor pollution is often the worst, especially if you have a gas cooker without adequate ventilation, so there is a lot you can do to improve the air you breathe (see pp. 128–30)
- sulphur dioxide given off by preservatives used in some food and drink (see box on p. 207)
- weather conditions particularly thunderstorms
- laughing, sighing, yawning, coughing or any other altered breathing pattern
- stress or anxiety
- strong emotions such as fear, anger or excitement
- situations or people that evoke unpleasant memories – including traumatic childhood memories; sometimes psychotherapy is needed to sort such problems out (see p. 233)
- exercise (because breathing hard dries out the airways)
- the allergens responsible for the asthma, e.g. cat allergen
- colds, flu and chest infections.

Recording your symptoms day-by-day should help to identify the triggers that are most powerful for you. Generally speaking, such triggers should be avoided, but this is not the case for exercise which does much more good than harm, in the long run – without exercise, your asthma will get far worse (see p. 41).

Take care with aspirin

Aspirin sensitivity can develop unexpectedly in asthmatics, especially those with allergic rhinitis and/or nasal polyps (see p. 28). It can produce a severe, even fatal, asthma attack. Remember to avoid all aspirin-like drugs (see p. 151).

Just a cough?

For some, coughing is the main symptom of asthma. Known as **cough-variant asthma**, this is not always diagnosed correctly, especially in children. For children with recurrent coughing (two or more episodes per year of coughing without a cold) it may be a long time before the doctor considers asthma. But other doctors may diagnose a coughing child as 'asthmatic' all too readily, without doing enough tests. The important point is that asthma involves episodes of bronchospasm – contraction of the airway muscles. Without this it is not asthma. Bronchospasm can be detected by medical tests such as peak-flow readings. Wheezing is one possible symptom of bronchospasm, but coughing is another.

If there is only coughing as a symptom, and never any wheezing, this is probably not asthma. Among children with this pattern of symptoms, allergies are unlikely to be involved. The cause of such coughing may be:
- in children, the effects of parental smoking
- in those with perennial allergic rhinitis (see pp. 28–9) mucus from the nose running into the lungs. This is called **post-nasal drip** and produces a persistent cough.
- in the middle-aged, **eosinophilic bronchitis**. This is caused by an influx of eosinophils (see p. 19) into the airway lining, causing inflammation. Allergies do not seem to play a part (it is no more common in atopics than anyone else) and the airway muscles do not contract abnormally. Treatment is with inhaled steroids.
- in atopics (those prone to allergies), a condition sometimes called **atopic cough**. It involves eosinophils congregating in the trachea (windpipe) and bronchi, but not in the lower airways. There is inflammation but no airway narrowing. Very little is known about this disease at present; it may or may not involve allergies. Again, inhaled steroids are effective.
- for a few people, habitual coughing. This is usually an expression of some underlying emotional difficulty and responds to psychological treatments. The cough often has a honking or barking sound.

Any of these can be misdiagnosed as asthma. For patients with eosinophilic bronchitis or atopic cough, this is no tragedy as they will probably get the right treatment (inhaled steroids) anyway. But if more exact diagnostic criteria are being used (e.g. a reversibility test – see p. 38) such patients will not be classed as asthmatic – this is more of a problem because they may not get appropriate treatment.

Treatment

The first and most important aspect of asthma is environmental control – to try and minimise contact with allergens and irritants. If you are asthmatic and you smoke, you must stop, because this will only make matters worse by stoking up the inflammation. Any other smokers in the family should accept that from now on this is an outdoor activity.

One of the aims of good asthma treatment is to calm the airways down, so that they are less sensitive and 'twitchy'. This means tackling the inflammation. You can do this with **preventer drugs** such as steroids or cromoglycate (see p. 157), or with the new anti-leukotriene drugs (see p. 159), or you can simply remove the basic source of the trouble, if it is a domestic allergen such as a cat, dog or house-dust mite.

Treating associated diseases such as sinusitis, hayfever, perennial allergic rhinitis, gastro-esophageal reflux (GER – see p. 38) and athlete's foot (where this is adding to the symptoms – see p. 16) can also help in reducing the airway inflammation. Eating a better diet may make a further contribution to calming the airways down (see p. 206).

The second strand of treatment is to deal with bronchospasm (contraction of the airway muscles) when it occurs. This is done with **reliever drugs** such as Ventolin and Atrovent (see p. 152). Note that these only relieve the symptoms of an asthma attack, and do not address the underlying problem of inflammation. What is more, if used too frequently (more than once a day) they may increase the risk of a fatal or near-fatal asthma attack (see p. 153).

At one time, reliever drugs were the mainstay of asthma treatment, and were perceived as entirely safe, while preventer drugs such as steroids were only given to those with severe asthma. All this has changed, and most asthmatics, other than those with very infrequent attacks, are now given a preventer. If your drug regime has not been reviewed for some time, make an appointment with your doctor and check that you are getting the best of the modern treatments.

Drug treatment of asthma is not something you can just hand over to the doctor – it requires a lot of personal decision-making. If you usually get worse when you have a cold, for example, you need to increase your dose of preventer as soon as a cold appears, to stop the inflammation before it starts. You also need to know when an asthma attack is serious enough to warrant calling an ambulance. A **management plan**, worked out with your doctor, is a useful aid in such decisions (see p. 96). Using a peak-flow meter, night and morning, to monitor your asthma will also be valuable (see p. 97).

The third strand of asthma treatment is to deal with associated problems:

• Panicky reactions during asthma attacks – which make matters infinitely worse – can be dealt with by meditation, yoga, relaxation techniques or martial arts training (see p. 222).

• Hyperventilation, which plays a much larger role in asthma than previously suspected, can be tackled by a variety of methods (see p. 228).

• The distortions of the rib-cage that develop in severe asthma can be treated with osteopathy.

• Losing weight, if you are very heavy, will help ease the burden on your breathing.

Exercise and asthma

Exercise-induced asthma is best tackled, paradoxically, by taking exercise. As your fitness improves, you don't pant so hard when exercising, so your airways dry out much less. Countless asthmatics will tell you that once you overcome the first hurdle – of wheezing the minute you start to exercise – things get a great deal easier. You will need reliever drugs, and possibly extra preventer, to help you over this hurdle, but it's worth it.

Warming up with a few sharp sprints, separated by a rest period, will also help. (If you get an asthma attack while exercising, however, you should always stop – carrying on regardless can be fatal. Always have your reliever inhaler with you when you exercise and use it if you get an attack.) Swimming is an excellent starting point for unfit asthmatics, because the moist air prevents the airways from drying out. Once you are fitter, regular strenuous exercise makes the breathing muscles stronger, which is of great benefit – this can also be achieved with operatic exercises, and with mechanical lung exercisers (see p. 231).

Don't underestimate asthma

Asthma can be fatal, so never take it too lightly. If you often wake up in the night with asthma, you cannot keep up with most other people your age, or are frequently breathless when climbing stairs or walking uphill, then your asthma is not under control. The same is true if you need your reliever inhaler more than once a day, or frequently need steroid tablets. Review your treatment with your doctor because you probably need more preventive treatment such as inhaled steroids (see p. 157).

Recognising an asthma attack and knowing when to call for help, or go to the hospital, is also crucial (see p. 100). Remember that fatal asthma attacks often come on very quickly – half those who die do so within two hours of the attack starting, a quarter die within 30 minutes. Those who die are generally people who have neglected their preventer medication, or have been exposed to very high levels of allergens.

Atopic eczema

A Greek word meaning 'to boil over' or 'to erupt' is the source of the medical term 'eczema'. It refers, of course, to the way in which the skin erupts into a rash, but it could equally well describe the eruption of controversy around this disease. No other allergic disease is quite such a cauldron of dissent – indeed, even the question of whether it *is* an allergic disease remains unresolved. These controversies directly affect the treatment of atopic eczema, so it is useful to understand them if you or your child have eczema.

The disagreement begins with the question of what causes atopic eczema.

Let's start with the one point that everyone agrees on: dry skin plays a fundamental role. Those with atopic eczema have dry skin, not just in the eczematous areas, but in other parts as well, sometimes all over the body. The skin cells are less efficient than normal skin cells at retaining water.

Everyone would also agree that there is **inflammation** of the skin – a reaction that is produced by the immune system. But when it comes to the question of what *starts off* the inflammation there are huge differences of opinion among specialists treating atopic eczema – these specialists include dermatologists, allergists and paediatricians.

Given that people with atopic eczema are atopic – that is, allergy-prone – and that most of them have huge amounts of the allergy antibody, IgE, going round in their blood, it might seem plausible that an allergic reaction to some external item kicks off the inflammation. And when skin-prick tests to common allergens such as house-dust mite are tried, there are usually a large number of positive results.

But many of these turn out to be false positives – when tested more directly, the allergen concerned does not actually play a part in causing the skin symptoms. This has led some specialists working with eczema, mainly dermatologists, to believe that allergic reactions play little part in either initiating or perpetuating atopic eczema.

In their view, the basic cause of atopic eczema is dry skin and a generally overwrought immune system, not specific allergic reactions. To these doctors, positive skin-prick tests are *all* false positives in atopic eczema – that is, irrelevant to the disease process.

A positive skin-test result, they believe, simply indicates that the skin of atopic eczema sufferers is in a highly sensitive state, not that the allergen concerned plays any causative role.

Allergists tend to take a different view – but even here a wide range of opinions exists. Just to

What the words mean

Eczema is not a disease in itself. The word refers to a certain type of reddish rash – a rash which can be caused in a variety of ways. The type of eczema that affects people of an allergic disposition (atopics), is called either **atopic eczema** or **atopic dermatitis.**

The word **dermatitis** just means inflammation of the skin. Most doctors consider it to be synonymous with **eczema**, but some give it a slightly broader meaning.

type of immune reaction (see pp. 18–19), or even a mixture of the two.

Research using direct challenge tests (see p. 90) has identified some of the things that could provoke such sensitivity reactions:

- cow's milk or other food – a prime suspect in babies and young children (see p. 68). Note that the response to food is usually delayed, occurring some hours after the offending item is consumed.
- house-dust mites, pollen or moulds
- cats, dogs, rabbits and other furry pets.

The eczema symptoms can be provoked either by airborne allergens falling on the skin, or by direct contact (e.g. mite allergens in the bed, skin contact with pets, lying on grass for those with grass-pollen allergy). The rash tends to occur on skin not covered by clothes. But it can sometimes be localised to the most sensitive areas of skin, for example in those who react to house-dust mite but have eczema on the eyelids only .

Additionally, experiments show that even when allergen is *only inhaled* it can sometimes provoke eczema symptoms. The allergen (or some pro-inflammation messenger chemical) reaches the skin in the bloodstream. This means that the skin reaction could occur anywhere on the body, not just on exposed skin.

The next step

Whatever causes atopic eczema, it provokes the most horrendous itching, as every eczema sufferer knows. The itch cries out to be scratched, and scratching is the major cause of the visible rash. *If left untouched, the skin does not erupt into eczema*, although it may well turn red, and there are still distinct changes in the skin that can be seen with a microscope.

Once eczema has erupted, the skin is no longer an intact protective layer that neatly separates 'in-here' from 'out-there'. The skin becomes more permeable and loses its own natural moisture far more readily, so the dryness gets worse. At the same time allergens and irritants penetrate far more easily, causing yet more inflammation.

Something else compounds the damage: once atopic eczema is established, the immune system starts making IgE antibodies to the body's own proteins, especially those found in skin cells. This helps explain why atopic eczema can become so severe and so entrenched.

The wandering rash

For a baby with atopic eczema , the face, and especially the cheeks, are commonly affected, but there may be a rash all over the legs, the backs of the arms, and the back. As the months go by, the rash settles on the lower legs, and spreads to the fold of the elbow, and then the fold at the back of the knees – by about three years of age, this **flexure eczema** is the main problem for most children.

In adults, eczema is often found in quite restricted areas, such as the hands, scalp, lips, eyelids or chest. It may be located around the nipples – a sensitive spot where rubbing by clothing is enough to initiate a rash.

Atopic eczema is always in a process of change, and different parts of the body may display different stages of the rash:

- The rash is red and usually dry at first, and there may be not a great deal to see. In this early stage the visible signs may be minimal, while the itchiness can be colossal. Sometimes there is oozing of clear fluid.
- Occasionally the first phase is more marked, with dense patches of small red bumps or tiny blisters. On the hands, these may merge to form much larger blisters.
- Infections tend to change the appearance of the rash (see p. 44).
- With time the skin becomes thicker, paler and scaly. It may form leathery patches (called **lichenification**), especially if there is habitual scratching or rubbing. This is **chronic eczema.**
- When the eczema clears, there may be an area of skin that is lighter in colour, or darker, than the surrounding skin.

Infections – another vicious circle

When eczema erupts and the skin barrier is breached, infections frequently become a problem. A regular source of trouble is the bacterium *Staphylococcus aureus*, the cause of the infection called impetigo. This microbe invades eczematous skin far more readily than healthy skin, causing a prolific ooze with golden-yellow crusting.

Staphylococcus aureus produces a toxin known as a 'super-antigen' which revs up the immune system to even more furious effort. This effort does not, unfortunately, oust the bacteria, but it does make the skin inflammation even worse. To add to their woes, many who are afflicted with atopic eczema start making IgE antibodies against *Staphylococcus aureus* toxins.

Infection with fungi (yeasts and moulds) is also a problem in atopic eczema (see p. 49), and there may be sensitivity reactions to these fungi.

The herpes virus, responsible for causing cold sores, can also invade eczematous skin, though this is much rarer. It worsens the eczema and produces flocks of small red bumps, each with a tiny dimple or blister at the centre – ***this needs urgent treatment***.

Irritants and stress

People with atopic eczema are far more susceptible to everyday irritants such as soap, traces of detergent left behind in clothes, wool and rough synthetic fabrics. Chlorinated water, either in swimming pools or from the tap, can also aggravate the skin, and even 'hard' water (found in areas with chalk or limestone bedrock) may be a factor.

Some air pollutants may play a part in atopic eczema. Researchers in Germany have found that children living close to busy trunk roads, or in homes with a gas cooker and no extraction hood (see pp. 128–9), were more likely to develop eczema. Formaldehyde fumes, often found in modern houses (see p. 129), are sometimes a factor when eczema affects the face and hands.

Various other things can irritate the skin and make atopic eczema flare up:

- cold weather
- dry air
- long car journeys
- sweating heavily; clothes or shoes that trap sweat may also cause problems
- dust mites, which can act as an irritant, even if not an allergen
- tobacco smoke
- solvents and other chemicals encountered at work
- skin contact with fruit (especially citrus), vegetables, and

sometimes other foods. The spray generated by peeling potatoes can even produce eczema on the face.

Anything which increases blood flow through the skin makes the itching worse:

- heat, especially a hot bath or being too hot in bed
- anger or embarrassment
- hot drinks of any kind
- coffee, tea, and alcohol because of the drug-like substances they contain
- vinegar and spicy foods
- chocolate, soy sauce, yeast extract, orange juice, tomatoes and other foods that are rich in amines (see p. 200).

Various changes in the body can make the eczema worse:

- teething, in babies
- colds and other viral infections
- in women, certain phases of the menstrual cycle.

Many eczema sufferers are aware that their skin gets worse when they are upset, stressed or anxious (just before examinations, for example). Like other allergic diseases, atopic eczema is not *primarily* psychological but, once it has begun, psychological factors can play quite a big part.

Contact sensitivity

People with atopic eczema can develop contact dermatitis (see p. 54) – to nickel, for example, or perfume. There is always this risk with regularly applying creams to your skin, especially anything containing fragrance or lanolin. Antihistamine and antibiotic creams also carry this risk.

Even the ingredients in the creams prescribed for eczema – such as moisturisers and steroids – can sometimes provoke contact dermatitis. Creams are more likely to contain sensitising ingredients than ointments. Very occasionally, the sensitivity is to a preservative or emulsifier that is widely used in different ointments and creams, which means that switching brands yields no improvement. Steroid suspended in petrolatum (white paraffin jelly) is the least likely to cause reactions.

The rash produced by contact dermatitis looks no different from atopic eczema, so this sensitivity will be far from obvious. It will just seem as though the atopic eczema is not getting better.

Talk to your doctor if you think there may be a problem of this kind. He or she can check by using the suspect cream on one side of the body, and a different-but-equivalent product on the other side. Patch tests (see p. 92) may also help to identify contact sensitivity.

The good news...

...for children and teenagers, is that if you have eczema as a child, your chances of developing acne during your teens are greatly reduced.

Diagnosis

There are five separate aspects to diagnosis:

1 Is this really atopic eczema? There are no clear-cut tests for atopic eczema. Instead the diagnosis is based on a 'points system' – how many of the typical features of atopic eczema are present? The doctor adds them up, and if there are enough, then it's atopic eczema. Sometimes all the typical features are there and this is obviously the right diagnosis, but in other cases there may be room for doubt. The doctor should rule out the possibility of contact dermatitis (see p. 54), especially if you have eczema only, or mainly, on the hands.

2 What avoidable irritants are making the skin worse ?

3 Is the eczematous skin infected? The signs of infection are usually clear, but not always, especially with fungal infections. Steroid creams can sometimes mask the overt signs of infections: if atopic eczema is not responding to treatment this possibility should be investigated.

4 Are there any allergic reactions to those infections? Or to the normally harmless microbes that live naturally on the skin (see p. 17)? Skin-prick tests or blood tests can reveal such allergic reactions where fungi are concerned. Adults with persistent atopic eczema which is getting worse rather than better are the most likely candidates.

5 Are there allergic reactions (or other sensitivity reactions) to food, or to allergens such as house-dust mite?

This fifth aspect of diagnosis is where controversy is rife. Many dermatologists feel that atopic eczema is treated quite adequately with moisturisers (emollients) and steroid creams. The search for allergic/sensitivity reactions – in other words, for basic causes – seems unnecessary for most patients, or more trouble than it is worth. Indeed, some dermatologists believe that looking for such sensitivity reactions is actually mistaken because they are not basic causes (see p. 42).

Other specialists disagree, and feel that allergic/sensitivity reactions are a basic causative factor in atopic eczema. They concede that there are many false positives, but in their opinion, there are enough true positives in the skin-prick test results to make it worth sorting them out from the false positives. Except for patients with very mild eczema, such doctors prefer to identify and eliminate the root causes, if possible.

Patch tests are now used by some of these doctors (see p. 69) – yet another contentious issue! The time-honoured use for patch tests is in contact dermatitis, and there is a lot of resistance to using them for atopic eczema. Traditionally, the immune reactions involved in atopic eczema and contact dermatitis are seen as entirely different – the former involving IgE and being a quick reaction (identified by skin-prick tests), the latter involving immune cells and being much slower (identified by patch tests). New research into atopic eczema shows this view to be overly simple (see pp. 18–19) and provides a rational basis for using patch tests.

If, as a patient or a parent, you are keen to search for fundamental causes, remember that this should *never* displace treatments to quell infection or restore the protective structure of the skin. When these treatments are neglected the whole problem can get far worse, because of the vicious circles that sustain atopic eczema.

Sweaty sock dermatitis

More correctly known as 'juvenile plantar dermatitis', this rash on the feet affects an awful lot of atopic children. It is frequently misdiagnosed as athlete's foot, and treated with anti-fungal drugs. The important clue can be found by looking between the toes: if there's no rash there, then it is not athlete's foot.

Treatment

Treatment for atopic eczema has five possible angles:

1 calming the inflammation
2 avoidance of scratching and rubbing
3 caring for the skin and restoring its normal structure
4 treating infections
5 avoiding allergens.

One or more of these aspects may be neglected, depending on what kind of specialist you are seeing. Some allergists may not put enough emphasis on skin care, for example.

Calming the inflammation

Steroid creams are the mainstay of atopic eczema treatment because they calm the inflammation in the skin. The creams do carry a risk of side effects, but are safe when used correctly (see p. 147). An over-fearful attitude to steroids creams can mean that the eczema never gets under control, and this can mean using more steroids in the long run. When treating an outbreak of atopic eczema with steroid cream, it is vital to continue applying the cream until the 'hidden healing' has occurred (see p. 146) – don't stop as soon as the skin *looks* better.

Tar-based ointments have a much milder anti-inflammatory effect, and can be helpful for areas of thickened skin. They were once widely used for atopic eczema, but are used less now, in part because they stain fabrics and smell unpleasant. Sometimes they irritate the skin, too, and there are concerns about safety: they contain carcinogens, and significant amounts are absorbed into the bloodstream. However no evidence has been found that these cause cancer, despite intensive searching.

Antihistamine tablets are sometimes used and while they may not help the eczema much, some evidence suggests that they could reduce the risk of asthma developing later (see p. 249).

Powerful drugs such as cyclosporin are sometimes used in severe cases of atopic eczema, to damp down the immune response. They must be taken by mouth, and can affect other parts of the body, not just the skin. Very careful monitoring is needed. A new immune-modulating drug called tacrolimus, which works when applied directly to the skin in a cream, may soon become available.

Sunlight is often beneficial, because it suppresses the inflammatory processes in the skin. However, not everyone improves with sun exposure – some get worse. Careful experimentation is the only way to find out: build up the length of sun exposure very gradually, starting with less than an hour a day.

Medical treatment with UV (ultraviolet) light can produce the same effect as sunshine and suppress inflammation. This treatment may be prescribed, but you should not try it for yourself with a sun-lamp. In PUVA treatment, a plant-derived substance called psoralen is given by mouth, or applied to the skin, to enhance the response to UV light.

Kicking the scratching habit

Scratching is a substantial part of the problem in long-standing atopic eczema. Experiments with healthy people and mechanical 'scratching machines' show that perfectly normal skin will erupt into eczema if it is scratched intensively.

There is no steroid cream powerful enough to counteract the effects of scratching. But if scratching stops, then the skin can – with the help of medication – heal up.

Note that 'scratching', in this case, includes rubbing the itch (directly or through clothes; using a hand, wrist, chin, leg, foot, or *any* other part of the body), touching or picking at the skin, rubbing against sheets, furniture or another person, or using a towel, flannel or hairbrush to rub the skin. All these activities can be habitual and *quite unconscious,* if atopic eczema has been present for more than a few months – you just don't realise you're doing it most of the time.

For many with atopic eczema, another problem creeps in – scratching without itching. This may be just habit, a response to boredom, stress or anxiety, or even part of the family dynamics, in which scratching has become a form of emotional expression. Scratching alone can set off itching, and a scratch-itch-scratch cycle ensues.

The first step in combating scratching (for an adult or older child) is simply to notice how often scratching occurs. Doctors at the Chelsea and Westminster Hospital in London issue their patients with little hand-held counting devices (tally-counters), and ask them to press the button on the device every time they scratch or rub. Over a period of days, patients discover – usually to their own amazement – just how often they do scratch. The point of the exercise is simply to become conscious of the scratching impulse, and to notice the situations which typically provoke scratching. You could use a small pocket-sized notebook and pencil to achieve the same end.

Once this awareness has been gained, then you are in a position to break the scratching habit. The methods involved – called 'habit reversal' – were first developed by a Swedish dermatologist, Peter Norén. It takes about 2–4 weeks for most people, but the change is long-lasting. Most eczema sufferers find that they recoup their time investment rapidly, once they are free from the chore of dealing with chronic eczema.

When you notice that you are about to start scratching, and before the urge to scratch overwhelms you, take control and do something deliberate with your hands – for example, clench your fists, while breathing deeply and slowly. Think cool non-itchy thoughts. The urge to scratch may pass. If it doesn't, then you can allay the itch by pinching the itchy area gently, or pressing your fingernail into it, or *lightly* applying a little moisturiser.

In the bath or shower, don't use flannels, and never rub or scrub the skin. Dry off by gently patting with a soft towel.

The aim is to get scratching episodes down to fewer than ten per day. In achieving this goal, relaxation exercises, stress management techniques, hypnotherapy or autogenic training (see p. 222) can also be very helpful, especially if you sometimes scratch in tense situations.

With small children, the parents have to do the noticing. Most are unaware just how much their child scratches or rubs the eczema – babies often rub against the side of the cot.

Once the awareness is there, a child over four can usually be taught the habit-reversal technique described above. With a younger child, the parents must distract the child when scratching is imminent, by talking or playing. If the child is scratching while asleep, parents should pick the child up and, very gently, hold the child's hands away from the body. Situations and activities which commonly provoke scratching should be avoided, or planned for. Give the child something to hold while dressing and undressing, for example – keep the hands busy. But *never* say 'Don't scratch' – it usually has the opposite effect in the long run.

For the first four days and nights, while you are trying to break the scratching habit, the child should never be alone, even for a minute – someone who is able to distract the child from scratching should always be there, and awake. Fortunately, children lose the habit far more quickly than adults.

Keep a child's fingernails very short, and smooth them with an emery board too, so that if any scratching does occur the effects are minimised. (Soft cotton mittens, to be worn at night, are often recommended, but the cotton itself can be used to rub the skin – observe your child carefully! The same is true of all-over cotton suits.)

For this anti-scratching programme to be effective in healing the skin, there must be a *determined effort with drug treatment at the same time*. You should be using a steroid cream of *sufficient strength*, twice a day, and plenty of moisturising treatment.

By taking this 'Combined Approach', as Dr Christopher Bridgett and his colleages at the Chelsea and Westminster Hospital call it, you should be able to clear the eczema completely, even if you have had it for years and have tried innumerable different treatments. Once this has been achieved, you can maintain an eczema-free state by watching carefully for any outbreaks of itching, redness or roughness, and treating them immediately with a short course of steroid cream (see p. 146).

Will it clear up?

Small children with eczema generally grow out of it by the age of two. Those who have eczema after this age tend to show a big improvement at puberty. Sometimes, however, the eczema can disappear at puberty, only to reappear later: so continue to be careful with your skin.

Atopic eczema is frequently the first sign of a tendency to allergies (see p. 22). Given this early warning sign, parents should take steps to avoid allergies developing, or at least reduce their severity (see pp. 244–9). One small piece of good cheer: atopic eczema and life-threatening food allergies are very rarely found together.

People with both asthma and atopic eczema frequently notice that when one improves the other seems to get worse. There is no explanation for this as yet.

Moisturisers – how to use them

Moisturisers (emollients) do two things: they increase the amount of water in the skin, and they lubricate the skin, making it less brittle.

A moisturiser is designed to leave an oily layer on the surface of the skin which stops the skin's natural moisture from escaping. The most effective preparations, from this point of view, are ointments made from white paraffin, such as Vaseline, which form an uninter-rupted waterproof layer: these are sometimes called **occlusives**. They contain no water, unlike creams. Although a cream forms a less formidable barrier to the escape of moisture from the skin, it does provide some moisture itself, which can soak into the skin.

The most important thing is to have something that you like using, so that you apply it regularly. There are lots of moisturisers available, so ask the doctor for different ones to try.

Applying moisturiser well is crucial:

- Apply moisturiser before your skin gets dry, as a preventive treatment.
- There's no need to rub in your moisturiser (this can be a form of scratching). Just apply it very lightly.
- A thin layer is all that's needed. A thick layer keeps in heat which aggravates the skin.
- Always apply within 3 minutes of a bath or shower.
- In addition, apply every 3–4 hours during the day. Carrying moisturiser around with you is helpful – the little plastic containers in which camera film is sold are useful for this.
- Ask the doctor to prescribe moisturiser in large quantities, to make sure you have enough. But beware of infecting big pots with *Staphylococcus* bacteria and then re-infecting your skin. Pump-action dispensers are safer.

Moisturiser can also be smeared onto bandages which are then wound around the affected areas at night to reduce the itch – or you can use ready-made 'wet-wraps' (ask your doctor about these). As long as the bandages/wraps are immovable, they will reduce nocturnal rubbing and scratching.

Avoid lotions, and any non-prescribed creams, as they could be irritating to the skin. Choose bath oils with care – some contain alcohol which is an irritant.

Skin care

Firstly, avoid all the irritants which you think may affect your skin. Give clothes an extra rinse cycle in the washing machine, to remove all detergent. Wash all new clothes before wearing them, to remove chemicals such as formaldehyde. Wear soft cotton or silk next to the skin.

Where eczema affects the hands, special care is needed (see p. 57).

Water can be both good and bad for eczema. When you soak in a bath, water is absorbed by the skin cells, which helps correct the dryness of the skin. But when you get out of the bath, and the skin dries, the outermost layer shrinks and develops microscopic cracks, making it even less waterproof than it was before. The way around this problem is to apply a moisturiser immediately after a bath or shower – gently pat the skin until partially dry, and apply the moisturiser immediately so that it can trap the water in the skin.

For anyone with a severe flare of eczema, current recommendations are:

- soak in lukewarm water for 20 minutes, twice a day
- pat dry
- quickly apply steroid cream to the eczematous areas, then moisturiser over the top, and to all other dry-skin areas
- make sure the moisturiser goes on *within 3 minutes of emerging from the water*.

This works well for some people, but not all. For a few eczema sufferers, the effect of taking natural oils out of the skin (which soaking does, to some extent) may outweigh the benefits of putting water in. Or they could be sensitive to something in the tap water – the chlorine, perhaps, or pollutants. It may not be obvious that this routine treatment is not helping. As Dr Michael Tettenborn, a British paediatrician with long experience of atopic eczema, observes: 'By the time they're referred to me, children are usually on the standard regimen of two-soaks-a-day. One of the first things I do, as an experiment, is tell the parents to just bathe them once a week and use a moisturiser and tissues to keep them clean the rest of the time. Some children do a lot better after that.'

Tackling infections

Where infection of eczematous skin occurs, antibiotics, anti-fungal drugs or anti-viral drugs (depending on the type of infection) are essential. Learn to recognise the early signs of an infection developing, and seek medical help promptly.

This is particularly important in the case of herpes (cold sore) infections: a severe infection of eczematous skin with herpes can even be life threatening. Avoid contact with anyone suffering from cold sores.

If you would prefer not to take antibiotic tablets, you could talk to the doctor about the possibility of using an anti-bacterial ointment containing the drug mupirocin. This is a relatively new treatment option.

Undetected fungal infections can be a cause of severe atopic eczema that does not respond to treatment. A recent study at the University of Virginia, USA, showed that for some adults with disabling eczema, a prolonged course of itraconazole (the drug which kills the widest range of fungi) can work wonders. Antibiotics may well be needed at the same time.

Infection of the hands with the fungus that causes athlete's foot can sometimes be the main factor in persistent hand eczema. Occasionally it is *only* the feet that are infected with this fungus, and the hands just 'come out in sympathy'. Treating the feet cures the hands. Contact dermatitis of the feet can produce the same strange 'echo' of eczema symptoms on the hands.

Occasionally overgrowth of yeasts in the gut, combined with an allergic reaction to them, appears to be playing a part in atopic eczema (see box on p. 83). Children whose skin is very red, and who are not responding to treatment, are likely candidates.

Allergen identification and avoidance

Where pollen is the culprit, there is usually a marked eruption of the eczema during the pollen season, so the link is obvious. By contrast, 75% of eczema sufferers who are sensitive to house-dust mite don't notice the connection because exposure is constant.

If you want to investigate the possible role of everyday allergens, and cannot get skin tests, then simply avoid the allergen and observe the effects.

Given that a child with atopic eczema is at high risk for developing other allergic symptoms later, it makes perfect sense to avoid these allergens anyway, especially house-dust mite. Follow the avoidance programmes described in Chapter 4.

The vexed question of investigating food sensitivity is considered on p. 68.

Assuming allergens have been identified, is there any alternative to avoidance? Unfortunately, conventional immunotherapy does not work well for atopic eczema: in fact it can make the skin worse. Doctors practising Enzyme Potentiated Desensitisation (see p. 211) claim good results with atopic eczema.

Additional treatments

Giving up coffee, or stopping smoking, sometimes clears atopic eczema symptoms completely.

There are a few reports of bacterial replacers (or 'probiotics') helping with atopic eczema. They are worth a try (see p. 205), especially if you have taken frequent courses of antibiotics.Some adults with hand eczema lose their symptoms when taking a supplement of Vitamin E.

Evening primrose oil helps some eczema sufferers (see p. 221). Chinese herbal treatments, taken as a tea, may also work for atopic eczema, but be very wary of 'herbal creams' (see pp. 220–1).

An unsuspected problem

Nickel, and other metals, if at high levels in the diet (see p. 55), can cause symptoms resembling atopic eczema in people who are sensitised. The fold of the inner elbow, the sides of the neck, and the skin around the genitals and anus are commonly affected. Recurrent episodes of hand eczema, especially if it is a blistering rash, may also be a sign of metal sensitivity.

Nettle rash and swelling

The resemblance of nettle rash to nettle stings is no coincidence: the liquid that the nettle plant injects into the skin with its spiky hairs contains **histamine**, which is also the main messenger chemical produced during allergic reactions.

The medical name for nettle rash is **urticaria**, which comes from the scientific name for a nettle, *Urtica*. Another term for this condition, used mainly in North America, is **hives**.

Histamine has many effects on the body (see box on p. 12), among them making the smallest blood vessels more leaky. Fluid seeps out into the surrounding area, producing a pale 'nettle-sting' swelling in the upper levels of the skin, called a **wheal**, and/or a swelling at deeper levels known as **angioedema** (*angio-* means blood vessels, *oedema* means swelling caused by excessive fluid). The histamine also causes intense irritation.

Nettle rash is a symptom that can be caused in countless different ways. The different triggers all activate mast cells (see box on p. 12) in the skin to release histamine.

These triggers can sometimes be very difficult to identify in the case of **chronic urticaria** and angioedema ('chronic' means that the symptoms have been present for some time). Prolonged and careful investigation may be needed (see pp. 51–3).

In **acute urticaria** and angioedema – a severe but short-lived reaction – the trigger is usually obvious. It is often an insect sting, a food, or a drug such as penicillin, for example, and the symptoms are due to an IgE-mediated allergy (see box on p. 12).

Because acute urticaria comes on immediately after the encounter with the food or other allergen, there is generally no difficulty in identifying the culprit – if a child takes a mouthful of egg and within minutes his lips and face are swollen and puffy, you know he's allergic to eggs.

Acute urticaria and angioedema are key symptoms of food allergy (see p. 62) and often form part of the catastrophic allergic reaction known as anaphylaxis (see p. 58).

A bed of nettles

A few unfortunate women suffer acute urticaria after sexual intercourse, due to an allergy to semen. In some cases it appears all over the body, not just around the vagina, and asthma or anaphylaxis (see p. 58) can develop. This problem is 'not readily recognised by the medical community', to quote doctors at the University of Cincinnati, USA, who have studied it intensively.

This is an IgE-mediated allergy, but it is usually an allergy to proteins supplied by the partner's prostate gland, rather than to the sperm themselves. Quite often (and this is a puzzle) it occurs on first intercourse. Skin-prick tests with the partner's semen should confirm the diagnosis.

Using condoms usually solves the problem. (If the symptoms persist in these circumstances, the possibility of latex allergy should be considered.) Immunotherapy using the partner's semen is also very effective. For women who have not had immunotherapy and want to conceive, artificial insemination with washed sperm, free of the offending allergens, can be used. The drug sodium cromoglycate (see p. 148) can be used within the vagina before intercourse and this, too, may allow conception.

Drugs, such as penicillin, taken by the male partner can get into the semen in trace amounts and cause urticaria, or even anaphylaxis, in women already sensitised to the drug. It is also believed possible that food allergens eaten by the male partner, and transmitted by the semen in minute amounts, could affect women with severe IgE-mediated food allergy. However, there is no concrete evidence of this.

There can also be IgE-mediated allergic reactions in the vagina to spermicides or to very low levels of *Candida* but these tend to cause more persistent symptoms of itching, or burning and irritation, rather than acute urticaria. This is often wrongly diagnosed and treated as if it were caused by a recurrent *Candida* infection.

Chronic urticaria

First the good news: if you have had chronic urticaria for less than six months, it may well clear up of its own accord – research shows that it does so in about 50% of cases.

Anyone who has been suffering for more than six months has a much smaller chance of spontaneous recovery (only 6%), so treatment is advisable. Those who see a conventional allergist about their problems may then be told the bad news: 'a cause can be determined in only 5–20% of chronic urticaria cases' to quote one authority or '90% of the time your physician will not be able to find the cause of your hives' in the words of another.

Luckily, it isn't true. Some research teams who are studying chronic urticaria intensively have, through sheer persistence in looking for causes, got the proportion of patients with unexplained symptoms down to 23%. Indeed, a recent paper from doctors at the University of Munich states 'there are probably few truly "idiopathic" cases of urticaria' – in other words, few cases where no cause can be found for the disease.

Some of the newly discovered causes for chronic urticaria are:

- a chronic infection elsewhere in the body, often unrecognised. Possible culprits include long-term sinusitis or throat infections, tonsillitis, infected teeth, middle-ear infections, intestinal parasites, inflammation of the gall bladder, kidneys, ovaries or uterus, athlete's foot or related fungal infections (intertrigo, onychomycosis, tinea), prostatitis, Epstein-Barr virus and cytomegalovirus. If there is diarrhoea and inflamed joints as well, *Yersinia* infection is a possibility. These infections seem to have a direct effect on the immune system which causes mast cells to release histamine.
- a reaction to a food additive or to alcohol; these may act by triggering mast cells directly as in false food allergy (see box on p. 67).
- a reaction to nickel in food among those with skin sensitivity to nickel (see p. 55)
- drug sensitivity – often to aspirin or aspirin-like drugs (see p. 151); but it could also be antibiotics, sulfonamides, morphine or other narcotics. A recent case of chronic urticaria in a child was found to be due to an aspirin-like drug in her teething gel.
- chemical intolerance (see p. 84)
- unusual sensitivity to histamine found naturally in wine and matured cheeses such as Camembert: some people with chronic urticaria cannot detoxify histamine in food. Histamine produced by bacteria in the gut can also cause problems, and this may be linked to gut flora imbalance.
- a reaction to the preservatives e.g. parabens, used in creams and ointments. (Where urticaria occurs in direct response to something on the skin, it is called **contact urticaria.**)
- sensitivity to food or pollen (both are relatively uncommon causes)
- contact with latex, pets, or other items (these too are uncommon causes)
- premenstrual changes in hormones
- problems with 'Candida' – this is highly controversial; some sufferers probably do have yeast overgrowth in the gut, but it may not be *Candida* yeast (see pp. 82–3).
- very rarely, chronic urticaria is an early and atypical symptom of adult-onset coeliac disease (see pp. 70–71).

Could it be the 'ulcer bug'?

Some research suggests that *Helicobacter pylori* in the stomach – recently identified as the dark horse of stomach ulcers – may also be a source of chronic urticaria. The data are conflicting on this point, but if other investigations have got nowhere, and you have an active *Helicobacter* infection (shown by antibodies in the blood, a breath test for urea, and a stomach biopsy) then it is worth trying an eradication programme. This is a tough treatment – you take three antibiotics together for 1–2 weeks, followed by another stomach biopsy, then a second round of antibiotic treatment if the bacteria are still found. Don't accept a less rigorous treatment programme than this.

These novel causes should only be investigated once you have checked out those causes that are well known and accepted by all allergists:

- in the 'physical urticarias', simple physical triggers such as cold, heat, superficial pressure, deep pressure (as from sitting on a chair, though the symptoms may not come on until some hours later), vibration, exercise, contact with water, exposure to light, sunlight or UV light. Sensitivity to pressure may result in dermatographism – skin that can be 'written on' because it produces a wheal in response to a fingernail being lightly dragged across it.
- in cholinergic urticaria, activity by the branch of the nervous system called the parasympathetic (see box on p. 235) which is thought to directly trigger mast cells. This type of urticaria has a typical rash with very small lumps surrounded by areas of redness. It is triggered by warmth, or by emotional stress, and is found mainly in teenagers and young adults, who seem to grow out of it in time.
- a type of autoimmune disease where the body produces antibodies against IgE, or against the receptors for IgE; these rogue antibodies can activate mast cells directly.
- a rare hereditary defect
- an equally rare disease called mastocytosis, in which the number of mast cells in the skin is abnormally high
- a cancer (the most unlikely of all these causes).

Allergists check for physical urticarias with an ice cube, heat, a UV lamp, water and other relevant stimuli. And they will eliminate the possibility of an inherited defect or a more serious underlying disease by taking blood tests and skin biopsies.

Should a cause for your symptoms, such as cold or exercise, be found by these tests, you will probably be advised simply to avoid these. This is good advice, especially for cold-induced urticaria which can get worse and develop into cold-induced anaphylaxis (see p. 59). However, many people with a physical urticaria have multiple causes for their symptoms, including intolerance to a commonly eaten food. Dealing with other causes – by identifying and avoiding the culprit food for example – may mean that cold, exercise or whatever is no longer a trigger. So an elimination diet (see pp. 194–7) is worth a try. For example, one patient with cold urticaria found that, by avoiding milk, she had no longer had problems with the cold and could even take up skiing.

The downside of this aspect of chronic urticaria is seen when both causes are intermittent. The fact that two (or even more) factors have to be present at the same time to produce symptoms can make identification of those causes very difficult.

Investigating chronic urticaria

Many with chronic urticaria will find it hard to get a referral for a thorough medical investigation, or may have to wait a long time for this. In the interim, is there anything you can do to help yourself?

You will probably have a good idea of the cause already if you have one of the physical urticarias (see left) and you could devise common-sense tests – with an ice cube, for example – to confirm your suspicions.

Look at the list of other possible causes on pp. 51–2 and investigate those that do not require specialised medical tests. Do your symptoms come on during the summer – could it be pollen, or just heat or sunlight? Is there anything you are in contact with regularly (such as ointments, creams, latex rubber or pets) that could explain your symptom pattern? These are not the most common causes of chronic urticaria, but they are ones you could track down for yourself.

Unfortunately, chronic urticaria comes and goes all the time, and can be affected by the temperature, emotional stress, and a range of other factors. There could be more than one trigger, with both needed to start the symptoms off. You will have to make an accurate daily record of your symptoms, and keep an open mind, to have any hope of puzzling this problem out.

Is it an allergy?

Acute urticaria is usually a symptom of IgE-mediated allergy (see box on p. 12) but chronic urticaria is a different matter. Although atopic people are rather more likely to develop chronic urticaria than non-atopics there is no firm link with true allergy. Where a food or drug is responsible for the chronic urticaria, no IgE antibodies are found to the offending item and skin-prick tests are of no value in diagnosis.

Food allergy can kill

An elimination diet may be useful for investigating possible causes of chronic urticaria, *but not for acute urticaria*. Those who have prompt reactions to food, symptoms in the lips and mouth, or positive skin-prick tests, should never undertake food testing without their doctor's agreement and careful preliminary testing (see box on p. 23). If you ever have suffered anaphylaxis, an asthma attack, or any swelling of the throat from a food, do not test it except under medical supervision with resuscitation equipment available.

Another self-help measure is to investigate the effects of dietary changes. Get your doctor's agreement before you start.

- First try an additive-free diet for 6 weeks. You must also cut out alcohol, spices and all aspirin-like drugs – see p. 151 for details.
- A low-histamine diet may be helpful: it is described on p. 200. A low amine diet (see p. 200) is also worth trying.
- If there is no response to this, or a partial response, go on to a low-carbohydrate diet, while continuing with histamine avoidance – the idea is to minimise the production of histamine by bacteria in the gut. The diet reduces the food supply of these bacteria by reducing starchy foods (bread, biscuits, cakes, potatoes, pasta, pizza, pastry, rice, etc.) and fruit and vegetables, especially those with relatively indigestible residues that go through into the intestine, such as spinach. This is not a particularly healthy diet, and is not recommended long-term. Should it help with your urticaria, take a probiotic to repopulate the gut with beneficial bacteria (see p. 205), and then experiment with gradually reintroducing various foods.
- For anyone with bloating, wind or an itchy anus, yeast overgrowth (see pp. 82–3) is a distinct possibility. Sometimes these typical signs are absent and chronic urticaria is the sole symptom of yeast overgrowth. Tackling this requires a no-yeast no-sugar diet (see p. 204) and a course of anti-fungal drugs from your doctor.

- You could also carry out an elimination diet to look for food intolerance (see pp. 194–7), but this is a rigorous diet, and food intolerance is a relatively unusual cause of chronic urticaria, so explore other possibilities first.

Drug treatment

Investigating the causes of chronic urticaria could take some time, and it is important to control symptoms in the meantime. The best treatment is a non-sedating antihistamine, as used for hayfever (see p. 139). Some doctors add another type of drug, called an H-2 receptor antagonist, normally used for those with stomach ulcers. It blocks a different kind of receptor for histamine and because the two drugs together block both kinds of histamine receptor (H-1 and H-2) the combination may achieve better control of chronic urticaria. (If you are sensitive to colourings, other additives, or to any foods, you should obtain special additive-free, food-free formulations of these drugs.)

Antihistamines can become ineffective if taken continuously for years. Switching to another kind of antihistamine may help.

The new anti-leukotriene drugs (see p. 149), currently prescribed only for asthma, appear to be potentially very useful for chronic urticaria. They have produced excellent results in patients with severe symptoms that were not controlled well by other drugs, even steroids.

Treating solar urticaria

In the case of severe solar urticaria – a reaction to sunlight – total avoidance is clearly very difficult and sunblock creams don't help. Even thin clothing may let through enough sunlight to cause a reaction. Often, however, there is a spectrum of light that inhibits the reaction, if given promptly after exposure. Careful testing will reveal the wavelength of light that has this curative effect. Alternatively, there are light treatments, similar to those used for atopic eczema (see p. 46), which can desensitise the skin. You will need a very good dermatologist to explore such treatment options with you.

High doses of antihistamines can also help, by reducing the itchiness of the rash, but your skin will probably still turn very red in the sun. Fortunately, solar urticaria seems to become less severe with the passing years. In particular, the hands and face, which are constantly exposed to light, become less sensitive.

Contact dermatitis

Like smallpox and dropsy, it is a disease that is now just history, but once it was among the most common skin conditions seen by doctors. The disappearance of this disease owes nothing to vaccination campaigns or improved diagnosis, but everything to a simple invention: tights. The female patient with two red itchy patches at the top of each thigh, directly underneath her suspenders, is now a thing of the past.

While Suspender Belt Rash may have vanished, the underlying problem – usually a sensitivity to the metal nickel found in the suspenders – has certainly not disappeared. If anything, with the vogue for pierced ears and other body-piercing, it is becoming ever more common.

This is just one form of **contact dermatitis**, a skin problem that affects millions of people worldwide.

As the name suggests, contact dermatitis is primarily a rash that occurs where the offending substance – the **sensitiser** – comes into contact with the skin. This sensitiser may be either:

• an irritant, which will produce contact dermatitis in anyone, given enough exposure. This is **irritant contact dermatitis**. The range of possible irritants that can cause this problem is huge. Cleaning products and chemicals encountered at work are fairly common culprits.

• an antigen which can provoke the immune system into a **delayed hypersensitivity** or Type IV hypersensitivity reaction (see p. 18). These sensitisers affect some people but not others. The reaction usually occurs about 48 hours after exposure. However, the time-lag can be much less (only 12 hours) if the reaction is severe or recurrent, and much more if the sensitivity is newly acquired.

The response provoked by this second type of sensitiser is sometimes known as 'allergic contact dermatitis', but given the tight definition of allergy being used in this book (see pp. 6–7), that term is not appropriate. There is no IgE involved, and the problem is no more common in atopics than in anyone else.

Cross-reactions

The immune cells that produce contact dermatitis recognise their antigen by means of receptors on the cell surface. These receptors work in much the same way as antibodies, and are therefore capable of cross-reactions (see p. 14).

Irritants are a far more common source of contact dermatitis than antigens, accounting for 80% of cases. Quite often both irritants and antigens are involved. An irritant may start the problem by making the skin more permeable and therefore more susceptible to an antigen.

Many different antigen sensitisers exist, but the most common ones are:

• nickel, cobalt and chromium. Much more rarely, silver and gold. The metal binds to some of the body's own proteins, and then elicits a reaction by the immune system. (This kind of sensitiser is known as a **hapten**.) Nickel leaches out of jewellery, the metal studs of jeans, and other items in contact with the skin. Chromium sensitivity is typically caused by working with cement.

• fragrances used in perfume, cosmetics and toiletries. This problem is becoming increasingly common.

• various other ingredients of cosmetics and toiletries such as lanolin and preservatives

• sunscreens, and medicinal drugs applied to the skin in

creams, including antihistamines, some antibiotics, benzocaine, and steroids. Likewise the preservatives and other necessary additives used in these creams. Acrylates and other substances used in dentistry can also sensitise.

• garden plants and weeds, particularly those of the daisy family, e.g. chrysanthemums, marigolds, dandelions and feverfew. These plants are so common that the source of the rash often goes unrecognised. *Primula obconica*, primroses, ivy, hydrangeas and tulip bulbs are also frequent culprits. With some plants the sap is the culprit, with others it is the leaves themselves, or hairs on the stems. In North America, the notorious poison ivy plant is a major cause of contact dermatitis: it is one of the most potent sensitisers known. In India, an introduced weed, *Parthenium hysterophorus*, causes severe contact dermatitis, and airborne particles from the plant create misery for many people – a constant exposure that they can't escape.

• plant extracts and other natural substances used in herbal medicines, and in many modern cosmetics and toiletries. Some of these cross-react with sensitising garden plants (e.g. feverfew), others cross-react with fragrances (a product can be labelled 'fragrance free' but still contain these), while some are just powerful sensitisers in their own right (e.g. tea tree oil and propolis).

• substances encountered at work. Synthetic chemicals are the main offenders, but some woods are also sensitisers e.g. Australian blackwood.

• substances used in handicrafts or hobbies e.g. glue, resin

• latex, used in rubber gloves, balloons, condoms, rubber bands, finger stalls, make-up sponges, and elastic. The substances that provoke a contact dermatitis reaction to latex are additives called rubber accelerators, whereas immediate IgE-mediated reactions (see box on p. 12) are to the natural proteins in latex.

• textile dyes, leached out of clothing and bed sheets by perspiration.

A sensitiser can be transferred to other parts of the body by the fingers. Sometimes those parts develop a rash when the hands do not, because the skin is more sensitive. Men urinating after touching a sensitiser may get a rash on the penis only. Women may have a reaction to nail varnish on the face or eyelids, where the fingernails have touched, but not around the nails because the skin is less sensitive there.

Pets or clothing can pick up the sensitiser, and then transfer it to the skin. Creams, including medicinal creams, can rub off onto another person, usually in bed at night, and cause contact dermatitis even though the original user of the cream is unaffected.

Getting into the system

Sometimes a sensitiser becomes airborne and is inhaled, then carried around the body in the blood. There is a widespread reaction affecting the skin of the whole body, but especially those areas of skin previously affected by direct contact. Medical workers sensitised to drugs, and then exposed to them in the air at work, are vulnerable in this way.

This is known as **systemic contact dermatitis**, because the sensitiser gets into the whole system.

If the sensitiser, or something very similar to it chemically, is found in food, or is taken as a medicine, this too can cause a systemic reaction. Some food (e.g. sweets, marmalade) may contain substances that are sufficiently like fragrances to provoke a cross-reaction in those already sensitised, but such reactions probably happen quite rarely.

Many doctors now believe that absorbing nickel from food may also produce systemic reactions in some patients, although this is a question that is far from settled, and some of the evidence is contradictory.

Patients with this problem vary greatly in terms of symptoms. At least five different symptom patterns are seen:

1 long-standing nettle rash (chronic urticaria) sometimes with swelling (angioedema) as well

2 a widespread rash that resembles atopic eczema. The distribution of the rash may be all over the body, or it may favour the fold of the elbows, the eyelids, sides of the neck, and skin around the genitals and anus.

3 an all-over itchy rash that does not fit any ordinary diagnosis

4 recurrent episodes of hand eczema, often a severe blistering rash. Sometimes the feet are also affected.

5 eczema mainly, or only, on the skin around the anus and genital area.

Most of those affected are young women, the group most likely to have contact sensitivity to nickel. More surprisingly, according to a recent and very careful study by Italian doctors at the Asola Hospital in Mantua, over 40% of the patients studied had never – as far as they could remember – suffered from any rash due to contact with nickel. However, they did show sensitivity to nickel when patch-tested.

The women in this study improved considerably on a low-nickel diet, and relapsed when given a test dose of nickel.

People who are sensitised to chromium or cobalt may also respond to these metals when eaten, and a recurrent blistering hand rash is especially likely. (As with nickel, the flare-ups may coincide with consuming larger amounts of the metal than usual.) Some of the most severe cases of this are seen in patients with a sensitivity to both nickel and cobalt. Note that chromium sensitivity is more common in men than women – the reverse of the situation with nickel.

If you have a long-standing and unexplained rash that fits one of the descriptions above, and if you have tried all the standard treatments without success, then it may be worth investigating this possibility by trying a low-nickel diet (see p. 199). Talk to your doctor first, and have a patch test with nickel – if this is negative a diet is unlikely to be of any benefit. (However, there are a few people with symptoms on the hands or in the ano-genital region who have negative patch tests but a positive reaction when the metal is taken by mouth.) A low-chromium or low-cobalt diet is more difficult (see p. 200).

Diagnosis

The **patch test** (see p. 92) is the only way of diagnosing contact dermatitis, apart from relying on your memory of everything that came in contact with your skin in the days and weeks preceding the onset of the rash.

Once the offending substance has been identified, you should be given:

- the name of the antigen, plus any synonyms
- typical places where it might be found, or substances in which it may be an ingredient
- instructions on how to avoid it
- where needed, substitutes or alternatives to the antigen, or to products that contain it.

Prevention

A survey of teenagers in Finland found that 31% of those with pierced ears were sensitised to nickel, compared with only 2% of the rest. The message is clear: avoid earrings containing nickel – which means any made of relatively cheap metal. High-carat gold or stainless steel are the best options. If you can't imagine life without jeans, the metal studs can be covered (on the back, where they contact the skin) with a piece of thick sticking plaster.

The Danish government has banned the use of nickel in jewellery, watches, spectacle frames, rivets and zip fasteners, because sensitivity to nickel is so common. Perhaps other governments should follow suit.

When shaving, use an electric shaver, not a razor. One study showed that razors treble the risk of developing fragrance sensitivity.

Wear gloves when gardening. Even if you are not yet sensitive to garden plants, there is always that risk. Avoid *Primula obconica* (a houseplant) which can sensitise you to all kinds of primroses and primulas.

Treatment

Once sensitivity has begun, it is probably going to be with you for ever, so avoiding the sensitiser is necessary. You may be able to protect your skin with clothing or gloves, but make sure the material used really will keep out the sensitiser concerned – ask your doctor (preferably a dermatologist) for advice. Barrier cream very rarely works.

If the skin is already inflamed, avoid using creams and ointments containing known contact sensitisers, such as:

- antihistamines
- neomycin and some other antibiotics used in creams
- benzocaine
- tea tree oil.

By using these medicaments you could perpetuate the rash or make it worse. Research shows that 10–20% of people with hand dermatitis have a superimposed contact sensitivity to a cream or ointment used to treat the rash. This problem is frequently unrecognised.

You may need steroid creams to get the dermatitis under control, and your doctor can prescribe something suitable. Occasionally steroid tablets are given for a short time. An immunosuppressive drug, azathioprine, is used in India for severe contact dermatitis to *Parthenium hysterophorus* (see p. 55), since those sufferers most severely affected would otherwise need year-round steroid tablets, but such drastic treatment is unlikely to be needed elsewhere in the world.

Sun spots

Some contact dermatitis sensitisers only produce a rash when the skin is also exposed to sunlight. The rash can be severe and last for several weeks. After it goes, the affected skin may still look darker than usual, and further exposure to sunlight can cause a fresh outbreak of dermatitis.

Hand dermatitis

Hand dermatitis is very common and often very disabling. Sometimes it is due to atopic eczema, sometimes to contact dermatitis. Both may be playing a part – or the cause could be uncertain.

A doctor can carry out patch tests for contact dermatitis (as well as ruling out other possibilities such as ringworm – a fungal infection – or psoriasis) but the cause of hand dermatitis frequently remains mysterious. However, the treatment of this problem is the same, whether atopic eczema or contact dermatitis is the cause. As long as ringworm infection (*tinea*) has been ruled out, exact diagnosis is not essential.

Caring for the hands is vital – they must be protected from irritants if healing is to occur. Housework is a major source of hand dermatitis – American doctors call it 'homemaker's dermatitis'. Bar staff, kitchen workers, nurses and hairdressers are also very susceptible because of the constant exposure to soapy water and other irritants. Paint solvents and other synthetic chemicals can irritate the hands too.

Rather than soap, use a non-soap cleanser (available from pharmacies). Ease up on hand washing: wear cotton gloves while at home, especially if doing vacuuming, dusting and other housework. This keeps your hands clean so that they need less washing, as well as protecting the skin from many irritants. Most pharmacies stock inexpensive cotton gloves that are especially designed for protecting sensitive skin.

When you need to do wet work or gardening, put on waterproof gloves over the cotton gloves. Vinyl (PVC) gloves are preferable because of the risk of latex (rubber) sensitivity: ask your pharmacist to order some if they are not in stock.

Make sure you have several pairs – there should be vinyl gloves available in the bathroom, the kitchen and anywhere else where wet work occurs.

Disposable vinyl gloves (available from pharmacies) can be useful for delicate jobs such as peeling or chopping fruit and vegetables. In particular, protect the skin from tomatoes and the juice and peel of citrus fruits.

If you are only able to get latex gloves, ensure that they are unpowdered (the powdered ones are highly allergenic). Always wear cotton gloves underneath anyway, to reduce the risk of latex sensitivity to a minimum.

Once you have the problem under control, and the dermatitis subsides, you can probably tolerate a lot more exposure because the skin is less permeable and therefore less sensitive. 'For a while, I had three pairs of cotton gloves in use,' says Lauren, who used to have severe hand dermatitis, 'one pair in the kitchen, for eating in, one pair by the loo, and one pair in my pocket, for use at all other times. I bought six pairs altogether – three in the wash, and three in use. That way, I managed to get through the whole day without washing my hands more than once. It was amazing how quickly my hands got better. Now I still use the cotton gloves a little, mainly for housework, but I don't need to be so obsessive about it. Gardening gloves and washing-up gloves are always a must, of course.'

You need to experiment a little to find a strategy that works for your particular lifestyle.

Remember that friction – from tools such as hammers, screwdrivers and wrenches – can irritate the skin almost as badly as chemicals. Dry frosty air is another hazard, so wear gloves (preferably leather ones) in winter.

In addition to these protective measures, you also need treatment with steroid creams. Follow the doctor's instructions carefully – don't use either too much or too little. A moisturiser is also useful, but get one prescribed rather than using ordinary hand cream.

Should the rash not improve despite good treatment, there may be some internal cause rather than (or in addition to) the external one. This is especially likely if the rash is on the palms of the hands, or along the sides of the fingers. Possibilities to consider include:

- sensitivity to food – this can be checked with an elimination diet (see p. 194)
- sensitivity to nickel or another metal in food and water (see p. 55). This is especially likely if there is a blistering rash that recurs regularly.
- an effect of cigarette smoking – this too can cause a recurrent blistering rash
- an effect of oral contraceptives or aspirin.

Anaphylaxis
ALLERGIC COLLAPSE

The Egyptian Pharaoh Menes was the first recorded victim of anaphylaxis, over 4000 years ago. Hieroglyphic inscriptions in his tomb reveal that he was stung by a wasp, and died soon afterwards.

The term anaphylaxis was coined in 1902, by a French doctor, who derived it from two Greek words. There is disagreement about how to translate it – 'repeated reaction' or 'excessive reaction' are two possibilities.

'Excessive' is an appropriate description, as anyone who has suffered severe anaphylaxis will confirm. The symptoms of anaphylaxis, roughly in the order that they occur, are:

- itching all over
- nettle rash or hives (see p. 50) anywhere on the body
- widespread swelling under the skin caused by fluid escaping from the blood vessels into the tissues (angioedema)
- sometimes hoarseness due to swelling of the larynx
- occasionally, sneezing and a blocked nose, and/or symptoms in the eye
- difficulty in breathing, swallowing or speaking
- a flushed face and a general feeling of warmth
- rapid pulse, palpitations
- anxiety, disorientation, and (most characteristically) a sense of doom
- cramping pains in the stomach
- incontinence or diarrhoea
- dizziness, faintness and collapse due to a sudden fall in blood pressure.

It may take less than an hour to progress from the first itchiness to the final – often fatal – symptoms. *Prompt action is vital* – read p. 98 *now* so you know what to do if the worst happens. Sometimes things go much more slowly, and anaphylaxis takes an hour or more to start, but it can still be a very serious reaction.

Another name for the later stages of this devastating reaction, including collapse, is **anaphylactic shock** – or it may be described as a **severe systemic reaction**. 'Systemic' means that it involves the whole body (owing to allergens travelling in the bloodstream) rather than just affecting that part of the body where the allergen made contact. A **cutaneous systemic reaction** is one that simply affects the skin, producing the first three symptoms only. (Note that some doctors use anaphylaxis in a narrower sense, to mean only anaphylactic shock.)

Anaphylaxis can kill in a variety of ways:

- the drastic fall in blood pressure
- the swelling in the throat
- a fatal asthma attack.

Recent research has shown that most of those who die are asthmatics. Heart failure during anaphylaxis, or due to treatment, is also a possibility, especially in older people.

For those who have near-fatal attacks, there is a risk of kidney failure or brain damage.

Recognising anaphylaxis

In the early stages of the reaction it may be difficult, even for a doctor, to be sure it really is anaphylaxis. Fainting or a panic attack can look very similar. But those who are simply fainting are pale and have a slow pulse, whereas those suffering anaphylaxis are usually pink in the face and have a fast pulse. If someone is just fainting, their blood pressure normalises and they start to recover when they lie down, but this is not true for anaphylaxis.

There are many different causes of anaphylaxis:
- food allergy (see pp. 62–7)
- insect-sting allergy or snake-venom allergy (see pp. 60–61). Even leech bites can provoke anaphylaxis.
- latex allergy, a problem that mostly affects hospital-workers, others who wear latex gloves for work, and children who have had a lot of surgical operations (e.g. those with spina bifida). Once sensitised, there may be a reaction to balloons, elastic bands, condoms and rubber gloves.
- drug allergy, most commonly to penicillin
- vaccines, although this is rare (see box on p. 249)
- the extracts used for immunotherapy (see p. 164)
- skin-prick tests, though this is rare; anaphylaxis is more common with intradermal tests.
- allergy to substances used in other medical procedures, such as radio-contrast media used prior to X-rays
- exercise – usually strenuous exercise, but some unfortunate people are affected by simply walking or raking leaves. As well as the usual symptoms of anaphylaxis, there may also be headache, extreme perspiration and choking. Some people are only affected if there are other triggers as well (see below).
- cold – this is a rare and extreme form of cold urticaria (see p. 52). Swimming in cold water is the usual trigger, and the anaphylaxis may lead to drowning – great caution about outdoor swimming is needed in those who have severe cold urticaria since this could progress to cold anaphylaxis.
- semen – anaphylactic shock can occur but the reaction is usually milder than this, and it is rare for semen allergy to be life threatening. There are effective treatments (see p. 50).
- the drugs known as beta-blockers, used for heart problems can transform a mild allergic reaction into severe anaphylaxis, by preventing the body from protecting itself (see p. 150).

Even when all these potential causes have been investigated by an allergist, there remain cases of **idiopathic anaphylaxis**, where no trigger can be found. Such mystifying patients are far from rare, and the cause is not psychological in the majority of cases. Fortunately, this unexplained condition is very rarely fatal.

With exercise-induced anaphylaxis, identifying the cause may be tricky. Some people only react to exercise if they have eaten beforehand, or eaten a particular food – shellfish, alcohol, tomatoes, cheese, celery, strawberries, wheat and peaches are the most common offenders, but it could be any food, and you may need an elimination diet (see p. 194) to pinpoint the culprit(s). Certain individuals require the additional trigger of aspirin-like drugs (see p. 151) or extreme weather conditions (heat, cold or high humidity) to react to exercise. You need to keep a detailed record of what occurred just before each attack.

Treatment

You should see an allergist, to confirm that you really have suffered anaphylaxis and to identify the cause if possible.

To protect yourself in future, carry an autoinjector containing adrenaline (epinephrine – see p. 150) and wear a Medic Alert bracelet or pendant, just in case you arrive in hospital alone and unconscious one day. This is particularly important if you are allergic to latex (surgical teams need to know that their gloves could kill you), penicillin, other drugs, or radiocontrast media.

Great caution about triggering factors is necessary, especially where anaphylactic shock has occurred. Make sure to tell all the medical staff you deal with – including dentists – if you have an allergy to drugs. Immunotherapy (see pp. 164–9) may be helpful for triggers that are hard to avoid, especially insect stings, but it must be done carefully.

Avoiding all exercise is obviously a bad idea. and by being careful about what they do most people with exercise-induced anaphylaxis can remain fit. Indoor exercise may be a good choice if weather extremes affect you. Drugs such as antihistamines (see p. 138) and cromoglycate (see p. 148), taken before you start, can be very helpful. Both are safe enough for daily use and it is better to take this preventive medication than to resort to adrenaline injections at regular intervals.

Make sure those you play sports with know about your problem, so they can ring for an ambulance in an emergency. Solitary jogging is a bad idea if you have ever had severe anaphylaxis. Those with exercise-induced asthma as well should take additional precautions (see p. 41).

Fortunately, exercise-induced anaphylaxis often clears up spontaneously after a time. The same is true of cold anaphylaxis, and some food allergies in children (see box on p. 23), but not the other kinds of anaphylaxis.

Anaphylactoid reactions

When there is a massive release of histamine from mast cells, but IgE is not involved, an **anaphylactoid reaction** ensues. This looks exactly like anaphylaxis, and can be just as deadly.

For example, the anti-venom given for snake bites, if anti-venom has been given before, will provoke such a reaction: the circulating immune complexes (see p. 13) are present in such numbers that they spark off a system called **complement**, which in turn triggers the mast cells. False food allergy and histamine poisoning (see box on p. 67) can also provoke anaphylactoid reactions.

Insect-sting allergy

'I'd been stung by bees before, but that time it was different. I started to itch like mad, all down my body, I felt sick and it was hard to breathe or talk. I went dizzy, and then the next thing I knew, I woke up in hospital.' Hilary was lucky to survive this experience – anaphylaxis (see p. 58) to a bee sting. It kills hundreds of people every year. The tragedy is that these deaths could, in most cases, be prevented.

Insect-sting allergy is caused by the body making IgE antibodies (see box on p. 12) against the insect's venom. Because the venom enters the bloodstream, there are symptoms in distant parts of the body – a **systemic reaction**. In its mildest form, this may just cause itching, nettle rash (urticaria) and swelling all over the body. A more severe systemic reaction can be fatal.

Very rarely, there are further reactions after the initial crisis has passed. Some people who have had a severe systemic reaction, or multiple stings, develop an inflammation of the blood vessels, the kidneys, or the nerves. This is due to circulating immune complexes – see p. 13.

Assessing the risk

Venom allergy is alarming, and you need to have a realistic idea of how great a risk is involved:

• The ordinary reactions to insect stings – itching, pain, redness and some swelling around the sting – are not due to allergy but to toxins in the venom.

• Anyone can develop an allergy to insect stings – you don't have to be atopic (prone to allergies). But atopics are more likely to have severe anaphylaxis if they become allergic to venom. Routine skin-prick testing of atopics is, however, not considered worthwhile because false positives are so common. Taking the general population, 10–30% of adults give a positive skin test to at least one venom, but only 1–5% of adults have a systemic reaction.

• Some people have more pronounced local reactions than is normal, with extensive swelling around the site of the sting,

peaking after 2–3 days. This may or may not be an allergic reaction (one involving IgE). About 10% of people affected in this way will progress to having a full allergic reaction.

• Suffering a lot of stings at once will produce a body-wide toxic reaction, from the sheer volume of venom injected. This is not the same as an allergic reaction, but the effects can be similar and emergency treatment may be needed. (Very occasionally, multiple stings seem to cure a pre-existing allergic reaction to venom, but it's just as likely to be the death of you, so don't try it.)

• A **cutaneous systemic reaction** is one which affects the skin in parts of the body far distant from the sting site, causing itching, nettle rash (urticaria) and swelling (angioedema). It indicates a genuine IgE-mediated allergic reaction. An adult who has had such a reaction may well progress to a severe systemic reaction, and would benefit from immunotherapy. This is not true for a child under sixteen: the risk of a severe systemic reaction next time is only 10%.

• A **severe systemic reaction** causes all-over skin symptoms, as above, plus anaphylactic symptoms such as swelling of the throat, wheezing and breathlessness, faintness, stomach pain, vomiting, diarrhoea and collapse. Someone who has survived one such reaction will not necessarily react in the same way again – the risk of a similar or worse reaction is, surprisingly, only 30–60%. But it is wise to be cautious.

• Children under ten have much less chance of a fatal reaction than teenagers or adults. Older people with heart conditions or bronchitis are most at risk of dying.

Diagnosis

If you have had a bad reaction to a sting, there are two effective forms of treatment – adrenaline and immunotherapy – which could save your life if stung again.

See the doctor as soon as you can and take the insect with you, if you have it, or the stinger. If not, try to identify the insect using a field guide.

Unfortunately, many people never see their insect assailant. In these circumstances, make a record of where you were at the time, as this may give vital clues. If a child is the victim, get as much detail as possible about what happened, when and where. Did they feel a stinger go in? On which part of the body? Try to locate the site, as this may assist with diagnosis.

Skin-prick tests (see p. 91) are the next step. The usual procedure is to test with all the venoms from stinging insects found locally. You may react to more than one, because the rate of false positives – a positive test but no allergic reaction – is high.

There are also rare individuals who are genuinely allergic but give a negative skin test. A blood test known as a RAST (see p. 92) may be positive but – very rarely – this too gives a doubtful result, with barely detectable levels of anti-venom antibodies.

Treatment

Prompt first aid can save the life of those with venom allergy (see p. 99). Most deaths occur within the first hour. (A severe reaction can also begin some hours after the sting, but never more than 24 hours afterwards.)

Anyone who has had a systemic reaction to an insect sting should be referred to an allergist. In the meantime, your GP should prescribe an auto-injector loaded with adrenaline (epinephrine), in case you are stung again. Make sure you have proper training in using it (see p. 150).

Avoidance of the insect is essential (see pp. 112–13). Wear a Medic Alert or similar bracelet or pendant (see box on p. 95), in case you are stung while alone, and fall unconscious.

Immunotherapy is invaluable for this allergic condition. It reduces the risk of another systemic reaction to a mere 3%, and for the unlucky few who do succumb again, the reaction is much less severe. Try to get this treatment if you can (see pp. 164–8). Bee-keepers do particularly well on immunotherapy, and most are able to go on keeping bees thanks to this treatment.

Mosquitoes and midges

The received wisdom on biting insects such as mosquitoes and midges is that, while inhaled particles from them can cause allergic symptoms in the nose and lungs (see p. 28), their bite injects little or no allergen – so allergic reactions to their bites are extremely rare.

New research is beginning to question this view. Doctors at the University of Manitoba in Canada have identified what they call 'Skeeter syndrome': a very large swelling around the area of the bite, plus fever. The problem is usually misdiagnosed as an infection deep in the skin (cellulitis), despite the fact that the swelling comes on within hours – much too soon to be an infected bite.

Conventional skin-prick tests for mosquito bites will probably be negative because the commercial test extract is made from the whole bodies of mosquitoes, and this contains very little of the allergen from the salivary glands. (The dedicated Canadian researchers made a test extract by carefully dissecting the salivary glands from no fewer than 370 mosquitoes!)

'Skeeter syndrome' is seen most often among young children and those with lowered immunity. It may well be a worldwide problem which is largely overlooked by doctors.

In addition, there is one report of an asthmatic who suffered asthma attacks in response to mosquito bites. Immunotherapy gave her protection.

Those with dermatographism (see p. 52) often show an unusually large local reaction to mosquito bites, but this is simply due to the general sensitivity of their skin.

Snake-venom allergy

Not all snake bites are instantly fatal. Some snakes, such as the European adder, deliver a bite that many people survive. But others do not – an anomaly that may be explained by allergic reactions. Research shows that those who are bitten once run the risk of developing IgE antibodies against snake venom. (If already sensitive to bee venom, there may be a greater risk.) This can result in anaphylactic shock if they are bitten again, on top of the symptoms caused by the toxins in the venom. The risk of death then shoots up dramatically.

Some doctors may not be aware of this possibility, and not offer appropriate treatment for the allergic reaction. The distinctive symptoms of anaphylaxis – symptoms that are not seen with ordinary snake-bite reactions – include itching, nettle rash, general swelling (angioedema), wheezing and breathlessness. (Reactions to the anti-venom given for snake bites are dealt with on p. 13.)

Food allergy

Could you be killed by a kiss? For those with very severe food allergy – the 'exquisitely sensitive' as doctors call them – a microscopic amount of the food is enough to provoke a severe reaction. A smear of the food left in a badly washed cooking pot can do it, or a trace left on a grill or work-surface. And the killer-kiss has *nearly* occurred on at least two occasions. A young man with fish allergy kissed his girlfriend shortly after she had eaten fried mackerel, and had to be given emergency treatment for the consequences. In another incident, a young boy was kissed affectionately by his aunt, who had just consumed a packet of peanuts. She had forgotten about his peanut allergy, and was horrified to see, within a few moments, his lips and face swelling with the allergic reaction.

Both these reactions were extreme examples of **IgE-mediated food allergy**, one of the **classical allergic diseases** (see box on p. 11). This kind of response usually occurs immediately after eating the food and first affects the lips, tongue and mouth, and often the throat. Much less commonly, it can occur some hours later, and affect the stomach and intestines – see p. 64. In babies with food allergy, a delayed reaction that manifests as stomach pain, vomiting, and diarrhoea is actually more common – see p. 65.

In its mildest form, IgE-mediated food allergy produces a tingling or itching of the mouth, sometimes with slight swelling of the lips, mouth and face. More severe reactions cause a dramatic swelling of the lips, tongue and throat. Both are described as **local reactions** because only the areas that contacted the food are affected.

When the swelling in the mouth is severe, there are often symptoms in more distant parts of the body as well, caused by food allergens that have entered the bloodstream. This is described as a **systemic reaction** because the body-system as a whole is affected.

The name used for systemic allergic reactions is **anaphylaxis** and, where it is severe enough to cause collapse, **anaphylactic shock**. It is important to be familiar with the symptoms of this (see p. 58) because it can kill remarkably quickly. Recognising the problem at an early stage, and taking the right sort of action, can prevent a death (see p. 98).

Anaphylactic shock is the most frightening of all sensitivity reactions to food. Because it is potentially fatal, many sufferers, or their parents, must live

Allergy not intolerance

Note that the next six pages deal with classical IgE-mediated food allergy, not with other immune reactions to food (see pp. 68–73) or with food intolerance (see pp. 74–7).

in a state of perpetual vigilance to avoid eating the food by accident. This is particularly difficult when extremely small amounts of the food provoke a full-blown anaphylactic reaction. Fortunately, the proportion of allergy sufferers who develop severe food allergies of this kind is relatively small.

One reason that doctors dislike the use of 'food allergy' as a loose term for food intolerance is that true IgE-mediated food allergy can be such a dangerous disease. Those affected by true food allergy need to be taken seriously (by canteen staff or waiters, for example), and it does not help if thousands of other people also claim to have 'food allergy' on the basis of reactions such as headaches or diarrhoea, which are certainly debilitating but not life-threatening.

Most food allergies begin during childhood, but there are also cases of adults suddenly developing an allergy to a food, such as cow's milk or sesame seeds, that had previously been eaten without trouble.

No one can react to a food the first time it is encountered: there has to be an initial contact to sensitise the immune system. But this initial contact can occur before birth (from food molecules reaching the foetus in the mother's blood), or during breast-feeding (from food molecules in the mother's milk) so a child can react to a food the first time he or she eats it. This is why women are now advised not to eat peanuts – a source of powerful allergens – while pregnant.

Will it get worse or better?

There are several different patterns with food allergy:
- Assuming they eat the same quantity of the food, most sufferers get the same degree of reaction – whether mild, moderate or severe – every time.
- Some children grow out of their allergy eventually, especially if it is to milk (80% of babies with this problem grow out of it) or egg (50% grow out of it). However, an aversion to the food may persist, quite understandably, due to the child's unpleasant early experiences of the food.
- A few sufferers experience mild reactions (e.g. itching and tingling of the mouth) at first,

but then go on to more and more severe reactions. The escalation can sometimes be very fast: it is even possible, though rare, to have fatal or near-fatal anaphylaxis with the second reaction to the allergenic food. For this reason, caution is always the best policy with food allergies.

One group of food allergy sufferers rarely gets any worse: those with **Oral Allergy Syndrome** (OAS). This is a tingling and itching sensation in the mouth on eating certain fruits and vegetables, caused by a **cross-reaction** from either pollen or latex (see box below). Oral Allergy Syndrome does not usually progress beyond mild reactions in the mouth. (What is more, simply cooking the fruit or vegetable substantially changes the characteristics of the allergen and this usually eliminates the reaction.)

However, there can also be severe anaphylactic reactions to some fruits. This is particularly true of plums, peaches, cherries and apricots. Kiwi fruit, an increasingly common source of allergy, can also provoke severe reactions.

Pollen and food

Pollen is the primary sensitiser in many cases of Oral Allergy Syndrome. Birch pollen is a common offender, and the plant foods that cross-react with birch are very diverse, ranging from apples and cherries to spinach and carrots. Long lists of potentially cross-reacting plant foods also exist for mugwort pollen (celery, carrot, apple, spices, melon, chamomile) and ragweed pollen (melon, chamomile, bananas, sunflower seeds). Fortunately, the reaction to the food is usually very mild, but occasionally severe anaphylaxis can occur, as with a little boy allergic to mugwort pollen, who reacted to his first ever cup of chamomile tea and almost died as a result.

Latex allergy, seen mostly in medical workers, can also generate cross-reactions to fruits and other foods (see p. 15).

Which foods can cause food allergy?

The range of foods that can cause food allergy is huge. But there is also a huge difference in the numbers of people affected – for every person allergic to garlic, fenugreek or buckwheat there are thousands allergic to cow's milk or peanuts.

This means that many doctors will only come across patients with allergies to these common allergens. Unfortunately, some non-specialists therefore believe that the more exotic food allergies simply do not exist. So a patient may be told, incorrectly 'You can't possibly be allergic to that – no one is allergic to that.'

Why are certain foods more likely to elicit allergic reactions than others? In the case of cow's milk, the early exposure of the foetus to large doses of milk allergen (carried in the mother's bloodstream), followed by feeding with cow's milk formula, may make the development of allergic reactions more likely.

Frequency of eating the food also seems to have some influence. For example, rice allergy is very rare in Europe and the US, but more frequently seen in Asia. In the Western world, the foods most likely to provoke IgE-mediated food allergy include several staples such as wheat, egg, milk and, increasingly, soy (now widespread in processed food).

Finally some foods, such as peanuts, may actually antagonise immune cells, so that IgE is produced rather than more innocuous antibodies (see p. 12). The same may be true of other nuts, sesame seeds and poppy seeds.

Unusual forms of food allergy

'I visited friends one evening, and they cooked moussaka. I enjoyed the meal, caught the train home, and went to bed,' Chris recalls. 'Then I awoke some time after midnight – about five hours after eating the meal – feeling ill. I vomited continuously until my stomach was completely empty, and continued to retch even when there was nothing to bring up. During this violent retching, I lost control of my bladder. I ended up in an exhausted state, sitting on the bathroom floor, barely able to move. Eventually I crawled to my bed. I awoke a few hours later with bad diarrhoea. No one else who had eaten the meal was ill. Then I recalled that the only time I had vomited before – in my adult life, at least – was after eating aubergines. They were something I never usually ate. I resolved to avoid them in future.

'Since then, I have been ill in this way three times, though never quite as badly. On each occasion, this has been some hours after a restaurant meal, and subsequent enquiries have revealed that the food did indeed contain some aubergine. The last time it happened, after I'd finished vomiting, I was aware of what felt like an enormous lump in my throat, making swallowing difficult. It was a bit frightening, as it appeared so suddenly. Swallowing was painful, and it took several days to subside. I have mentioned these incidents to my GP, but I don't think he knows what I'm talking about. It was only from reading a book that I found out you can be allergic to the digestion products of certain foods.'

For Chris, and others who react to a digestion product of the food rather than to the food itself, it may take many years to get an accurate diagnosis. Like all rare conditions, this one is very likely to be overlooked, misdiagnosed, or simply dismissed as 'psychosomatic'. This unusual form of food allergy seems to be particularly common with soy allergy.

Some people only react to their food allergen if they also take exercise soon afterwards – one form of exercise-induced anaphylaxis (see p. 59). An allergic reaction to food can also vary with emotional stress, alcohol or a virus (viral) infection, but this is unusual.

Some people with food allergy do not react to the allergen when it is cooked. This happens frequently with fruits, vegetables and tuna, less often with other fish, and occasionally with eggs (they must be hard-boiled to become harmless – see box on p. 186). Much more rarely, cooking creates an allergen (see box on p. 186).

Most allergens are proteins, but a recent report describes allergy to a starch called inulin, found in Jerusalem artichokes. This starch is also widely used as an additive, and the unfortunate allergy sufferer had experienced reactions to a number of different foods, including margarine and sweets.

Diagnosis

This is one allergy where diagnosis is usually very easy because the reaction is so prompt. Even so, your doctor will probably want to confirm your suspicions with skin-prick tests.

Make sure the medical staff have made adequate preparation for anything going wrong. If you are extremely sensitive to your culprit food, you could experience an adverse reaction, even anaphylaxis, to a skin-prick test. There are no recorded fatalities, but caution is still advisable. Resuscitation equipment should be on hand. The test solution should be greatly diluted, not used at its normal strength.

Skin-prick tests always require some careful interpretation (see p. 91). A positive test does not necessarily mean that there is an allergic reaction on eating the food. In other words, the rate of **false positives** (see p. 91) is quite high.

Some allergists maintain that the rate of false negatives is, on the other hand, very low – so that a negative test result rules out the possibility of food allergy. This may be true for some allergens, such as peanut, but the picture is less clear for other allergens. Some doctors think that false negatives do occur reasonably often and they are concerned about patients being told, very firmly, that they are 'not allergic' to a particular food, despite repeated bad experiences after eating it.

Not many people find themselves faced with this problem, so don't worry about it unless you have already had a negative skin-prick test. If you are in this situation, what do you do? The problem for the doctor is that some people do develop a psychological aversion to food which will produce exactly the same pattern – the patient says there are terrible symptoms from eating it, but the skin-prick tests are negative. The only way to show that this is not what's happening for you is to undergo a food challenge test, where you eat the food in a disguised form (a double-blind trial – see p. 90). You are more likely to be given such a test if you seem an unlikely candidate for psychological explanations, so deal calmly with difficult questions (or expressions of disbelief) from the doctor.

Diagnosing food allergy in babies

In contrast to food allergy in older children and adults, where symptoms usually affect the lips and mouth, the symptoms for babies tend to be in the lower parts of the digestive tract (vomiting and/or diarrhoea – sometimes with blood and mucus). Atopic eczema may also be among the symptoms of true food allergy for some children (see p. 68).

Anaphylaxis is less common in babies than in older children or adults with food allergy, but it does sometimes occur.

The diarrhoea produced by food allergy in babies can induce secondary lactase deficiency (see p. 79) which adds to the symptoms. Even when the allergen is removed from the diet, the secondary lactase deficiency may persist for a while, until the lining of the digestive tract recovers.

The allergen is usually cow's milk protein for bottle-fed babies. For those being breast-fed it may be any food that the mother is eating: tiny amounts get through into the milk. Common allergens such as cow's milk are the prime suspects.

For confirming true food allergy and identifying the culprit food, skin-prick tests may be useful in infancy, but there are quite often false negatives (a negative test despite a genuine reaction). False positives (a positive skin-prick test but no actual reaction to the food) are relatively rare in babies.

As a rule, the disease is more likely to be IgE-mediated if the symptoms occur very rapidly after a feed. It may help the doctor with the diagnosis if you have made a careful note of the timing of symptoms and any other details that seem relevant.

Some babies with ulcerative colitis (characterised by diarrhoea with blood and mucus) are reacting to food. Such infants may be diagnosed as having **food-induced colitis.** This is a form of true food allergy, and skin-prick tests should show which foods are at fault. The colitis will probably clear up in time, but other classical allergic diseases, such as asthma, may follow.

Diagnosing food reactions in babies is especially difficult because there are so many different kinds of food sensitivity in this age group – many of these are not true food allergy but another kind of immune reaction (see pp. 68–73). Often it is impossible to discover exactly what is going wrong, or to give the disease a name.

Alternative formula for babies

The ordinary brands of infant formula are made from cow's milk, and will affect babies with any kind of sensitivity to cow's milk, including those who are unable to digest lactose (see p. 79). The alternative infant formulas described here are not only useful for babies with true food allergy, but also for those with other forms of sensitivity to cow's milk. Many different types of alternative infant formulas are now available:

Lactose-free formula for those with lactase deficiency. Infant formula is also available that is both lactose-free *and* suitable for babies with cow's milk allergy – ask your paediatrician or pharmacist about this.

Soy-based formula, which often helps babies at first, but can create more problems in the long run because soya itself is a potential allergen. The parent of a child with soy allergy faces a lot of difficulties because soy creeps into just about everything these days – once the child is weaned you will be slavishly reading labels and discovering that almost every ready-made packaged food is out of bounds. One of the other alternative formulas is therefore a better choice.

Hydrolysates, which are derived from cow's milk but with the proteins (i.e. the substances that provokes sensitivity reactions) partially broken down by a cunning processing technique that mimics digestion. The effect is to destroy most of the potential for provoking either allergy or other forms of immune sensitivity. However, small pieces of the cow's milk proteins do survive the processing, and the occasional baby will react to these because the piece that survives happens to contain the epitope (see box on p. 15) to which the baby is sensitised. A baby may react to one brand but be fine with another, so it is worth experimenting. Brand names of hydrolysates include Alimentum, Nutramigen.

Amino acid formula is the most drastic of the alternatives. Rather than taking cow's milk proteins and breaking them down, the approach here is to take the constituents of the proteins – amino acids – and mix them up in the right proportions to get the nutritional equivalent. Amino acids are too small to evoke a reaction from the immune system, so these really are foolproof, unlike hydrolysates. Unfortunately, some of the amino acids taste diabolical, so this is the least palatable option. Brand names of amino acid formulas include EleCare, Neocate.

These alternative infant formulas can be used for both diagnosis and treatment. If there is some doubt about the existence of the sensitivity to cow's milk, your doctor should be able to prescribe one for a while, just to see what happens. Try a second brand if the first does not help.

Treatment

Emergency treatment

For first-aid treatment of anaphylaxis see p. 98. Remember that emergency hospital treatment is also vital, even if injectable adrenaline (epinephrine) is available and has been given.

Just occasionally, a severe allergic reaction to food can appear to be over, but the symptoms then recur between four and eight hours later. So you should be kept in hospital for several hours just in case: there have been a few deaths as a result of people being sent home prematurely.

Routine treatment

Food allergy can only be treated at present by strict food avoidance – and strict means *strict* here (see pp. 110–11). This really could be life-or-death.

For a few very sensitive individuals with food allergy, even inhaling airborne molecules of the food is sufficient to spark a reaction. Someone opening a jar of peanut butter nearby, or a packet of peanuts, can do it for those with peanut allergy. So can the smell in a fish market, or the cooking fumes from fish or vegetables for those with the appropriate sensitivity. This can be alarming, but be reassured by the fact that no fatal reactions have ever been recorded from airborne food.

If you have ever suffered a systemic reaction (anaphylaxis – see p. 62), you should be carrying injectable adrenaline (epinephrine) for emergency use, when the offending food is eaten by mistake. Make sure you get this *and that you know how to use it properly* – research has shown that the training given by some doctors and other professionals is far from adequate (see p. 150).

An adrenaline inhaler may be useful for those whose throat swells, or who also have asthma as well as systemic reactions to food – they should use it *in addition to* an adrenaline injector (see p. 98).

Conventional immunotherapy (see pp. 164–9)) is not used at present for food allergy, mainly because of the risk of an anaphylactic reaction during the treatment. The protection given is also far from certain, and there is concern about giving sufferers a sense of false security.

All this may soon change, as new vaccine-type treatments, using modified food allergens, become available. These are intended to produce good tolerance of the allergen without serious risk of anaphylaxis during treatment (see p. 168).

Drug treatment offers limited protection in true food allergy, unfortunately. Although sodium cromoglycate, which blocks the degranulation of mast cells, may reduce sensitivity, the risks of it not working when needed far outweigh the advantages.

The exceptions to this rule are those difficult cases involving multiple IgE-mediated food allergies and delayed reactions such as diarrhoea (which may be reactions to digestion products of the food – see p. 64). For anyone with problems of this type, life can be tough, especially if new allergies develop at regular intervals. The symptoms can often be eased, and the rate of development of new allergies reduced, with the judicious use of sodium cromoglycate (see p. 148). Food avoidance is still needed, but the reactions to accidental ingestion are less severe. Some people who suffer with this type of problem also seem to benefit from treatment to improve the balance of the gut flora (see pp. 204–5) but there is no strong evidence to support this.

Mimicking food allergy

Two different conditions produce symptoms that look just like true food allergy: false food allergy and histamine poisoning.

False food allergy involves mast cells but is produced without any allergic reaction. It is due to substances found naturally in foods that can trigger mast cells directly.

Some of these substances bind to the IgE receptors on the surface of the mast cell, so cross-linking the receptors and making the mast cells degranulate (see box on p. 12) – it is the immune equivalent of picking a lock.

The symptoms of false food allergy are indistinguishable from true food allergy because the same basic mechanism – release of histamine by mast cells – is involved. However, it is unknown for this reaction to be fatal. False food allergy is generally regarded as less common than food allergy itself.

Some people are far more susceptible to false food allergy than others, for reasons that are not yet understood. As regards diagnosis, skin-prick tests are usually positive, but do not distinguish false food allergy from true IgE-mediated food allergy. A modified form of the RAST (a blood test – see p. 92) can distinguish the two.

Food avoidance is the only treatment. The usual culprits are beans, strawberries, tomatoes, fish, pork, chocolate, egg white and tartrazine (a food additive used for its yellow colour). Pineapple and papaya, which contain powerful protein-digesting enzymes, may also trigger mast cells directly.

Histamine poisoning is another reaction that can resemble a true allergy to food. Fish such as mackerel and tuna, if stored badly before eating (or before canning), can have a very high histamine content, due to bacterial action. Histamine is histamine, whether it comes from a mast cell (see box on p. 12) or is consumed with food, so the fish evokes a severe and unpleasant reaction. This is referred to as **anaphylactoid shock**, to distinguish it from true anaphylactic shock (see box on p. 59). It can be fatal, so watch out for fish that looks slightly discoloured and has a sharp, peppery or metallic taste. If you've only eaten a mouthful you should be fine – it's the quantity consumed that counts here.

Other foods, such as well-ripened cheeses, also contain histamine, but in much smaller amounts. Most people can happily eat such foods, detoxifying the histamine in the liver. A few people seem to lack this power to break histamine down, and may be badly affected by these foods. Sometimes this can cause chronic urticaria or other symptoms. A low-histamine diet may be worth trying (see p. 200).

Food sensitivity
IN ASTHMA, ECZEMA AND OTHER ALLERGIC DISEASES

In 1995, medical researchers in North Carolina, USA, asked over a hundred dermatologists how they treated atopic eczema. All used standard treatments such as moisturisers and steroid creams, but only 14% mentioned the possible role of food to the parents of children with eczema.

Between them, the dermatologists in this study treated about 17,000 children with atopic eczema per year. Using the most widely accepted estimates for food sensitivity in atopic eczema – 38% of eczematous children are sensitive to food – one can calculate that there were over 5000 children in this study area who might perhaps have benefited from avoiding a problem food, but whose parents were never told about this treatment option.

North Carolina is by no means unique. The situation is much the same in other parts of the world, which adds up to *millions* of children and parents not even being told about a treatment that is frequently effective.

Other allergic diseases (see right) can also be triggered by food, although the percentage of patients affected is much lower than for atopic eczema. Here too, many doctors are unaware of (or sceptical about) the possible role of food.

These reactions are best described as 'food sensitivity'. They cannot be called food allergy (see p. 62) if there are no symptoms in the mouth or gut and if skin-prick tests are negative – as is often the case. Negative skin tests suggest that the reaction is not IgE-mediated (see box on p. 121)

However, in some children with atopic eczema, the skin-prick tests to culprit foods are positive. When these foods are eaten after a period of avoidance, such children sometimes suffer an immediate reaction, with symptoms typical of true food allergy. For these individuals, their atopic eczema seems to be a symptom of IgE-mediated food allergy.

How can an atopic eczema reaction in response to food be IgE-mediated in one individual and not in another? Research is finally beginning to answer this question (see pp. 18–19).

The allergic conditions that may sometimes be induced, or simply aggravated, by a *non-immediate* reaction to food are:
- atopic eczema (atopic dermatitis)
- asthma
- perennial allergic rhinitis (constantly blocked or runny nose)
- chronic sinusitis
- secretory otitis media ('glue ear').

In all of these conditions, many other causes exist. Except in the case of eczema, *the other causes are far more likely* than sensitivity to food. This fact will weigh heavily with your doctor, whose instinct, quite sensibly, is to look for likely causes first.

Taking asthma as an example, food sensitivity is relatively unusual as a primary cause, whereas allergy to airborne items, such as pollen or house-dust mite, is very common. Food probably affects only 8–10% of asthmatics overall, but is much more important for those with brittle asthma (the most severe and unstable form), affecting as many as 60%, in a recent study.

The pollen connection

People who suffer from both birch-pollen allergy and atopic eczema may have worsening eczema when they eat certain fruits and vegetables, e.g. apples and carrots. These same foods cause Oral Allergy Syndrome (see box on p. 63) in some with birch-pollen hayfever, but they can aggravate eczema *without* causing Oral Allergy Syndrome.

Diagnosis

Consider other likely allergens first. Look at p. 28 for the airborne allergens that could play a part in perennial allergic rhinitis, chronic sinusitis, secretory otitis media ('glue ear'), and asthma. Only in the case of children with atopic eczema is food a prime suspect (between 38% and 69% of children with atopic eczema are affected by food), but even here there are a lot of other factors to consider (see pp. 43-4).

If you do decide to investigate the role of food, don't abandon basic treatments in the meantime. By neglecting these, you could make the whole problem a great deal worse.

There are various clues that food is at fault:

- If you have other symptoms that suggest food intolerance (see p. 76). These problems often seem to go together with food-induced asthma or rhinitis.
- If you have noticed that a particular food makes your symptoms worse. Where there is intolerance to one food, there could well be intolerance to another, which you have not noticed.
- If you have exercise-induced asthma (see p. 41) and sometimes respond severely to exercise but sometimes have little or no reaction. Sensitivity to a food or foods may be instrumental in changing the response to exercise.
- If you have brittle asthma – but you must get your doctor's consent for an elimination diet. *Foods must be tested under medical supervision as severe life-threatening asthmatic reactions can occur on testing*.
- If there are also digestive problems such as diarrhoea, vomiting or belching. This is a strong clue in the case of children with atopic eczema. Symptoms such as diarrhoea frequently *precede* atopic eczema, and it seems likely that a reaction to food in the gut increases the leakiness of the gut wall, allowing more food molecules through to the blood.
- If there is pronounced eczema around the mouth in children (but this can also be due to constant licking).
- For adults with atopic eczema, if there is a persistent rash on the hands, or the lips. Where there is a blistering rash on the hands that erupts at regular intervals, food is often the problem – or it may be metal contaminants of food such as nickel (see p. 55). In general, food sensitivity is rarer among adults with atopic eczema than it is among children.

Skin-prick tests (see p. 91) for commonly eaten foods are worth trying in all the diseases – if they give a positive result, they should be noted, but if they give a negative one, they should be disregarded. The many alternative tests being marketed (see p. 93) are highly inaccurate and unlikely to help.

Research from Tampere University Hospital in Finland suggests that babies are much more likely to give false-negative skin-prick tests for food than older children and adults with atopic eczema. The Finnish researchers found that 52% of babies with atopic eczema give a negative skin-prick test despite having a genuine reaction when tested by food challenge. In an attempt to tackle this problem, they have devised a patch test, similar to those used for contact dermatitis. The patch test, in which food is applied to intact skin and left there for two days, gives false negatives in only 39% of babies.

The best way to detect food-sensitive eczema, according to Dr Erika Isolauri, who heads the Finnish research team, is to use both tests, and take note of a positive reaction to either. This detects 80–90% of eczema-causing food reactions in infants.

Few other doctors are currently using patch tests for atopic eczema, because so much controversy surrounds this topic, and no standardised method has yet been devised. You may be lucky and find a specialist who does these tests.

To confirm the role of particular foods in atopic eczema, a food challenge test is essential, having first avoided the food carefully for two weeks. Great care is needed in testing (see p. 198).

If you cannot get suitable tests done, a simple elimination diet will be needed (see p. 198).

Treatment

There is a choice here, between avoiding the offending food, or eating normally and controlling the symptoms with drugs.

The difficulty comes when parents have to make this decision on behalf of their children. Unfortunately, there is insufficient evidence as regards the consequences of this decision. Treating food sensitivity can reduce the eczema symptoms substantially in the short term, but it does not necessarily improve the long-term prospects for the child. Orthodox doctors tend to think that eating a normal diet is much better for a child nutritionally and socially, and they have a point.

Doctors with a special interest in food sensitivity generally believe that treating the problem at source, rather than just suppressing the symptoms with drugs, must take the pressure off the child's immune system, and give the child a better chance of growing out of sensitivity reactions in the long run.

The decision is yours – but it is vital that the diet is not more of an encumbrance than the disease itself, and that the child's interests come first (see pp. 170–71). Whatever you do, don't allow a child to become malnourished (see p. 198).

Coeliac disease

During World War II, there was no bread to be had in the Netherlands and people were forced to eat tulip bulbs. 'My mother roasted them,' one survivor recalls, 'and they tasted delicious then, because we were so hungry I suppose. I cooked some years later, just to taste them again, and they were absolutely disgusting.'

While most of the population was thin and unwell on this starvation diet, a few children were actually healthier than before. An observant Dutch doctor noted that these were the children who, before the war, had suffered from constant diarrhoea, fatigue, poor growth and muscle wasting. They were suddenly stronger and, his enquiries revealed, their diarrhoea had vanished. But when the food situation improved at the end of the war, all their old problems returned. By carefully experimenting with the diet of these patients, the doctor discovered that eating wheat and rye caused the symptoms. Subsequent research has revealed that both contain a collection of proteins, referred to as **gluten**, which are the source of coeliac disease.

Belly disease

Coeliac disease (or celiac disease) is an old name which simply means 'belly disease'. It is derived from the Greek word for 'belly' – *koilia*. Once the cause of the symptoms became understood, a new name was devised – **gluten-sensitivity enteropathy** – but it has not really caught on. Other terms that you may come across are **non-tropical sprue** and **coeliac sprue**, based on the close resemblance of the symptoms to those of tropical sprue. This disease, found in those who live or have lived in the tropics, is probably caused by bacterial infection. There is no causal link with coeliac disease.

Symptoms

The symptoms of coeliac disease are:
- diarrhoea, with pale, bad-smelling stools
- in a few patients, constipation rather than diarrhoea, but this is very rare
- bloating and wind
- damage to the lining of the intestine. This is of a characteristic type: the complex folded structures (the **villi**) of the intestinal lining are destroyed. Additionally, huge numbers of immune cells are present.
- the loss of the villi results in failure to absorb nutrients from food (**malabsorption**) causing poor growth in babies, and weakness and weight-loss in adults.
- poor appetite, especially in babies. This can greatly reduce the diarrhoea.

Coeliac disease usually appears in babies during weaning, a few weeks after cereals are introduced, but it can also begin for the first time in adults. The tendency to coeliac disease is genetically inherited, so it runs in families.

Where coeliac disease runs in the family, another disease, **dermatitis herpetiformis**, is also likely to occur. Dermatitis herpetiformis has the same basic mechanism as coeliac disease but very different symptoms:

- an intensely itchy rash, sometimes with tiny blisters; the rash is symmetrically distributed on the buttocks, shoulders, scalp, and the outer surfaces of the knees and elbows
- the same characteristic damage to the lining of the intestine as seen in tests for coeliac disease, though generally less severe
- diarrhoea, in some cases, but not all.

About 5% of those with coeliac disease actually go on to develop dermatitis herpetiformis. Most people have either one or the other.

Both diseases are caused by the same gene, which results in sufferers developing antibodies against one of their own proteins, an enzyme called tissue-transglutaminase. The job of this enzyme, which is found in the intestines, is to assist with the breakdown of gluten.

If no gluten is present, the enzyme does not arouse the interest of the immune system. It is the process of gluten digestion, in which a particular peptide is produced from gluten, that provokes the autoimmune reaction. (A **peptide** is any short length of protein chain, obtained from the complete protein chain by digestion.)

What seems to trigger the autoimmune reaction is this enzyme–peptide combination: the offending peptide, newly-produced and still attached physically to the enzyme. There is something about the particular 'chemical picture' that this combination makes which outrages the immune system of individuals with a particular genetic make-up.

The impact of this autoimmune reaction on the intestinal lining is severe in coeliac disease, less so in dermatitis herpetiformis. What causes dermatitis herpetiformis is a particular type of antibody, called dimeric IgA, which is transported by the bloodstream from the gut to the skin. It is deposited in the skin all over the body, but for some reason only provokes inflammation in certain areas.

In rare cases, an IgE-mediated food allergy to wheat can co-exist with coeliac disease, making reactions more severe.

Secondary problems

Paradoxically, while the damaged gut lining of untreated coeliac disease makes a poor job of absorbing specific nutrients (e.g. iron and vitamins) in a form that the body can use, it also lets through far more intact, or partially digested, food molecules. These get into the bloodstream in such numbers that they can lead to idiopathic food intolerance (see p.74). Sensitivity to soy is a common problem, because it is so heavily used in gluten-free bread and other prepared food. Those with coeliac disease who have not improved fully, despite a strict gluten-free diet, often benefit from an elimination diet (see p. 194). This must be done under medical supervision.

Another possible effect of the intestinal damage is lactose intolerance (see p.79), producing a sensitivity to milk.

The frequency of schizophrenia is higher among those with coeliac disease than among the general population. Coeliacs not following a strict gluten-free diet are also vulnerable to other psychological problems. These might be linked to the effects of food-derived exorphins (see pp. 76–7) and other peptides on the brain. The increased permeability of the gut could play a part in this, allowing more exorphins to reach the bloodstream.

Diagnosis

A biopsy (see p. 92) is the only really reliable form of diagnosis. *It is crucial that this is done before removing gluten from the diet*, because the damage is repaired if gluten is avoided and the healing process is fairly rapid for some people (though in others it takes many months). If the intestinal lining reverts to a normal appearance quite quickly, an accurate diagnosis is never obtained, which can have serious consequences: if you or your child are coeliac, you need to know.

New blood tests can also be helpful in diagnosis, but they do not give the unequivocal result obtained with a biopsy.

Research from the US suggest that coeliac disease is under-diagnosed in some countries compared to others – for example, Italy screens children routinely but the US does not. Some authorities suspect that there is a great deal of 'hidden' coeliac disease in the US, and this could be true in other countries as well. There is no routine screening of children in Britain.

The symptoms of coeliac disease are not always distinctive. Many cases are first detected when patients with rather non-specific symptoms are discovered, by a blood test, to be anaemic.

Treatment

There are no drug treatments for coeliac disease and avoiding gluten religiously is the only way to remain well. Those who are lax about their gluten-free diet may be more vulnerable to certain cancers of the digestive tract.

A strict gluten-free diet is not easy to follow (see p. 177). The most severely affected coeliacs are so sensitive to gluten that they react violently to even a tiny amount: this is known as **coeliac shock** and can be fatal.

A gluten-free diet is also the treatment for dermatitis herpetiformis, but at the outset the rash can be controlled with the highly effective drug, dapsone.

Other immune reactions to food

'When I finally found someone who could say what was wrong with me, it was such a relief. I can't tell you how much ill-health and pain and misery I'd had up to that point. I'm immensely grateful to the doctor who sorted the problem out for me. My life has been transformed.'

Richard has eosinophilic gastroenteritis, one of the rarer immune reactions to food. Like all rare diseases, it can escape diagnosis for a long time. IgE (the allergy antibody – see box on p. 12) is sometimes involved in eosinophilic gastroenteritis, but it is not an essential part of the reaction. Those who, like Richard, do not make IgE antibodies to the problem food will not give positive skin-prick tests. For them, the possibility of food being responsible for their symptoms may well be overlooked.

Another difficulty for patients such as Richard is that most of the non-IgE immune reactions to food affect babies and children exclusively. A few of them can also occur in adults, but this is very rare, so it's not something that automatically springs to mind when the doctor is searching for a diagnosis.

Eosinophilic diseases

The key event in these diseases is the arrival of large numbers of immune cells called eosinophils (see p. 19) in the walls of the digestive system. If the eosinophils converge on the tube leading down to the stomach (the oesophagus) the disease is called **eosinophilic oesophagitis**, and the symptoms include reflux (regurgitation) of food, occasional vomiting, refusing food (in babies), stomach pain and disturbed sleep.

If the stomach is the focus for the eosinophils, this is **eosinophilic gastritis**, and there is vomiting, pain, poor appetite and therefore poor growth. There can also be obstruction of the stomach outlet which may, in a few babies, produce pyloric stenosis (the main symptom is projectile vomiting).

When eosinophils flock to the intestines as well as to the stomach, the disease is called **eosinophilic gastroenteritis**. In terms of symptoms, the picture is not much different from the previous condition, but there can be diarrhoea as an additional symptom, and babies may be irritable and puffy in appearance.

These conditions are most common in babies, but sometimes they continue through childhood. Only eosinophilic gastroenteritis is known to occur in adults too.

Heiner's Syndrome

This disease affects babies only, and is very rare. It is a severe form of cow's milk sensitivity leading to wheezing and haemosiderosis (bleeding into the lungs). The child usually seems sickly, growth is slow, and there may be recurrent bouts of pneumonia. A full diagnosis requires blood tests to check for anaemia, examination of sputum under the microscope, and a biopsy or lavage (see p. 92) from the lung. The only effective treatment is to completely remove cow's milk from the diet. Needless to say, this must be done under full medical supervision.

Other reactions to food

The cause of these diseases is not fully understood, but the immune system is clearly involved.

Dietary protein entero-colitis syndrome

In babies, the symptoms begin with general irritability and vomiting between one and three hours after a feed. Unless the offending food – usually cow's milk – is withdrawn promptly, there will be bloating, diarrhoea (usually containing blood), anaemia, and poor growth. Older children have similar symptoms, while adults suffer terrible nausea, plus stomach pains and vomiting.

Nickel in food

Nickel and other metals in food may cause immune reactions for those with sensitivity to such metals (see p. 55). The symptoms are usually in the skin, but there can be a few digestive symptoms too.

Dietary protein enteropathy

The main symptom here is diarrhoea, usually very severe. Often babies vomit their feed as well. Most have little appetite, and if the offending food is not withdrawn they suffer from poor growth, anaemia and other signs of malnutrition. This is because damage to the lining of the gut prevents nutrients from being absorbed properly. Older children show similar symptoms.

Dietary protein proctitis

This is a far less severe problem. The babies with this disorder look healthy, but there is inflammation in the bowel and small amounts of blood are passed with the faeces.

Diagnosis

There are two aspects to diagnosis:

- what kind of disease is it?
- what food or foods are causing the reaction?

Your doctor will probably try to answer the first question by looking inside the digestive tract with special equipment (endoscopy) and by taking a small sample – a biopsy (see p. 92).

A blood sample may also be taken to look for raised levels of immune cells and antibodies. Skin-prick tests or RAST tests (see pp. 91–2) will be tried to rule out the possibility of true food allergy – and because IgE can play a small part in these other forms of food sensitivity (as in the eosinophilic diseases, for example).

Often the tests yield no very clear answers, especially in babies, and an exact diagnosis is not possible. But failure to answer the first question does not mean that the second question should be ignored. Pinpointing the culprit food or foods is vital.

Identifying the food is easier the younger the child, simply because the range of foods eaten is so much smaller. Cow's milk is the most common offender when the disease affects young children – particularly bottle-fed babies, since standard infant formula is made with cow's milk. Your doctor will prescribe an alternative formula (see box on p. 66) for you to try. For older children and adults, an elimination diet will probably be required to identify the food concerned. Among young children, likely offenders include soy, egg, wheat, rice, chicken, or fish. A simple elimination diet, similar to that used for atopic eczema (see p. 198) may be adequate. You must have full medical supervision for this.

In the case of eosinophilic reactions, skin-prick tests may help identify the foods concerned, but are usually of limited value, so an elimination diet is again necessary. Where adults are affected by eosinophilic diseases, sensitivity to several different foods is likely, so identifying the offending foods usually requires the most exacting form of elimination diet, using an elemental diet for the exclusion phase (see box on p. 196). The symptoms are very slow to disappear: it can take up to 8 weeks of avoiding the foods before your ailing digestive tract recovers. Don't give up too soon.

Treatment

Avoidance is the only way here. Special infant formula (see box on p. 66) is required for cow's milk sensitivity in babies.

In the case of eosinophilic reactions, some doctors may use steroid tablets as an additional treatment, just for a few weeks, to get the inflammation under control.

Controversial topics

According to some doctors, a reaction to food may, on rare occasions, produce **vasculitis** (inflammation of the blood vessels).

Vasculitis itself is a well-recognised condition. The blood vessels are damaged by inflammation, and become more leaky. Symptoms often begin with a general swelling (angioedema), and an outbreak of small red blotches deep in the skin – especially on the legs – where small amounts of blood have escaped. These blotches later turn purplish, then yellow, before fading. This type of rash is known as **purpura**. Sometimes there are larger emissions of blood, resulting in spontaneous bruising.

Many different conditions can cause vasculitis, but few doctors would agree that food sensitivity is one of them. Those who believe in the existence of food-induced vasculitis suggest that the inflammation could be caused by circulating immune complexes containing food antigens bound to antibodies (see p. 13).

Equally controversial is the suggestion that food sensitivity can be the cause of trouble for some children with kidney disorders. Some research groups have found that a few children with certain kinds of kidney disease recover on an elemental diet (see box on p. 196) . All those affected have a classical allergic disease such as asthma or atopic eczema as well, and they tend to be sensitive to several different foods, plus pollen or other airborne allergens. Circulating immune complexes might be involved here, but no one is sure.

Some cases of food-related rheumatoid arthritis and palindromic rheumatism (see p. 76) could be due to immune complexes involving food molecules becoming deposited in the joints, but it is not the mechanism in all, or even most, of those affected.

Food intolerance

The comments of those who have recovered from food intolerance after many years of ill-health are always memorable. 'It's like getting my life back again,' said one woman. 'I had actually forgotten what it felt like to be well,' said another, 'the effect of cutting out certain foods was just amazing.'

For most of those with food intolerance, the disease begins very subtly and gradually – first one symptom (persistent and unexplained diarrhoea, perhaps) then, some years later, another (migraine or headaches) and then, when a few more years have passed, another symptom (such as joint pain or muscle aches). Steadily increasing levels of irritability, 'fuzzy-headedness' or inexplicable tiredness may accompany this decline in health.

Most patients have no idea that all these symptoms are connected until they try an elimination diet, and everything clears up at once, quite dramatically. As one former sufferer described it: 'Some of the stuff that got better – well, I'd been like that so long I thought it was just the way I was – grumpy and exhausted, and feeling terrible if I didn't eat meals on time. It was an absolute revelation to feel completely OK again.'

What does 'food intolerance' mean?

In this book, **food intolerance** means any reaction to food where the immune system has no proven central role.

All the people I have described so far have **idiopathic food intolerance**, which means, *food intolerance with no established mechanism* – in other words, doctors can't say exactly how it is caused. This is a highly controversial area.

The definition of food intolerance used in this book means that it also includes **metabolic abnormalities**, which do have a well-established cause. These are due to defective enzymes (see upper box on p. 75).

The question of what words mean is a key part of the debate over idiopathic food intolerance. At one extreme, you may come across doctors who call this problem 'food allergy', using the original meaning of the word 'allergy' (see p. 6). (Some of these doctors use terms such as **delayed food allergy** and **masked food allergy**, to point up the distinction from true food allergy, but not all do.) Using the word 'allergy' in this context causes a lot of aggravation and confusion, so the term 'food intolerance' has, for a long time, been widely accepted as a useful one that avoids unnecessary conflict.

You will also hear the term 'food intolerance' used to mean idiopathic food intolerance only – this is probably the most common usage. When the term is used in this way, metabolic abnormalities are being thought of as a separate entity altogether.

A new twist has recently been added to this long-standing wrangle over meanings. When mentioning food intolerance in their literature, some of the major medical organisations (those who dispute the very existence of idiopathic food intolerance) now say simply 'food intolerance e.g. lactase deficiency'. To anyone familiar with this field, it looks suspiciously like an attempt to re-define 'food intolerance' so that it means nothing more than 'metabolic abnormalities'. The idea seems to be that, if you deny a disease a name, it will go away!

In the medical wilderness

The main text of this article is about idiopathic food intolerance, a disease with a distinctly dubious reputation among doctors. Because it is so controversial, few doctors actually look at the evidence that it exists – which is in fact quite strong (see box on p. 77). Such evidence is simply ignored in most of what is written by the major medical organisations debunking idiopathic food intolerance.

This lack of medical recognition is very unfortunate for patients with idiopathic food intolerance, whose debilitating symptoms could be eliminated, rather than simply being treated (usually to little effect) with drugs.

This prejudiced attitude to idiopathic food intolerance also plays into the hands of those offering bogus diagnostic tests and phoney treatments, often at a very high price. These practitioners – who have moved in to fill the gap left by conventional medicine – are a considerable part of the problem, helping to give idiopathic food intolerance a bad name.

The waters are muddied even more by the fact that some people who believe themselves to have food intolerance are actually suffering from psychological problems, which they prefer to attribute to food. Such patients are a good source of revenue for the less scrupulous fringe practitioners and are unlikely, therefore, to be discouraged from their beliefs.

Fortunately there are enough conventional but open-minded doctors, often GPs, who have come to realise, through experience with their own patients, that elimination diets have a remarkable curative effect for some people. The ones who benefit are often the doctor's 'old faithfuls' – those with long-term multiple symptoms, who have been referred to innumerable specialists and treated with all kinds of drugs, but who never get much better. The conventional view of such patients is that they have psychological problems that are being expressed as physical symptoms. This may well be true for some – but others have idiopathic food intolerance.

One of our enzymes is missing

Metabolic abnormalities are a distinct type of food intolerance. Unlike other kinds of food intolerance, metabolic abnormalities have a clearly understood cause: an enzyme that carries out a crucial task in the body's metabolism is either missing or inept. The problem is generally caused by a defective gene and is therefore inherited.

The most common metabolic abnormality is **lactase deficiency** leading to lactose intolerance (see p. 79) – this may or may not be inherited. Other metabolic abnormalities include:

trehalase deficiency, lack of the enzyme which breaks down a substance in mushrooms and most other fungi, including yeast

galactosaemia, a defect in the enzyme which processes galactose, one of the sugars found in milk (cow's or human). This is a serious disease and sufferers must avoid milk scrupulously.

fructose intolerance, which is extremely rare. Those affected have an unpleasant taste in the mouth on eating fruit and other sources of fructose, so avoidance is no particular problem.

phenylketonuria, also very rare. Those affected are usually identified early in life, by a routine blood test.

Is it just placebo effect?

Doctors who doubt the very existence of idiopathic food intolerance will say that people who recover on an elimination diet are just experiencing **placebo effect** – a psychological response that operates with any treatment, whether effective or ineffective, simply because people believe that the treatment will work. But this is to ignore certain facts:

• Placebo effect produces a fairly small improvement in most people – you have to be very suggestible to feel enormously better. By contrast, when people respond to an elimination diet (the standard method for diagnosing idiopathic food intolerance – see p. 194) they usually have a sudden and dramatic improvement.

• Most of those with idiopathic food intolerance have had it for years and tried all sorts of treatments. They have often experienced some small benefit from these, probably placebo effect. When they try an elimination diet, they have a response that is in a completely different league.

• The idea that all the different symptoms are linked has never occurred to many people who try an elimination diet – they are often trying it for just one symptom, and are staggered when everything clears up. Placebo effect relies on expectation.

• Placebo effect doesn't last very long – it fades over the ensuing weeks and months. Avoiding the culprit food usually produces a lasting improvement for those with idiopathic food intolerance.

Symptoms

The symptoms of idiopathic food intolerance come on slowly after eating the offending food, and the foods to blame are often those eaten very regularly, such as wheat or milk. Consequently, the symptoms from one meal tend to overlap with those from the previous meal and people with idiopathic food intolerance are more-or-less unwell for most of the time. It is usually not obvious that food is at fault.

All the symptoms of idiopathic food intolerance are common ones that can be caused in other ways. And no two patients have exactly the same set of symptoms.

(As far as doctors are concerned, neither of these attributes gives the disease a respectable air.)

These are some of the symptoms commonly reported:
- headache or migraine
- diarrhoea, sometimes with bloating and wind; this is often diagnosed as irritable bowel syndrome (IBS)
- in children, stomach aches
- occasionally constipation
- nausea and indigestion
- joint pain
- aching muscles
- a constantly runny or blocked nose (this could be perennial allergic rhinitis linked to food – see p. 68)
- glue ear (see p. 29)
- fatigue and a general feeling of vague ill-health.

Asthma and eczema, triggered by specific foods (see p. 68), can also be part of the picture.

In babies, colic is often caused by food intolerance, including foods the mother is eating which come through into the breast milk in tiny amounts (see p. 202).

Less common symptoms include:
- recurrent mouth ulcers
- stomach or duodenal ulcers
- chronic urticaria (see pp. 50–53)
- swelling (angioedema).

The following diseases have also been linked to idiopathic food intolerance in some patients:
- Crohn's disease
- palindromic rheumatism (intermittent episodes of joint inflammation)
- rheumatoid arthritis.

Psychological problems such as depression, anxiety, or hyperactivity in children can sometimes be due to food (see p. 80) but it is rare for such psychological effects to occur without any physical symptoms.

Remember that every single one of these symptoms and conditions can be caused in some other way. However, the constellation of migraine/headache, joint pain and diarrhoea is highly characteristic of idiopathic food intolerance.

How might intolerance be caused?

No one knows how idiopathic food intolerance is caused. There are probably many factors involved, with a slightly different mix of factors in each patient. This would help to explain why the symptoms are so extraordinarily varied, with no two sufferers exactly alike.

Although symptoms accumulate over the years, some people can in fact pinpoint the moment when their problems began. 'I had this terrible bout of diarrhoea from eating too much melon. I lived near a farm and they were free, because of a glut, so I just gorged myself on them. Although I was over the diarrhoea in a couple of days, I was never what you'd call "regular" after that, and the least thing would upset me. Eventually the doctor said it was irritable bowel syndrome. When the other problems began, ages afterwards – headaches and hypoglycaemia and fatigue – it seemed like something quite separate. I never associated them in my mind with the diarrhoea.'

Bad diarrhoea can clear the intestines of their beneficial bacteria, known collectively as the **gut flora** (see p. 204), and this is probably what initiates food intolerance in such cases. Large doses of antibiotics (as are sometimes given before an operation, e.g. a hysterectomy), or prolonged and repeated courses of antibiotics, given for glue ear or acne, can also disrupt the gut flora and lead to food intolerance. A study of hysterectomy patients has shown that antibiotic treatment before the operation tends to result in irritable bowel syndrome – a common symptom of idiopathic food intolerance – afterwards.

A few interesting observations suggest that minor metabolic abnormalities – a defect in certain detoxification enzymes – may sometimes play a part in idiopathic food intolerance. This is especially likely where there is intolerance to food additives, or where there are behavioural symptoms (such as hyperactivity) or symptoms involving the nervous system (such as migraine).

A third factor that could play a part for some patients are **food-derived exorphins**. These are fragments of proteins (called **peptides**) produced by the digestion of food proteins. They happen, probably by pure coincidence, to resemble the substances called **endorphins** that we all produce for ourselves. Endorphins are our internal painkillers. They modify nerve impulses in the body and brain, reducing sensations of pain, and improving the sense of well-being. The receptors to which they bind are the same receptors that bind morphine and heroin – it is the intensive stimulation of these receptors that makes these drugs so effective.

Food-derived exorphins may sound like the stuff of science fiction, but they have actually been demonstrated in the digestion products of wheat and milk. They may exist for other foods as well. They are nowhere near as strong as morphine, but do seem to improve mood.

These exorphins may explain the strange observation (made repeatedly, by a great number of initially sceptical doctors) that patients with idiopathic food intolerance often eat huge amounts of their offending food, and 'can't live without it'. Often they eat the food several times day, sometimes at every meal. With a ubiquitous ingredient like wheat or milk, this is not particularly difficult – wheat cereal and milk for breakfast, a cheese sandwich at lunchtime, pasta with a creamy sauce for supper, a milky drink and biscuits at bedtime.

Any of these abnormalities is likely to be just one factor in a multi-factorial disease.

Diagnosis

Unfortunately there are no simple accurate tests for idiopathic food intolerance. The kind of tests you may see offered commercially (in advertisements in health magazines for example) are very inaccurate, and a waste of money. Consequently, the only way to diagnose idiopathic food intolerance is through an elimination diet, in which you cut out all the foods you commonly eat, and then – if you get better – test them one by one.

It sounds easy but it isn't, so make sure you read all the instructions for doing the diet before you start (see pp. 194–7). You should also see your doctor and get his or her approval. Some symptoms – such as severe diarrhoea or headaches – should be investigated by conventional methods first, in case there is some serious underlying cause.

The first step in diagnosis is to decide if a food really is the cause of the symptoms, and the second step is to identify the food or foods concerned.

The first step is crucial. One of the problems with the diagnostic tests that are advertised – such as those using samples of hair or blood – is that they begin with the second step. In other words they assume that food is the problem (see p. 93).

When it comes to the second step, remember that although common foods are often the culprits, almost anything that is eaten can cause idiopathic food intolerance. Every patient with this problem is different in the foods they react to.

Treatment

Avoidance of the food is usually the best treatment for idiopathic food intolerance – however most people do not have to avoid their problem foods for ever. After a while – it could be six months or it could be three years – you can usually go back to eating it again, but in moderation. You must never start eating the food in large amounts again, and it is best not to eat it every day – certainly not at almost every meal, which is the usual pattern for cow's milk and wheat in the Western diet.

If you find the restrictive diet too difficult, you could try desensitisation treatment (see pp. 210–13). This can work very well.

The patients who should avoid the culprit food indefinitely are those with Crohn's disease and rheumatoid arthritis: a severe and irreversible relapse can occur otherwise.

The evidence

The evidence for idiopathic food intolerance is more substantial than its opponents would have you believe.

One very well-conducted and interesting study involved children with severe migraine who were investigated by a research team at Great Ormond Street Hospital in London. These are children who are very difficult to treat successfully by normal means. On an elimination diet, 88% of those children got better – an astonishing number. Not just their migraine, but all sorts of other symptoms as well, including aching limbs, runny noses, asthma, eczema, diarrhoea, wind, mouth ulcers and hyperactivity. Some of these children also had epileptic fits, and even this symptom cleared up on the diet, recurring when culprit foods were tested.

A notable feature of this study is that, of the five researchers involved, four were deeply sceptical at the outset. Their report notes that they 'embarked on this study believing that any favourable response, such as that claimed to substantiate the dietary hypothesis, could be explained as a placebo response. The positive double-blind controlled trial…provides clear evidence that a placebo response was not the explanation.'

Other studies with good scientific credentials have demonstrated a role for idiopathic food intolerance in adults with migraine, and for sufferers from irritable bowel syndrome and Crohn's disease. There are also good studies of individual patients with rheumatoid arthritis and palindromic rheumatism (an episodic form of inflammatory arthritis) who have responded dramatically to avoidance of a particular food. Some of these patients were given several double-blind challenges and showed changes in certain immunological tests, as well as joint symptoms, when challenged with the offending food. This suggests that the immune system could be playing some part in these food reactions.

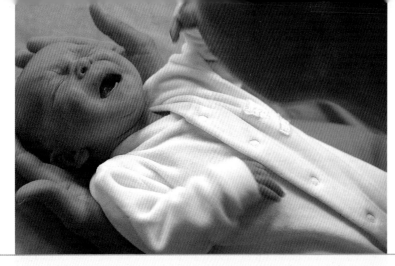

Colic

A baby who wails loudly for hours every day is enough to shatter the nerves of any parent. To most mothers it seems clear that the baby is in acute distress. But if you speak to the doctor or health visitor about crying, you may find that you get little help or support. The idea that it is 'normal' for babies to yell the house down still prevails. Since crying is 'normal', asking for help suggests to the doctor that you are an inexperienced, over-anxious young mother and – shades of catch-22 here – that means you are probably causing the crying with your nervousness and lack of confidence in dealing with the baby.

By the time you have your second child, you will have learned not to mention crying to doctors, which helps to confirm their belief (widely taught in medical schools but based on no evidence whatever) that first babies cry more. Which, of course, makes sense, when crying is due to mothers being inexperienced and anxious…

The fact is that a lot of crying babies have colic, a sharp pain in the intestines which can be due to food intolerance. If the child draws up its legs and goes red in the face when crying, this strongly suggests colic. Sort out the diet and the crying often stops – provided, of course, that the baby has the other basics of infant life, such as warm dry clothing, enough food, plenty of cuddling, reassuring skin contact, and a reasonably consistent and predictable environment.

Colic is often called '3-month colic' because it tends to clear up when the baby is about 10–12 weeks old. The standard explanation is that all mothers, *regardless of their individual circumstances*, suddenly become less anxious when the baby reaches this age and the babies stop crying accordingly. A more plausible scenario, which is backed up by a certain amount of evidence, is that the baby's system partially adapts to the problem food and stops responding with the acute symptoms of colic.

But while the colic abates, the baby continues to react to the food in other, more subtle ways. Eczema may begin soon afterwards, or there may be diarrhoea or other symptoms. Some of these children go on to develop a persistent and troublesome allergy to the food in question.

Overcoming colic

Stage 1: Stop smoking

If you smoke, stop now. Your partner should stop too. Babies with smoking parents are much more prone to colic.

Stage 2: See the doctor

Ask your doctor to examine the baby for intestinal obstruction, and for acid reflux (stomach acid coming up into the oesophagus). If there are no serious problems such as these, talk to the doctor, in general terms, about the possibility of a reaction to food. It is useful at this stage to have some idea of how your doctor reacts to such ideas. If you get a hostile or dismissive reaction, go very gently and be diplomatic. You need to keep the doctor on your side. Make it clear that you are not fixated on the idea of food as the problem, but have an open-minded approach.

Stage 3: Could the problem be caused by lactose?

All milk, whether human or animal, contains a virtually tasteless sugar called **lactose.** This sugar should be digested in the intestines by an enzyme called **lactase,** and then absorbed into the bloodstream. If there is too little lactase, a lot of the milk sugar remains unabsorbed, to the delight of some of the bacteria found naturally in the baby's gut. They have a big party on the excess milk sugar, causing colic and/or diarrhoea. This condition is known as **lactose intolerance**.

All babies produce the enzyme lactase, except for the few who are unlucky enough to suffer from **primary lactase deficiency**. This rare condition, in which little or no lactase is produced, is usually detected soon after birth because the child gets severely ill on any kind of milk. (Note that some babies are diagnosed as having primary lactase deficiency when they actually have a sensitivity to the proteins in the milk – see p. 202. This may be the explanation if the baby does not improve even on a lactose-free formula.)

Children who stop having dairy products once they are weaned lose the capacity to produce lactase. In the Far East, where milk is not part of the traditional diet, older children and adults get diarrhoea if given milk because they have no lactase. But a regular intake of milk may eventually induce tolerance.

Lactose intolerance in adults

Lactose intolerance affects older children and adults as well as babies. If you have primary lactase deficiency, you need to avoid lactose completely, or take a lactase replacer (see p. 205). If you have secondary lactase deficiency, due to an infection, or to some other form of food sensitivity which has caused diarrhoea, then you need to avoid lactose until you are better.

Even regular milk drinkers can find themselves without enough lactase after a bout of diarrhoea, because the lining of the intestine is depleted and takes a while to recover its ability to make lactase. Known as **secondary lactase deficiency**, this problem can affect people of any age. So if a baby has an infection that causes diarrhoea, drinking milk during or just after the infection can lead to further diarrhoea and/or colic.

Finally, it is possible that some babies have enough lactase to cope with an ordinary feed, but their lactase capacity is overwhelmed by a very large feed. This may be why they suffer colic more in the early evening, which is when the king-size morning feed reaches the intestine.

Armed with these facts, you are in a position to investigate lactase deficiency:

- Babies who have suffered severe symptoms from birth should be tested by the doctor for primary lactase deficiency. There are sophisticated tests that can distinguish between primary and secondary lactase deficiency – ask if these can be carried out. The routine tests do not make this distinction, which can lead to misdiagnosis (see p. 202).
- If your baby has recently had diarrhoea, suspect secondary lactase deficiency. Babies who are being bottle-fed can switch temporarily to formula feeds that are free from lactose. Ask your doctor or pharmacist about these. Mothers who are breast-feeding should continue to do so, even though their milk contains lactose, as breast milk contains antibodies that fight disease and is therefore the best option on balance.
- Where colic occurs at any time of day, try giving smaller feeds more frequently. The baby may have enough lactase to cope with small feeds only.
- Evening colic can often be relieved by making the morning feed smaller. If you are bottle-feeding, this is no problem. If you are breast-feeding, try any of the following:

1 Express some milk before the feed and freeze it for later.

2 Give a little boiled water first to help fill the stomach.

3 Feed from one breast only, and then from the other, rather than switching sides several times.

4 If your milk is abundant, feed from one breast only in the morning. Note that this will reduce your total supply of milk.

Stage 4: Investigating other possible causes

Should there be no improvement during the first three stages, then it is time to think about a different type of sensitivity reaction – one involving the proteins found in milk or other foods (see pp. 202-3).

Psychological reactions to food

In his book, *Not All In The Mind*, Dr Richard Mackarness tells the story of a former colleague, a psychiatrist, who attended one of his lectures on idiopathic food intolerance. Dr Mackarness mentioned that severe fatigue could be a symptom of food intolerance, and that people with food intolerance often experience a craving for the offending food. The psychiatrist had suffered serious fatigue for some time, and medical investigations had revealed nothing. He was profoundly sceptical about food intolerance, but prepared to give anything a try. The only food he ever craved was bacon, so it was easy enough to give this up.

The result astonished him. After feeling worse for a few days, he improved – in fact his fatigue lifted completely. Of his colleagues, all but Dr Mackarness himself reacted with utter disbelief to this news. Intent on proving that the whole thing was **placebo effect** – an outcome of wishful thinking on his part – the sceptics secretly asked the hospital cook to slip some slivers of bacon into the steak pie she was making for lunch.

The unsuspecting psychiatrist began his lunch, but halfway through his head started to nod. Pushing his plate aside, he laid his head on the table and fell fast asleep.

As Dr Mackarness recalled: 'The doctors who were in on the experiment were impressed and some of them even admitted that there might be something to it after all.'

Dr Mackarness's book was published over 30 years ago, but its message has made little headway – the idea that sensitivity to food can cause psychological symptoms is still deeply unacceptable in medical circles.

Crying and epilepsy

Occasional reports linking psychological symptoms to food do reach the medical journals. One was of a patient with epilepsy induced by beef. The reaction occurred reliably in a double-blind placebo-controlled trial (see p. 90), and could be recorded objectively with an EEG, which measures electrical output from the brain.

A patient who reacted with violent crying fits after consuming milk was tested with the same type of rigorous double-blind trial. In this case, giving the drug sodium cromoglycate beforehand stopped the reaction. Sodium cromoglycate blocks the firing of mast cells (see p. 148), so this suggests that a true allergic reaction was taking place.

In both these cases, the very careful testing that was done places the role of food beyond doubt. However, those conclusions are applicable to those particular patients only, not to others with epilepsy or crying fits. And most doctors would consider these cases to be highly atypical and extremely rare.

Exactly how rare they are is a subject worth discussing. If doctors and psychiatrists believe that food sensitivity is fantastically rare in patients with psychological symptoms, they don't go looking for it – time is precious, and there are better things to do. So the odds of a patient getting the kind of intensive and careful testing used for the two described above is extremely remote. In other words, the fact that such reports are very rare tells us little about how rare the phenomenon itself might be.

Having said that, absolutely no one would argue that cases like this are either common or typical. Psychological symptoms, which affect a great many people at some time in their lives, mostly have psychological causes (see p. 236).

The links with food

It is very unusual for food sensitivity to generate psychological symptoms alone – eating the culprit food almost always produces some physical symptoms as well.

A link with food has sometimes been observed for the symptoms listed below. In addition, psychological symptoms are occasionally a feature of coeliac disease, and food has been cited as a possible cause in Chronic Fatigue Syndrome (CFS) and autism (see p 85).

Depression and anxiety

Some patients who recover from physical symptoms during an elimination diet also experience a lifting of their former depression. This seems to be more common when the depression is accompanied by excessive fatigue.

Anxiety can sometimes be a symptom of idiopathic food intolerance. Too much caffeine (from tea, coffee and cola) can also induce anxiety and other symptoms, even severe psychological disorders. Hyperventilation – breathing too quickly – may play a part in anxiety, and this is especially likely if there are panic attacks (see p. 227). Sometimes there is a complex interplay between idiopathic food intolerance and hyperventilation, with the culprit food contributing to the hyperventilation. Caffeine can also trigger hyperventilation.

Minor mental symptoms

Among the symptoms that have cleared up during an elimination diet and have recurred on food challenge are: tension, nerviness, insomnia, dizziness, confusion, memory lapses, mental fatigue and poor concentration.

Bed-wetting

If children over the age of six wet the bed, the cause is usually a psychological one. But some children who begin following an avoidance diet for other symptoms – ordinary physical symptoms in most cases – stop wetting the bed when on the diet and start again if they eat the offending food. This may be a direct effect on the muscles of the bladder. It is most unlikely that bed-wetting would occur alone, without any other symptoms typical of idiopathic food intolerance (see p. 76).

Schizophrenia

There are occasional reports of patients with a long history of complex psychological problems improving remarkably on an elimination diet and then falling ill again when given their food in a disguised form. Such patients have usually been given various psychiatric diagnoses including schizophrenia.

When gluten-free diets (or gluten-free, milk-free diets) have been tried for schizophrenic patients, a small minority respond very well. Some researchers believe that exorphins or other peptides produced from the wheat or milk (see p. 76) may be at fault here.

Attention Deficit Disorder (ADD)

This problem is also called hyperactivity or Hyperkinetic Syndrome. The problem mostly affects children, but can continue into adulthood and typically includes:

- short attention span and poor concentration
- impulsive, fidgety, restless behaviour
- irritability and sometimes aggression
- sudden mood changes, outbursts of crying or temper
- frustration at any difficulty or obstacle
- clumsiness and lack of coordination
- difficulty in sleeping.

The potential causes of this problem are many. Because drug treatment with methylphenidate – Ritalin) has helped many children (or at least helped their parents) it is widely assumed that ADD is a disorder of the brain chemistry. But Ritalin increases concentration and mental focus for anyone, including perfectly normal adults, and the fact that it improves matters for these children proves very little. A percentage of children with ADD do appear to have some kind of subtle damage to the brain or a deficit in brain function, which could be inherited.

It seems likely that many different causes can produce symptoms that earn the diagnosis of ADD. Some children with this label may simply be normal, lively children with parents who were expecting something quieter and more orderly. Others may have genuine behavioural problems that can be traced back to difficulties within the family, or lack of attention from one or both parents. Or there may be other psychological problems of the child that are not directly related to current circumstances.

The potential role of food or food additives in ADD is a highly contentious issue. After several decades of work in this area, the collective experience of doctors suggests that a few children with ADD have idiopathic food intolerance and improve on an elimination diet. They are likely to have other symptoms suggesting food sensitivity as well, such as asthma or eczema induced by food (see p. 68) or some of the typical symptoms of idiopathic food intolerance (see p. 76).

Despite all the publicity given to the Feingold diet, food additives do not seem to be especially important in ADD – only a few children with ADD are genuinely sensitive to them. However it is still a possibility that is worth investigating, as part of a general elimination diet.

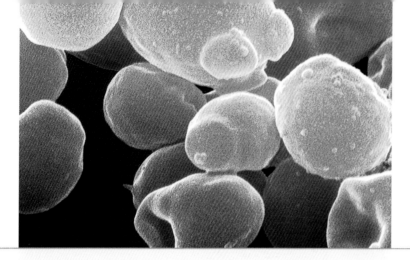

'Candida'

Spores of the fungus, *Candida albicans*, a focus of medical controversy.

'As a small child Jason was plagued with ear infections which led to many courses of antibiotics,' Hannah Mitchell recalls, 'Eventually he started to get symptoms such as an upset stomach, itchy bottom, flu-like symptoms and extremely itchy eyes. The GP prescribed eye drops and when I put them in Jason screamed his head off. In the morning every single eyelash had fallen out. Jason's health deteriorated and a few months later his eyebrows started to itch. Within two days every single eyebrow hair had fallen out. His eyes were worse and I was offered steroid eye drops again. Reluctantly I accepted.'

'Putting the drops in caused Jason extreme pain. The red patches of skin around his eyes spread and the itching increased. I was at the end of my tether when I came across a book in the library about food-related illness...'

What Hannah discovered from her reading was that, for many with diarrhoea, bloating, wind and an itchy bottom, the cause can be an overgrowth of yeasts in the gut, caused in part by repeated courses of antibiotics which kill off friendly gut bacteria in the **gut flora** (see p. 204) and allow yeasts to flourish. This is not mainstream medicine, which is why none of the doctors who had seen Jason mentioned the possibility of yeast overgrowth.

Yeasts are microscopic fungi, so anti-fungal drugs are needed to kill them. However, reducing the intake of sugar in the diet is also very effective because yeasts living in the gut thrive on sugar. Hannah took matters into her own hands, and tried out a diet containing no sugar and no yeast. (The reason for avoiding yeast in food is discussed below.) There was some improvement and, encouraged, she went back to the doctor and asked for anti-fungal drugs.

The doctor agreed, and to Hannah's immense relief, the combination of diet and drug treatment worked for Jason – it cleared the diarrhoea, wind and itching, and eventually allowed his eyelashes and eyebrows to grow back. (Note that few other patients with yeast problems suffer hair-loss – this is a very exotic symptom – but yeast overgrowth can produce some other quite unusual reactions.)

The elusive culprit

So far, you will notice, I have not mentioned *Candida*. Among those doctors who study and treat this condition, this particular yeast was once considered the prime suspect. Indeed, the disease itself was called 'candidiasis'. But the role of *Candida* is now considered doubtful by many.

Researchers such as Dr John Hunter, of Addenbrooke's Hospital in Cambridge, have tried to find *Candida* in their patients without success. 'I think now we have to reject the idea of *Candida* causing the symptoms,' says Dr Hunter. 'But I do believe that there is an imbalance in the gut flora – the micro-organisms that live in the gut. I believe that's at the root of so-called "candidiasis".' This new evidence has not yet affected beliefs about 'candidiasis' and 'Candida' in the complementary health field.

The fact remains that anti-fungal drugs have proved very helpful to many patients with the typical cluster of symptoms – diarrhoea, wind, bloating and an itchy anus – that were previously attributed to *Candida*. Given the effectiveness of these drugs, it seems probable that yeasts of some kind are playing a large part in this condition. So the term 'yeast overgrowth' is being used, rather tentatively at the moment, as a label for this condition. The yeasts concerned have not, as yet, been identified.

The facts about *Candida*

This box is about *Candida* as understood by conventional medicine, rather than 'Candida' and 'candidiasis' as understood by alternative medicine.

The yeast known as *Candida* lives naturally in the gut, usually causing no trouble. Problems are usually caused by *Candida* only when it sets up home in the throat, vagina or penis ('thrush' infections). Such localised infections have well-defined symptoms and, in most cases, are easily treated with anti-fungal drugs. Patients with damaged immune systems, caused by anti-cancer drugs or AIDS, often develop more widespread *Candida* infections, but this *never* happens to people with a normal immune system.

Inhaling steroids and not rinsing out the mouth afterwards can make asthma sufferers more susceptible to *Candida* infections in the throat (see p. 145).

Other symptoms that have been linked to yeast overgrowth are:

- fatigue
- poor concentration
- irritability, depression and confusion
- headache or migraine
- severe premenstrual problems
- recurrent cystitis
- skin rashes
- aching muscles
- chronic urticaria.

Sometimes there is constipation rather than diarrhoea. Recurrent thrush – a genuine *Candida* infection in the vagina – can also be a feature of this problem. Occasionally allergic symptoms such as asthma seem to get worse with yeast overgrowth.

Is there an allergic reaction to the yeast?

Those with symptoms typical of yeast overgrowth may give a positive skin-prick test to *Candida*, but what this means is debatable. For one thing, not everyone with this condition gives a positive test. For another, some entirely healthy people give a positive skin-prick test to *Candida*. To complicate matters, there are a lot of cross-reactions (see p. 14) between different kinds of yeasts and moulds, due to similarities in their chemical constituents. So the positive skin-prick test does not mean that *Candida* itself triggered the original IgE-response.

The question of whether some kind of sensitivity reaction to yeasts is occurring in those with yeast overgrowth, and contributing to their symptoms, is an interesting one. The benefits from avoiding yeast in food (see Diagnosis and treatment) suggest that it may be – but this is a question that cannot be answered at present.

Diagnosis and treatment

Unfortunately, this is one of those 'suck-it-and-see' conditions, where diagnosis and treatment are the same – you try the treatment for yeast overgrowth, and if it works you assume that the disease is, or was, yeast overgrowth. This is far from satisfactory, but is the best that can be done at present.

It is only worth trying this treatment if you have quite a number of the symptoms listed. Bowel problems and an itchy anus are characteristic, and if you have neither of these it is unlikely the treatment will help you.

A key part of the treatment is a no-yeast-no-sugar diet (see p. 205). This diet has been developed on a largely pragmatic basis, and seems to work – but why? The rationale for cutting out sugar is clear – it feeds yeasts in the gut. But why avoiding foods containing yeast should help is uncertain. Possibly the yeasty food supplies some special nutrient that benefits the yeasts living in the gut. Alternatively, there might, for some people, be a sensitivity reaction to the yeast in food (see left).

If it seems that you are on the right track, because there is some improvement with this diet, ask your doctor for anti-fungal drugs. You should take these in addition to the diet. Nystatin (see box below) is very safe for most people, since it is not absorbed from the gut. Bacterial replacers (see p. 205) may also be useful.

You may need a referral to a doctor who is knowledgeable about yeast overgrowth but try to avoid those doctors and alternative therapists who are part of the 'Candida' craze, and think that 'candidiasis' explains a huge variety of illnesses. You may not have yeast overgrowth at all, so you need someone with an open mind.

Eczema and yeasts?

Doctors have found that some children whose eczema looks very red, and is not responding to treatment, have IgE in the blood against a range of yeasts and other fungi (*Candida, Trichophyton, Saccharomyces* and *Pityrosporum*). Given the tendency to cross-reactions among fungi (see main text) it is not clear exactly what these reactions indicate. A proportion of these children get much better on anti-fungal drugs, including a drug called nystatin, which is not absorbed through the gut wall – so cannot reach the skin. The eczema improves, and at the same time there is a fall in levels of anti-fungal IgE in the blood. In other words, a treatment that can only affect fungi living in the gut benefits the skin. Exactly what is going on here is unknown, but the important point is that the treatment seems to work. This is a controversial topic, but since nystatin is an extremely safe drug, your doctor may be prepared to try it out. A course of 3–4 weeks is the minimum needed.

Chemical intolerance

'To start with, I just used to get this irritation in my throat when I was reading a magazine. Over the years it got much worse, and there was a dreadful burning feeling, not just in my throat now, but also in my eyes and nose. Sometimes I could scarcely breathe. My doctor said it couldn't be magazines and diagnosed asthma. Twenty years on, I can't look at a magazine, even for a few minutes, and other things affect me now too. If I go in a room with a photocopier running I start to choke and can't breathe. Whenever I describe this problem to anyone – apart from the doctor, that is – they almost always say they know someone else who has a similar problem. But the doctors still say that what happens to me can't happen.'

Mary has chemical intolerance, which is also known as chemical sensitivity, environmental illness or idiopathic environmental intolerances. It is a condition that arouses more passionate controversy than any other described in this book. Many believe that it simply does not exist, or rather that people who claim to have chemical intolerance are actually victims of psychological problems, which express themselves as physical symptoms. Careful studies show that, while some people with supposed chemical intolerance do fall into this category, others do not – they have no psychiatric problems, but they do appear to have valid symptoms when exposed to certain synthetic chemicals.

'People with MCS are desperate. They will go to great lengths and do almost anything to find a doctor, anyone, who believes them.' So speaks one sufferer from **MCS (Multiple Chemical Sensitivity)**, the most extreme form of chemical intolerance. It is often severely disabling, with symptoms such as exceptional fatigue, nausea, headaches, poor memory and concentration, dizziness, muscle aches, joint pain, chest pain and digestive problems. Those with MCS react to a very wide range of chemicals, and very often to foods and food additives as well.

These severely affected patients are a small minority, however, and many more people are like Mary, with sensitivity to just one or two types of chemical exposure. Surveys in the US suggest that about 30% of the population are affected in this way. The authors of one such survey note that 'the widespread idea that chemical sensitivity is a condition of educated, urban housewives was not supported by our study. The region surveyed was rural…and individuals who reported chemical sensitivity were found in all age, gender, income, race and employment groups.'

The chemical exposures that are identified as triggering symptoms include:

- perfumes
- pesticides
- cigarette smoke
- paint fumes
- petrol
- exhaust fumes
- cleaning products
- newspaper ink
- plastics, especially those with a strong smell
- glossy paper (e.g. in magazines).

Typical symptoms, in those with sensitivity to just one or two chemical products, are:

- a blocked or runny nose
- sore throat
- irritation of the eyes
- sinus pain and congestion
- headache
- breathlessness and wheezing
- nausea
- skin rashes
- extreme fatigue
- dizziness.

How does chemical intolerance begin?

For some of those with MCS, the problems began with a sudden over-exposure to a toxic chemical, such as a chemical spill, or pesticides from a crop-spraying plane. Others are first affected by regular doses of pesticide at lower levels, such as spray drift from nearby fields or from a neighbour's garden. It seems as if, for these people, their inborn ability to detoxify both natural and man-made toxins is overwhelmed by an unusually heavy exposure, and never fully recovers. Although there have been no systematic studies of this – it is difficult to imagine how they could be done – the wealth of well-documented cases is convincing. And studies of those exposed to high levels of pesticides in accidents at work support the idea that this can cause lifelong sensitivity to *very small* doses of some synthetic chemicals. Sensitivity to alcohol and caffeine usually increases enormously too.

In some cases, classical allergies also feature in the range of symptoms for those with MCS. If they had an allergic tendency before the accidental exposure to pesticides, this is especially likely: after the accident, along with chemical intolerance, they have far more pronounced allergic reactions to common allergens.

The loss of tolerance to everyday chemicals may be related to some kind of damage to the enzymes in the liver that carry out the important task of detoxifying toxins that enter the blood-stream. This detoxification system evolved to deal with natural toxins, such as those in plant foods, and those produced by bacteria living naturally in the gut. These enzymes can also detoxify the widely used synthetic chemicals, when these are encountered in relatively small amounts, but the enzymes are overwhelmed by large doses.

Chronic Fatigue Syndrome (CFS)

This is a disease that probably has multiple causes rather than a single cause. The main symptom is fatigue that is not relieved by rest. Many people with CFS also have a slightly raised temperature, problems with concentration and memory, headaches, sore throat and swollen lymph nodes ('swollen glands'). The lymph nodes are part of the immune system, so this symptom suggests some disturbance of immune function. Other findings, related to immune cells in the blood, also support this idea. However, there are often minor abnormalities in the brain as well, with some loss of the insulating material around the nerves (myelin).

For many patients, the disease develops in the wake of a viral infection, but for others the origin may be unclear. Whatever the origin of the disease, avoiding synthetic chemicals is very helpful in many cases. Some sufferers also find an elimination diet helpful (see pp. 194-7). Doctors working in this area say that there is no sharp demarcation between patients with Chronic Fatigue Syndrome (CFS) and those with MCS.

Autism

In the search for a cause of autism, many possibilities are being investigated. The consensus now is that there is a genetic predisposition which, when combined with certain trigger factors, leads to autism.

What are those trigger factors? Some researchers suggest that autistic children have poorly performing detoxification enzymes and are therefore sensitive to synthetic chemicals, both in food and the environment. The suspicion is that these chemicals affect the developing nervous system.

Other researchers pinpoint food as the culprit. They believe that children who develop autism are affected by exorphins (see p. 76) produced from the proteins in wheat and/or milk, and that these damage the child's developing nervous system. There are claims that a dairy-free and gluten-free diet can help, but that it must be ultra-strict to work, and may need to continue for at least 6 months before any improvement occurs. You must have your doctor's approval for this.

Before starting them on such a diet, some doctors also give a course of anti-fungal drugs to those autistic children who have been treated repeatedly with antibiotics. This combined treatment is reported to have very good effects for some children.

Treatment

Assuming that you really do have chemical intolerance rather than some deep-rooted psychological problem – and you have to be honest with yourself here, because otherwise you will never get better – then careful avoidance of the offending synthetic chemicals is the only effective treatment. If you have eliminated everything that obviously affects you and are not much improved, then try tackling common indoor pollutants (see pp. 128–30) as well.

Such measures are of value to some with chemical intolerance but may not be adequate for those most severely affected. If you need to take more radical steps, you may benefit from the bedding, paints and other household items manufactured for those with chemical sensitivity. Once you reduce the level of synthetic chemicals in your everyday environment, you may find that you can tolerate occasional exposures much more.

Some doctors recommend taking supplements of vitamins and minerals to speed your recovery. These (especially antioxidants – see p. 206) may be helpful for some people, but be sure to get nutritional advice from someone with good medical qualifications, rather than a self-styled 'nutrition therapist'.

Neutralisation therapy (see p. 211) seems to be effective for some people with chemical intolerance, but you will still need to avoid the offending substances. Hyperventilation (see p. 236) can make chemical intolerance much worse.

medical help and self-help

The days when doctors wanted their patients to obey orders and ask no questions are largely gone. Patients with allergies and other forms of sensitivity – or their parents – have to play a key role in managing the disease. Most doctors now recognise this, and encourage their patients to learn about their illness, its diagnosis and treatment, and to be partners in their own medical care.

Quite apart from this, there are aspects of allergy management where few doctors can afford the time to become experts. The nitty-gritty details of dust-mite avoidance or food labelling practices are good examples. You can usefully supplement your doctor's treatment here, by informing yourself.

But where should this process stop? That is a difficult question which doctors are increasingly forced to consider. One modern phenomenon, being discussed in many medical journals at present, is the abundance of medical information on the Internet. Some doctors dread the arrival of patients who have logged on the night before their appointment and are armed with a huge number of facts about their illness – some accurate, some utterly wrong and some highly debatable. But other doctors welcome the fact that patients are actively interested in their health problems.

The reactions of doctors to 'Internet patients' highlights an issue that also runs right through this book – that of medical orthodoxy. Who decides what is true and what is false in medicine, and how do they do it? Make no mistake – this is a deep and abiding problem which afflicts not just scientific medicine, but science in general.

If a doctor, confronted with a web-page claiming that allergies are caused by space aliens intent on destroying Western civilisation, snorts 'Rubbish!', he or she is not, strictly speaking, taking a scientific approach. In science, you should consider all the different hypotheses.

In theory, science works by questioning everything and taking nothing on trust – but you can't make much practical progress if you stick rigorously to that approach. Neither scientists nor doctors start their careers by running experiments to establish the truth of everything they were ever taught. At some point in science, and in scientific medicine, you have to assume that certain things are probably true, and proceed accordingly. If you make significant progress working on those assumptions, then the chances are they were correct. But a good scientist always remembers that they are only assumptions.

Scientific medicine rests on a huge number of assumptions. Some of these are clearly accurate – for example, that eating wheat triggers coeliac disease – and it would be time-wasting to argue about them. But this 'fact' about coeliac disease began as just a theory (see p. 70), and a highly debatable one. It has taken time for it to become substantiated by more and more evidence.

Some medical assumptions become enshrined as facts rather too quickly. Fifty years ago, orthodox medicine accepted as a 'fact' that many asthmatic children had 'intrinsic asthma', which was psychological in origin. Research since then has shown that there is almost always an allergy underlying childhood asthma. Many other examples could be given of medical 'facts' that are overturned by subsequent research.

Doctors thirst for certainty, something that is quite understandable when they are faced with so much human need. A significant part of the healing power of medicine comes from **placebo effect** (see p. 233), and that relies on patients having faith in the doctor. The traditional way for doctors to cultivate that faith was by assuming an air of absolute certainty – about their diagnosis of the patient's illness, about the treatment, and about medicine in general. This need for certainty has always hastened the transformation of assumptions into facts.

The fatherly authoritarian attitude of old-fashioned doctors was, in large part, a reflection of how little they had in the way of useful treatments, and how much they relied on placebo effect. Modern doctors have far more genuinely effective remedies to offer and can afford to take a different approach. Many now rely on a different kind of authority, one based on intelligence, good information, flexibility, curiosity and openness. It's a form of authority that allows a doctor to say 'I could be wrong...' or, 'Let's try this and see what happens...' without losing face.

Unfortunately, there is another powerful force at work in this complex situation, and that is quackery – the age-old business of selling phoney cures (see p. 209). Official bodies within the medical community try to curb quackery by weighing the evidence about novel treatments and coming to decisions on their validity. This can be very useful. But in deciding what is, and what is not, good scientific medicine, medical organizations always run the risk of mistaking their own unverified assumptions for facts.

Establishing criteria for good treatment is essential in medicine, but when this develops into dogmatism, that is decidedly unhealthy. Among the treatments that are being dismissed as valueless today, there are several that deserve a fairer hearing.

Some of these treatments have been shown to work by the most excellent of scientific methods. The use of elimination diets in Crohn's disease is a good example – for some patients, there is a huge and sustained improvement, suggesting that their disease was caused, at least in part, by food sensitivity. The tactic used by those who want to reject this evidence, is simply to ignore it. When scientific review papers (summaries of all the current knowledge and latest research) are written about Crohn's disease, the research on diet is usually not mentioned. Evidence that is routinely ignored in this way slips into oblivion because most doctors only have time to read the review papers, not the original research reports.

Occasionally – and this is even more shameful – good scientific evidence that goes against the grain of current orthodoxy is actually misreported in review papers. This happened with an impeccable scientific study showing the benefits of an elimination diet for some patients with rheumatoid arthritis. By missing out certain key facts, a review author managed to give the impression that the results of this study supported the conventional view on the subject (that diet makes no difference to rheumatoid arthritis), whereas they actually disputed the conventional view.

Unthinking rejection of new treatments often occurs with currently untreatable diseases such as autism and Chronic Fatigue Syndrome (CFS). Such medical problems always attract experimental treatments, just as they always attract sheer quackery, and sorting out one from the other is not easy – it takes time, and a clear-headed approach, not knee-jerk dismissal.

Getting the right medical help

Expertise is obviously a prime requirement of any doctor, but communication skills come a close second. This is particularly important with long-term health problems, such as allergies and asthma, where you – as a patient or a parent – shoulder a lot of responsibility for day-to-day management and treatment.

This is how a recent article on asthma treatment in the *British Medical Journal* put it: 'The patient should be the primary manager of chronic disease, guided and coached by a doctor or other practitioner to devise the best therapeutic regimen. The practitioner and patient should work as partners, developing strategies that give the patient the best chance to control his or her own disease and reduce the physical, psychological, social and economic consequences of chronic illness.' So does your doctor work as a partner with you? That approach requires a particular attitude towards patients that comes more easily to some doctors than others.

Fundamental elements in that attitude include:
- respecting your intelligence
- taking the time to listen
- understanding your priorities in relation to health issues, and planning the treatment accordingly
- being prepared to explain medical issues in non-technical language.

Another important quality in a doctor is empathy. Some doctors have blind spots about certain illnesses – for example, they may dismiss atopic eczema in babies as a 'minor problem' or 'just a skin rash', and overlook the intense discomfort that it causes. Patients with unusual allergy symptoms, and those with illnesses such as food intolerance which are viewed with scepticism by orthodox medicine, are especially likely to encounter such dismissive and unsympathetic attitudes. Sometimes it is possible, with persistence and good communication skills (see p. 237), to improve the relationship, but frequently the only answer is to find another doctor.

Simply switching to another GP within a group practice might be a solution, but if the doctors in the practice work closely together, you may encounter the same attitudes again. In that case, look for other GP practices that cover the area where you live. If there is a choice available, find out as much as you can (see below) before deciding on a practice.

Changing specialists may also be possible, with your GP's agreement and help. Under the new National Health Service Trusts, there is sometimes the option of seeing a specialist outside your geographic area.

Choosing a GP

If you are moving to a new area, and you have a choice of GP practices within your area, find out everything you can about the different practices before making your decision. Some doctors may be prepared to meet you, before you have registered with them, so that you can talk over your medical concerns, see for yourself what facilities are available and judge how well you and the doctor get along. During this visit, you could ask the doctor how much experience he or she has with the type of allergy problems affecting you or your child. Also enquire about any particular services that you need, or may need in the future.

Seeing a specialist

Do you need to see a specialist (a 'consultant'), or can your GP give you all the help you need with your allergies? This varies, depending on the nature of your allergic reactions. Some people with allergies do need treatment by a specialist – such as an allergist, a paediatrician, a dermatologist, or a chest specialist.

Specialists working within the National Health Service are always based at a hospital. Many of these doctors also see patients privately, for a fee. In addition, there are specialists who only work privately and maintain their own clinics outside the hospital system.

In order to get specialist treatment under the National Health Service, your GP must refer you to the specialist. Although your doctor makes this decision, you can bring some pressure to bear if you feel you should be seeing a specialist. The information below will help you to decide if this is necessary.

Generally speaking, you will be able to see a specialist quite quickly, usually within a few months. But if you are referred to an allergist, you may find that you have a very long wait. It can be as long as two years for non-urgent cases. Even urgent cases – patients who have suffered anaphylaxis – may wait up to seven months. Indeed, a great many people who would benefit from seeing an allergist are not referred at all. This is due to the dire shortage of consultant allergists in Britain, compared to other countries in Europe. For example, there are 60 consultant allergists for every million people in Germany, while in Britain there are fewer than three. Some parts of Britain do not even have an allergy clinic to which patients can be referred.

The lack of allergists in Britain is the usual reason for the non-referral, although your doctor will probably not want to admit this, and may say that a referral is unnecessary. Indeed, many GPs *do* think it is unnecessary, simply because they are so accustomed to the current British situation, where hardly any patients see an allergist. In an effort to fill the gap, some doctors who are not allergists now do skin-prick tests (see p. 91). These doctors include some GPs, and some specialists in other fields, such as paediatricians, chest physicians or ear-nose-and-throat specialists.

Hayfever and perennial allergic rhinitis
Most cases can generally be dealt with adequately by GPs. You should be referred to a specialist if there are additional problems such as recurrent 'glue ear' or chronic sinusitis.

Food allergy and insect-sting allergy
If you have ever suffered anaphylaxis, especially anaphylactic shock (see p. 58), you should be seeing an allergist. Be persistent about this if your GP does not refer you: it really is important.

Asthma
Research from the United States shows that when asthma patients are cared for by asthma specialists, they have fewer symptoms, need emergency treatment less often, and feel significantly better. You should be seeing a specialist if:

- you have ever had a life-threatening asthma attack
- your asthma is not under control despite following your treatment schedule carefully
- you have chronic sinusitis or repeated chest infections
- you need high-dose inhaled steroids
- you sometimes need steroid tablets
- the diagnosis of asthma is uncertain.

Most asthmatics will probably see a chest physician or, if they are under 18, a paediatrician. For those with severe allergies, and/or other allergic symptoms such as eczema, referral to an allergist would be preferable. Talk to your GP about which specialist he or she thinks is best for you, and ask about things such as skin-prick tests (see p. 91) and immunotherapy (see p. 164).

Chronic sinusitis
Referral to an ear-nose-and-throat specialist is required here. Ask your GP to refer you to someone with a lot of experience of chronic sinusitis *and* with an interest in allergies.

Atopic eczema
Except in very mild cases, specialist help is probably advisable for atopic eczema. You may be referred to a dermatologist, an allergist, or – for a child – a paediatrician.

The emphasis of the treatment could be very different, depending on the type of specialist you see. You could use the information given on pp. 42–9 to fill in the gaps – but it is vital to do this in a spirit of cooperation with your doctor.

Contact dermatitis
You should be seeing a dermatologist if you think your problem could be work-related or if you have severe symptoms that are not responding to treatment.

Getting skin-prick tests
If you are unable to see an allergist, and your GP does not do skin-prick tests, it could be worth paying to have the tests done privately. For anyone who is unable to identify their allergens, this is recommended. Should you decide on this, ask your GP to recommend a specialist, rather than having skin-prick tests done by someone who is not a qualified doctor – some alternative practitioners offer skin-prick tests, but are unlikely to have the necessary experience in interpreting the results (see p. 91).

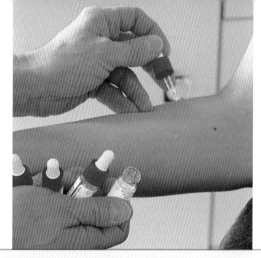

Accurate diagnosis

The simplest and most certain test for any sensitivity reaction is to expose the person concerned to the substance under suspicion and see what happens. This is known as a **challenge test**. Wiith true allergies, challenge tests are powerful tools, but they are also alarmingly close to reality. The risk of provoking a severe reaction requires a very cautious approach.

By comparison, an indirect test – a roundabout way of seeing how the body responds, such as the skin-prick test (see p. 91) – has the advantage of rarely producing dangerous reactions. The downside is that indirect tests can be misleading, precisely because they are not like the real-life situation. No indirect test is perfect – there are always false positives and false negatives (see box on p. 91).

Challenge tests

If you undergo a challenge test with food or an airborne allergen, you will also be given dummy challenges with an innocuous substance which is indistinguishable from the item being tested. Neither you, nor the tester who is scoring the reaction, should know which is which. This is called a **double-blind trial** because, to eliminate all possible bias, both of you are in the dark. (The full name is a 'double-blind placebo-controlled trial' – the dummy challenge is also called a 'placebo challenge' or 'control challenge'.)

The double-blind trial is a standard medical procedure and does not imply that the doctors think you are faking symptoms. Psychological forces are powerful things, and just thinking that you might react to a test can be enough to produce a reaction – the process that generates the symptoms is largely unconscious.

Food challenge

A food challenge – eating the food that is under suspicion – is a key test for food intolerance (see p. 197). It is sometimes used for food allergy and other forms of food sensitivity too, as a follow-up to skin tests. Some allergists use a food challenge only if the skin test is at odds with actual events reported by the patient. Other allergists use food challenge more readily, to confirm skin-test results, and to assess the severity of the reaction.

Extreme caution must be exercised with immediate food allergy, because of the considerable risks involved. *The test must be done under medical supervision with resuscitation equipment to hand*. A challenge test should never be done for true food allergy without some careful preliminary tests on the face and the lips (see p. 23). Even if these tests produce no reaction, only tiny amounts of the food should be eaten to begin with.

Bronchial challenge

This type of test involves inhalation of an airborne allergen – such as pollen – suspected of causing asthma. Bronchial challenge carries the risk of provoking a severe asthma attack, and few doctors use it unless there are compelling reasons to do so – such as demonstrating that someone's asthma is due to an allergen encountered at work.

Skin-prick tests

This is an indirect method of detecting true allergic reactions. It is one of a family of skin tests that use a similar approach. The different tests in this family are known as:

- skin-prick tests or prick tests
- puncture tests
- scratch tests.

For the skin-prick test – the technique most commonly used in Britain – a small drop of liquid containing an allergen, such as grass pollen, is placed on the arm. The doctor makes a small prick in the skin, under the drop of liquid, allowing a minuscule amount of the allergen to get into the skin. A positive reaction is recorded if a red bump develops soon afterwards. For accuracy, the bump must be compared to positive and negative controls (see below).

The puncture method is very similar to the skin-prick test but uses a slightly different technique for breaking the skin. The term **prick-puncture test** covers both techniques.

With the scratch method, the skin is scratched lightly, and the allergen solution is then applied over the scratch. This method gives less consistent results than prick-puncture testing.

It is important to include a **negative control** in the test – a skin-prick test with plain salt water (saline). This should not produce much of a bump – if it does, the skin is clearly over-reactive and the tests more difficult to assess. The doctor should also include a **positive control** – a skin-prick test with histamine, the substance that plays a central role in allergic reactions. This should always produce a bump. If it does not, the skin is decidedly under-reactive, and the tests are invalid.

Taking antihistamines will make the skin under-reactive, and you should stop taking them before the testing, for a period ranging from a day to several weeks – it varies depending on the particular antihistamine. Ask your doctor for specific instructions about stopping these and other drugs before testing.

Skin tends to be over-reactive to testing in people with dermatographism (see p. 52). Blood tests known as **RASTs** (see p. 92) are needed for anyone with this condition. Eczema sufferers with a rash over large areas of the body may also require blood tests, simply because there is too little clear skin for testing.

Skin-prick tests can produce both false positives and false negatives (see box below). Some allergic diseases will give a lot of false negatives and relatively few false positives, while for others the reverse is true. The allergen itself influences the rates of misleading reactions: for example, tests for soy allergy are notoriously unreliable, whereas those for peanut are far more accurate. The age of the person being tested also makes a difference. With all these influences at work, interpreting the test responses is a real art, and the doctor's experience counts for a lot.

All sorts of people offer skin-prick tests, including alternative practitioners. Get them done by a qualified doctor, preferably by an allergist, who will know how to make sense of the reactions.

The safety record of skin-prick tests is very good. Occasionally a systemic reaction (anaphylaxis) occurs with these tests, but there are no records of any deaths. Nevertheless, if you have severe asthma or have experienced anaphylactic shock in the past, it is advisable for the doctor to have resuscitation equipment available. Taking beta-blockers (see p. 150) increases the risk of a life-threatening reaction.

False positives and false negatives

Apart from challenge tests, none of the tests used for allergy works with 100% accuracy. Most give both false positives and false negatives.

A **false positive** means that there is a positive test but no actual reaction when the allergen is encountered (e.g. eaten or inhaled). A **false negative** means that there is a negative test result despite a genuine reaction (as shown by a challenge test, for example).

A test that gives relatively few false positives has **good positive predictive value** – in other words, if it suggests you are allergic to something, you probably are.

A test that gives relatively few false negatives has **good negative predictive value**. If it comes up negative, you are probably not allergic to that allergen.

Some tests for allergic reactions show good positive predictive value but poor negative predictive value, while for other tests the reverse is true.

Intradermal tests

These tests (also called 'intracutaneous tests') put allergen more deeply into the skin than prick-puncture tests. The skin tends to react more when penetrated to this depth, so there are more false positives. There is also a greater risk of a serious reaction which may require emergency resuscitation. Don't undergo these tests if you are taking beta-blockers (see p. 150).

Radio-allergosorbent tests (RAST)

A blood sample is required for this kind of test. It is sent to a laboratory which uses a very accurate test for IgE (the allergy antibody). Specific types of IgE are measured – for example, IgE against cat allergens, cow's milk or birch pollen.

Research shows that RASTs are no more accurate than skin-prick tests in confirming real-life allergic reactions. However, they are useful for patients who can't discontinue their antihistamines without developing severe symptoms, and for those with dermatographism or very severe eczema (see p. 91).

Patch tests

These tests, used primarily for contact dermatitis, are similar to straightforward challenge tests, because the suspect substances are applied directly to the skin.

The test substances are placed on the skin – usually on the back – in small chambers. They are held in place with sticky tape, and left there for several days. Ideally, the reaction of the skin should be checked three times: after two days, again the next day, and again the day after that. It really is worth going back for all these separate visits, because the accuracy of the test increases greatly with repeated checking.

The substances chosen for testing are a standard set of antigens that most commonly cause contact dermatitis. This standard set will pick up 60–80% of all sensitivity reactions in contact dermatitis. If you have substances that you suspect may be causing symptoms, such as cosmetics, the doctor can usually test for these too.

You should not be tested while you still have a rash, as the testing will probably make the existing rash flare up, even though the test patches are applied well away from the rash.

Use of steroid creams and any light treatments (including exposure of the test area to ordinary sunlight) must stop at least a week before testing starts, or the results will not be accurate.

Interpreting patch tests requires a huge amount of skill, plus extensive knowledge of the finicky details of the different test substances. You need a dermatologist with considerable experience in this area.

False positives (see box on p. 91) can occur, especially if you react very strongly to one of the substances tested – some people develop what dermatologists call an 'angry back', and this generates false positives to various other substances being tested at the same time. Should you be told that you are sensitive to a great many different things, you may want to query this reading of the test. Ernest N. Charlesworth, an allergist and dermatologist at the University of Texas, describes patients who 'develop into environmental cripples' after being told that they are definitely sensitive to multiple antigens, on the basis of misinterpreted false-positive patch tests.

False negatives (see box on p. 91) are also possible, even with very careful testing. Should this occur, a type of challenge test known as a ROAT (Repeat Open Application Test) is possible. The suspect substance is applied to the inner fold of the elbow twice a day for a week. Get your doctor's agreement before trying this test.

Endoscopy and biopsy

Miniaturised cameras and sophisticated fibre-optics have allowed modern doctors to do something that their predecessors could never have imagined possible – look right inside the human body. This procedure is called **endoscopy**, and it has a useful role in a few sensitivity reactions.

Looking inside the sinus cavities can assist in understanding exactly what is going wrong in chronic sinusitis. Inspecting the digestive tract can be valuable in several of the non-IgE immune reactions to food, such as coeliac disease (see p. 70) and eosinophilic gastroenteritis (see p. 72).

A **biopsy** is often carried out at the same time as endoscopy. This involves taking a small sample from the affected area, such as the lining of the gut, and studying it in detail under a microscope.

One purpose of a gut biopsy is to look for characteristic types of damage to the lining of the gut – such as the distinctive changes produced by untreated coeliac disease. A biopsy can also reveal what kind of immune cells are present. Abnormal numbers of certain immune cells, for example, eosinophils (see p. 19), may suggest a particular diagnosis.

Another way of looking at what kind of immune reactions are going on, used for lung diseases, is a **bronchoalveolar lavage** – literally a 'washing out' of the airways and lungs, allowing immune cells to be collected and studied. This diagnostic technique is used for Heiner's Syndrome (see p. 72).

Tests for food intolerance

The only really effective way of testing for food intolerance is an elimination diet (see pp. 194–7). This is the gold standard. However, it is neither easy nor quick – which has led to a constant search for alternative tests.

The proposed alternatives are all indirect tests, that is to say, non-dietary. The results of the tests are used as a basis for an avoidance diet. In other words, the foods that give a positive test result are avoided.

Some of these tests use samples of hair or blood, others use pulse testing, pendulums, or muscle strength tests ('applied kinesiology'). A few of these tests do show some promise. Pulse tests, and a blood test called the 'lymphocyte transformation test' for example can give a general indication of sensitivity reactions – *sometimes*. However, even in the most expert hands, these do not give a result that is accurate enough to be useful.

Of the other tests that are available, most have not been evaluated at all objectively.

Many of them are advertised directly to the public, and one of the problems with this approach is that the testing company starts by *assuming* that food is the problem. The same is usually true of 'dietary therapists' and others in the alternative health field offering tests of this kind.

Almost everyone who undertakes such tests is given a fairly long list of foods which have come up positive in the tests. This does not fit with the evidence from medical trials in which a group of people with irritable bowel or migraine (typical food intolerance symptoms) undertake an elimination diet. A significant proportion of them always find that they do not have food intolerance. Of the rest, many find that they react to one or two foods only. The long lists of foods produced by the commercial tests are, to put it mildly, implausible.

With tests that require a sample of blood, sending off two blood samples from the same person, under different names, is a simple way of assessing the tests' validity. This exercise has been tried several times with different testing companies, and every time two completely different lists of foods have been sent back.

Covert studies of this kind have also shown that the tests overlook genuine reactions. In one alarming case, a woman with a true allergy to peanuts was assured by a 'dietary therapist' that she really could eat peanuts safely.

Many people with food intolerance will tell you that they did well after following a diet based on such tests – and they may well have done. Given that common foods such as wheat and milk are regular offenders in food intolerance, and that these foods very frequently feature on the lists of positive test results generated by commercial testing companies, quite a few people should do well. The problem is that these people may also be avoiding many other foods quite unnecessarily.

Furthermore, if people have sensitivities to some other foods that are *not* on the list, they will be missing out. They could enjoy a far better level of health if *all* the foods causing symptoms were identified and removed from their diet.

In the end, an elimination diet is both cheaper and far more likely to give the right answers.

Testing for IgG antibodies

In diagnosing food intolerance, some doctors offer tests for a type of antibody called IgG. This antibody is formed to any food molecules that get into the bloodstream after a meal – and some do, even in entirely healthy people. So finding IgG antibodies to food molecules is not indicative of *any* disease at all. It occurs in everyone and is perfectly normal.

Nevertheless, some doctors feel that by measuring the level of IgG antibodies to foods, they can get a general idea of the permeability of the gut wall (which might *possibly* be true) and of particular foods that could be causing intolerance reactions (very doubtful – the tests just tell you what you eat most, and you know that already).

This test does have a genuine basis – it is measuring something real, unlike some of the alternative tests for food intolerance. But the relevance of what it measures to the health of the individual concerned is partial and indefinite.

In short, blood tests for IgG antibodies to food molecules seem like very poor value for money, and potentially misleading, whereas an elimination diet is a far more precise way of pinpointing food intolerances.

Taking care of yourself

Tony had suffered from hayfever since childhood but rarely took any medicines. Outside the grass-pollen season, he was fine, free of allergies and very fit. Then, when he was 35 he bought a run-down cottage in the country. The cottage was very damp and dirty.

The previous owner of the cottage, an elderly man, had died, and everything was much as he had left it. Tony moved in with his wife in late summer, and they began pulling out all the old carpets and furniture. Many of the windows would not open and there were dank musty cupboards and attics to be cleared. Dust filled the air – and Tony's nose. He began to sneeze a little and within a few days he had a strange and unfamiliar feeling of tightness in his chest. During the following weeks, harvesting began in the surrounding fields, with several huge combine-harvesters working away all day and night. Tony noticed that, when out of doors, his eyes began to stream and the tightness in his chest became more noticeable. A few more days passed, and Tony found it harder to breathe, so he reluctantly went to see the doctor. The diagnosis was asthma. Skin-prick tests showed that Tony had allergic reactions to house-dust mite and moulds.

Tony's case shows how someone who is already sensitised to an allergen – pollen in this case – may be vulnerable to developing new sensitivities, and new symptoms. It was almost certainly the dust mite and mould spores in the cottage that sparked off the trouble, followed by the mould spores from the cereal leaves, dispersed during harvesting.

For people with a tendency to allergies, the dangers of heavy exposure to potential allergens are something to bear in mind. It is surprising how many people with asthma had their first major attack while away from home, sleeping on an old sofa or in a friend's dusty spare room. The dose of dust-mite allergen that you get from an ancient mattress or eiderdown can be massive.

Managing your allergy symptoms

As well as avoiding the development of new allergies, you need to manage your existing symptoms, and make sure that they interfere with your life as little as possible. For this you need good information and advice, support from your doctor, optimal drug treatment, and careful avoidance of your allergens.

Quite often people have all the information and drug treatment they need, but they still don't stay on top of their health problems. There can be two distinct reasons for this: either they are not wholehearted about wanting to be well (ambivalence) – or they have never really accepted that they are ill (denial).

Ambivalence

Sometimes being ill has certain benefits – or being entirely well has certain disadvantages. Our state of health determines how people treat us, especially within the family, and the expectations people have of us. It may be comforting to be ill because others are more supportive then, or it may be less risky, because we are not forced to try things (such as sports or other physical activities) at which we might fail or look foolish. Being ill as a child often sets up a pattern for how we interact with the world, which revolves around caution, the comforts of familiarity, and holding back from new situations.

These habitual patterns can survive in the mind long after any real advantages have evaporated. Many people become stuck with a way of thinking and living where ill-health is a cornerstone of their existence. Doctors at the Chelsea and Westminster Hospital in London, who have developed a radical programme for treating atopic eczema (see pp. 46–7), have noticed this in their patients. 'Old habits die hard and living with a little bit of eczema is a very tempting prospect for many patients, rather than clearing the skin completely…. As atopic skin disease begins for many in the first year of life, causing sometimes understandable alarm and despondency in the parents, the child learns how relevant their condition can be in their relationship with the external world, and with their parents in particular. Before they are able to speak, they have a powerful means of gaining parental attention which can have long-standing effects in the development of their personality. For some, to live without eczema is understandably a daunting prospect. This can be consciously appreciated and spontaneously referred to by some patients, while for others the issue will be buried from view, deep in their unconscious.'

If any of this rings bells with you, try to tackle the problem at source. Such mental blocks are not immovable. Indeed, simply recognising that the block is there can start to change things for some people.

Others may need professional help to overcome these long-standing habits of mind. Counselling or cognitive therapy can be very valuable, and your doctor may be able to help in locating a suitably qualified person for this.

Denial

At the opposite end of the spectrum are those who want to deny that they have any kind of health problem. Often these people cannot quite accept that they have a long-term disease, such as eczema or asthma, so they forget to take their drugs, apply creams to their skin, or carry their inhalers. Ironically, these people frequently wind up having far more trouble with their allergies than they need to, and a very poor quality of life, simply because they neglect preventive treatments.

To be really well, you first have to admit that you do have allergies, and then sort out your conflicting feelings about what this means. Again, counselling, cognitive therapy or some other kind of psychotherapy can be helpful.

Dealing with doctors

The decisions that your doctor makes about your treatment are ones in which you should be fully involved. Quite a few allergy patients don't feel happy about their doctor's treatment plan, but they never say so to the doctor's face.

The usual pattern is to accept what the doctor prescribes without any argument, but then halve the dose of tablets, or only put the cream on once a day instead of twice, or not use the inhaler at all. Some people stop and start their drugs in a random way because they never quite make up their minds about whether drugs are a good thing or not.

This approach to allergies invariably leads to worsening symptoms. The risks are greatest with complex problems such as atopic eczema or chronic sinusitis, where a vicious circle can easily be set up if the disease is not brought under control, and for those with a life-threatening condition such as asthma. In the case of asthma, neglecting preventative treatment can be fatal.

It is far better to say what you think in the surgery, and discuss any misgivings you may have about drugs with the doctor. That way you can agree on a treatment regime that you are prepared to stick to – which may or may not involve drugs. Most doctors would far prefer a little plain speaking at the outset to having a patient who is half-hearted about following the treatment plan and never really improves.

A more serious form of communication breakdown occurs when a doctor stops believing what a particular patient says. This usually occurs because the doctor has decided that some or all of a patient's symptoms are due to psychological rather than physical causes. (This is far more likely to happen to those with intolerance or unusual forms of allergic reaction than to those with classical allergic diseases.) Sometimes doctors say what they think, but often they don't – they just start treating the symptoms in a different way, or acting impatiently, or saying rather puzzling things that leave the patient trying to guess what is going on.

If you find yourself in such a situation, the main thing to do is stay very calm and be very rational. Getting upset, or challenging the doctor's opinion in a manner that seems at all aggressive, instantly confirms the 'psychological' diagnosis. Unfortunately, insisting firmly that the symptoms are not psychological *also* confirms the diagnosis as far as many doctors are concerned (see p. 237) which can be extremely frustrating. To begin with, deal with the situation by informing yourself about your illness. Be tactful and patient but persistent with the doctor, trying all the time to keep the relationship pleasant and the channels of communication open. If, after giving it a fair try for some weeks or months, this approach isn't working, you should look into the possibility of changing doctors (see p. 88).

Emergency alerts

An emergency alert bracelet or pendant should be worn by anyone who:

- is allergic to latex rubber, or to drugs such as penicillin
- has a severe allergy to insect stings
- suffers from exercise-induced anaphylaxis, or anaphylactic shock as a result of food allergy
- has very severe asthma attacks.

Key information is engraved on the bracelet, along with a telephone number which gives medical staff access to a computer database containing vital medical data about you. This valuable service is provided by a non-profit-making company called Medic Alert. For contact details see p. 255.

How should you use this book?

As everyone knows, a little knowledge is a dangerous thing. You can use the information in this book to help yourself, but it's important to remember that there is no substitute for the comprehensive understanding of the human body that your doctor gained during many long years at medical school. Always check with your doctor before changing your diet, stopping your drugs, practising breathing exercises, taking a non-prescription medicine or trying any other experimental treatment.

The information about disease, diagnosis and treatment in this book falls into four categories:
- basic information about the disease that no doctor would disagree with
- the findings of new research, or research that has not become widely known, but which falls within the accepted medical model of the disease concerned. Your doctor may not know about some of this research (there is a *terrifying* amount of new information bombarding doctors every week, and no one can keep up with it all) but he or she won't find it unbelievable.
- evidence from research that is entirely valid, but which is widely ignored or dismissed because it falls outside the accepted medical model of the disease concerned (see pp. 86–7)
- information based on the repeated observations of doctors, or of patients – this does not amount to scientifically valid evidence, but it's included here if it seems plausible and if it could be useful to some readers.

You should be able to tell, from the context in which it is presented, which category any item of information falls into. When talking to your doctor about items that belong in the last two categories above, be prepared for a certain amount of scepticism or possibly outright dismissal.

The important thing to ask the doctor is if there is good reason why you should not try the suggested measures, in addition to your usual treatment – is there any *risk* involved, given your particular state of health? Make it clear that you want to try the additional treatment with an open mind and drop it if it is not helping. Ask for the doctor's help in assessing the effects of the treatment objectively.

Managing asthma

Of all the diseases described in this book, asthma is among the most difficult to live with, especially severe asthma. Learn to recognise asthma symptoms before they get out of hand, and take immediate action.

Studies of patients who die from asthma attacks find that the deaths could, in almost all cases, have been prevented. Factors contributing to fatal attacks include:
- heavy exposure to allergens just before the asthma attack
- cigarette smoking
- failure to use preventer drugs
- repeat prescriptions for inhalers being given without the patient seeing a doctor
- delays in seeing an asthma specialist
- depression in the asthmatic leading to neglect of treatment.

For the day-to-day management of asthma, you should have a written **management plan** prepared by your doctor or asthma nurse.

This should tell you how often to take your drugs under normal circumstances, and what to do if your symptoms change or you develop a cold or chest infection. The actual brand names of your drugs (or the colour of the inhaler) should be included on the management plan. Assuming you have a peak-flow meter – and you really should have one – specific peak-flow values should be included on your management plan, with instructions for how to respond if your peak flow falls to these levels.

Your plan should tell you how to recognise a severe attack coming on, and what to do at the various stages of the attack. (This personal management plan is specifically geared to you or your child. Although pp. 100–101 give generalised advice, your own plan is invaluable.)

Be sure that you know exactly how the advice in the plan relates to the sort of real-life situations you experience. No matter how good your plan, real life can sometimes be far more complex than anyone anticipates, so there may be times when it is difficult to know what to do. When this occurs, make a note of the situation, and the reasons why you are unsure how to implement the plan. Call your doctor immediately if your asthma is getting worse, and get the asthma attack under control. Save your notes and, at the next opportunity, check with the doctor what you *should* have done in those circumstances. This will help you to build up your detailed knowledge of how to manage your asthma, or that of your child.

Research shows that asthmatics can, with training, develop a greater awareness of how narrow their airways are – this helps you to detect worsening asthma before things get too serious. You can train yourself in this art by guessing what your peak flow will be and writing your guess down *before* you use your peak-flow meter (see right) each day. Over a period of weeks, you should find your guesses getting closer to the true value.

A key part of asthma control is having everything with you that you need in case of an attack. It's tedious, but you have to do it. You should take your reliever inhaler with you wherever you go. Those with severe asthma can also benefit from carrying a collapsible spacer (ask your pharmacist or see p. 255 for contact details of suppliers).

For a long day out, or a stay away from home, check that you also have:
- your management plan
- your peak-flow meter
- your preventer inhaler
- steroid tablets, if you sometimes need these
- your doctor's phone number.

A little lateral thinking may be needed regarding the problem of carrying all this kit around. One asthmatic friend of mine carries his inhalers in a trendy-looking camera bag that goes everywhere with him. Mothers of asthmatic children have solved the problem by making an 'inhaler pouch' from a sunglasses case and attaching it to a favourite belt or by enlarging the pocket in a teenager's jacket to accommodate inhalers.

Anyone with severe allergies to food or insect stings should take similar steps, so that carrying their auto-injector everywhere is a simple matter.

Peak-flow meters

A peak-flow meter can detect narrowing of your airways – the beginnings of an asthma attack – before there are any obvious symptoms. It measures the maximum speed at which you can force air out of your lungs. The signs of worsening asthma include:
- a morning reading which is less than 75% of the evening reading
- average readings less than 75% of your best-ever reading. (If they get to less than 50% of your best reading, this is a severe and possibly life-threatening attack.)

To use a peak-flow meter:
- push the pointer to zero and hold the meter horizontally
- keep your fingers away from the scale and the pointer
- breathe normally before you start
- stand up and take a deep breath, but don't puff your cheeks out and don't hold your breath before you blow
- seal your lips tightly around the mouthpiece
- blow hard into the meter, as if blowing out candles on a birthday cake; don't move your tongue while doing this
- repeat three times, and record the highest reading of the three.

You must learn how to use a peak-flow meter from your doctor or asthma nurse, who should also check your technique regularly – it is very easy to get into bad habits.

Dealing with emergencies

Let's hope it never happens – but if it does, knowing what to do could make the difference between surviving and not surviving. The sensible thing is to read these pages – or whichever parts are relevant to you or your child – *before* you encounter an emergency. It is often helpful to rehearse the procedure in your mind and actually imagine yourself going through the actions described here.

Find out in advance what the local ambulance service is like, and ask your GP for advice about who to contact in an emergency. These are the different options:

- Call your GP. If the doctor is nearby and the hospital or ambulance station a long way off, this may be the best decision. Doctors in rural areas may have supplies of adrenaline for emergency treatment, and oxygen for those suffering a severe asthma attack.
- Call an ambulance. Where the local ambulance service is dependable, this is *always* the best option. The ambulance crew will have adrenaline and oxygen.
- Go by car or taxi to the nearest hospital emergency department. This is not usually a good plan, because your condition may quickly get worse, and you have no emergency treatment available. But there may be situations where it is a sensible decision.

Remember that emergencies can occur when you are away on holiday or on business. Never stay anywhere without a phone – and check that it is working as soon as you arrive. Make sure you know where the nearest hospital is and that you have the phone number of a local doctor. A remote holiday cottage can be a dangerous place to develop an asthma attack or anaphylactic shock.

Anaphylactic shock

This is an extremely serious emergency, requiring immediate medical help. The signs of anaphylactic shock are listed on p.58. In the case of food allergy, there are additional signs in the mouth, lips and throat (see p. 62).

Use **adrenaline (epinephrine)** straight away if you have it – *but get emergency medical help as well*. With injectable adrenaline (see p. 150), remove the cap and push firmly into the outer thigh, going straight through any clothing. Never inject into any other part of the body – this can be dangerous.

If you have an adrenaline inhaler you can use this first to treat symptoms in the mouth, throat and airways, and then use the injector if you still have symptoms. For those who have relatively mild reactions normally, this is a good approach. (Improvise a spacer – see p.100 – if there is difficulty in inhaling the adrenaline.)

Anyone whose reactions tend to be severe should use the injector first and follow up with the inhaler if necessary.

Overdosing with adrenaline is possible, *and can be fatal*, but using the inhaler as well as the injector is safe as long as you don't have a heart condition. (Don't exceed the maximum number of puffs allowed for the inhaler, because the propellant can cause problems.)

If you do not improve after using the injector, a second one can be used, 10–15 minutes later. In situations where medical help is not yet available and the symptoms are not abating, another shot of adrenaline can be given every 15–20 minutes. But the maximum number of shots recommended by your doctor should *never* be exceeded. Keep count of how many you've had, and tell medical staff.

An asthmatic who does not have an adrenaline inhaler can use a beta-2 reliever inhaler such as Ventolin (see p. 152) as well as the adrenaline injection, although it probably won't help very much.

Suppose you know for sure that you have encountered your allergen, but you don't have any symptoms yet? In Britain, the usual advice is to wait for symptoms, but US doctors say go ahead and use the adrenaline injector if you have reacted very badly in the past. In general, for people with no other health problems, it is better to give an adrenaline injection which isn't needed than to delay giving one that is needed.

Following anaphylactic shock, you should be kept in hospital for 6–12 hours even when everything seems fine. Attacks have recurred as much as 8 hours later. Corticosteroids reduce the chance of this happening – ask if these have been given. If you are discharged early and it is a long journey home, consider waiting in the hospital, or nearby, until 8 hours after the original reaction.

First aid for anaphylactic shock

A badly swollen tongue or throat can cause suffocation. If there is visible swelling and the person is unconscious or turning blue, try to keep the top of the trachea (the main airway leading from the throat) open. Use the handle of a spoon – one that has *very smooth edges*. Slide it carefully over the top of the tongue and into the throat. Press down gently but firmly to open the airway.

If there is swelling in the throat and difficulty breathing, a sitting position is generally better than

A first-time attack

The first allergic reaction you ever experience can be very mild – maybe no more than tingling or itching of the mouth in the case of food allergy. Stay near a phone for an hour or so, in case you need to call for medical help. Often the symptoms just wear off, and that's it. Keep well away from the food, insect or whatever, read pp. 58–9, and see your doctor soon. If symptoms worsen, and if they affect the body as a whole, (for example, widespread nettle rash) or if your breathing is affected, then you need emergency medical help.

lying down. A person who is losing consciousness should be put in the standard recovery position (see any first-aid manual) to reduce the chance of them inhaling vomit – a particular risk with food allergy.

Insect-sting allergy

If you don't have an adrenaline injector, get medical help immediately.

If you've had a **cutaneous systemic reaction** (see p. 60) in the past, use the adrenaline injector if there is any difficulty in breathing, hoarseness, stomach cramps, diarrhoea, nausea, faintness, dizziness or confusion. If you are unsure, remember that, unless you have a heart condition, it is usually better to over-react (i.e. use the adrenaline unecessarily) than to under-react.

If you've had a **severe systemic reaction** (i.e. anaphylactic shock) in the past, use an adrenaline injector at the first sign of any reaction other than immediately around the sting.

If there is a honeybee stinger left in the skin, scrape or flick it out sideways, using a fingernail, knife blade or credit card – *the venom sac is attached and will go on injecting venom for up to 10 minutes if you leave it there*.

Don't try to pull the stinger out – this squeezes the venom sac and pumps more venom into the skin.

Get emergency medical help, and follow the other measures for anaphylactic shock (see left).

Don't go alone

If you suffer vomiting or diarrhoea during anaphylaxis, and have to go to the toilet, tell someone to call an ambulance *and take someone else with you* to the toilet. Do not go in alone and lock the door, in case you collapse.

Asthma attacks

Even those with mild asthma, who have never had a serious attack before, can quite suddenly get into difficulties and require emergency treatment. Don't be over-anxious about this, because it is unlikely to happen – but do be prepared. Not having your reliever inhaler with you when a severe attack starts is a recipe for disaster – *always take it, wherever you go*.

Deal with an attack promptly. The sooner you act, the fewer drugs you'll need in the long run to control the attack. Most asthmatics wait too long and then under-treat their asthma.

The important thing is *recognising* an asthma attack, and knowing when it is getting out of control. Not all attacks are the same – some come on fast, some come on slowly.

Rapid asthma attacks come on in a matter of hours. You may have been fine all day, but then start to feel very breathless and wheezy, or begin coughing badly. Less than an hour later, despite using the reliever, the breathlessness is worse and it is a struggle to speak or walk across the room. *This is a severe attack: don't delay in getting medical help*.

Slow asthma attacks come on over a period of days. At first you are more breathless and wheezy than usual, and your reliever inhaler is not helping much. Asthma wakes you up at night, and you are far more breathless than usual in the morning. This could be the beginning of a severe attack, so don't delay in getting medical help. If you get to the point where your asthma is disturbing your sleep every night, and in the morning you have difficulty in speaking or walking about, this is a very serious situation – *you must see your doctor or go to the hospital now*.

A few asthmatics have great difficulty recognising when they are increasingly breathless, and for them, using a peak-flow meter (see p. 97) every day is essential. Indeed, most asthmatics find that monitoring peak flow is a valuable way of spotting attacks in advance. However, if your peak flow seems normal, and yet you feel breathless and have a tight feeling in your chest, *pay attention to your symptoms and get medical help*.

Your response to your reliever inhaler is another helpful sign in assessing asthma attacks. Things are serious if:

- the reliever inhaler does not seem to be working at all within 10 minutes of taking a puff
- it does not work as well as usual
- it works, but the effect wears off in less than 3 hours.

If you have an asthmatic child, give everyone who normally takes care of the child detailed written instructions for recognising and dealing with an asthma attack. People forget verbal instructions, especially in an emergency. A child who is exhausted or upset by an attack should always be given medical care.

Taking action

If your reliever inhaler is not working well (see above), take another puff to open up your airways – *and then take further action*, as described below.

If you seem to be in the early stages of a slow asthma attack, check your management plan, and if your peak flow has fallen below the recommended level, double the dose of inhaled steroids (twice as many puffs each time) now. Add any other medicines (e.g. steroid tablets) as recommended by the management plan.

Those who don't have a peak-flow meter or management plan should double the dose of inhaled steroids and make an urgent appointment to see the doctor.

If you are suffering a rapid attack, or a slow attack that has got out of control, you need emergency medical help. Ring for an ambulance, ring your doctor, or go to the hospital – the ideal course of action will vary, depending on where you live (see p. 98).

Use your reliever inhaler until medical help arrives. You can take a puff every 5–10 minutes if needed, but keep a count of how many puffs you've had and stop after 30. Some doctors suggest taking up to 30 puffs all at once. (If you have a heart condition, this dose might be dangerous: follow your doctor's advice.)

If it is difficult to inhale, use a spacer – this can make all the difference, especially for children.

You can improvise a spacer from a plastic cup, a plastic bottle, or a paper bag. Make a hole in the bottom of the cup or bottle, or in one corner of the paper bag, and insert the mouthpiece of the inhaler here. The open end of the cup, bottle or bag goes in or over the mouth – with the bag, you have to bunch it up and hold it around the mouth. Squirt the inhaler repeatedly into the improvised spacer, while breathing steadily in and out.

Recognising an asthma attack in a very young child

With a young child, these signs indicate a severe asthma attack:

- the nostrils are flared
- the shoulders are unusually high
- the child can say only one or two words between breaths
- the ribs are pushed out, and the spaces between the ribs, and below the chest cage, are sucked in during breathing
- you can hear wheezing (a whistling noise)
- the lips, tongue or fingernails are blue.

If wheezing stops, without any other apparent improvement, this is a very bad sign – it may mean that the airways are now so narrow that no air is passing through them. This is called a 'silent chest', and indicates an *urgent* need for medical attention.

The six golden rules for asthma attacks

• Breathe as slowly as possible and concentrate on breathing out, not on breathing in. Exhale as fully as you can and your in-breath will follow automatically.

• Never panic – if you do, you may start hyperventilating, and this makes matters much worse (see p. 226). Panicky parents are the worst possible thing for an asthmatic child during an attack.

• Adopt a position that makes breathing as easy as possible. Propping your arms up at about shoulder height can help – for example, sit back-to-front on a dining chair, with your arms folded and resting on the back. Or put pillows on a table, sit in an upright chair, and rest your head and arms on the pillows. Don't lie down, as this makes matters worse. Open a window, as long as the air outside is not cold, polluted or loaded with pollen.

• Avoid factors that can make an asthma attack worse, for example, vigorous activity, cold air, irritants and allergens.

• Drink plenty of water, fruit juice or other liquids as a lot of water is lost through the surface of the airways during an asthma attack, and you can become dehydrated.

• Don't take anything to help you sleep, even herbal pills. If your asthma gets worse during the night, you need to wake up so that you can get more air.

After an attack

Asthmatics who have suffered a severe attack are occasionally sent home from hospital before they are completely better. A few people have died as a result of being discharged too soon. So if you feel breathless or otherwise unwell after you leave hospital, don't hesitate to go back – or seek other medical help.

See your GP or specialist within a few days of any emergency treatment. Don't be over-confident just after a severe attack – this can be a very vulnerable time. Take more rest than usual and drink plenty of fluids, as you may be dehydrated. Keep taking your preventer inhaler at the increased dose – reducing the dose now could lead to another severe, possibly fatal, attack. Keep taking steroid tablets if you have been given them.

If you produced a lot of mucus during the attack, try to clear it, but without violent coughing. Mucus can sometimes form solid plugs which block small airways. Treatment by a physiotherapist would help, and expectorants – drugs which help loosen mucus – can also be useful (ask your pharmacist about these). Don't take ordinary cough medicine (see p. 163). There are also some breathing exercises which can help to clear mucus (see p. 231).

An asthma attack represents a chance to learn more about preventing asthma – so think about what went wrong. Had you forgotten to take your preventer inhaler regularly? How long is it since you had your medicines reviewed by the doctor or asthma clinic? Have you been using your peak-flow meter daily? Were you exposed to a high dose of allergen or an irritant?

A reaction to aspirin-like drugs

Aspirin sensitivity can begin quite suddenly in someone who has previously taken aspirin without trouble. If you have unexplained chronic urticaria, or polyps in the nose, plus asthma and/or rhinitis, the development of aspirin sensitivity at some time in the future is a distinct possibility (see p. 151).

A sensitivity reaction to aspirin or aspirin-like drugs usually begins between 30 minutes and 2 hours after the drug is taken. You will have some or all of these symptoms:

• a runny or badly blocked nose, and red eyes
• a feeling of warmth, flushing and sweating
• a general rash
• a sensation of tightness in the chest, a dry cough, increasing breathlessness
• malaise and exhaustion
• vomiting or diarrhoea
• swelling (angioedema) and/or nettle rash (urticaria).

If you have such symptoms **get emergency medical help immediately** because the reaction can quickly develop into severe asthma, shock, collapse and unconsciousness.

If you have asthma, use your reliever inhaler as much as required (up to 30 puffs) until medical help arrives. Anyone who has an adrenaline (epinephrine) autoinjecter, or an adrenaline inhaler can use this as well – up to 30 puffs of the inhaler, or whatever maximum dose is given in the instructions. Tell the ambulance crew and doctors exactly what you have taken.

Helping children to cope with their illness

Suffering from a long-term illness, especially if it is severe and sometimes limits activity, can easily make a child feel different from other children, and 'not good enough'. Children with allergies, especially those with severe asthma or food allergies, may also be very frightened and anxious. At the same time, such children often feel that they have to protect their parents by not revealing their fears.

Children may also think that their illness is a punishment for something they have done wrong. Their guilty feelings can be so powerful that they may not confide in you unless you spend time talking with them about their illness, and encourage them to share their feelings with you.

One of the most valuable things you can do for children with allergies is to build up their self-esteem. This is especially important when they first start school, because they have to adjust to other children there, and learn how to deal with questions about their illness, as well as some unkindness.

For children whose allergies limit what they can do physically, or restrict some normal activities, try to find other interests and hobbies that the child can do well. When talking with the child, always emphasise the positive things – the difficulties that you have overcome together in the past, the measures that the child can take to keep the symptoms under control (such as stopping scratching, applying creams, or using a preventer inhaler) and the areas of life where he or she is particularly successful. As the child gets older, introduce the idea that coping with illness makes you a stronger, kinder and more resolute person, one who can cope with any of life's challenges. Show the child how much you value their maturity and perseverance.

Pay attention to what the child's friends are saying – a bit of eavesdropping is allowed – and be prepared to counteract any negative messages. Teach your child to be strong and self-confident about choosing their friends, and to prefer those who are sensible, understanding and supportive. Ask casually about what schoolteachers and other adults say when you are not around, because they can, without meaning any harm, undermine a child's confidence with thoughtless remarks.

For children with problems that are potentially life threatening, such as true food allergy, your natural anxieties as a parent can lead you to be overprotective. This can make the child feel smothered, but letting go is far from easy. You somehow have to find a middle path that works for you both.

With asthmatic children, focus on letting them live as normal a life as possible. Avoid saying 'no' automatically to things that might induce an asthma attack – such as running around outdoors in cold weather. Take some small risks, and let the child make the decision sometimes – he or she will gain a lot from taking the responsibility, *especially* if the decision is the wrong one.

This is the only way for children to learn how to manage their own condition. The sooner you can begin letting go, the better the child will cope in his or her teenage years, when it really will be necesary to make some difficult decisions without your help.

A pitfall for parents

In bringing up a child with allergies, remember that there should never be any 'secondary gain' from illness – absolutely no advantages to having the eczema get worse (easily done by scratching) or starting an asthma attack (some children can bring one on by breathing in a particular way).

If your child has to take time off from school because of ill-health, ask the teacher for work that can be done at home, and check that it really is done. Children who are allowed to benefit from being ill can establish an unhealthy pattern for dealing with life's difficulties (see pp. 94–5), which may be long-lasting. Such a mind-set can seriously limit a child's development.

Incidentally, the 'secondary gain' from illness may be quite altruistic in nature. It can include stopping parents from arguing, or from nagging a naughty brother or sister, as well as more obvious things such as getting a parent's attention – so be aware of all the circumstances in the family that are affecting the child.

Sometimes a child realises, unconsciously, that attending to illness gives a parent welcome distractions from emotional problems and a comforting feeling of being needed and useful. The allergies can become part of the structure of a family, the glue holding everyone together.

Conversely, long-term illness can tear families apart: according to recent research in the United States, divorce is more common in families where a child suffers from severe asthma. Doctors frequently notice that severe eczema also can create a lot of tension in the home.

If you feel that a child's illness is affecting the family badly – in whatever way – talk to your doctor, or someone else who you trust. You may need the help of a counsellor or family therapist to sort things out.

Children and medicines

Parents often feel very anxious about all the medication an allergic child uses. On the whole, the drugs prescribed for allergy are very safe, and only children with severe disease are at risk of significant side-effects. These children will be carefully monitored by the doctor.

Needless to say, if you can cut down on the drugs by reducing allergen exposure, avoiding irritants (e.g. tobacco smoke) and implementing some of the other measures described in this book, you should do so. But if the child still needs drugs to control the symptoms, it is far better to accept them than to let the child struggle with all the discomfort, limitations and distress that the illness imposes.

Parents who are very concerned about drugs should talk openly to the doctor about their fears. If there are differences of opinion about drugs within the family, try not to expose the child to the disagreements. Sort out a joint policy in advance and always present a united front to the child. Be consistent and reassuring about drug use, otherwise the child may feel confused and anxious about the situation – or may even learn to manipulate it.

The asthmatic child

Children with asthma should have a management plan (see p. 96) and may benefit from using a peak-flow meter (see p. 97). Once your child is old enough to comprehend the difference between preventers and relievers, explain that using the preventer regularly keeps asthma under control, which means no sudden attacks and less need to use the reliever in public – something which most children find intensely embarrassing. You should oversee the child's treatment closely until the age of seven or eight, then gradually let the child take over some of the responsibilities.

Coping with food allergy

The following concerns true food allergy (see p. 62), which can be life threatening, not idiopathic food intolerance (see p. 74).

Protecting a child with severe food allergies is a major task. You will find it enormously helpful to be in contact with other parents who are facing the same challenge. The practical details are everything here, and you can benefit from other people's ingenuity in solving day-to-day problems. Several support groups exist (see p. 255), offering a wealth of advice.

For very small children, the main task is to ensure that everyone who looks after the child understands exactly what can and can't be eaten. Child-minders and baby-sitters should spend time with you as 'apprentices' seeing what is involved in preparing food for the child – this is *far* better than just giving verbal instructions. Also make sure that everyone knows how to use the adrenaline auto-injector (see p. 98).

Once children start going to parties, you should always stay at the party for the whole time, and supervise your child closely. Take food that your child can safely eat, but which other children can also share. Some parents put a label on toddlers warning other adults that certain foods are taboo – for children under reading age this is probably acceptable, and does allow you to relax a little, but with older children the dangers of being teased or stigmatised should always be borne in mind.

Plan ahead all the time. Keep a snack box in the car containing food that the child can safely eat. Whenever you go on a trip, however short, have some safe foods with you, in case you get stuck somewhere and the child gets hungry. If you go out to eat, exert maximum caution about the restaurant food (see p. 111). Some parents take along a guaranteed-safe, but super-delicious sandwich or burger, and ask the restaurant to warm it up in a microwave (where appropriate) and serve it at the same time as the other food. If you do this, be sure the staff understand that the food must not touch any other food.

At home, some parents opt for everyone eating the same allergen-free food, on the basis that this makes for being 'a real family'. Others, finding this too problematic or expensive, make a virtue out of the allergic child having a different meal. 'I try to make her feel special about having her own food. The allergen-free dinner or cake always looks and tastes really good.'

As children get older, and more independent, you need to educate them thoroughly about avoiding the offending food. Equip them for difficult situations by role-playing. Act out being offered a tempting item of food by another child, and being jeered at for refusing. Act out suffering an allergic reaction to food and getting help quickly, even though people around don't understand and are uncooperative.

Allergies and schools

When your child starts at a new school, crèche, or kindergarten, request a meeting with staff and teachers to talk about the child's allergies if there is any likelihood of these becoming a problem. Do this well before your child starts at the school, so that any necessary changes can be made. If your child has a serious food allergy or severe asthma, you may have to make several visits because there are usually a number of different people you should meet, and follow-up sessions may be needed with some staff. If all this sounds daunting and 'not my style' then you need, for the sake of your child, to develop your skills in dealing with people and being assertive. Talk to a counsellor, or look for suitable training courses.

In addition to ensuring that the school takes good care of your child's health (see below), you should also discuss wider issues of adjustment to school life. Teasing or bullying can be a problem for children with any kind of health problem. Ask the teacher to keep an eye on your child and ensure that he or she is coping well – for example, that there is no difficulty about using an inhaler in front of other children when necessary.

Eczema

Ensure all staff realise that the skin rash is not infectious, and that they are aware of the need to communicate this to other children. The appearance of the skin can create a lot of problems with class-mates, and teachers need to be alert for taunting remarks or hurtful nicknames.

Unfortunately, children with eczema are very susceptible to infections caught from others, such as impetigo (see p. 44) but you can't really protect children from such infections without isolating them socially. The best way to tackle this problem is to deploy all the available treatments so that your child's skin becomes stronger and more resistant.

Food allergy

If your child has food allergy, go and see the catering manager personally. It may be helpful to take some printed material on food allergy with you, plus lists of synonyms for food ingredients (see pp. 172–4) where appropriate. Concentrate on building up a good relationship with catering staff, while ensuring that they understand how dangerous certain foods can be to your child.

Many parents feel more relaxed if they supply their child with a packed lunch that they know is allergen-free. This is often a good strategy, but don't be complacent. Most allergic reactions in schools involve food given or traded by another child with entirely good intentions. Some schools with food-allergic children have set up a 'no trading food' policy, which seems to work well. Other schools establish milk-free or nut-free tables in the canteen, so that friends can sit together and trade food safely. (The mothers of the other children sitting at these tables need to be well versed in food avoidance, of course, so that their packed lunches are as safe as your own.) In the United States, schools have sometimes tried banning nuts or peanuts altogether, where there is a nut-allergic student, but this does not work well.

Some parents prepare a printed information sheet about their child's food allergy, with a photograph of the child, and put these up at strategic points around the kitchen and canteen area. This information can include instructions on how to deal with anaphylactic shock (see below) and who to contact in an emergency.

Finally, include the art teacher in your rounds – foodstuffs are often used in art and craft projects.

Anaphylaxis

For children with severe food or insect-sting allergies which can lead to anaphylaxis, check that everyone at the school understands the potentially fatal nature of this condition. Key staff must know how to recognise anaphylactic shock and exactly what to do: show them how the adrenaline injector kit works. You could take along an old one, so that they can practise (see p. 150). Injector kits and adrenaline inhalers must be within easy reach, never locked in a cupboard.

Repeat this educational process at the beginning of each new school year, and before school trips. As an additional precaution, your child should wear a bracelet or pendant (see box on p. 95) that informs medical personnel about his or her allergies – this is also vital for children with latex or drugs allergies.

Asthma

If your child has asthma, ask what arrangements are made for inhalers. Children who can take responsibility for their own treatment should keep their inhalers with them. For younger children, the inhaler should be in the classroom, somewhere that is easily accessible (**never locked away**) and should be taken along during breaks and mealtimes. The child must always be able to get to the inhaler quickly: even a small delay in using it when an attack occurs can have dire consequences. Make sure everyone at the school understands this, that they know how to recognise an attack, and how to react. Assure the teacher that there is little danger of an asthmatic child overdosing, and if other children take a few puffs they will come to no harm.

If the teacher seems to believe that asthma is a psychological problem (some still do), go and see the head. Suggest that a local asthma nurse or doctor comes in and talks to the staff and pupils about asthma.

Ensure that the teacher knows about the effects of cold air and exercise on asthmatics. Talk to the games teacher or sports coach, and the playground attendants. It is vital that the games teacher is encouraging but understanding towards asthmatic children. They should never be told to continue exercising if they feel breathless.

Allergens and irritants in school

Schools today often have soft furnishings and carpets – these may be full of dust mites. If your child is allergic to mites, and if allergy symptoms are frequent at school, have a look around the classroom and see if this might be the cause. Before discussing the problem with the school, learn all you can about dust mites (see p. 114–117) so that you can assess whether proposed solutions to the problem would actually work.

Pets are common in classrooms and they can cause allergic reactions in sensitised children. Moulds flourish in many school buildings, and will affect a child with mould allergy. Poor ventilation is sometimes a major problem in school buildings, especially those where windows cannot be opened.

Irritants in school air include glue, paint, the solvents from felt-tip pens, disinfectants, air fresheners and the fumes produced during science lessons. Make sure the science teacher is aware of the risks and always uses a fume cupboard if irritant gases such as nitrogen dioxide or sulphur dioxide are likely to be given off during an experiment

Applying sunscreens to children's skin is now routine in many schools and preschools. Teachers probably won't think to ask permission, so if your child is sensitive to any common ingredients of creams or sunscreens, let them know in advance.

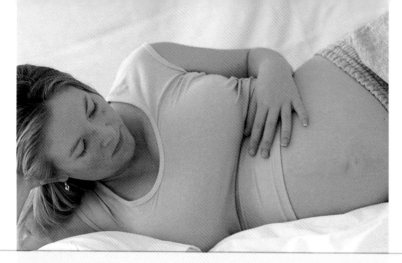

Allergies and pregnancy

Great care is taken in prescribing drugs during pregnancy. This is something that doctors are now exceedingly cautious about, but do tell the doctor *as soon as you decide to try for a baby*. The foetus is most vulnerable to damage by drugs during the first three months, and especially the first few weeks after conception.

Your prescription will be changed if the drugs you are currently taking could pose any threat to the unborn child. A drug that has not had sufficiently rigorous testing for safety during pregnancy, or lacks a long track record, will probably be withdrawn. New drugs are generally considered to be slightly more risky than the tried-and-true older drugs: rare side-effects may not come to light during the testing which precedes release of a drug, but they do become apparent once the drug is in widespread use for a long time (see pp. 136–7).

If you are already pregnant as you read this, don't worry too much. With a few notable exceptions – certain antihistamines and antibiotics – most of the drugs used for allergic diseases do not pose any major risk to the unborn child. There is probably nothing to worry about, but see your doctor as soon as you can – and talk to a pharmacist, in the meantime, if you are concerned. Don't panic, and don't stop taking your drugs unless you are absolutely sure that you can do without them. *Do not stop taking your drugs if you have asthma.*

Some non-prescription medicines are best avoided during pregnancy. Read the packet carefully, and talk to your pharmacist if you have any doubts.

From the moment you start trying for a baby, remember to tell *any* medical personnel who treat you, and any pharmacist you buy medicines from, that you are pregnant.

Immunotherapy and skin testing
Immunotherapy should not begin during pregnancy, because of the risk of anaphylaxis (see below), but pregnant women who are already undergoing immunotherapy can continue.

The safety procedures described on p. 167 should be followed with meticulous care.

Most doctors continue immunotherapy at a steady 'maintenance dose' because there is always a small risk of anaphylaxis with immunotherapy when the dose is increased. Some doctors are even more cautious and reduce the maintenance dose during pregnancy, but give more frequent injections – this minimises the chance of bad reactions.

Many doctors do not give skin tests for allergy during pregnancy, as these also carry a very small risk of anaphylaxis. If you do have skin tests, there must be resuscitation equipment available. Intradermal tests (see p. 92) are best avoided.

Severe allergic reactions (anaphylaxis)
Special care should be taken to avoid anaphylaxis during pregnancy as this may increase the chance of a miscarriage.

Injecting adrenaline during the first three months of pregnancy may carry some small risk of malformation of the baby. But the evidence here is uncertain, whereas the danger to your own life, if you don't use adrenaline when you need it, is both certain and substantial. If you have an adrenaline self-injection kit, talk to your doctor now about what you should do in an emergency. The best policy is to be ultra-careful about avoiding your allergen, so that anaphylaxis does not happen.

Women who suffer from exercise-induced anaphylaxis (see p. 59) generally play safe by exercising less strenuously while pregnant. The problem can get worse during pregnancy, but it does not usually do so. Labour itself is very strenuous of course, but problems during the birth are uncommon. If anaphylaxis does occur, the reaction is usually quite mild – nettle rash only – and the baby is delivered alive and well. However, many women find that the attacks of exercise-induced anaphylaxis are more frequent and severe when they start exercising again after the baby is born. It is best to resume exercise very gradually.

Eczema and other skin problems

Atopic eczema may improve during pregnancy, probably because the body produces slightly more of its own natural steroid, hydrocortisone. Contact dermatitis may either improve or flare up.

Stretch marks often itch a great deal, and widespread itchy skin, with or without a rash, is a common problem during pregnancy. These are not usually allergic reactions, and no cause can be identified in most cases. The skin tends to recover a few days after the birth.

If there is itching in the vulval area, this could be due to a *Candida* infection (your doctor can prescribe a safe treatment) or it might be just another of those unexplained itches of pregnancy.

Hayfever and other nasal allergies

The natural hormone changes of pregnancy affect the nose, which can become more blocked. If you have allergic rhinitis this will add to your woes. See your doctor and make sure that your drug treatment is adequate (see p. 29). The nose-clearing exercises on pp. 230–31 might also help.

Asthma

Severe asthma can be bad for both the pregnant mother and the unborn child. Uncontrolled asthma increases the risk of the baby being born prematurely – and premature babies are more likely to develop asthma themselves. The death rate for newborn babies is also higher if the mother has poorly controlled asthma.

Treating a severe asthma attack promptly helps to prevent any damage to the baby, so don't hesitate to call an ambulance – and tell the operator you are pregnant. The ambulance should be carrying oxygen which is particularly important for helping the unborn baby through the attack.

If you have asthma, don't stop using your drugs or reduce the dose unless advised to do so by a doctor. Because it is so important to keep asthma under control during pregnancy, your doctor may want to add, or increase, preventer drugs such as inhaled corticosteroids or sodium cromoglycate (see p. 148). It also makes sense to monitor your peak flow twice a day (see p. 97) so that you have advance warning of serious attacks.

Unfortunately, some asthmatics – usually those who have severe asthma to begin with – get much worse during their pregnancy. In such cases, careful monitoring and increased use of preventer medicines are essential. The symptoms usually increase from week 24 to week 36 of the pregnancy. The last four weeks tend to be much better, and things are back to normal by about three months after the birth.

Some women with asthma have fewer symptoms while they are pregnant, and for others their asthma stays about the same.

Asthma can also appear for the first time during pregnancy, and may be quite severe. However, a relatively mild breathlessness can be due simply to the fact that, as the pregnancy advances, the chest cavity, and therefore the lungs, become compressed. This is not necessarily asthma.

This simple physical effect can also add to the difficulties of women who were already asthmatic before they became pregnant.

GER (acid reflux) – see p. 38 – can contribute to asthma during pregnancy, and treating this problem may help.

Asthma attacks during the birth

Severe asthma attacks very rarely occur during labour, but it is still important that all the medical staff in attendance know you have asthma. They should also be told if you have taken steroid tablets during the previous two years. A record of when you took steroids, how long for, and at what dose, will be valuable. You may need a low dose of steroid to get you through the physical stress of labour (see p. 142). Some doctors believe that patients who have been using high-dose inhaled steroids should be treated in the same way.

Smoking

Smoking is a bad idea if you have allergies or any allergic tendency in the family. Smoking is a very bad idea indeed if you are pregnant, or a parent. This is the moment, if ever there was one, to give up.

Enlist your doctor's help, and ask if counselling, psychotherapy or other forms of support are available. If you have tried all this before, and failed, then talk to your doctor about the possibility of using nicotine patches. Some doctors believe that, for pregnant women who smoke 20 cigarettes or more a day, the advantages of nicotine patches outweigh the risks to the foetus. Nicotine levels in the blood are lower with patches than with heavy smoking, and your baby is not enduring the hundreds of other toxins found in cigarette smoke.

Chapter 4
avoiding allergens and irritants

Many countries have special schools for children with severe asthma and other allergies. Italian children are sent to one in the Italian Alps, where there is no trace of pollen, house dust mite, or animal allergens. After nine months these children are a great deal healthier and more active – all their lung function tests are vastly improved. Blood tests show that they are actually less allergic to common allergens than before.

You may not be able to do quite this well at home, but all allergens and irritants can be avoided to some extent. Even if you can't eliminate them completely, you can certainly reduce your exposure.

Before you start, it is important to be clear about exactly what affects you, otherwise you will be wasting a lot of effort. For example, people who are allergic to dust-mite often think that a dusty house will necessarily be worse for them than an apparently clean house, but this is not so (see p. 115). Or they may say 'Oh, I got asthma on holiday, because the roads were so dusty and I'm allergic to dust,' forgetting that only house dust contains dust mites. The road dust may have acted as an irritant, and helped to spark the asthma attacks or it may have contained pollen or mould spores – but it does not contain dust mites or their allergens. Blaming the wrong thing for the asthma attack means that the real culprit is not identified.

If you are not absolutely sure what causes your allergies, skin-prick tests (see p. 91) can identify the allergen. These are especially recommended if your reactions to the presumed allergen are inconsistent, or you don't respond to the anti-allergen programmes described here. For example, a few people who react to house dust are not allergic to dust mites, but to something else in the dust such as wool fibres or mould spores, or particles from cockroaches, house flies, carpet beetles or a long-departed cat. Even pollen that has accumulated in house dust can provoke allergic reactions – if you are not an over-keen duster, it can still be there long after the pollen season.

If you have hayfever, knowing which pollens cause your symptoms (and learning to recognise the plants concerned) is useful. You will probably need skin-prick tests to be sure. 'Hayfever' can even be a seasonal mould allergy in some people (see p. 27).

Tackling allergens is now big business. There are a lot of people out there competing for your money and false claims are common, especially for anti-mite products. Only a few manufacturers are deliberately misleading, and most false claims probably stem from ignorance or wishful thinking, but be very sure you know the facts about your allergen before you buy.

Air filters are a good example. A really good quality air filter (called a HEPA filter – High Efficiency Particulate Air filter) is an expensive purchase and, as the advertising tells you, it takes out very small particles with staggering efficiency. But this is entirely irrelevant if the source of those particles is no distance at all from your nose – your mite-infested pillow, for example, or the cat on your lap.

Something else that advertisements for air filters rarely mention is that unless you take measures to reduce allergen production – tackling mould growth in the house, for example, or keeping the dog outside – the filter can't help much. In short, filters do have their uses for *some* allergens, but they can't work miracles.

The products mentioned here, if not available in your locality, can be bought mail-order from specialist suppliers of anti-allergy products (see p. 255). Note that some offer both very good products and distinctly doubtful products, so judge each item on its individual merits. Ask to see scientific evidence that it works.

Don't be taken in by vague statements such as 'anti-allergenic' – get the facts. This label is often used on pillows with synthetic filling, for example, and people assume that it refers to dust-mite allergy, whereas it simply means that the pillow does not contain feathers. But unless you are allergic to feathers, there is no reason to avoid feather pillows. (In fact, if not covered with mite-proof covers, synthetic pillows collect *more* dust-mites than feather pillows, because the fabric used for the cover is less tightly woven and the mites and skin particles get in more easily.)

Bad advice is also a hazard. Some of it just wastes your time and effort, but some could actually increase your exposure to the allergen. Advice to vacuum floors daily, or to vacuum beds, is commonplace but this achieves little and it means breathing much more allergen unless you have the right kind of vacuum cleaner. One health magazine even advised its readers with dust-mite allergy to 'air mattresses by regularly turning them'. This will not affect mite numbers at all, but it will shoot *massive* amounts of mite allergen out of the mattress and into the nose and lungs.

Ridding your house of allergens and irritants is, in itself, a hazardous procedure because more of the offending substances will be released into the air during the work. If you take up carpets or remove mattresses, dust-mite allergens and mould spores will be churned up in their millions. Just bundling up a duvet will produce invisible clouds of dust mite allergen – and cat allergen, if your pet once slept on the bed.

Ideally, the allergic individual should not do the work, nor be in the house until it is 100% complete *and* the house has been very thoroughly aired. This is particularly important for those with chronic sinusitis and mould growth in the house, because of the risk of fungal infections in the sinuses (see p. 32).

If you are an allergy sufferer and have absolutely no choice but to do the work yourself, or to be present, then you should get a good quality dust mask and wear it throughout – only take it off when you go outdoors. Those with atopic eczema and sensitivity to airborne allergens should cover their skin carefully – with clothing, not barrier cream.

An ordinary hardware-shop dust mask is not adequate for most allergens – it only takes out really big particles and lets through all the common airborne allergens except pollen. You need a more serious sort of mask, designed for workplace use and conforming to official standards. Before buying one, ask what is the smallest size of particle that it filters out (at 90% efficiency, or better). Compare this with the particle size of your allergen (given in the articles that follow).

You must be able to breathe well through the mask when physically active, and it must fit tightly against your face, forming a seal at all edges. Beards and moustaches tend to prevent this – as does stubble.

Masks that combine an activated carbon filter with a dust filter, will take out gases and chemical vapours as well as particles. Cycle shops now sell such masks - or try an industrial supplier. Such a mask can be useful if you are affected by traffic exhaust or industrial pollution as well as an allergen, for example, or if you are exposed temporarily to wet paint or other fumes at home. Activated carbon masks should also filter out the irritant substances from oil-seed rape plants.

Some people who try the anti-allergen programmes feel much better quite fast. But generally these are long-term strategies – you may not reap any benefits for a few weeks, and the improvement may be small at first. Sometimes it takes several months for the full effects to be felt, so be persistent.

Allergens in food

Anyone with true food allergy or coeliac disease needs to be very careful about avoiding certain foods. The information given here is aimed mainly at such people, rather than those with food intolerance (see p. 74), who can usually tolerate small amounts of their offending foods. However, some of the basic information given here is relevant to those with food intolerance as well.

There are different levels of sensitivity even among those with true food allergy. The 'exquisitely sensitive' can react to unbelievably minute traces of the food, and for them life is especially difficult. The same is true of some coeliacs, who can be affected by the tiniest quantity of gluten.

These people are a small minority. The level of vigilance required of such people will not be necessary for most people reading this book, so don't get things out of proportion. While it is vital to be sensible about avoiding your problem food, it is also important not to become over-anxious.

Buying basic ingredients

Cooking for yourself is the safest way to eat for those with true food allergy and coeliac disease. There are relatively few hazards, but do beware of well-meaning assistants in health-food shops who try to sell you some exotic package of grain or flour – spelt or kamut or triticale, for example – reassuring you that it is 'definitely not wheat'. Be well informed about the different forms of your problem food and the names under which it is sold (see pp. 172-5).

Oils made from foods such as corn or peanut sometimes cause concern. Ordinary refined oils have been so thoroughly processed that they actually contain no allergenic proteins, so you can safely use these. Bottles of gourmet walnut oil and almond oil are a different story however, and should be avoided if you have nut allergies. Sesame oil is not purified either and can provoke serious reactions. With any oil, if you are unsure how safe it might be, go by the smell. Oils that smell or taste like the food from which they are made could well contain allergens.

Those with allergy to tuna can usually eat tinned tuna because the processing makes it safe. The allergens in fresh fruit and vegetables are generally inactivated by cooking too, so jams and tinned fruits tend to be safe – but test very cautiously. Cooking does not have much effect on other food allergens, apart from eggs. In rare cases, cooking can create allergens (see box on p. 186).

If you share your kitchen with others, and are highly sensitive, check that all cooking utensils are truly clean before use. Coeliacs should watch out for breadcrumbs in the butter dish, jam or toaster. Where small children are allergic to a food, it may be best to keep the culprit out of the house entirely.

Genetic engineering and food allergy

Many people with food allergies are very concerned about the possibility that genetic engineering could introduce allergens from one plant species into another. This concern seems to be shared by government officials and those in the food industry, who are being extremely vigilant and cautious at present. As long as this attitude continues, there should be little danger to food allergy sufferers.

Finding food in funny places

If you are suffering some inexplicable reactions to non-food items, it might, just possibly, be a food reaction. Some latex gloves contain the milk protein casein, for example, added as a manufacturing aid.

Buying packaged foods

There are several different issues here:

- the need to read labels carefully for allergenic ingredients described by unfamiliar names (see p. 172)
- errors in the packaging used (see pp. 174-5)
- contamination by minute traces of a food substance due to processing machinery not being cleaned adequately. Cartons of fruit drink have occasionally been contaminated with traces of milk because the same production lines were used for packaging milk drinks. Tofu desserts made in ice-cream factories can also become contaminated with milk. These tiny traces of a food will only affect the most highly sensitive individuals, but contamination by nuts can involve large pieces and affect anyone with nut allergy (see p. 174).
- foodstuffs which are used as part of the production process and leave a tiny residue in the finished item (see p. 174).

Be very cautious indeed about ready-made food that is unlabelled, such as that from bakeries and home-made stalls. Egg is frequently used as a glaze on baked products, nuts may lurk within, and milk or wheat can turn up in the most unlikely places.

Restaurants, cafes and takeaways

The majority of fatal and near-fatal incidents involving people with true food allergy are due to restaurants, cafeterias and canteens. Takeaways can also be a problem except in the case of the large chains such as McDonald's, where ingredients are standardised. It is alarming that highly allergenic foods (e.g. peanut) are sometimes used – yet far from obvious – in recipes and sandwich fillings where they would simply not be expected. Anyone with peanut or shellfish allergy should be ultra-cautious about Chinese, Thai or Malaysian cooking – but those with milk allergy should find a haven here, because milk is not part of these culinary traditions.

The simplest solution is to eat very plainly when you go out – steak and salad, for example. Steer clear of casseroles and thick soups, where you can't see what's in it (the occasional chef throws in peanut butter to thicken the mix…). Food wrapped in pastry is best avoided for the same reason. Desserts and cakes are risky for anyone with nut, egg or milk allergy.

You must insist on accurate information about the food before you taste it. If the counter staff, the waiter or the waitress is unsure of the ingredients, ask them to check with the chef, or with the label on pre-packaged food. Be persistent and never eat anything unless you are sure. Make eye contact with the person concerned, and learn to be a good judge of character. Your life could depend on telling the difference between the waiter who knows the facts about the food and the waiter who is being blandly reassuring for the sake of a quiet life.

It is a great mistake to pick out the pieces of offending food – kiwi fruit from a fruit salad for example – and eat the rest. There is often enough allergen left behind to cause anaphylaxis in the highly allergic individual.

Those who are extremely sensitive to the offending food must also consider the problem of contamination in the kitchen. Grills and fryers in restaurants and canteens can become contaminated with fish allergens or nut allergens (e.g. from nut cutlets) and these can be transferred to fried potatoes or other foods, provoking anaphylaxis in the highly allergic individual. One person with fish allergy died in this way. Sesame seeds can also contaminate equipment, work-surfaces or bakery counters.

Parties and buffets

Milk, egg, shellfish or nut allergies can make it especially hazardous to eat buffet or party food. Regard everything with suspicion. Cocktail snacks with nuts or peanut paste hidden inside are a particular problem.

When fish allergy isn't fish allergy

Anisakis is a parasitic worm that infests fish and can sometimes survive the cooking process to infect humans. The worms are easily thrown off by the human immune system, but the body is primed to make IgE antibodies should it ever encounter *Anisakis* again. Another meal of parasitised fish – even if the *Anisakis* worms are all dead this time, and only the allergens remain – will provoke a massive IgE-mediated reaction, leading to anaphylactic shock. This problem is usually misdiagnosed as allergy to fish itself.

Other inconsistent reactions to food can be due to contaminants such as antibiotics, preservatives, other food additives or (especially in the case of shellfish) naturally occuring toxins.

Bees, wasps
AND OTHER STINGING INSECTS

'Know your enemy' is always a good motto, but particularly for those with insect-sting allergy. Being allergic to wasps or hornets, for example, is enough of a problem without panicking every time you encounter a hoverfly as well.If your reaction to this is 'What's a hoverfly?' then you need a good field guide or a friend who knows a little about natural history. These common insects have yellow-and-black stripes to mimic those of wasps, giving them some protection against predatory birds. They fool a lot of people as well as birds, but it isn't difficult to tell the two apart – hoverflies are a different shape from wasps, hold their wings differently at rest, and fly in a completely different way (for one thing they hover, unlike wasps). Being able to tell one from the other will make life much more relaxing.

If you did not see the insect that stung you, ask the doctor which skin tests came up positive (see p. 61), and use a field guide to check exactly what the insect(s) looks like.

As well as knowing what your problem insect looks like, you need to know a little about its habits and tastes.

These are the general characteristics of stinging insects that you need to know about:
• The most dangerous thing you can do is to disturb the nest – all stinging insects go into attack mode when this happens. If there is a nest in or around your house, call in a pest control expert to destroy it. Never tackle this job yourself, nor allow anyone else to do it while you are in the vicinity.

• If you think there may be an insect nest in or around your house, call in a pest control expert to do a survey. Regular annual check-ups of your property are advisable if insects have nested before.
• Insect repellent works only for biting insects, such as mosquitoes. It does not repel wasps, bees or other stinging insects.
• Insecticide spray can be useful, but make sure the insect is really dead before you touch it. A groggy poisoned insect may well sting.
• A small but thick blanket can be useful for catching bees or wasps that have flown into cars. Don't try to do this yourself unless there is no alternative. Ask a passer-by to help you if you are alone.
• Always stay as calm as possible.

Honeybees and bumblebees

- When it stings, a bee loses part of itself – the stinger and venom sac – and therefore dies. So stinging is very much a last resort. Most honeybees are not aggressive, and only sting if their nest is attacked, or if they are threatened when feeding.
- Bees feed on nectar from flowers. They may be attracted by brightly coloured clothes, especially red, orange and yellow, and flower-prints, mistaking these for flowers. Wearing dull colours is advised.
- Some perfumes, shampoos and scented cosmetics or lotions may also attract bees. If bees do approach you, never swat at them, and don't panic. The best thing is to brush them away very gently.
- Bees often feed on clover, which grows in lawns and other grassy places, and it is easy to tread on them in this situation. Walking bare-foot outside is therefore dangerous.
- Bees are attracted by water, including swim-ming pools and paddling pools.
- Although large, bumblebees are also very placid and rarely sting.
- Swarming bees are dangerous because they have the queen with them. If you see a swarm, keep well away.

Africanised honeybees

If travelling abroad, you should remember that Africanised honeybees – found in South and Central America, Texas, Arizona and parts of California – will sting with much less provocation than ordinary bees.

They are hybrids between domestic honey-bees and an aggressive variety of wild African bee mistakenly introduced to South America. While they are much more pugnacious than ordinary bees, Africanised honeybees are only intent on defending their hive, and do not maliciously hunt people down as some horror movies have implied! They inject slightly *less* venom with each sting than a normal bee, but multiple stings are more likely because more than one bee is usually involved.

Wasps and hornets (vespids)

- If you react to one species of vespid, you may well have a cross-reaction to other species in this group, so take care.
- Wasps like sweet foods (e.g. jam, honey, cakes) and you should avoid taking these on picnics. They will also crawl into open cans of beer or soft drinks. Never *ever* drink from the can, as you can get a mouthful of cross wasp with your drink.
- In spring and early summer, wasps collect protein-rich food for their young, and may be attracted to meat. If eating outdoors, as far as possible keep food covered.
- Wasps come to fallen fruit in the autumn. They get very sluggish and bad-tempered late in the year, and will sting with little provocation. They may crawl into crevices or hollow logs as winter approaches. Be very careful about picking up fruit or dead leaves, or working in the garden – always wear thick gloves.
- Wasps are often on the ground, especially in late summer and autumn. Wear shoes and socks for protection. If working outside where there may be wasps, long trousers and long-sleeved shirts are also advisable.
- Rubbish bins and litter bins are also very attractive to wasps. Make sure your own bin has a tightly fitting lid, and that no rubbish accumulates around it. Ask neighbours to do the same. Keep away from litter bins, and from picnic sites, orchards and tea gardens, all of which are havens for wasps.

Cross-reactions between insect stings

There are cross-reactions between the venoms of wasps, hornets and related insects (vespids), so if you are allergic to one, you may react to another. Cross-reactions are very unlikely between bee and wasp venoms.

Honeybees and bumblebees have very similar venom and these cross-react (but honey-bee immunotherapy does not work for bumblebee allergy – see p. 168). Surprisingly, there is some cross-reaction between honeybee venom and snake venom.

The usual suspects

Wasps, hornets and bees are the most common source of allergic reactions worldwide. (If travelling to North America, remember that common wasps are known there as yellow-jackets and are very troublesome.)

Locally, there are allergic reactions to various other stinging or biting animals. Fire ants are a particular problem in the southeastern United States. Hopper ants are a cause of anaphylaxis in Australia, and allergy to leech bites has been reported from Tasmania.

A few people are allergic to the kissing bugs (*Triatoma* spp) – also called cone-noses, 'big bed bugs' or 'Mexican bed bugs' – that are found in South and Central America, as well as rural areas of North America. These large insects creep into beds and bite painlessly, by night. The bite injects allergen and can cause a systemic reaction, even anaphylaxis, though this is rare.

House-dust mite

AND INSECT PESTS

Because house-dust mites are a major source of allergic reactions they have been studied intensively, and various ways of killing them devised. But simply killing the mites is not enough. Their allergens will remain, and continue to cause allergic reactions for years. The allergens have to be either removed or inactivated – that is, changed chemically so that they are no longer recognised by the immune system.

Tackling dust mite is easier if you know certain key facts:

1 Dust mites prefer humid conditions. They do not drink, but absorb water from the air. When the relative humidity falls below 50%, the mites gradually dry out and are killed.

2 Mites feed on our skin scales, but only if they have been broken down first by moulds. High humidity (70–90% relative humidity) is a particular problem, for anyone with an allergy to house-dust mites, because it favours the mould that suits dust mites best.

3 Dust mites live inside mattresses, pillows, upholstery, cushions and soft toys. The allergens are blasted out when you settle into an armchair, get into bed, or turn over in the night.

This is when you inhale the biggest dose of allergen, or get the maximum dose to your skin. Carpets also contain dust mites, but the numbers are generally lower.

4 Dust-mite allergen is relatively heavy, compared to cat or mould allergens for example. Little of it floats around in the air, and the most significant exposure is inhaling it close to the source – from a pillow, mattress or teddy bear. This is why air filters are of little value for anyone with dust-mite allergy.

5 Dust mites are everywhere, and are carried around in clothing. Even if you could eliminate all the mites from your house, new ones would soon appear. A new mattress will usually be colonised by dust mites within four months.

The size of the allergen particles

The droppings of the dust mite, not the mites themselves, are the main cause of symptoms. The droppings are 4–20 microns in size, but they can crumble into fragments of 1–3 microns, and the tiniest bits are only 0.5 microns across. The pores of mite-proof covers (which really means mite-*allergen*-proof) should be less than one micron across, and preferably less than 0.5 microns. Dust masks (see p. 109) should also filter out particles of this size to be effective. The mites themselves are much bigger, 200–300 microns long. (A micron is one thousandth of a millimetre.)

The basics of mite warfare

- A temperature just above boiling point kills dust mites and inactivates Der p1, which is the troublesome allergen for most asthmatics. However Der p2, the other mite allergen, is not affected by heat. (Note that the carpet treatments advertised as 'steam cleaning' generally just use hot soapy water, not steam. Because they leave the carpet very damp, they can *increase* the numbers of dust mites.)
- Washing with detergent at 55°C (130°F) or above (i.e. a 60°C wash cycle) kills mites and removes the allergen.
- Cooler washes will not kill mites, but will remove the allergen. This can be useful if the mites have already been killed by some other means. Regular cool washes of clothing or sheets will also remove human skin scales, reducing the mites' food supply. (This is beneficial if you have eczema, because flaking skin adds to the problem by giving dust mites even more to eat.)
- You can buy mite-killing substances (see p. 255) to add to cooler washes, so that the mites are killed – the chemicals are rinsed out at the end of the wash, so are pretty safe.
- Dry-cleaning kills mites and it removes some of the allergen, but the amount removed is variable (20–70%).
- Freezing for more than six hours kills mites. Three hours strong direct sunlight in dry air will kill mites living in rugs and blankets. Neither treatment removes allergen.
- Mites hang on to the carpet fibres when the vacuum cleaner passes overhead, and about 65% of them remain afterwards. An ordinary vacuum cleaner sprays mite allergen into the air as it goes. The amount in the air – and therefore available to be inhaled – is *three times higher* after vacuuming.

Combating mites

Bear in mind that mites are the enemy – not dust itself. A house may be thick with dust but, because the windows are open a lot and the air is dry, it will have few mites. Another house may look perfectly clean, but be seething with mites because it is thoroughly draught-proofed, warm and slightly humid. The mites will be thriving in the carpets, beds and upholstery. Vacuuming and dusting every day, if done with an ordinary type of vacuum cleaner and a dry duster, will stir up the allergens and ensure that the air is full of them. So a person with mite allergy would feel far worse in the apparently very clean house than in the dusty one.

One crucial aspect of a mite-reduction programme is making the air drier – see p. 119 – so that mites no longer flourish.

Most of the other measures – described below – will involve stirring up dust-mite allergens, so the allergic person should not do the work, nor be in the house (see p. 109).

Too dry or too moist?

It is a well-established fact that the air in most modern houses is too humid, encouraging dust-mites and moulds. Yet many people fit humidifiers because they believe that the air is 'too dry' and that this irritates the nose. Some very good scientific studies have shown it is indoor pollutants plus overheating that is the problem here, not dryness – even very dry air is not irritating as long as it is clean. Should your nose feel dry and ticklish, try to reduce indoor pollution (see pp. 128–9).

It is true that during an asthma attack, dry air does makes matters worse, and very moist air helps. Inhaling steam from a bowl of hot water can be used to ease the attack.

The bed

Begin with the bed because this is the main exposure zone. A Danish study showed that just fitting mite-allergen-proof covers to the mattresses and pillows of dust-allergic children worked well. After a year the children had much less asthma at night, used half as much inhaled steroid, and gave better peak-flow readings.

The best approach is to buy a new mattress and new pillows before putting anti-mite coverings on them. These covers keep skin scales and mites out, which should prevent a new mattress or pillow becoming recolonised. The modern covers have tiny pores which allow perspiration to evaporate – this makes them comfortable to sleep on.

These pores are small enough (see box on p. 114) to keep any mite allergens inside, so they will also work with an old mattress, keeping the existing allergen inside. But the mites themselves will also thrive inside (there's enough old skin there to keep them in business for years) and there is always the risk that, if a small tear develops, the stores of allergen in the mattress will come pouring out again. So start with a new mattress if you can.

Another possible option is to arrange for a contractor to heat-treat the bed, the mattress and all bedding. This is a new specialist treatment (see p. 255), where the bed is enclosed in a plastic tent and heated to very high temperatures. It is designed to kill all mites, even those right inside the mattress, and inactivate the allergen. (The contractor can also do your living room suite.)

If the covers are for a small child, check with the manufacturer that they pose no threat of suffocation. Mattresses and bedding with built-in covers may be safer.

Buy a new duvet (or wash or dry-clean your existing one) and put an anti-mite cover on it. Alternatively, buy a duvet and pillow that can be washed at 60°C (130°F), and wash them once a month. You must have the use of a tumble dryer, because mites will flourish if bedding is not *completely* dry.

An upholstered bed base will have its own (much smaller) population of mites. Buy a simple wooden or metal bed frame if possible. Or you could enclose the upholstered base in a mite-proof cover, or in plastic sheeting completely sealed with heavy-duty tape.

Wash all sheets and blankets at 60°C or more, or have blankets dry-cleaned – or buy new ones. From now on, wash sheets once a week and blankets once every two weeks.

Get rid of any other bedding such as patchwork quilts or fleecy underblankets. Alternatively, you can wash or dry-clean them regularly.

Electric blankets can be cleared of mites by washing them, and are very useful in keeping the bed free from moisture. This prevents mites from setting up home in the *outer* surface of your new mite-proof covers, so that you don't need to wash the covers, sheets and underblankets so frequently. Leave the electric blanket on at a high setting, with the bed made, for at least twelve hours (check that there is no fire risk first). *Note that some mite-proof covers might be damaged by this procedure* – check with the manufacturer. If you have not yet purchased mite-proof covers, there are some made from Egyptian cotton which can tolerate this level of heat without damage (see p. 255).

Children's beds and toys
Where children share a room, all the beds and bedding should be dealt with. Even then, an asthmatic child should never sleep in the lower half of a bunk bed, because mite allergens will shower down from the bed above.

All soft toys should spend at least six hours in the freezer once a week, to kill the mites. The first time, wash the toys immediately afterwards to remove any existing allergen and dry thoroughly in a tumble dryer.

A hot wash, or the freezing/washing treatment, should also be used for 'comfort blankets', dressing-up clothes, dolls' clothes and any other fabric items.

Sheepskins, sometimes used for babies' cots, especially in New Zealand and Australia, contain huge amounts of dust-mite allergen. It is advisable to discard these.

The next steps
Clothing is often full of mites, especially sweaters, coats and woollen trousers. Dry-clean all such items, or wash using a mite-killing wash, then store them in a well-heated place so that they are always *very* dry.

Dandruff consists of skin flakes, and may help to feed mites. Using an anti-dandruff shampoo may help. Semen also gives mites nourishment.

From now on, be careful about exposing your airways to dust. Get someone else to empty the vacuum cleaner bag – and they should, of course, do it outdoors. If you are stripping wallpaper, wash it down first to remove dust. Moving house, going into the attic, spring cleaning, turning out cupboards or moving furniture should all be avoided – unless you have a good mask on.

Do not use fan-heaters or convector heaters which churn up mite allergens from the carpet. Seal off any hot-air ducts from centralised heating systems, as these blow mite allergens around the room.

If possible, invest in a vacuum cleaner that keeps in all the allergens, or vents them outside, rather than spraying them out into the air. Make sure that the vacuum cleaner you buy really

What about sprays?
Chemicals that kill mites (known collectively as acaricides) are sometimes useful but have various limitations. They do not penetrate inside upholstered furniture, cushions or mattresses, so make little difference to the total population of dust mites. Even on carpets, sprays won't reach most of the mites unless you rub the spray in really hard. (And 'anti-mite' carpet shampoos are *completely* ineffective.)

The safest chemical is benzyl benzoate – so safe that it is used directly on the skin for treating scabies infections. It can cause skin irritation at these doses, but rarely does so at the concentrations used in anti-mite sprays.

However, the idea of constant spraying, over a period of months or years, is worrying. Doctors generally advise against spraying bedding, and carpets or furniture where babies or small children play, to avoid close and prolonged contact with the spray residue.

Even more alarming are sprays containing a pyrethroid (pyrethrum) compound. The latter is derived from a plant and is therefore sold as 'natural', but pyrethroids are potentially toxic with prolonged exposure, and they quite often provoke allergic reactions too. They should definitely be avoided.

Sprays that inactivate allergen (rather than killing mites) sometimes have their uses. There are two kinds and both should work against a variety of allergens, not just dust mite. Polysaccharide sprays stick the allergen particles together, so that they don't float about and get inhaled. Tannic acid sprays change the allergen chemically, making it non-allergenic. Because tannic acid is found in tea it is assumed to be harmless, but the sprays available vary a lot and often contain many impurities, so it is hard to be sure about their long-term safety. Don't use these sprays on bedding.

Carpets and bedding covers with built-in pesticide are also on sale, but are probably best avoided.

does its job well – a lot of machines now claim to be 'allergy' vacuum cleaners but they are not all equally good. Very few have been adequately tested (see p. 255). Alternatively, cover the bed with a clean sheet and open the windows whenever you vacuum, leaving them open for half an hour afterwards. After closing the windows, allow the dust to settle for another half hour, then carefully remove the dust-cover from the bed.

For dusting, use a damp cloth and add a few drops of eucalyptus oil which deters mites. Alternatively, use a special anti-mite duster with an electrostatic charge that holds the dust.

Above all, keep the moisture levels in your house down. Ultimately, this is the key to eliminating dust mite. Look at p. 119 and check you are doing everything possible.

The bedroom in particular should be kept dry. Air your bedroom whenever it's dry and sunny. Remove pot plants and fish tanks. Don't dry clothes in the room and don't shampoo the carpet. Avoid using Calor gas heaters, as these produce a lot of moisture. If your bedroom has an en suite shower, fit a powerful extractor fan, or open a window wide during and after showers – or just stop using this shower. En suite basins may also generate moist air.

Do you need to do more?

Give it some time before deciding if you have done enough. In one study, it took *eight months* for the full benefits of an anti-mite campaign to be seen.

If you are still not as much improved as you hoped, then you could try a more drastic mite-elimination programme.

Thoroughly clean the bedroom, getting rid of any dust along skirting boards or picture rails, on top of wardrobes or behind furniture. Remove anything stored under the bed, so that vacuuming is easier in future. During this cleaning operation, completely cover the bed.

Get rid of the bathroom carpet, if you have one. In the bedroom, either remove the carpet or buy a special anti-mite steam cleaner that kills mites in the carpet and inactivates the allergen. To work properly, the device must produce steam at a temperature above boiling point, by means of high pressure. Make sure you are buying the right kind of device.

If you take out the carpet, you will need to mop the floor, with a wet or oiled mop, several times a week, as the dust will quickly build up, and is easily made airborne from an uncarpeted floor. One of the advantages of carpet is that it 'holds' dust at floor level.

Wash the curtains, or dry-clean them, or replace them with blinds of a kind that can be easily wet-dusted. If you have bought an anti-mite steam cleaner for the carpet, use this on the curtains every 2–3 weeks.

Remove dirty clothes from the bedroom, clean out drawers and shelves, and dry them thoroughly. Only store freshly laundered clothes in the room.

Remove all upholstered items from the bedroom, such as padded headboards, cushions, armchairs, or stools with padded seats. Draught excluders, fabric lampshades and anything covered in velvet should also go.

A different approach

If you are even more allergic to housework than you are to dust mites, consider buying a really powerful dehumidifier, designed for killing mites. This makes the air too dry to breathe (its relative humidity or RH goes down to 25%), so you leave it on in the bedroom during the day, with the bedroom door closed. You must eliminate all sources of moisture that will counteract the dehumidifier, and have fairly tight seals around your windows and doors for it to work. In the evening, turn the dehumidifier off and leave the bedroom door open for an hour or so before going to bed.

Of course, all the allergen which was already there in the bed, carpet, curtains, clothes and soft toys will still be present. You need to either eliminate or inactivate this allergen using the methods described above. But once you have got your daily dehumidifier routine going, you do not need to rewash everything regularly because mites will be a thing of the past, so no new stocks of allergen will be produced.

The rest of the house

A completely mite-free house is hard to achieve, but if you are determined, you can come close. Everything so far described for the bedroom, such as reducing moisture in the air, and dealing with carpets and curtains, is applicable to the rest of the house.

The exception – and the toughest nut to crack – is the upholstered furniture in the living room. Fixed upholstery (i.e. everything other than removable cushions) is a safe haven for mites that is especially hard to deal with.

One option is to give all such furniture a specialist heat-treatment, if this is available locally (see p. 115). The mites inside will be killed, and the allergen inactivated. If you drastically reduce moisture levels at the same time – with a powerful dehumidifier used at night, perhaps – you should avoid serious reinfestation.

Alternatively, you could replace all your existing upholstered furniture with leather-covered or vinyl-covered furniture. Both are impenetrable to mites. Furniture made of wood or bamboo with loose cushions and no fixed upholstery can also work. Fit the cushions with tailor-made mite-proof covers (hard to get, but ask around) when new. Then put the ordinary covers on top, and wash these regularly.

Cockroaches and other insects

Compared to the huge amount of research that has been done on dust mite, very little effort has gone into elimination methods for cockroaches and their allergens. This is a real tragedy, because these insects are responsible for a great deal of allergy, especially in urban areas of the United States. Several other countries have now recognised a problem with cockroach allergy, including Israel, South Africa and France, but it seems likely that this is only the tip of the iceberg.

In Britain, cockroaches are usually killed by the winter weather. In spite of this, they may infest some tower blocks. Because numbers build up during the summer and dwindle in the winter, cockroaches may cause seasonal allergies which are often mistaken for hayfever.

Cockroaches are miniature six-legged vultures, feeding on our leftovers. The allergens are found in their sloughed skins, their droppings and saliva.

To get rid of cockroaches, you must:

- Clear up all food scraps and crumbs promptly and wash dishes straight after each meal. Keep all food in cockroach-proof containers, and take garbage out daily.
- Eat only in the dining area, and keep the floor there very clean. Never eat in the bedroom.
- Eliminate any pools or drips of water which the cockroaches can drink. Repair leaky plumbing, and prevent condensation on the pipes. Wipe up any spills of water or other liquids immediately.
- Seal all the cracks and holes through which cockroaches enter
- Use bait stations to kill cockroaches, replacing them every 2–3 months. Boric acid or diatomaceous earth can also be used to kill these pests, especially in kitchen cabinets, and under sinks and appliances.

While cleanliness is important, sometimes the problem is structural, and cockroaches persist in a house despite vigorous cleaning. You need expert help from a pest exterminator if this is the case.

Blocks of flats pose a particular problem. It is impossible to eliminate cockroaches from your flat unless the whole block is treated, because they will come back in from neighbouring flats. HEPA air filters are of little value with cockroach allergen.

Unfortunately, even when cockroaches have been eradicated, a great deal of cockroach allergen often remains in the home, despite thorough cleaning. The reason for this is unclear, but it should not discourage you from trying to combat cockroach allergen, because even just reducing your exposure a little can have big benefits. In one American study that looked at asthmatic children who were allergic to cockroaches, the levels of the allergen at home determined how severe the asthma symptoms were. All the homes had cockroach allergen – not surprisingly, since this is what had caused the allergy. But children exposed to the highest levels of cockroach allergen at home were three times more likely to be hospitalised for asthma. They also missed more school due to asthma, and had more sleepless wheezy nights.

Cockroach allergens in food?

Flour is frequently contaminated with cockroach allergens. Cooking decreases the level of allergen, but does not destroy it entirely. It is possible that contaminated flour could provoke a reaction when eaten by someone with cockroach allergy.

Other insects

Almost any insect that infests houses can cause allergic reactions in some susceptible individuals. Houseflies and carpet beetles (their larvae are called 'fuzzy bears') have both caused allergies occasionally, and in some parts of Europe the Berlin beetle is a problem. Outdoor insects, including midges, mosquitoes, caddis flies and mayflies, can cause allergies if they are especially abundant – as they are around the Great Lakes area of North America in the breeding season, for example.

Mouse hazard

Until recently, no one had investigated the possible role of mice in causing allergies. Now researchers have shown that 18% of children in inner city areas of the United States have an allergic reaction to mice, and that this can contribute to asthma.

Tackling humidity indoors

In the modern drive for good insulation, one crucial thing has been forgotten – ventilation. Huge amounts of water vapour are generated in a house, and if it can't escape it creates humid conditions that are ideal for moulds and dust mites. Apart from the steam generated by cooking and showering, you give off about 1 litre (2 pints) of water in sweat each night.

A household of four people pushes 70–140 litres (130–250 pints) of water into the atmosphere around them every week. Combine this with modern draught-proofing and the result is air that is much too moist.

There are two distinct problems to be tackled:
- the overall level of moisture in the house
- localised areas of condensation, which are especially problematic with mould allergy because they create damp surfaces where moulds can grow.

The first step towards reducing moisture is to take out any humidifiers, repair any plumbing leaks and rectify any structural problems, such as cracks in walls, a leaking roof or rising damp. Make sure there is no water penetration in the cellar. Remember to look behind furniture for unnoticed damp patches.

Keep the kitchen door closed when cooking, turn off kettles as soon as they boil, and always use lids on saucepans to reduce steam. Think about having an extractor fan fitted, for use when cooking. Alternatively, open a window while you cook, and leave it open for a while afterwards.

Try to dry clothes outside, or use a tumble dryer. Failing that, dry them in a well-ventilated utility room with the door into the house closed so that the moisture goes out, not in.

Either fit a powerful extractor fan in the bathroom, or just open the windows wide after baths or showers. (Baths are better as they produce less steam.) Wipe down tiles and grouting with an old towel after showers, and leave towels and bath mats to dry elsewhere, not in the bathroom.

Note that all extractor fans and tumble dryers most be vented to the outside (not, for example, to the attic).

Most important of all, ventilate the whole house whenever the air is dry outside. You should open several windows so that a draught blows right through. In addition, unblock any air bricks or other fresh-air vents, and reduce the amount of draught-proofing, to improve ventilation. If there are overshadowing trees, or tall bushes around the house, cut them back to improve air flow.

Consider having an open fire in the sitting room. This improves ventilation considerably: as warm air and smoke go up the chimney, the fire pulls in clean air from outdoors.

To eliminate condensation in colder rooms, heat all parts of the house to the same temperature. Loft insulation will help to keep ceilings warm and so avoid condensation upstairs. Keep cupboard doors open if they have any tendency to dampness, and/or warm the interior with a low-powered heater.

In the bathroom, strip off any vinyl wallpaper, and gloss or eggshell paints, as these are impervious to water. Replace with emulsion paint (preferably with a mould-inhibitor added) or with ordinary wallpaper. Both allow moisture to be absorbed into the wall and eventually to escape to the outside. Vinyl paper and gloss paint keep condensation on the surface encouraging mould growth there. For the same reason, tiles should just be used where needed, not all over the walls.

Don't have carpets in bathrooms, or in basement areas.

Take out any metal window frames and replace with wood or PVC frames, as cold window frames encourage condensation. If possible, fit double-glazing, which gives a much warmer glass surface.

Wipe away any condensation that does occur around windows, or on windowsills, every day, and dry the cloths outside or in a utility room.

A device known as a hygrometer, which measures the relative humidity (RH) of the air may be useful. Some garden centres and hardware shops sell them, as do a few specialist allergy suppliers (see p. 255). Aim for an RH of less than 50% or (even better) less than 40%.

For new houses, or those that have just been completely renovated, ventilation is even more important. As much as 1360 litres (300 gallons) of water is used in the construction of a house, mainly for plastering. This will take about a year to disperse. Using a dehumidifier may be worthwhile during this period, especially if there is a lot of rain, but do not speed the process up too much as this can cause damage to the plaster, concrete or timbers.

Moulds

AND OTHER FUNGI

The air around us is full of bits and pieces that are mostly too small to be seen without a microscope – pollen grains, mould spores, fragments from plants, fibres from clothing, specks of ash from smoke, skin flakes and diesel particles. Of these, mould spores are by far the most abundant.

Except in very dry climates, there are more mould spores in the air than anything else. In Britain the record count is over 160,000 spores per cubic metre of air, compared to a record pollen count of only 2800 grains per cubic metre. Luckily, mould spores are not particularly allergenic or even more people would be suffering as a result of inhaling such huge quantities of them.

Spores are produced by moulds and other fungi, and they are to the fungus what seeds are to a plant – they can grow into new fungi. Doctors generally speak just of 'mould allergy' because moulds are the most common offenders, but larger fungi – mushrooms and toadstools – also produce allergenic spores. For example, a bracket fungus called *Ganoderma*, that infests dead trees and produces spores prolifically in mid-June, has been found to affect 16% of asthmatics in one part of New Zealand. Bracket fungi occur all over the world, but until recently no one had suspected them of causing allergic reactions, so the extent to which they cause allergies has not been investigated. The same is true of other large fungi.

Yeasts (single-celled fungi) are also found in the air, and it is possible – though this has not been investigated – that people with an allergy to yeast in food would also react to inhaled yeasts.

Indoors and out

Mould spores are a particular nuisance because they can be produced both indoors and out. There are different species of mould in different places, and you may be lucky and only react to one or two uncommon species. But many moulds grow in a very wide range of situations, both indoors and outdoors. There are also cross-reactions (see p. 14) between some of the moulds, unfortunately, which means that people generally react to a great number of different moulds. You will probably need to reduce mould growth inside your home as well as avoiding mould-rich places outside. Changes to your garden that eliminate havens for moulds, such as leaf piles, may also be helpful.

Moulds may only be growing in one part of a house – the cellar perhaps – but can be carried all around the house on air currents.

Avoiding outdoor moulds

Moulds live in the soil, and grow on any decaying plant matter, such as dead leaves, dying plants, fallen trees, hay and straw. Spore counts are highest in the autumn. A thick covering of snow reduces the numbers of mould spores in the air dramatically. Once the snow melts in spring, moulds flourish on the plants killed by the cold, so spore counts soon rise again.

The effect of the weather on spore release is very complex. Some moulds like to release their spores when it is dry and windy, but others favour fog, mist or dew. Rainfall washes a lot of spores out of the air, but it stimulates the release of some small spores.

A few pollen information services also give current mould-spore counts, but predicting spore counts for the following day is well-nigh impossible.

Drastic avoidance measures, for those who are severely sensitive, include moving to a desert or semi-arid area where there are far fewer mould spores in the air.

Listed below are the mould-rich situations and activities which could provoke your allergy symptoms. If they do, you should avoid them, or wear a mask that will prevent the spores being inhaled (see box on p. 120).

Places

- Near fields of cereal crops in late summer, because of moulds growing on the cereal leaves. Symptoms are likely at harvest time, when combine harvesters disperse the spores.
- In forests and old orchards, in gardens with compost heaps or piles of dead leaves, and in greenhouses.
- Near springs, waterfalls, and other damp, shady places.

Times

- During late summer and autumn, when moulds flourish outdoors on fallen leaves and fruit.
- Following the first frost of autumn, which triggers spore release by fungi in the soil.

Activities

- Disturbing compost heaps, damp straw or hay, piles of grass clippings or heaps of fallen leaves, all of which are absolutely full of moulds.
- Collecting up fallen leaves or fruit.
- Watering the garden because mould spores are released when water hits the dry soil.
- Mowing grass, if the clippings were not cleared up after the last mowing. Unless the weather is very dry, the clippings tend to go mouldy.
- Removing dead leaves or flowers from plants.

A dangerous mould allergy

Anyone with asthma who also has allergy to the mould *Alternaria* should – with their doctor's agreement – increase their dose of preventer inhaler (e.g. steroid or cromoglycate) during the spore-producing season. Research shows that severe near-fatal asthma attacks often occur during the *Alternaria* spore season among those allergic to this mould.

Spore release by *Alternaria* usually occurs in the summer or autumn, but the timing varies from one part of the world to another, so check with your doctor or a local pollen/spore monitoring service. *Alternaria* can live outdoors in soil, and on seeds and plants. Indoors, it is a denizen of window frames, carpets and textiles.

Indoor moulds

These are the indoor situations that can be difficult for mould-sensitive people. You should either avoid these, wear a mask, or tackle the problem at source – for example, by reducing damp-ness (see p. 119).

Places

- Buildings that are damp, because moisture encourages mould growth. Never sleep in a room which has mould growing on the walls or window-panes. In addition to damp houses – now very common – you may encounter moulds in old churches and church halls.
- Buildings that are near lakes, rivers or the sea, because of the dampness of the air. Rooms with humidifiers.
- Bathrooms and shower rooms, unless well ventilated, owing to the steam and condensation.
- Rooms that are generally left unheated, and are therefore colder than the rest of the house, as these tend to suffer from condensation.
- Buildings with dry rot or wet rot. Not all mould-sensitive people react to the spores of these dreaded timber-rotting fungi, but some do.
- Buildings where old timbers are being removed, as this stirs up huge numbers of spores.
- Buildings where central heating has recently been installed, as the warmer temperatures in the building stimulates the existing moulds to release their spores.
- Buildings with lots of indoor plants. There are moulds you cannot see growing on the surface of the soil around a potted plant.
- Cellars and basements. Conservatories can also be full of moulds if not well maintained.
- Antique shops, farms, mills, holiday cottages.

On the first day of Christmas...

Christmas trees usually have moulds (which you can't see) growing on the needles. When the tree is brought indoors, the warmth encourages these moulds to shed their spores.

Times

- During the winter, when there are usually more moulds growing indoors due to condensation.

Activities

- Handling clothes, curtains or furnishings that smell mildewy: they may be dry now but they will still be full of mould spores.
- Handling vegetables or fruit that have been stored a long time, or in damp conditions (e.g. in plastic wrapping). Note that this can include mushrooms – they often have white moulds growing on them, which can be quite inconspicuous.

If looking around your house for moulds, bear in mind that they vary a great deal in colour. Bread, vegetables, cheese and other foods that are past their best grow green, grey or white moulds, often furry, and these are the ones most people are familiar with. But the black stuff on the walls of bathrooms and in the door seals of refrigerators is also mould. In some situations it takes a practised eye to spot this type of mould – around window frames for example, or in the patterns of bathroom-window glass, it can easily be mistaken for ordinary dirt. On shower curtains and cubicles you may find pinkish-red moulds as well as these black kinds. Garden plants and crops can have bright orange moulds (called 'rusts') on their leaves, as well as the more familiar grey or black kinds.

Combating indoor moulds

The crucial task here is to reduce dampness and condensation in the house – see p. 119 for the details – as this encourages mould growth on all kinds of surfaces, including walls, ceilings, windows, bathroom tiles, shower curtains, and even carpets. Once you have reduced the humidity, then you can have a big clean-up and remove the spores that have been left by moulds.

If your allergy symptoms are very bad, and you need some immediate relief, then you could get someone to clean away the mould growth and spores first, then tackle the damp problem, *then* repeat the cleaning operation. Obviously, this is less efficient, but it may be the best approach if you are severely affected.

Note that the cleaning will, in itself, stir up a massive but unseen cloud of spores, so the allergy sufferer should not be at home during this work (see p. 109).

Cleaning away moulds and stopping regrowth

There are two aspects to this task:

- a one-off effort to clear the accumulation of mould growth and old mould spores – trillions of them are probably lying around your house – since these spores are the cause of the allergic reaction
- an ongoing effort to prevent the regrowth of moulds in problem areas such as the bathroom.

Get rid of any furniture that smells 'mildewy': it is packed with old mould spores. Fabric items that have this smell should be washed thoroughly. Old clothing, books and newspapers may also be a source of mould spores.

Any carpets or other porous materials (e.g. ceiling tiles, wall panels) that have ever been soaked by flood or storm waters should be disposed of now – and, unless everything can be dried within 24 hours, this should be always be done if there is water penetration in the future. Research shows that such materials quickly become infested with moulds. Check above the flood line, as water can seep upwards through the walls or panelling.

On fridges and freezers, clean out the rubber seals around the doors, going into all the crevices to get out the black mould that lives there. Also clean out the drip-pans of fridges, freezers and dehumidifiers. Keep shower heads and air conditioning equipment (including the filters) very clean. This all needs to be done regularly from now on.

Clean off all the mould growing around windows, or on walls and ceilings, tiles or other surfaces. Alcohol (e.g. white spirit or surgical spirit) kills it very effectively, without the use of water, and it takes a long time to grow back again. You could, alternatively, wash the walls down with a mix of one part bleach to two parts water. (But note that chlorine fumes may be irritating to the airways of those with rhinitis or asthma.) Special anti-mould sprays are also available, but try them out cautiously as they too may be irritants. Do not brush mould growth off with a dry cloth, as this simply disperses the spores. In the future, keep an eye out for new mould growth, and remove it promptly.

Buy a new shower curtain and replace it regularly, or clean it thoroughly with an anti-mould spray.

Can foods and mould spores cross-react?

Some people with mould allergy appear to be affected by eating mushrooms, or foods that contain yeasts or other fungi, e.g. certain well-ripened cheeses, dried fruit, soy sauce and vinegar. There has been little scientific investigation of these claims.

No cause for concern

The drug penicillin – which can cause severe allergic reactions – comes from the *Penicillium* mould. Fortunately, there appears to be no cross-reaction between the drug and the spores of *Penicillium*.

Cut down on the number of houseplants, and find a new home for any that need constant moisture. With the remaining plants, take off dying leaves and flowers promptly, and remove the top layer of soil occasionally, replacing it with fresh soil or – even better – sand or grit. Pot-pourri should also be evicted, as it can be full of mould spores.

Use vegetables and fruit promptly, and do not allow bread to go stale, or jam to go mouldy.

What to do if these measures fail

Where there is an invincible damp problem, a really powerful dehumidifier used during the day in bedrooms, and at night in the sitting room, will kill off most moulds and defeat their efforts to regrow. Close all the doors and windows in the room where the dehumidifier is operating, and shut off air vents. Note that air conditioning will also reduce the humidity of the air, but not as much.

Keeping mould spores out of the airways

Ordinary house dust can contain a lot of mould spores. The allergic individual should not dust, vacuum clean, sweep floors or make beds until the anti-mould measures have begun to bite. Ideally the allergic person should go out while housework is done, and the house should be thoroughly aired before their return. If this is impossible, then wearing a good mask all the time is essential. A special vacuum cleaner that retains allergens, or vents them outside, may be helpful *in addition to* the mask.

Even though you have cut down on moisture and condensation, and tackled mould growth, there could *still* be a lot of mould spores around, especially in an old house, one that has been very damp in the past, or one that is close to water. If symptoms persist, then think about hiring or buying a high-quality HEPA air filter (see p. 108) to take mould spores out of the air.

Do not use fans or fan heaters, as these churn up mould spores from the floor and other surfaces.

Beating athlete's foot

Allergenic fungi can grow on your body, as well as in your house (see pp. 16–17). If athlete's foot is playing a part in your allergies, it is vital to treat the infection thoroughly with drugs, because the fungus grows deep into the skin and can quickly stage a come-back if not completely destroyed. You should also be careful not to re-infect yourself:

• always dry your feet very thoroughly, especially between the toes; kitchen roll does a better job than towels, and can be discarded, reducing the risk of re-infection
• wear cotton socks and shoes made of leather or canvas, which allow sweat to evaporate; only wear trainers or gumboots, or any other footwear that makes your feet feel sweaty, when you really need to
• when your feet get wet, change your socks and shoes promptly
• launder all towels and bath mats at high temperatures when you start the course of anti-fungal drugs, and again when you complete it
• never share towels, bath mats, socks, sandals or shoes
• wear flip-flops at the swimming pool or sauna, and in changing rooms; if any other member of the household has athlete's foot, take the same precautions in the bathroom at home – and make sure they seek treatment.

Occasionally athlete's foot is a misdiagnosis for atopic eczema of the feet, which is a common problem among allergy-prone children (see box on p. 45). If the skin between the toes is not affected, it's unlikely to be athlete's foot and more likely to be eczema.

Cats, dogs
AND OTHER PETS

If you or your child are allergic to your pet, you should really find it another home. But a survey in the United States showed that more than a third of people with cat allergy still keep their cat – so there is detailed advice below for those who want to keep the pet, as well as those who decide to part company.

Often people with severe allergies find that, although they miss their pet badly at first, the vast improvement in their symptoms makes that difficult decision seem like a good one in the long run. Finding a home for an adult pet is often difficult, as most people want kittens or puppies, but try advertising locally, and explaining in your ad exactly why the pet needs a new home. Family and friends may be happy to help by offering your pet a home. Ask around among your older neighbours too – they may value having a mature pet that is calmer and already house-trained.

Cats

You can't *see* cat allergen – many people wrongly assume that it is cat fur that is allergenic, or flakes of skin. The main allergen is a protein found in the sweat and saliva of the cat, which wafts about in the air in microscopic specks. These lightweight allergen particles are carried throughout the house.

So small are these particles that they remain airborne for six hours or more, however still the air. If they do finally settle, they are easily made airborne again by the least little breeze. Simply walking around a room is enough to disturb them.

Parting with the cat

After your cat has gone, there will be allergens everywhere – on and in the armchairs, sofas, and cushions, on shelves and lampshades, in the carpets and even stuck to the walls and curtains. They will also be *inside* the mattress if the cat once slept on the bed, and will shoot out every time you lie down.

Once the cat has gone, air the house very thoroughly to shift all the allergen that is just hanging in the air. Wait a couple of weeks, and see how much your symptoms improve, before going further. If you still have troublesome symptoms that are worse at home, then you need to:

• Buy a high-suction vacuum cleaner that retains allergen particles (these are marketed for dust mites – make sure it is a good one) so that you can vacuum your furnishings without redistributing the allergen everywhere.

• Wash anything that can be washed: duvets, sheets, curtains, loose covers, cushions and their covers, duvet covers, pillow cases, bedspreads etc. Cat allergen is not affected by heat, so a cool wash is as good as a hot one – but you must wash all the allergen away, so run the rinse cycle twice. No one knows if dry-cleaning removes cat allergen.

• If the cat ever slept on your bed, then consider buying new pillows and duvet. Covers designed for dust-mite avoidance (see p. 115) are an alternative option. They will keep some of the cat allergen from escaping into the air, but not the very smallest particles.

• The seat cushions of sofas and armchairs can be sprayed with tannic acid or a polysaccharide (see box on p. 116) to deactivate the allergens. Vacuum clean very thoroughly first to remove as much allergen as possible, then spray repeatedly for a few weeks or months.

A clean getaway

The allergic individual should go out while this work is done, and stay out for at least six hours afterwards (see p. 109).

Even after the cat has gone, and you have cleaned up meticulously, you may still sometimes have symptoms. Unfortunately, cat allergen is carried about on the clothes of cat-owners and gets into schools, cinemas, buses, banks and even the padded seats in hospital waiting rooms. However, only the most highly sensitised people are affected by these low levels of allergen.

Keeping the cat

Bear in mind that keeping the pet will result in significant continued exposure however hard you try with the methods described.

- Improve the ventilation in your house as this will reduce the amount of allergen in the air. If your house is tightly sealed against draughts at the moment, this will actually make a huge difference. Air the house regularly. Always keep a window slightly open whenever the cat and/or the allergic person is indoors. You could use a HEPA filter to clean the air, instead. These work fairly well for cat allergens because these are very small lightweight particles which easily become airborne, so there is quite a lot of allergen in the air most of the time. Of course, an air filter cannot do anything to protect you from a cat sitting on your lap (though advertisements have sometimes implied that they can!).
- Put the cat outdoors when it begins washing itself, as this generates a lot of airborne allergen. Provide the cat with a shelter outside where it can sleep and wash, to reduce the amount of allergen in the house. Make it as warm and comfortable as possible, feed the cat there, and provide a little catnip to make it more attractive.
- If your cat is still allowed indoors, remove all soft furnishings and fitted carpets. Buy leather- or vinyl-covered armchairs which can be wiped clean of cat allergen.
- Keep the cat out of the bedroom entirely. If it has been in the habit of sleeping there, wash all the bedding and buy new pillows. The mattress and duvet should be replaced or covered with anti-mite covers (see p. 124).
- If you have an un-neutered tom, consider having him neutered: the amount of allergen produced declines when male cats are neutered.

The following measures are sometimes recommended, but in fact they don't work:

- treating the cat with acepromazine, an animal tranquilliser
- using a spray called Allerpet-C, which, so it is claimed, reduces the amount of allergen released. Scientific trials by a research group in Detroit have shown that it does not work.
- giving the cat a shower – i.e. drenching it in water. After a cat has had such a shower, the washing water contains a lot of cat allergen, so everyone assumed that this meant less cat allergen in the air. New research shows that the amount of allergen in the air around a cat after showering is no less than before. However, actually immersing the cat for three minutes followed by rinsing in clean warm water does reduce the allergen level in the air considerably. Unfortunately, the cat probably renews its stocks of allergen very fast, as a washed dog does (see below) so you need to repeat the wash at least once a week to reduce the allergen level in the air.

Dogs

Most of the advice given above, for cats, applies to dogs too because their allergens are also small and lightweight. Dogs produce less allergen than cats, and it seems to be less potent. However, you would still need to clean up thoroughly after the dog has gone, assuming you decide to find it another home.

If you decide to keep your dog, HEPA filters can be very useful, although you need also to take other measures, such as excluding the dog from bedrooms and keeping it outside for more (or most) of the time. Washing dogs thoroughly in a bath, using dog shampoo, reduces the amount of allergen in the air, but it builds up again to its former level within three days. You would need to wash the dog twice a week to achieve a useful reduction in allergen levels.

Other pets and domestic animals

Horses produce very powerful allergens, and those with allergies to horses are often so sensitive that even clothing that has been worn while riding and then brought indoors can elicit symptoms. Old furniture or mattresses stuffed with horsehair can sometimes cause problems too.

In the case of small mammals, such as mice and guinea pigs, it is usually the urine that causes allergic reactions. Proteins in the urine become airborne, and are carried around the house. You may be able to keep the pet if it is in a well-ventilated utility room or caged outside.

With snakes, lizards and other reptiles the allergens are found in tiny skin particles that float in the air. The same is true of stick insects and other insect pets.

Pollen

Do you ever wake up in the middle of the night with an attack of hayfever or pollen asthma? And do you ever wonder why this should happen? The explanation is that warm air, rising up from ground level on a summer's day, takes pollen with it high into the Earth's atmosphere. When the air cools down after sunset, this pollen slowly descends again – an invisible 'pollen shower'.

This pollen shower falls quite quickly in the countryside, reaching ground level between 8 p.m. and 10 p.m. but hot city pavements and buildings keep upward air currents going, and pollen stays aloft for longer. Most pollen lands on the city between about midnight and 2 a.m. That's why you wake up sneezing or wheezing – especially if you sleep with the windows open.

Understanding facts like these about pollen can help you to substantially reduce exposure. Pollen is by far the most difficult allergen to avoid, but don't believe the defeatists who tell you 'You can't do anything about pollen.'

Pollen counts and forecasts

Pollen counts are based on the amounts of pollen collected at specific sites earlier in the day, or on the previous day.

Forecasts for the coming day are really just informed guess-work, based on the present pollen count, the time of year, the temperature and rainfall over the last few days, and the weather forecast for the next day. At best, pollen forecasts are only as good as the weather forecast.

Forecasts of pollen can be useful in deciding when to start taking antihistamines for hayfever or when to increase your asthma preventer drugs (steroid or cromoglycate inhalers). The start of the grass-pollen season is now predicted quite accurately.

Avoiding pollen outdoors

One thing that really can help here is an air-conditioned car. In an ordinary car, closing the windows (and perhaps fitting a filter to the air intake) helps a lot, but the heat is terrible.

The size of the allergen particles

The pollen grains that cause allergies are between 10 and 40 microns in size, with the majority between 20 and 35 microns. An ordinary dust mask takes out particles larger than 5 microns, so it will be adequate for most pollens. However, a few plants – including rye grass – produce tiny allergenic fragments, some no bigger than half a micron. These are about the same size as cat allergen and will therefore need much better masks. For these fragments, it is worth using a HEPA air filter, and getting a high-quality vacuum cleaner.

A good cycle mask will keep out pollen grains and fragments during peak pollen times. Just wearing a scarf over the mouth and nose will also give some protection.

Another option is to smear a little Vaseline just inside each nostril and breathe through your nose only. Much of the pollen coming into your nose will stick to the Vaseline.

Timing is everything

Pollen release occurs at different times of day for different plants. Grasses release pollen from about 7.30 a.m. onwards, but if the ground is damp the release will be delayed until the moisture has evaporated. Unfortunately, a few species of grass wait until the afternoon, so there will be some pollen entering the air all day. If you get up at 6 a.m. for a walk or run, you can be safely home by 7.30 a.m. Alternatively, go out in the early evening, after grasses have finished releasing pollen, and before the 'pollen shower'.

Birch is an afternoon pollen: release peaks between noon and 6 p.m. Unfortunately, there is no information at present for other types of plants.

All types of plants favour warm sunny days for releasing pollen, and they all avoid rainy weather. On cloudy days there is a build-up of pollen in the flowers, so a massive release of pollen occurs on the next day of good weather.

Avoiding pollen indoors

Pollen grains have one huge point in their favour: compared to other allergenic particles, they are big and heavy. This means that they settle more quickly from the air. In a room with 3-metre-(10-foot-) high ceilings, all the pollen will settle within four minutes, as long as the air is completely still. In other words, if you close all the doors and windows, block off any draughts, and sit fairly still, within four minutes you will be breathing pollen-free air.

This does not mean that all your symptoms will instantly vanish, because the 'Late Phase Reaction' (see p. 13) can go on for up to 24 hours. But you should feel better and, by not starting a new cycle of allergic reaction, you are improving the prospects for the next day. Escaping from pollen for a few hours every day should produce a general improvement in the long run, with your nose and airways becoming less inflamed.

The bad news is that some plants produce allergenic fragments much smaller than the pollen grains themselves. Rye grass, ragweed, Japanese red cedar and Australian white cypress-pine do this, and there may be others as well. These tiny particles take much longer – up to six hours – to settle from the air.

Some plants even produce 'volatiles' – airborne chemicals that provoke symptoms. Birch trees release volatiles from their buds in early spring, weeks before the pollen itself is released, and they affect a great many people, including some who are not allergic to birch pollen. Volatiles can only be removed by masks or air filters if they contain an activated carbon filter (see p. 109).

The notorious effects of oil-seed rape on the nose are also due to volatiles, not pollen. These volatiles are simply irritants and there is no allergic reaction.

To cut down on the amount of pollen you inhale at home:
- Dry all your laundry indoors during the pollen season, to stop it collecting pollen.
- Pets bring in pollen on their fur, so keep them outdoors during the pollen season, and avoid stroking them or getting too close. Brushing them thoroughly before they come in is another option, but the allergic individual should not do this.
- Close the windows when your offending pollen is being released, and during the evening 'pollen shower' (see p. 126).

- Change your clothes when you arrive home, since they will be coated with pollen, and wash or rinse your hair. Keep some clothes for indoor use only.
- Aim for still air (no draughts, no fans and no vigorous movement) in the rooms where the allergic individual studies, sits or sleeps. Air currents stir up pollen from the floor and furnishings. (No draughts means poor ventilation, of course, which is acceptable during the pollen season – but ventilate again afterwards, to discourage moulds and dust mites.)
- If tranquil air is an impossibility, consider getting a high quality air filter, or air conditioning. Alternatively, wet-dust and vacuum every day (using a vacuum cleaner that keeps allergen particles in – see pp. 116–17) to reduce the amount of pollen residue. Those who are very sensitive may need to do this as well as having an air filter.
- Cover your armchair and bed with a dust sheet during the day. In the evening, fold this up *very* gently and wash it. This removes the layer of pollen that accumulates on furniture during the day, before it is disturbed and inhaled. If you are studying, cover your desk and books when not working.

Places to go, places to avoid

- For the grass-sensitive, mown grass is usually fine (it won't flower) although some people react to skin contact with grass (see p. 43). Unmown grass does flower, and will cause symptoms. Wheat, barley and oats, although they are grasses, release little pollen and rarely cause problems. Rye and sugarcane do release pollen, and may affect some people, but maize (corn) has heavy pollen that does not travel far, so it rarely causes much trouble.
- The levels of most pollens do not differ much between town and country. In fact, high up in a tower-block may be one of the worst places, because of pollen rising on warm air.
- The seaside is often pollen-free thanks to onshore breezes. Mountain peaks and ridges are also good, but deep mountain valleys can be pollen traps.

Roses are not the problem

The pollens that cause allergic reactions almost all come from plants with inconspicuous greenish flowers. These plants are pollinated by the wind, which is why there is so much of their pollen wafting about in the air. Colourful and scented flowers are pollinated by insects and have big sticky pollen grains that don't float about and rarely cause allergies. However, strong scents can irritate the nose of those who already have hayfever, and make their symptoms worse.

Avoiding air pollution

Air pollution plays a variety of roles in allergic reactions. Some pollutants irritate the nose and airways (and sometimes the skin) making them more sensitive to allergens. These pollutants can worsen existing allergic symptoms and may promote the development of allergies in children, by making the airway membranes more permeable. Other chemical pollutants may affect the immune system directly, increasing any existing tendency to allergic reactions.

Indoor pollution

For many of us, the air in our houses is much more polluted than any outdoor air. Several of the indoor pollutants irritate the nose and airways, and some can trigger asthma attacks. A few of the pollutants found indoors can also make allergies and asthma more likely to develop in young children.

Background pollution

One of the worst irritants in indoor air is **tobacco smoke**. Other people's cigarette or pipe smoke can trigger asthma attacks in the short term, and makes asthmatics generally worse in the long run. Passive smoking might also affect the immune system making allergies more likely to develop, though this is not proven. Do whatever you can to eliminate tobacco smoke from your home.

Everyone is different

This article considers air pollution from the point of view of someone with classical allergies (e.g. hayfever or asthma). Those with chemical intolerance (see p. 84) may well be more severely affected by air pollution.

If you smoke yourself, there are many good reasons for giving up:

- If individuals from atopic families (see p. 8) smoke, they have a far greater chance of developing allergies and/or asthma when exposed to an allergen in the air.
- For those who had asthma as children and have grown out of it, cigarette smoking doubles the chance of it coming back.
- Parents of asthmatic children who smoke indoors make their children's asthma worse. Teenagers can be just as badly affected by passive smoking as young children.
- Smoking during pregnancy significantly increases the risk of a woman's baby developing allergies and asthma. (Smoking also leads to more prematurity, still-births and cot deaths.)

If possible, have an electric cooking stove rather than a gas one – or fit a powerful extractor fan. Cooking with a gas stove generates a lot of **nitrogen dioxide**, a gas that you can't smell or see but which affects the airways. This same gas also comes from motor traffic, but peak levels of nitrogen dioxide in kitchens with gas cookers are often ten times the average level on city streets, and frequently exceed standards for outdoor air set by the World Health Organisation. Other sources of nitrogen dioxide include cigarettes, gas fires and kerosene-burning stoves.

For some people with allergies, nitrogen dioxide enhances their response to the allergen. So if you inhale dust-mite allergen together with nitrogen dioxide, it may have more effect than the

Smoke screen

Smoke particles from coal or wood do not seem to make allergies more likely to develop – in fact, quite the reverse. In rural areas of Germany, researchers have found that children with coal or wood stoves in their homes were less likely to have allergies or asthma. An Australian study made a similar finding. Bronchitis and pneumonia are more common in those with wood and coal stoves and these infections may stimulate the immune system in such a way that allergies are less likely to develop later.

allergen alone. Breathing sulphur dioxide (see below) and nitrogen dioxide together boosts the reaction to allergen more powerfully than either gas alone.

Nitrogen dioxide might also make asthma attacks more likely, but the evidence on this is conflicting.

For young children, a high level of nitrogen dioxide at home may make the development of allergic reactions more likely. A recent Canadian study showed that children exposed to high levels of nitrogen dioxide in the home – usually from gas cookers – were *ten times* as likely to develop asthma as those breathing low levels of nitrogen dioxide. If a dog, cat or other furry pet was kept, *and* there were high nitrogen dioxide levels, the risk of developing asthma shot up even higher, to 25 times that of children with low nitrogen dioxide and no pets. (Other studies have not produced the same spectacular results, but their methods of measuring nitrogen dioxide exposure were less precise.)

Try to eliminate materials that produce **formaldehyde** fumes, or seal the items with a good coat of paint. Formaldehyde is given off by chipboard and to a lesser extent by MDF (medium-density fibreboard). Injected cavity wall insulation can also produce persistent formaldehyde fumes, and is very difficult to get rid of – moving out is often the only option. A recent study from Australia showed that children exposed to formaldehyde, especially in the bedroom, were more likely to develop allergic reactions: the higher the level of formaldehyde exposure, the more severe the child's allergic sensitisation.

Those with asthma have more frequent symptoms if exposed to high formaldehyde levels. A recent study from Finland shows that easy-to-clean plastic wall-covering and flooring increases the risk of asthma in children.

A Canadian study found that children whose first home was less than 20–30 years old were 50% more likely to develop asthma than children living in older houses. One possible explanation for this lies with the materials used in the construction and fitting of new houses, especially the plastics, wood preservatives and insulation materials. Solvents, and chemicals such as formaldehyde, are still being given off by these materials some years later.

Air fresheners provoke asthma attacks in some people. For a few individuals they can cause general symptoms of ill-health that are similar to those described for mild chemical intolerance (see p. 84). Those affected generally don't realise that the air freshener is the source of the trouble. This malign effect is not entirely surprising, since air fresheners work by giving off a chemical that targets part of the brain – the part involved in processing sensory input from your nose. The chemical 'freshens the air' by partially disabling your sense of smell. Better to open a window.

Cleaning products, furniture polish and deodorant were never intended to go into the nose and airways, but that's what happens when they are sprayed from an **aerosol**, and they can trigger asthma attacks. Steer clear of aerosols as much as possible – there are usually alternatives.

Pollution peaks

Read the instructions and ingredients lists on all products carefully. It is not just a question of what's in them, but also what gases they might give off when used. One asthmatic died within minutes when the de-rusting agent she was using on her dishwasher produced a large amount of **sulphur dioxide** gas: her airways tightened up so much that she couldn't even use an inhaler to save herself. 'Sulphuric', 'sulphate' or 'sulphite' in the list of ingredients should ring warning bells if you have asthma: sulphur dioxide gas could be given off by this product.

Bleach, and other **chlorine**-based cleaning products, such as toilet cleaner and scouring powder, should be used sparingly, and with plenty of ventilation. These products release chlorine gas which, in large amounts, can irritate the airways of asthmatics. Never allow bleach or toilet cleaner to become mixed with any other product. Take care with any product containing hypochlorite, chloramine, ammonia, acids or morpholine and with the chemicals used for swimming pool water. All these can trigger asthma attacks.

If doing repairs or DIY work about the house, take special care. Always ventilate the work area well, and wear a dust mask if sawing or drilling.

The smell of **paint** is due to solvents, and these can act as irritants to the nose and airways. When decorating, ventilate well, and use low-odour water-based paint. Some of the best low-odour paints, tested and shown to be safe for paint-sensitive asthmatics, are only available by mail order: see p. 255.

'Instant foam' kits sold for DIY insulation can provoke asthma in those who were not asthmatic previously. Two different substances are mixed to create the polyurethane foam, and during the mixing process, **isocyanate** is released – this is one of the most powerful asthmagens known (see box on p. 132). The level of isocyanate can breach the safety limit set for factories.

Avoid using fly spray or other **insecticides**: look for other methods of pest control. A study from Ethiopia showed that people using an insecticide in their houses were twice as likely to develop allergies. A study of Canadian farmers suggested that asthma might be linked to the use of carbamate insecticides (e.g. carbofuran). The sprays used for cockroaches can act as irritants for those with allergic rhinitis or chronic sinusitis.

If advised that your house needs spraying with insecticide, for woodworm or other wood-boring pests, ask for more information before you go ahead. Is the spraying really necessary? What will happen if the house isn't sprayed? How quickly will it happen? Is there any other method of eradicating the pest? Spraying is often done when it is not really essential – houses remain standing even with woodworm holes all over them. Unless you have a heavy infestation that is threatening the structure of the house, you are probably better off not having the house sprayed. The heavy and ongoing exposure to insecticide that spraying of a house involves is something you and your family should avoid if at all possible. All the sprays used are toxic to some extent – don't believe those who tell you otherwise. A heavy exposure to pesticides can sometimes make allergic symptoms worse or precipitate chemical intolerance (see p. 85).

The garage, workshop or garden shed can also be very polluted. Petrol, kerosene and paraffin can affect some people with rhinitis or asthma, and can bring on their symptoms. These fuels should always be kept in airtight containers. Paints sold for cars often contain isocyanates, among the most common causes of work-related asthma (see box on p. 132). If using such paint, wear a mask with an activated carbon filter *and* make sure the area is well ventilated. Avoid prolonged or repeated exposure.

Outdoor pollution

Some of the pollutants in outdoor air can make allergic reactions worse and can trigger asthma attacks in people who are already asthmatic. A study of hospital admissions in London, Paris, Barcelona and Helsinki found that high levels of pollution increased hospital admissions for asthma by about 3%.

The pollutants that matter to those with allergies are:
• **ozone** which soars to high levels on sunny days, mainly in country areas that are near large cities. The reason for this is a chemical reaction which occurs when car exhaust fumes are exposed to sunlight, producing ozone, a highly reactive form of oxygen. Further chemical reactions, involving another ingredient of exhaust fumes, then break the ozone down again. Thanks to this second reaction, there is usually little ozone in city air. But in a relatively rural area 20 miles or so upwind of the city, the pollutants are too dispersed for the second reaction to occur, and the ozone from the urban traffic can accumulate.

Ozone levels in the air tend to peak in the late afternoon and early evening – but it takes 4–24 hours for ozone to produce its effects on the airways. Indoors, ozone breaks down very quickly because of contact with other gases inside the house.

Ozone can increase the effects of allergens, such as pollen, on the nose and airways.

In addition, ozone makes the airway muscles contract, even for people without asthma. Healthy people tend not to notice these effects, whereas some asthmatics may have more symptoms, and may need more drugs, on days when ozone levels are unusually high.

• **diesel particulates**, which can become a problem in town centres, and close to main roads used by vans and lorries. Unlike ordinary petrol, diesel fuel contains oil, so when it burns it produces tiny black particles. These consist of flakes of carbon (soot), coated with complex chemicals that are produced by the

But what about the ozone layer...?

Is ozone good for us or bad for us? People often get confused about this, because of all the discussion about 'the destruction of the ozone layer'. But that layer (which screens us from harmful ultraviolet light) is a natural phenomenon and it is thousands of feet up, well away from our lungs. At ground level, in the air we breathe, ozone is unnatural and potentially damaging .

partial combustion of the oil. It is probably these surface chemicals, rather than the soot particles themselves, that have such bad effects on the nose and airways.

Some research suggests that diesel particulates might increase the risk of allergies developing – to pollen for example. Additionally, when levels of diesel particulates are high, asthmatics tend to have more symptoms. If levels rise above 50 micrograms per cubic metre there is a sharp increase in asthma attacks – and a recent study in Birmingham showed that such levels are regularly reached at roadsides.

• **sulphur dioxide**, which often reaches high levels in areas of heavy industry, particularly near coal-fired power stations and coking plants. It acts as an irritant to the airways and can trigger attacks in asthmatics, who are far more sensitive to sulphur dioxide than healthy people (see box on p. 207). However, at the sort of concentrations normally encountered, even in quite polluted air, sulphur dioxide does not have any effect on most asthmatics.

• **nitrogen dioxide** which is produced by all types of vehicles, and by power stations and some factories. In towns and cities with heavy traffic, nitrogen dioxide can build up to high levels. This gas is also found indoors (see p. 128) – often at far higher levels.

Oil refineries and cement works

In addition to these widespread pollutants, there are localised areas of air pollution, around industrial sites, that are frequently accused of causing health problems, including high rates of asthma. The kinds of industrial sites regularly mentioned include:

- oil refineries and oil-burning power stations,
- cement works that use waste solvents for fuel
- dock areas where oil is loaded into tankers

None of these accusations has been investigated in any detail, so it is impossible to say if there is a real link with asthma.

Avoiding outdoor air pollution

If you live in the kind of area that experiences high levels of ozone (see p. 130), plan your outdoor activities, especially jogging or playing sport, to avoid summer afternoons and early evenings.

Those who live very close to a main road, with a lot of lorries going past, would probably improve their own health, and reduce the chance of their children developing allergies and asthma, by fitting air conditioning or high-quality HEPA air filters – or by moving house. However, the benefits, in terms of decreased risk, are not enormous, and it is important to take other preventive measures as well (see Chapter 8).

When driving, if you stop behind a lorry or bus, keep your distance, close the window and turn off the fan. Diesel vehicles often emit a thick cloud of particles as they set off, and this can come straight into your car, setting off severe attacks for some asthmatics.

A car with air conditioning will reduce your exposure to diesel particulates while driving. When buying a new car, you can make a contribution to air quality by choosing a non-diesel vehicle, preferably one with a catalytic converter fitted. Alternatively, buy a diesel vehicle with a particle filter on the exhaust (now fitted as standard in Germany).

In Britain, the Vehicles Inspectorate of the Department of Transport encourages the public to report lorries and buses seen pumping out black smoke (look in the phone book for the number).

If you are asthmatic, breathing through your nose may help as this can filter out some damaging pollutants before they reach the airways in your lungs. (If your nose is usually blocked, try the exercises on pp. 230–31).

When levels of ozone or sulphur dioxide are high, taking a supplement of Vitamin C and eating plenty of foods that contain Vitamin E and beta-carotene (see p. 207) can protect your airways.

Allergens and irritants at work

Some workplaces have very high concentrations of allergens in the air, especially if proper safety procedures are not being followed. Occupational allergies can begin with symptoms in the nose, such as sneezing, blockage or constant streaming (allergic rhinitis). You may also suffer with itchy or watery eyes (conjunctivitis), a cough, sweating and a feverish feeling. Alternatively, direct contact with the allergen can produce a skin rash (dermatitis) or itchiness and swelling (contact urticaria/nettle rash and angioedema).

If you work somewhere with an allergy risk (see pp. 133–4), be vigilant for such symptoms and see your doctor immediately. These symptoms can be the forerunners of **occupational asthma**, which is a serious and potentially irreversible problem. Some allergens, such as latex, can even produce anaphylactic shock (a life-threatening allergic collapse).

Skin-prick tests (see p. 91) can show if you have developed an allergy to a substance encountered at work.

Acting promptly gives you the best possible chance of recovery and is vital if you have occupational asthma. Only if exposure to the allergen stops promptly do you have a good chance of shaking off the asthma. See your doctor as soon as possible and ask for a referral to a chest specialist, so that a definite diagnosis can be made. This is essential if you are going to make a claim for compensation.

Far too many people with occupational asthma are just sent off with an inhaler when they first see their doctor. By delaying the moment when work is identified as the source of the problem, and the exposure to the allergen is stopped, drug treatment can turn occupational asthma into a disabling lifelong problem. Although drugs can be helpful in

Other hazards

This article deals mainly with **allergens** at work, that is, substances which provoke classical allergies.

In addition, there are skin irritants and antigens which can provoke **contact dermatitis** or **contact urticaria**: hairdressing involves several of these. Protective clothing and gloves are needed – but do not use latex gloves, especially the powdered variety, or you run the risk of developing latex allergy (see pp. 133–4).

Some of the most dangerous workplace substances are chemicals which bring on asthma but are not allergens. These are usually called **low molecular weight asthmagens**. The most notorious of these are:

- platinum salts
- isocyanates (used in cement, in the manufacture of foam, plastics and varnishes, and for spray-painting cars, aeroplanes and boats)
- colophony (used as a solder in electronics)
- glutaraldehyde (used in hospitals for sterilisation procedures)
- persulphate (used in hairdressing).

Powerful respiratory equipment, supplying air from outside the area (see p. 135) is needed if you work with some of these substances, e.g. isocyanates for spray-painting.

speeding your recovery *once exposure to the allergen has ended*, they should *not* be seen as a way of allowing you to go on working with the offending allergen or asthmagen.

If it seems plausible that your allergies or your asthma are related to your work, your doctor should be able to give you a sickness certificate, so that you can have some time away from the workplace, to see if you recover.

The medical service at your workplace may be better at diagnosing occupational asthma than your own doctor, but be cautious. In some workplaces they offer genuinely confidential treatment. But there have also been cases of information being passed to the management, and workers with the early signs of occupational allergies and/or asthma being dismissed on spurious grounds, or made redundant, to avoid a possible compensation claim. Most occupational health services claim to be independent, but they have to actually earn the trust of the workforce. Before you make any move, ask your colleagues for their views, especially those who have worked there for many years.

Choosing a job

If you have any tendency to allergies, or come from an allergy-prone family, you should be very choosy about where you work. Try to avoid workplaces where there is heavy exposure to allergens:

- Bakeries and flour mills, where the allergens concerned may be wheat proteins in the flour, or enzymes added to the flour mix. These allergies can take years to begin.

- Other food-processing works, particularly those dealing with tea, soybeans, others beans (e.g. gram flour), shellfish and fish (especially if automated gutting machines are used without adequate ventilation).

- Farms, docks and cotton mills – or any other workplace generating dust from plant products. In the case of farms, it is the dust from grain and hay that is often responsible, although mould spores (see p. 121) can also be the culprit. Allergies to mites in hay, grain and flour sometimes occur and eczema is the most common symptom – this is often called simply 'grain itch'.

- Saw mills and joineries, because of the wood dust, especially that from hardwoods and from red cedar (*Thuja plicata*).

- Paper recycling plants, if there is a lot of paper dust in the air.

- Detergent and pharmaceutical factories handling enzymes – these are added to 'biological' washing powders and are potential allergens. The risks are greater if the enzymes are in powder form, rather than granules.

- Factories processing natural products such as psyllium or ispaghula, which are used as laxatives. Anyone who has been sensitised should avoid taking medicines containing the offending substance in the future.

- Hospitals and clinics, mainly due to latex rubber, used in gloves and equipment. Although nursing staff and surgeons are most susceptible, hospital administrative workers

Making the workplace safe for everyone

Note that these choices about employment are for the *individual employees* to make for their own protection – an employer cannot refuse to take anyone on because they have allergies or come from an atopic (allergy-prone) family.

The reasoning behind this is that the workplace should be safe for everyone, as far as possible. As many as one in three of the population may be susceptible to allergies, and it is clearly wrong to bar all such people from major industries. Current thinking, in most countries, is that the focus should be on getting allergens and asthmagens out of the air, not keeping the more vulnerable workers out of the workplace.

can occasionally be affected. Fears about the spread of the HIV virus has led to a huge increase in the use of latex gloves in medicine and dentistry, and a consequent epidemic of latex allergy. Other workers who regularly wear latex gloves at work (e.g. food handlers) are also at risk. The main problem is with powdered latex gloves which release 15,000 times as much allergen into the air as unpowdered gloves. Unpowdered, low-allergen gloves greatly reduce the risk of latex allergy developing, and vinyl gloves are even better.

• Factories making or using rubber items may also expose workers to the risk of latex allergy.

• Chiropody and podiatry clinics, where there is a risk of allergic reactions to the fungus that causes athlete's foot. It is inhaled on skin flakes from the patients' feet.

• Laboratories and other workplaces where animals are kept. In the case of mice, rats and other rodents, the allergen is found in the animals' urine, and becomes airborne as the urine dries. Insects and spiders (e.g. those reared for biological pest control), are also allergenic due to small airborne particles from their bodies. Those working closely with bees (either honeybees or bumblebees, now reared for pollinating glasshouse crops) are liable to be stung frequently, and this can lead to sting allergy (see pp. 60–61).

Taking a risky job

If circumstances force you to take a job with an allergy risk, observe all the safety procedures that are in place, and where you have the option of turning on extractor fans, wearing protective gear, or simply opening doors and windows, always do so. If the safety procedures seem inadequate, talk to your trade union Safety Representative, or the local Health and Safety Executive which can run a check on safety procedures in your workplace. This will be presented to the employer as a routine check, so they need never know that a member of the workforce has contacted the HSE.

Whatever you do, if you are in a risky job, don't smoke. At a salmon processing plant in Scotland, 40% of the smokers developed allergies (resulting in asthma) to the fish allergens in the spray from the fish-gutting machine. Non-smokers – who formed the overwhelming majority of the workers – were not affected at all. In United States cotton mills, smokers are affected by levels of cotton dust in the air that are legally defined as 'safe', while non-smokers remain unaffected.

Passive smoking at work is also an important issue. A recent American study showed that non-smokers were more likely to develop asthma if they worked alongside a smoker. Your employer has a duty to provide you with clean air. This includes ensuring that other employees do not impose their cigarette smoke on you.

Respiratory equipment

Where respiratory equipment is needed, your employer must provide this, and it must be the right equipment for the job. It should be inspected, tested, cleaned and repaired after each use, and filters should be replaced regularly. All this is your employer's responsibility, but check that it is being done, and always look the mask over before you put it on.

Two different types of respiratory equipment are currently in use:

• Those that give you a supply of air from outside the work area, either from a compressed-air cylinder, or via an air-hose (airline) supplied with fresh air from outdoors. In Britain these are called **breathing apparatus**.

• Those that use the surrounding air but filter it to remove allergens and asthmagens. In Britain these are called **respirators**. (In some countries this term describes any kind of respiratory equipment.) Ordinary respirators may pose problems for some asthmatics because they cannot breathe in strongly enough to draw sufficient air through the filter. Powered respirators can be the answer: they have a battery-powered unit to help with pulling in the air.

There are government regulations concerning the type of equipment required for each type of allergen and asthmagen. Large companies generally follow these regulations, but small businesses, such as local sawmills, joineries and car-repainting workshops, may not even know about them.

Any respiratory equipment that has a face mask must form a tight seal with your face. Facial hair will prevent this, and so will stubble, so shave carefully. Faces vary enormously in shape, and if your face mask does not fit, ask for a different type of mask or a different type of respiratory equipment. Persist until you get one that's right for you.

Carry out a 'fit check' each and every time you wear the mask. For example, with respirators, you can check the fit by covering the air intake completely with your hand and breathing in sharply: if the mask fits properly, it should collapse onto your face, and remain stuck to your face for several seconds. Look

at the manufacturer's instruction booklet as there may be a specific fit check recommended for the equipment you are using.

If there is any difficulty in breathing through the respiratory equipment, the replaceable filter cartridge or the equipment itself should be replaced. You should also take action immediately if you can smell the substance being handled – but never rely on this as a danger sign, because an extremely small amount, way beyond the detection capacity of the human nose, may be very damaging indeed to your health.

Keep your mask on throughout the work period. If you find this impossible, talk to your employer or line manager about getting a different kind of respiratory equipment – a powered device, for example, that assists the inflow of air.

No form of respiratory equipment provides complete protection against allergens and asthmagens: there is always the chance of some small amount getting through. This is why respiratory equipment should not be used by those who have already developed occupational asthma but want to stay in their job.

Those who really cannot change jobs (e.g. farmers) are sometimes able to use a powered respirator helmet, which allows them to go on working despite the allergen. But this is not an ideal solution from a purely health point of view. Farmers can also improve matters, where moulds are the source of allergens, by keeping all harvested crops dry and thoroughly ventilated.

drugs and immunotherapy

'With my children, both of whom have allergies and asthma, I have always worried about the possible side effects of using Becotide, Ventolin and various antihistamines. But it seems to be a case of being "between the devil and the deep blue sea" – in other words, *not* using the drugs is far more risky than using them. I'm concerned about the effect of steroids on Michael's growth rate and bones, and about the effect of Ventolin on his heart. I've always wondered, when doctors have tried to reassure me, just how long these drugs have been around and if doctors could possibly know what the effects are on someone taking them for, say, 40 years. In the end, I've come to the conclusion that doctors simply don't have an answer to that question.'

Rachel's concerns about drugs are probably shared by most parents of allergy sufferers – and by those who have allergies themselves. Their fear and suspicion of drugs is often fuelled, paradoxically, by the fact that doctors tend to be blandly reassuring, and rarely mention side effects when prescribing. Rachel is not the only one to feel unhappy with this approach.

The reason for this apparent lack of honesty is quite simple: being frank about potential minor side effects, such as headaches and nausea, greatly increases the number of patients who actually suffer from them. The power of the human imagination is such that it can produce a wide range of minor side effects from a completely inert dummy pill, if side effects are expected. This is the flip-side of the **placebo effect,** whereby a dummy pill can produce a distinct improvement if the doctor seems confident that it will help. So doctors tend to keep quiet about side effects when they first prescribe a new drug – which

does not mean that they are either complacent or ignorant about them.

If you want to know about all the possible side effects of the drugs you are taking, that information is available here, along with information about how the drugs work, and advice on using them to the best possible effect.

Before you start reading about the side effects of your drugs, please bear in mind that none of the **major side effects** – the ones that seriously damage health – is likely to happen to you. Only a few of the drug treatments for allergy – long courses of steroid tablets, for example, or high doses of theophylline – are *commonly* associated with major side effects. Some of the major side effects mentioned here are so vanishingly rare that you probably have more chance of being struck by lightning. What is more, even with the more hazardous treatments, you can tip the odds in your favour by being sensible – using your drugs correctly, taking the precautions suggested here, and keeping an eye out for warning signs.

Remember that all the most common reactions are just **minor side effects**. In other words, they may be unpleasant or inconvenient, but they do not indicate that the drug is doing you any serious damage. These common side effects are noted during the safety trials that precede the release of a new drug, and studied closely to check that they are not a cause for concern. Careful testing is carried out on the patients involved in safety trials, to exclude the possibility of any dangerous unseen side effects on the liver, heart, kidneys and other vital organs. Carcinogenic effects are ruled out at an even earlier stage.

Unfortunately, these pre-release trials cannot

possibly identify all major side effects. We vary in our response to drugs, because we are all so different at the chemical and cellular level. A drug might have a serious side effect that only affects one person in 10,000, and no safety trial can hope to identify such a rare response. Only when a drug is released, and becomes widely used, do such side effects come to light. Other unanticipated side effects can sometimes arise when people taking the new drug are much older than those in the safety trials, or belong to a different ethnic group with different susceptibilities. Combining the drug with certain other drugs can also be a potential source of trouble, although pharmaceutical experts can often predict such problems from a detailed knowledge of the chemistry of drugs and how they are broken down in the body. Side effects that take several years to develop – more than the timespan of most safety trials – will also fail to show up until the drug has been released.

All this may sound very alarming, but in fact severe reactions to new drugs are not that common. And there are various safety nets in place – doctors keep a close eye on patients taking new drugs, and a special reporting system ensures that, if unexpected side effects do show up, the information is quickly shared with others in the medical community.

In order to relate the information here to a particular medicine that you take, you need to know what drug category it belongs to. Does your inhaler contain a beta-2 reliever, a steroid, a cromoglycate-type drug or an anti-cholinergic, for example? If you are not sure, ask your pharmacist.

Those are the **category names** for drugs: they denote families of drugs which are similar chemically and work in roughly the same way. Within each category, or family, there are a number of individual drugs. The individual drugs should, ideally, have a standard internationally agreed name – this is known as the **generic name**. Unfortunately, a few of the drugs used for allergies and asthma have more than one generic name – salbutamol is known as albuterol in some parts of the world, and adrenaline is called epinephrine.

Finally there are the **brand names,** which are the ones most patients are familiar with. These are always shown with a capital letter, unlike the generic names. Long-established drugs are usually made by several different pharmaceutical companies, and therefore marketed under several different brand names. A newer drug, which is still covered by the patent of the pharmaceutical company that developed it, will be sold under only one brand name.

The issue of brand names is important, because a different brand name might make you think you are taking a different drug, when in fact it is exactly the same drug being marketed in a different guise. If you have suffered side effects from a particular drug in the past, and wish to avoid it in future, take note of its generic name, rather than its brand name.

Sometimes the generic name is used as the brand name, in what are called **generic drugs**. These are relatively inexpensive copies of popular drug brands – they are just the same chemically, but they cost less because there is no advertising of the brand to doctors, and profit margins have been cut to a minimum. In order to reduce National Health Service costs, doctors are now asked to prescribe generic drugs whenever possible.

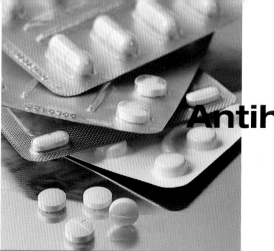

Antihistamines

Antihistamines were first introduced in 1947, and are very widely used, so their safety – at least in the case of the older antihistamines – is beyond doubt. Most of the antihistamines have no major ill effects, and no one should feel concerned about taking them. At worst they produce some rather annoying minor side effects, such as drowsiness, which often wear off in time.

These drugs are particularly valuable for **hayfever** and other allergies in the nose (**perennial allergic rhinitis**). They are also used for **chronic urticaria**, sometimes in combination with another histamine-blocking drug – see p. 53.

Antihistamines are not much used for **asthma.** They have relatively little effect, probably because so many other messenger chemicals are involved in an asthma attack. However, doctors in Japan do use antihistamines for asthma, and it is possible that people of Asiatic origin react differently to them. Only one antihistamine, ketotifen, is widely used for asthma in the West, and this has other effects besides blocking histamine (see p. 159). A new role may soon develop for antihistamines in the treatment of asthma, combined with anti-leukotriene drugs (see p. 159).

If you suffer from **anaphylaxis** you might be given antihistamines in a liquid or chewable form, for use in an emergency. These are *not enough* in themselves to treat this dangerous condition – *you must have an adrenaline injector* (see p. 150).

In the past, some doctors prescribed antihistamines for **atopic eczema**, mOinly for their sedative effect (see p. 139) which was thought to help children to sleep better and scratch less at night. This treatment has largely gone out of favour, because its value is in doubt. But a recent study has revealed that the non-sedating antihistamine cetirizine may be useful for very young children with atopic eczema, not only in treating their skin, but also in reducing the chance of them developing asthma (see p. 249).

Most people take their antihistamines in tablet or capsule form. Syrups and sugar-free elixirs are available for children.

Antihistamines can also be applied directly, in the form of nasal sprays or eye drops. These are mainly used to treat hayfever and the conjunctivitis (inflammation of the eye) which often accompanies it. Levocabastine (brand name Livostin) is particularly effective for the eyes.

Antihistamine creams are also sold, without prescription, for the treatment of insect bites – i.e. the normal non-allergic reaction to such bites. These creams are not recommended for atopic eczema or other allergic conditions affecting the skin. Not only are they unlikely to help, but they may make matters worse because, with regular use, skin sensitisation to the antihistamine occurs very readily (see pp. 54–5).

Some common brand names
Common brand names include:

non-sedating antihistamines – Clarityn, Semprex, Zirtek; Mistamine, Mizollen, Telfast, Terfenadine. The first three are available without prescription.

older (sedating) antihistamines – Atarax, Dimotane, Optimine, Periactin, Piriton, Tavegil, Vallergan

eye drops – Emadine, Livostin, Optilast

nasal sprays – Livostin, Rhinolast

How antihistamines work

Of the messenger chemicals released when an allergic reaction occurs, the most important is **histamine.** This does its work by attaching to specialised **receptors** in certain parts of the body, and so triggering various reactions (see box on p. 12). The action of antihistamines is very simple: they bind to the same receptors as histamine, but they do not trigger any reaction. Histamine cannot bind to the receptor because the antihistamine is already there.

Unfortunately, the reverse is also true: if the histamine is already there, the antihistamine cannot elbow it off the receptor, which is why it is important to take the antihistamine *well before* the allergen is encountered. Taking antihistamines at the first sign of a snuffle or itch can also work, but the effects will not be nearly as good as taking them in anticipation of an exposure.

The best approach to treating hayfever, for example, is to start taking the antihistamines at least a week before the pollen season begins, and preferably two to three weeks before. You should then take them continuously until it is over. This will make a huge difference to the degree of symptom control you achieve.

Side effects of these drugs

The older types of antihistamine, such as chlorphenamine (brand name, Piriton) are relatively non-specific in their effects – they bind to several different kinds of receptors, not just those for histamine. As a result they can have some unwanted effects, such as causing drowsiness and poor coordination. While these sedative effects are no cause for concern in themselves, they can, of course, be hazardous if you work with dangerous machinery or drive. Avoid both until you are sure how you react to the antihistamine. Note that the effects of alcohol may be increased.

Very occasionally antihistamines have the opposite effect, causing stimulation rather than sedation; this is most likely to occur in children and old people. Lowering the dose may solve the problem.

The other possible side effects of the older antihistamines – all of which are minor ones – are headache, dry mouth, blurred vision, difficulty in passing urine, nervousness, shaky hands, upset stomach or diarrhoea. A few men suffer impotence while taking antihistamines, but this disappears when the drug is stopped.

The minor side effects of antihistamines, including drowsiness, often wear off after a while, although the benefits of the drug remain. So it is worthwhile persisting with an antihistamine, even if it causes some problems at first. Many people experience side effects from certain antihistamines but not from others, so try several different types to find one that suits you.

The problem of drowsiness has been reduced, in recent years, thanks to the development of new drugs that are far more specific for histamine receptors, the **non-sedating antihistamines**. A few people do get drowsy even with these drugs. Again, the effects vary from one drug to another, so if the first one disagrees with you, try a different one.

It is worth noting – since some people may still have the odd packet in their medicine cabinet – that two of the non-sedating antihistamines that were available without prescription a few years ago proved to be unsafe for a small minority of people. One was astemizole (brand names: Hismanal, Pollon-eze), which has now been withdrawn from use altogether in Britain. The other was terfenadine (brand names: Triludan, Seldane, Terfenadine) which is still available, but only on prescription.

There are several special precautions relating to terfenadine:
- Never exceed the correct dose.
- If you have ever had any kind of heart problem, talk to your doctor before taking terfenadine.
- Stop taking the drug if you have palpitations, or if you feel faint; see your doctor promptly.
- Do not take terfenadine if you are taking the antibiotic erythromycin, or anti-fungal drugs such as ketoconazole (Nizoral) or fluconazole (Diflucan), used to treat vaginal thrush.
- Do not take terfenadine if you have liver disease.
- Do not drink grapefruit juice while taking terfenadine: something found naturally in grapefruit interacts unpleasantly with this antihistamine.

In addition to these special precautions concerning terfenadine, *any* antihistamine should be treated with caution by those suffering from epilepsy, Parkinson's disease, glaucoma, prostate enlargement, kidney problems, urinary retention, a gastric ulcer, a thyroid disorder, porphyria or liver disease. Check with your doctor before taking antihistamines if you have any of these conditions.

It may be inadvisable to use antihistamines if you are taking sleeping tablets, anti-depressants or anti-anxiety drugs – again, see your doctor.

Stop taking antihistamines if you suffer any unusual kind of rash, or if your skin becomes more sensitive to sunlight.

If you are breast-feeding, note that, because they go through into the milk, the older antihistamines may make the baby sleepy. However, they do no harm.

Rescue treatment

Most antihistamines perform very badly if you take them once the allergic reaction has set in, but acrivastine (Semprex) can be good in these circumstances and is non-sedating. No prescription is required for this drug.

Steroids

Few drugs create quite so much alarm as **corticosteroids.** To some extent, this alarm is justified – if over-used, they have dangerous side effects. But rejecting them entirely is a great mistake, because they are safe at the right dose, and *immensely* useful for a variety of allergic symptoms. With the information given here, you can use steroids as safely and effectively as possible.

Although their proper name is corticosteroids, these drugs are commonly – and rather inaccurately – called **steroids**. This name adds to their doubtful reputation by confusing them with the notorious anabolic steroids (see box on p. 142). However, the term 'steroids' is used for corticosteroids in this book, simply because that is the name most people recognise.

Steroids do not deal with the allergic reaction itself, unlike antihistamines (see p. 138) or cromoglycate (see p. 148). Instead, they tackle the consequences of the allergic reaction, **inflammation.**

What exactly is inflammation? The visible features of this phenomenon – for example, if it occurs in the skin, around a scratch or cut – are redness and slight swelling. There is also soreness, and some warmth. All these effects are produced by an influx of immune cells, intent on protecting the broken skin from infection. These immune cells generate messenger chemicals (see box on p. 10) which boost the inflammation, as well as attracting yet more immune cells to the area. When inflammation affects delicate membranes, as when you suffer a sore throat for example, there can be a great deal more swelling and discomfort.

The inflammation that follows allergic reactions is very similar to that provoked by infection, although the balance of immune cells and messenger chemicals is slightly different. Eosinophils (see p. 19) play a particularly important role in sustaining the inflammation produced by allergies.

This influx of eosinophils and other immune cells, which lights the fires of inflammation, occurs some hours after the allergic response itself. It is known as the **Late Phase Reaction** (see p. 13). Steroids work well for allergies because they curtail the Late Phase Reaction and have a calming effect on various immune cells, especially the eosinophils.

Steroid phobia
So many patients have a profound objection to taking steroids that doctors call it, half-jokingly, 'steroid phobia'. One of the hazards of giving information about potential side effects – as in this book – is that it may encourage 'steroid phobia'. That would be a tragedy, because steroids really are useful drugs that can do you a lot of good and very little harm, if used correctly. The risks are very small when the steroids are used at low to medium doses, and targeted directly onto the inflammation. Even with high doses, the serious side effects can generally be avoided. Please don't use the information here to scare yourself – instead, use it to protect yourself while getting the most from steroid treatment.

Mimicking nature

All corticosteroids are chemically very similar to a substance known as **cortisol** that is produced naturally by the body. Cortisol – which is a hormone made in the **adrenal glands**, located near the kidneys – has a great number of different effects, apart from damping down inflammation. It regulates the action of the kidneys, moves proteins out of the muscles and bones, and alters the pattern of fat distribution.

Like other hormones and chemical messengers that the body produces, cortisol achieves its effects by binding to **receptors** on target cells (e.g. immune cells, muscle cells and the cells that make up the kidneys). These receptors vary a little, which gives researchers scope for making a synthetic version of the hormone, cunningly modified so that it binds well to one kind of receptor (the one on the immune cells, for example) but not so well to another (the one on the kidneys).

Hydrocortisone, the original steroid drug, is identical to cortisol, but the newer steroids have been modified chemically to have the maximum effect on inflammation and minimal effects on other body processes. While hydrocortisone can only be used for allergies at very low doses (as in non-prescription hydrocortisone cream), the modified steroids can be used at higher doses.

The side effects of steroid drugs are of two basic kinds:
- those due to suppression of inflammation (the desired effect of the drugs) because this partially reduces immunity to disease
- those due to the effects of steroids on other body processes – undesirable effects which have, as far as possible, been designed out of the modern drugs.

These different side effects are discussed in more detail on p. 142. First, it is important to look at the crucial difference between taking steroids in tablet form and applying them directly to the affected area. Much unnecessary anxiety can be avoided by understanding this difference.

Targeting steroids

The risks of steroids fall dramatically if, instead of taking them in tablet form, you put them exactly where they are needed: that means drops for the nose or eyes, inhalers to get the drug into the airways, or creams and ointments to target the skin.

The medical term for this is **topical application**, and it is infinitely preferable to taking steroid tablets. When a drug is swallowed, it does its job by being absorbed through the stomach lining into the bloodstream, and then being carried around the body in the blood. This is called **systemic treatment** because it reaches the whole body-system via the blood.

The areas that need the drug – the itchy skin or inflamed airways – get their dose, but so does every other part of the body. In order to get a useful amount to the afflicted parts, a fairly large total dose has to be taken which inevitably affects the rest of the body, making the drug far more hazardous.

When a drug is targeted precisely, in sprays, drops, creams or inhalers, the dose used can be very much smaller. Some of the drug does get into the bloodstream, by penetrating the skin or the membranes of the nose or airways, and entering the tiny blood vessels that lie just below. But the amount reaching the bloodstream is usually minuscule compared with the amount in the blood when you take steroid tablets. **Systemic side effects** – those due to the drug going round in the blood (see below) – are usually avoided, although there may be some local side effects, where the drug is applied.

Only with very powerful doses – as in the steroid inhalers used for severe asthma, or high-potency creams for eczema – do topical steroids reach the bloodstream in sufficient amounts to cause systemic side effects. You have to be on these treatments for a long time, or be overdoing the dose (a possible hazard with creams for eczema), to run the risk of systemic side effects .

Steroid tablets

Short courses of steroid tablets – which means three weeks or less – are pretty safe. They are usually sufficient to get the inflammation under control, and can be taken three or four times a year without creating any problems.

Even if you have no choice but to take steroid tablets on a long-term basis, remember that the serious side effects can usually be avoided, or reversed if caught early (see p. 143).

Side effects of steroid tablets

Apart from changes that may (rarely) occur in the stomach lining, the side effects of steroid tablets are all **systemic side effects**.

In the early days of steroid use, a set of side effects that resemble a disease known as **Cushing's Syndrome** were frequently seen. The side effects included deposits of fat on the shoulders and abdomen, and around the face, producing a 'moon face', water retention resulting in puffiness, weakening of the bones, easy bruising, acne and muscle wasting. All these changes are due to the unwanted effects of steroids on other body processes, not to any effect on inflammation.

With the new and improved steroids (see left), plus a much more watchful approach by doctors, these severe side effects have become very rare, but they can still occur in those on high-dose steroid tablets. As long as they are noticed in good time (see p. 143) the problem can be reversed.

A few effects on other body processes remain, even with the new steroids:

- Raised blood pressure – this can occur even with short-term use of steroids.
- Children may stop growing, or grow more slowly. Usually they make up for this later.
- Quite commonly, there is increased hunger (though you don't actually need more food, and will put on weight if you eat more than usual). Insomnia and an agitated, edgy feeling during the day may occur. These are minor side effects, and no cause for concern.
- Side effects in the eye can occur: there is an increased risk of glaucoma and, with prolonged use, cataracts.
- Long-term use can also result in loss of minerals from the bones, leading to thinning and fragility (**osteoporosis**).
- Psychological changes may occur. Some people experience euphoria or greatly increased energy levels – with the opposite effects occurring when the course of steroids ends. At worst, steroids can trigger paranoia or severe depression and suicidal feelings. (These effects are more likely to occur in those with a history of mental illness. If you are concerned about this aspect, discuss the possible risks with your doctor before taking steroid tablets.)
- Epileptics may suffer more frequent or more severe seizures.
- Very rarely, stomach ulcers develop, or other side effects in the digestive system.
- The skin may become thin, and the small blood vessels beneath it more fragile, leading to easy bruising and stretch marks (striae). This is also a potential problem with steroid creams (see p. 146). Elderly patients are much more susceptible to this side effect.
- Some diabetics need more insulin. In addition, anyone with the potential to develop diabetes is more likely to do so, but only if taking steroid tablets long term. The diabetes usually goes when the steroids are stopped.
- A few men suffer impotence, but only with long-term use of tablets. This can be treated, so see your doctor. Women may have irregular periods.
- Damage to the hip bones may rarely occur, usually with excessive doses of steroid tablets. This is called avascular necrosis and may require hip replacement.

In addition to these effects on other body processes, there are also some side effects that arise from the steroids' suppression of the inflammation. These can occur even with short courses. Again, however, these problems can almost always be prevented, or treated, or reversed if detected at an early stage.

- Skin wounds may be slow to heal, and are more likely to become infected because of reduced immunity. This is not a serious problem – just keep all cuts as clean as possible.
- Infections by viruses and fungi (e.g. *Candida* – see box on p. 83), may occur more readily.
- Some infections may be masked initially because fever is suppressed by the steroids.
- Chickenpox and measles can be far more serious – even fatal – if steroid tablets are being taken, *or have been taken for more than three weeks within the last three months*. This is something to be very careful about (see item 15 on p. 143).
- Prolonged use can increase the risk of chest infections.
- Vaccination with live vaccines can cause problems.
- Older people who once suffered from tuberculosis (TB) may find it comes back.
- Steroids can lead to pregnancy if using an IUD, because IUDs work by inducing mild inflammation in the womb.

The most insidious effect of steroids – and remember again that this is only a hazard of *prolonged high-dose treatment* – is **adrenal suppression**. When steroid tablets are taken for more than three weeks, the adrenal glands' own ability to produce cortisol (see p. 141) starts to be slightly suppressed. The longer the course of steroids, the greater the effect. Stopping the steroids abruptly leaves the body without enough cortisol to protect itself, which, in the very worst cases, can lead to collapse. Less obviously, there may be greater vulnerability to the effects of accidents, serious illnesses, surgery or childbirth – demanding events that would normally stimulate a rise in cortisol production to help the body cope with the stress.

If you take a short course of steroid tablets during this period, there is more risk of side effects than normal. Adrenal suppression can last for 6–12 months after steroid treatment ends. It may be two years before the body can cope with surgery unaided and you will need low doses of steroids to get you through stress of this kind.

Will I look like a weight-lifter?

Absolutely not. The steroids taken by unscrupulous athletes to pump up their muscles artificially are **anabolic steroids**. They are entirely different from the corticosteroids used to treat allergies.

Using steroid tablets safely

Those taking steroid tablets for more than three weeks, or taking a lot of short courses, can protect themselves from serious side effects in the following ways:

1. Weigh yourself every day. Should your weight suddenly start to rise, despite eating normally, consult your doctor: this may be a sign of water retention.

2. If you develop hip pain, swollen ankles, muscle weakness, or acne tell your doctor.

3. Get your blood pressure checked regularly by the doctor.

4. Get your eyes checked regularly by an optician, who can detect any problems before there is irreversible damage.

5. In the case of children, make sure the child's growth is being monitored carefully by the doctor.

6. Stay as active as possible, with plenty of vigorous exercise, to protect against osteoporosis. Avoid getting too thin, as this is also a risk factor for osteoporosis. Reduce your salt intake and don't drink too much alcohol. Ask your doctor to order a bone-density measurement periodically. Following the menopause, women on steroid tablets should consider taking hormone replacement therapy (HRT) as this protects against osteoporosis.

7. Persistent unexplained back pain must be reported to your doctor: this can be a sign of osteoporosis. If you fracture your wrist in a fall (a Colles' fracture) make sure your GP knows about this, and prescribes urgent drug treatment for osteoporosis.

8. See your doctor if you are over-tired, thirsty, or need to pass urine much more frequently – these can sometimes be signs of diabetes.

9. Take your tablets after food to protect the stomach. See your doctor if you have persistent indigestion: coated forms of the tablets may help.

10. If you ever produce black, tarry stools, call your doctor immediately. This is generally a sign of bleeding from the digestive tract.

11. With your doctor's permission, take all your daily steroids as a single dose in the morning. The long gap between one dose and the next stimulates the body to maintain its own steroid-making abilities and so reduces the risk of adrenal suppression. It can also protect against growth problems in children. Even greater protection comes from taking steroids on alternate days – one day on, one day off – although not everyone can keep their symptoms under control with this regime. Obviously, you must consult your doctor before you try. Your dose may need adjusting.

12. Adrenal suppression puts you at risk during any medical procedure. Tell your doctor, dentist, and anyone treating you in an emergency – ***even if you stopped taking steroids up to two years earlier***. You should also carry a Steroid Card at all times, in case you are unconscious. These cards are available from your doctor.

13. Ask the doctor what you should do if you develop any kind of infection or suffer an accident. It is often necessary to increase the dose of steroid tablets.

14. Tell your doctor if you have ever had TB, as this can recur.

15. If you or your child have *not* had measles or chickenpox, avoid contact with anyone suffering from these diseases – or from shingles (herpes zoster) which is caused by the chickenpox virus. ***See your doctor promptly if there is any contact with someone infected.*** Emergency treatment to combat the virus must be started promptly.

16. When being vaccinated, remind the doctor or nurse that you are taking steroid tablets.

17. Never stop taking steroid tablets abruptly if you have been taking them for more than three weeks, as some degree of adrenal suppression may already have begun. Your body needs time to recover its natural level of activity, so reduce the dosage gradually. Get precise instructions from your doctor about how to do this.

18. If you are asthmatic, at the end of any course of steroid tablets lasting more than three weeks, be extra careful about exposure to allergens and asthma triggers. You may be more vulnerable to severe asthma attacks for as much as a year after long-term steroid tablets are stopped, or the dosage reduced.

Watch out for adrenal suppression

If you develop any of the following symptoms after stopping steroids, or while reducing the dose, call your doctor as soon as possible:

- muscle weakness; muscle and joint pain
- feeling 'under the weather'
- mental changes
- scaly or flaking skin
- breathlessness
- lack of appetite; or nausea and vomiting
- fever and weight loss
- painful itchy lumps on the skin.

Note that, very rarely, withdrawal of steroid tablets, or lowering the dose, can unmask a disease called Churg-Strauss Syndrome (see p. 160).

Steroid nose drops and sprays

Most steroid nose drops and nasal sprays contain very low doses of the drug, and produce no significant side effects when used for short periods of time. The safety of these preparations is such that several are available without prescription.

Steroid drops and sprays for the nose are a very effective way of treating hayfever and perennial allergic rhinitis. They can be used after the symptoms have begun, or in advance of encountering the allergen.

Steroids nose drops are also useful in reducing the size of nasal polyps (see p. 30) but only if the drops are inserted correctly. Kneel down and, bending your neck forward as much as possible, put the crown of your head on the floor. Now put the drops in and stay in this position for several minutes while the drops reach their target. Once the polyps have shrunk, the drops can be replaced by a steroid spray which will keep them under control.

Always stick to the stated dose, as with any drugs – don't use the drops or spray more often than you should. If you have a cold or other infection in the nose, stop using steroid drops and sprays until it is better. Following surgical operations on the nose, ask your doctor's advice before using steroid drops or sprays.

Side effects

Minor short-term side effects may include dryness and irritation in the nose and throat, and disturbances of smell and taste. Nosebleeds might occur and should be reported to your doctor. When inserting the drops, try to keep them away from the central partition of the nose (the septum), as this is the part most vulnerable to bleeding. If you are a long-term user of steroid nose drops, your doctor should check the membranes in your nose regularly, to be sure that they are not becoming thinned. Eye checks may also be advisable with long-term use, as glaucoma can occur.

Allergic reactions to the steroid are possible, and they can cause bronchospasm (contraction of the airway muscles) though this is unusual. You should obviously stop using the drops and see your doctor if this occurs.

With very high doses of steroids in the nose, or prolonged treatment, some systemic side effects might occur. The main cause for concern is children's growth (see box on p. 145) – their height should be checked regularly.

Steroid eye drops

Steroid eye drops are sometimes given for severe inflammation of the eye during the hayfever season. However, the eye is vulnerable to infections if treated with steroid drops, and such treatment requires close medical supervision.

Side effects

Be extremely careful about infections – don't rub your eyes with your fingers, for example, or dry around your eyes with a towel unless it is absolutely clean. Follow your doctor's instructions very carefully, and go back immediately if your eyes become more uncomfortable, if redness increases, or if you have any other cause for concern.

Steroid eye drops are rarely used for more than a few weeks. With prolonged use, there is a risk of two serious side effects, glaucoma and cataract.

Using two lots of steroid

Allergy sufferers who need steroid nose drops or a nasal spray, as well as a steroid inhaler, often worry that they are getting too much steroid overall.

In fact there is no cause for concern, unless you are taking very high doses of inhaled steroid, in which case talk the matter over with your doctor. The amount in most nose drops and sprays is quite small and the same is true of steroid eye drops. In all cases, relatively little gets into the bloodstream.

If you have allergies in the nose, this may well be making your asthma worse, and using steroid nose drops can be very helpful for the asthma symptoms (see p. 39).

If an asthmatic child inhales relatively high doses of steroids for many years, his or her growth can be stunted. However, only a small number of children need these high doses, and with low to moderate doses most children's growth is unaffected. They may experience a short-term slow-down in growth, but their eventual height should be normal.

Unfortunately, there are a few children whose growth is stunted even by relatively low doses of inhaled steroids – and it is impossible to predict which children will respond in this way. However, if it is noticed in good time, and if the steroids can be withdrawn safely, the child's growth rate will almost certainly recover.

Your GP or paediatrician should be monitoring your child's growth. You can also measure this yourself, and go back to the doctor if you are concerned. Keep the risks in perspective – uncontrolled severe asthma also stunts children's growth, as well as endangering the child in far more serious ways, so don't stop using the steroid inhaler.

Steroid inhalers

Inhaled steroids are a key part of the modern treatment of asthma (see p. 157).

Side effects

As with other topical treatments, inhaled steroids are a great deal safer than steroid tablets. However, some of the drug does get into the bloodstream, and with high-dose inhaled steroids taken for several years, the levels can be high enough to cause systemic side effects such as osteoporosis (see p. 142).

The dose is the crucial factor here. The packaging or information leaflet that comes with your inhaler will tell you how much of the drug is delivered with each inhalation. To interpret the information about side effects correctly, you need to know your total daily consumption of inhaled steroid, and whether this corresponds to a low, medium or high dose:

- For budesonide or beclomethasone, two of the more common steroids, less than 400 mcg (micrograms) per day counts as a low dose for adults and children over the age of five. A moderate dose is 500–800 mcg per day, and more than 800 mcg a day is a high dose.
- For fluticasone (Flixotide), halve these figures (i.e. 400 mcg a day is a high dose).
- In the case of children under five, all these figures should be halved (e.g. a high dose of beclomethasone is more than 400 mcg a day).
- For other steroids, check with your pharmacist.

Anyone taking a low or moderate dose has very little to worry about as regards systemic side effects. Only those inhaling high-dose steroids for many years need feel concerned.

If you may be at risk of systemic side effects, follow the protective measures described for steroid tablets on p. 143. Apart from growth suppression in children (see box above) the most likely effects are osteoporosis, adrenal suppression, and a recurrence of tuberculosis.

You can minimise the risk of systemic side effects from steroid inhalers by swallowing as little as possible of the steroid. Always rinse out your mouth, gargle, *and spit out the water* after using your inhaler. Using your steroid inhaler morning and evening, just before brushing your teeth, will make it much easier to remember to do this.

Bear in mind that inhaling steroids regularly will help you avoid the need for steroid tablets. Asthmatics who are worried about side effects sometimes skip doses of their inhaled steroids, then find their asthma is much worse and that they need a course of steroid tablets. Frequent courses of tablets increase the risk of serious side effects.

Minor local side effects of inhaled steroids include hoarseness and short-lived coughing due to direct irritation of the throat. These are no cause for concern.

If you are regularly inhaling steroids from a nebuliser, make sure the mask fits really well (see p. 163).

Because steroids reduce the immune defences a little, one common side effect of inhaling them is a throat infection by *Candida* (see box on p. 83). Oesophageal infections with *Candida* can also happen but these are rare; the symptoms are heartburn and indigestion. Gargling with warm water after each inhalation will help prevent *Candida* infections. There are also anti-fungal lozenges, if you are still having trouble.

Keep inhaled steroids away from your lips if you suffer from cold sores (herpes infections around the mouth). These can be made worse with steroids.

Fortunately, other infections are no more common when using inhaled steroids. This includes chest infections.

Steroid creams and ointments

Steroid creams and ointments are used for both atopic eczema and contact dermatitis. By delivering the drug to the place where it is needed, they reduce the dose required to an absolute minimum and, if used correctly, are very safe. Dr Ernst Epstein, a dermatologist at the University of California, observes 'All too often I encounter children who are miserable with uncontrolled atopic dermatitis because of their parents' unjustified fears of steroid side effects. It is cruel to the child and the family to forgo topical medication.'

It is very important to use a steroid cream of the right strength. For example, applying a 1% hydrocortisone cream (available without prescription) to severe atopic eczema will be of no value. Similarly, only applying a prescribed cream occasionally, or only once a day when the doctor said three times a day, will mean that the rash never really succumbs to the treatment.

Keeping old tubes of steroid cream in the bathroom cabinet, and using these rather than the newly prescribed cream, is another frequent mistake. If the earlier prescription was for a weaker steroid cream, that is not quite up to the job, you won't get the symptoms under control.

Inadequate treatment means that the rash goes on longer, so you probably apply *more* steroid in the long run – which exposes you to a *greater* risk of local side effects. It is far better to use a moderately strong steroid cream for a short period of time and get the inflammation fully under control.

Remember that steroid creams are absorbed far more effectively immediately after a bath or shower, so this is a good time to apply them (see p. 48).

Don't stop using steroid creams too soon. The skin looks healthy and happy long before it is completely healed underneath. You must continue until the 'hidden healing' has occurred. As a rough guide, the point when the skin looks good is just the halfway point: so the steroid creams should be continued for the same length of time again. If it took three weeks to get to the point where the skin looks fine, then you should go on applying the steroid creams for another three weeks after that.

Generally speaking, it is a good idea to phase steroid creams out slowly, especially after using them for a long period of time. Stopping abruptly may cause the rash to flare up again – this is called a **rebound effect.**

Once you have atopic eczema under good control, you will still need some steroid cream at home for dealing with relapses. As soon as you notice any rough, itchy skin, apply the cream twice daily for three days, then once daily for another three days. This should be enough to curb the outbreak of eczema before it really gets going.

Side effects

To assess the risk of side effects from your steroid cream or ointment, you need to know how strong it is. Four grades are recognised:

- mild (corresponding to non-prescription hydrocortisone cream)
- moderately potent
- potent
- very potent.

Ask your doctor or pharmacist which grade corresponds to your cream, so that you can make sense of the information given below.

Unfortunately, if steroid creams are not used correctly, there are some quite serious local side effects. Any steroid cream that is strong enough to work is also strong enough to produce side effects if over-used, so this is a delicate balancing act. The main local side effects are thinning of the skin and striae (stretch marks). Teenagers and pregnant women are particularly susceptible to stretch marks if using steroid creams.

It is important to take care because these side effects can be irreversible. The stretch marks, for example, may fade in time but never entirely disappear. Sustained over-use of steroid creams can produce permanent thinning of the skin. Thinning of the skin on the face may produce redness, with small blood vessels showing through. The fingertips may develop painful cracks.

Note that these side effects can come on very gradually. Some may be mistaken for symptoms of the disease itself.

Other local side effects may include an outbreak of spots that look rather like acne. Increased hairiness or change in skin colour are also possible. Fortunately these effects are reversible.

To avoid side effects, always follow the instructions for using steroid creams carefully, and don't apply too much or too often. If you have not been given clear instructions by your doctor on the quantity to use, go back and ask for more information. Ideally, you should actually be shown the correct amount of the cream to use each time. Remember to wash your fingers after applying steroid creams.

If potent or very potent steroid creams are slapped on with abandon, enough is absorbed into the bloodstream to produce **systemic side effects**, comparable to those that can occur with steroid tablets (see p. 142).

With very potent steroid creams, used for a long period of time, there is some risk of slight systemic side effects even though the instructions for use are carefully followed. Young children are more susceptible. Bear in mind that covering the skin with bandages after applying the cream increases the amount absorbed into the bloodstream. The degree of adrenal suppression caused by using the cream (see p. 142) is probably going to remain unnoticed in everyday life, but a major illness, accident, childbirth or a surgical operation might reveal the problem – so tell medical staff what you have been using.

Different areas of the body respond differently to steroid creams. The skin of the face, and within skin folds, is more sensitive and generally requires a lower-strength cream, while the palms of the hands and the soles of the feet require a higher strength. The genitals and the area around the anus are particularly sensitive, and can become *permanently* damaged (and then a source of intense discomfort) by strong steroid creams: some dermatologists recommend using nothing stronger than 1% hydrocortisone.

Make sure you see your doctor regularly when using steroid creams continuously, especially if:
- you are using very potent steroid cream
- you are applying a potent or moderately potent steroid cream over more than 20% of your body for more than a month
- you are applying potent steroid cream to a baby or young child.

The vehicle – the cream or ointment base in which the steroid is carried – is important because sensitivity reactions can occur to certain of its ingredients (see p. 44). Eczema sufferers can even become sensitised to the steroid itself, and this problem is difficult to diagnose because patch tests with steroids often give false negatives (see p. 91). If you are not getting better, ask the doctor if this could be the explanation. (**If a rash gets worse and starts to spread** when you begin using steroid creams, go back and see the doctor very promptly – you may have an infection called *tinea*, or ringworm, which flourishes all the more when steroid creams are applied.)

Some common brand names

Common brand names of steroids include:

nose drops – Betnesol, Vista-Methasone

nasal sprays – Beclometasone, Beconase, Flixonase, Nasacort, Nasonex, Rhinocort Aqua, Syntaris

eye drops – Betnesol, Cloburate, Maxidex, Predsol, Vista-Methasone

inhalers – Aerobec, Becloforte, Beclometasone, Becotide, Flixotide, Pulmicort

tablets – Betnesol, Cortisyl, Dexamethasone, Medrone, Prednesol, Prednisolone,

creams – Adcortyl, Betnovate, Dermovate, Fucibet, Synalar

Other anti-allergy drugs

An allergic reaction is a lengthy, complex process, and the various anti-allergy drugs all work on different stages of that process. That is why it often makes sense to use several different drugs for the same allergic condition: they each tackle the problem in their own way.

Steroids (see p. 140) intervene at a very late stage, quelling the inflammation that follows on from an allergic reaction. Using a steroid is rather like calling the fire brigade to put out a fire, whereas using an antihistamine (see p. 138) is like having fire-proof doors, to prevent the fire spreading at an early stage. Cromoglycate-type drugs (see below) intervene at an even earlier stage. They are like basic fire prevention – teaching children not to play with matches, or fitting smoke detectors.

Anti-leukotriene drugs (see p. 149) work at roughly the same stage of the process as antihistamines but tackle an entirely different aspect of the allergic reaction.

Cromoglycate-type drugs

These drugs are also referred to as mast-cell stabilisers or mast-cell blockers.

There are three drugs in this group, sodium cromoglycate (also spelled cromoglicate), nedocromil sodium, and lodoxamide. All operate at an early stage of the allergic reaction, stopping it before it actually starts. They stabilise the outer membrane of the mast cells (see box on p. 12), which prevents the allergic response from occurring.

This is a far more satisfactory way of dealing with an allergic reaction than trying to tackle it after the reaction has occurred. But from a purely practical point of view, it has a drawback. In order to work at all, these drugs must reach the mast cells *in advance of* the allergen. They are of very little use if taken after the allergic reaction has begun.

For those who are taking cromoglycate-type drugs on a regular schedule, several times a day, it is very important to be conscientious about taking them on time. This maintains the protective effect of the drug, without any gaps.

If you are using these drugs on an 'as-needed' basis, you should take them 30 minutes before an allergen is encountered, or 30 minutes before a bout of exercise, if they are being prescribed for exercise-induced asthma. (Note that children sometimes respond differently, getting protection from these drugs immediately.)

The effect of these drugs takes time to build up. You should take them regularly for at least four weeks before deciding whether they are helping you or not.

One point in favour of cromoglycate-type drugs is that they are extremely safe, with few or no

Some common brand names
Common brand names of cromoglycate-type drugs include:
  inhalers – Cromogen Easi-Breathe, Intal, Tilade
  eye drops – Hay-Crom, Opticrom, Rapitil, Vividrin, Viz-on
  nose sprays – Rynacrom, Vividrin
  capsules – Nalcrom

side effects in most people. Sadly, they do not work for everyone. A fairly high percentage of children respond well to them, but the response rate is much lower for adults. Nevertheless, adult allergy sufferers, especially those who need steroids to control their symptoms, should always be given the opportunity to try out these drugs. When cromoglycate-type drugs do work, they are very effective and almost always trouble-free, so they are a good alternative to steroids.

Both sodium cromoglycate and nedocromil sodium are available in inhaler form for asthma (see p. 157). Sodium cromoglycate is also available as nose drops for hayfever and other nasal allergies.

All three drugs are available as eye drops. Recent evidence suggests that sodium cromoglycate drops are less effective than the other two, particularly for the treatment of severe allergic conjunctivitis (inflammation of the eye).

Sodium cromoglycate is available in capsule form for food allergy. Note that these capsules are of very limited value in food allergy, and are certainly not a substitute for food avoidance. They do reduce sensitivity a little and can sometimes be helpful for those with multiple food allergies (see p. 67).

Side effects of these drugs

There are no serious side effects at all for nedocromil sodium. Cromoglycate can, very rarely, cause joint pain and swelling. An allergic reaction to the drug itself is even more uncommon. Stop taking the drug and see your doctor promptly if either of these occurs.

The only other side effects that have occasionally been reported are headache, nausea and vomiting. None of these indicates any damaging effect by the drugs – they are all minor side effects.

Eye drops containing these drugs may cause stinging and burning when inserted, but this is a minor side effect and usually wears off. Flushing and dizziness have sometimes been reported with lodoxamide eye drops.

Nose drops may also cause local irritation. This could be due to the drug itself, in which case it is a minor side effect. Alternatively, the irritation may be due to the preservative used or some other non-drug ingredient (see box on p.33).

Occasionally cromoglycate nose drops cause bronchospasm – contraction of the airway muscles – but this tends to wear off quite quickly. Bronchospasm can also occur when cromoglycate-type drugs are inhaled (see p. 157).

Anti-leukotriene drugs

These drugs, which have a set of very specific effects (see p. 159), were originally designed to treat asthma. Their potential for treating other allergic diseases is currently being explored:

• Several studies show that they work well for **perennial allergic rhinitis**. In one trial involving people allergic to cats, taking an anti-leukotriene drug regularly for a week reduced the symptoms brought on by cat allergen.

• They are especially useful for both rhinitis and asthma in patients suffering from **triad** (see p. 28). Research shows that they also reduce asthmatic reactions to very small test doses of aspirin, but they don't give protection against anaphylaxis brought on by normal doses.

• They have also been used successfully in cases of **chronic urticaria** and for some patients with **delayed pressure urticaria.** It seems plausible that they would also be helpful for chronic urticaria linked to aspirin sensitivity.

• Preliminary trials suggest that zileuton (brand names Leutrol, Zyflo) could perhaps be useful in **atopic eczema**. This anti-leukotriene drug helps to keep eosinophils (see p. 19) away, which may explain its beneficial effects. Eosinophils show up in the skin once eczema is well established, and help keep inflammation going.

For side effects of these drugs see pp. 159–61.

More powerful anti-allergy drugs

Occasionally people with severe allergies, who are on constant high doses of steroid tablets, or who fail to respond to steroids, need treatment with powerful anti-inflammatory drugs, such as methotrexate or cyclosporin. These drugs suppress the immune system, and extremely careful monitoring for side effects is needed. Various new anti-allergy drugs may soon become available. One of these, omalizumab (Xolair) blocks allergic reactions by binding to IgE (see box on p. 12) and inactivating it.

Adrenaline (epinephrine)

Anyone who has suffered anaphylactic shock (see p. 58) should be carrying a special syringe, called an auto-injector, loaded with adrenaline. The injector is very simple to operate and is designed for emergencies. Most allergy sufferers, even children, can give themselves the injection – or a parent or other adult can give it.

Some asthmatics, and those with food allergy who suffer swelling of the throat, may be given adrenaline in inhaler form as well. This can be useful as an additional treatment but it's definitely not a substitute for an injector.

Detailed instructions for using adrenaline in a crisis are given on pp. 98–9.

Wherever you go, take your injector with you. Always keep it close at hand: you need to be able to use it within minutes of the allergic reaction starting. You may be unable to speak (and therefore unable to ask someone else to fetch it) quite soon after the attack begins. The injector can be damaged by sunlight and excess heat, so don't leave it in a parked car on a summer's day.

If you are going camping or hiking somewhere remote, ask your doctor for a second injector, or one that can deliver multiple injections. Also ask about the maximum number of injections that can be given, and never exceed this total.

It is vital that you are shown exactly how to use the auto-injector. Canadian researchers discovered that only one out of four health professionals got the technique entirely correct when demonstrating how to use an auto-injector. In this study, pharmacists

were much the best bet as regards accurate instructions. Dummy injectors are useful for training purposes and most pharmacies have them.

When the adrenaline auto-injectors expire, they can be very useful for practising with, or for showing a new baby-sitter or teacher – practise on an orange or grapefruit.

Side effects of this drug

The important side effects of adrenaline involve the heart. Anyone with a heart condition should be given special advice by their doctor about using adrenaline. The same goes for people with diabetes, hyperthyroidism or high blood pressure, and anyone taking tricyclic anti-depressants. Bear in mind that if you are taking beta-blockers for a heart condition, adrenaline may not have much effect. The crucial thing, in all these cases, is to talk to your doctor *in advance* of an emergency, and get appropriate advice.

There are quite a few minor side effects from adrenaline, such as anxiety, trembling, nausea, sweating, dizziness and cold hands and feet. These soon wear off.

Drugs that can make you worse

Aspirin and its relatives have a very bad effect on some people with rhinitis and/or asthma (see box on p. 151). Unfortunately, recent research shows that **paracetamol** is not safe either. It makes asthma more likely to develop in those who do not yet have the disease, and increases the severity of asthma symptoms for those who do. Unlike aspirin, paracetamol affects everyone, because it lowers the levels of a natural antioxidant, called glutathione, which the body makes to protect the lungs from oxidants. The greatest effects are seen in people who take paracetamol regularly (once a week or more), but even an occasional dose makes some difference.

All the other drugs that can make you worse are prescription drugs, and your doctor should be alert to the dangers. But doctors are overworked and sometimes forget, so it is sensible to know about the risks for yourself. If you have any doubt about the drugs you are taking, ask a pharmacist.

Beta-blockers are a major hazard for people with allergies. They can make the airways contract, and can bring on a serious asthma attack. They also make anaphylaxis more likely in someone who already has allergic reactions (see p. 59) and they increase the risk of a severe reaction to immunotherapy (see p. 166) or skin-prick tests (see p. 91). Beta-blockers are prescribed for high blood pressure, angina and other heart problems, migraine and thyroid disease. There are alternative drugs in all cases. Sometimes asthma develops in people who have been taking beta-blockers for years. The beta-blockers are not responsible for this, but once asthma has begun, they will make symptoms worse. Eye drops for the treatment of glaucoma may also contain beta-blockers and can have a bad effect on asthmatics.

ACE inhibitors, used for heart conditions, may cause a cough and airway narrowing. They may also increase the risk of a severe reaction to immunotherapy.

Female hormones affect asthmatics, so taking the **contraceptive pill** or **hormone replacement therapy** (HRT) may make asthma worse. Progesterone-only contraceptive pills tend to cause fewer problems.

The drug **isoniazid** (INH), prescribed for tuberculosis, makes the body far more susceptible to histamine in foods (see p. 200).

An allergic reaction to a specific drug (e.g. penicillin) can also occur in some people, resulting in urticaria, or even anaphylactic shock.

Aspirin sensitivity

Aspirin sensitivity is not an allergic reaction, because neither IgE nor mast cells are involved. What causes this problem is a metabolic abnormality – a malfunction in one aspect of the body's chemistry. The details of this are very complicated: you may want to skip the next three paragraphs and simply read about how to cope with the problem.

The exact nature of aspirin sensitivity is still far from clear, but it seems to involve a relatively poor production of **prostaglandins**, combined with a plentiful production of **leukotrienes**. Both these substances are **messenger chemicals** which, broadly speaking, promote inflammation. But the details of their pro-inflammatory activities differ. It seems that, ideally, the body should have a harmonious balance between the two, and an imbalance produces problems.

Both prostaglandins and leukotrienes are manufactured from certain fats that are found in the diet. These fats, the raw materials, are worked on initially by two different **enzymes** – one that leads to the production of prostaglandins and another that leads to the production of leukotrienes.

If one of these enzymes is defective, it may mean that the other is oversupplied with raw materials, resulting in a serious imbalance between prostaglandins and leukotrienes. In those with aspirin sensitivity, or at risk of developing aspirin sensitivity, the enzyme that produces prostaglandins seems to be defective.

Even in the absence of aspirin, this imbalance in the production of prostaglandins and leukotrienes causes problems. It leads to symptoms such as chronic urticaria (see p. 51) or rhinitis, nasal polyps and asthma (a cluster of symptoms that is commonly called **triad** – see p. 28).

Taking aspirin can make the imbalance between prostaglandins and leukotrienes even worse in a person with this underlying abnormality. Aspirin exerts its painkilling effects by disabling the main prostaglandin-making enzyme – the enzyme that is already defective.

When someone with aspirin sensitivity takes aspirin, they may suffer worsening asthma, a severe asthma attack or – the worst-case scenario – collapse. This is a potentially fatal reaction, similar to anaphylaxis, requiring emergency medical treatment (see p. 101).

The greatest puzzle about aspirin sensitivity is why it often takes so long to develop in someone who already has the symptoms of triad – indicating the basic metabolic abnormality. It may be as much as 20 years from when someone has their first triad symptoms to when they begin reacting badly to aspirin.

If you have triad symptoms already, but no aspirin sensitivity yet, what should you do? Unfortunately, there are no safe tests for aspirin sensitivity at present – taking a small dose of aspirin and seeing what happens is very hazardous. It is probably best to assume that you are going to become sensitive to aspirin at some stage, and avoid all aspirin and aspirin-like drugs. Caution is the best plan here because aspirin sensitivity can come on very suddenly, and be life threatening the very first time it occurs. Note that some triad sufferers have polyps and rhinitis but no asthma until they actually develop aspirin sensitivity – a dose of aspirin suddenly brings on their first asthma attack plus other symptoms of aspirin sensitivity.

Avoiding aspirin itself is not difficult, but aspirin-like drugs pose more of a problem. Every year there are a number of deaths from these drugs. Some cases occur because a busy doctor momentarily forgets that a patient should not take these drugs. The drugs that need to be avoided are all known as **non-steroidal anti-inflammatory drugs** (NSAIDs), **COX-1 inhibitors** or **COX-2 inhibitors**. However you will not see either of these names on the packet. These drugs are very widely used for pain relief (e.g. in headache and backache remedies such as Nurofen), for the treatment of arthritis, and for several other inflammatory diseases.

There are dozens of non-steroidal anti-inflammatory drugs available, and many are sold under several different brand names. The list grows every year, as new drugs or new brands are launched. The only way to avoid these drugs is to be very cautious:

• When buying any cold- or flu-remedies, painkillers, medicines for sprains or sports injuries (including those you apply directly to the skin), headache tablets or migraine tablets, always buy them at a chemist's shop rather than a supermarket, and check with the pharmacist that they do not contain aspirin or aspirin-like drugs.

• Be cautious also about remedies for an upset stomach. A few (e.g. Alka-Seltzer) contain aspirin.

• Don't take any drugs unless you are 100% sure of what they contain. Remember that the ingredients of a familiar brand name can sometimes change – read the label every time.

• When a doctor prescribes any new drug, always mention that you are sensitive to aspirin, or that you have triad symptoms. Alternatively, check with the pharmacist when the prescription is filled.

• Aspirin-free painkillers almost always contain paracetamol, a drug which can cause a severe reaction (similar to the collapse induced by aspirin itself) in about 5% of those with aspirin sensitivity. If you are taking paracetamol for the first time, start with half a tablet. Be sure that, for the next 2–3 hours, you have a way of getting to hospital quickly should you start to feel ill. (Note that paracetamol has an entirely separate effect, increasing the severity of asthma, and it is best not to take it too often – see box on p. 150.)

Avoiding all aspirin-like drugs will prevent you having anaphylaxis or severe attacks of asthma. Unfortunately, triad symptoms will not go away however careful you are about avoiding aspirin.

It is well worth trying the new anti-leukotriene drugs (see p. 149), especially if you have aspirin-induced asthma. They seem to help with triad symptoms by curtailing the activities of leukotrienes and so redressing the balance between leukotrienes and prostaglandins.

Drugs for asthma

The drug treatment of asthma is far more complex than for any other allergic disease. Drugs prescribed for asthma fall into two basic categories: those that open up the airways by relaxing the airway muscles, called **relievers,** and those that treat the inflammation in the lining of the airways, called **preventers**. The former offer a 'quick fix' – like taking an aspirin when you have a headache. Just as the actual cause of the headache is not treated by an aspirin, so the actual cause of the asthma attack is not addressed by relievers. Preventers, on the other hand, tackle the basic problem – the inflammation that triggers the contraction of the airway muscles (see p. 36).

In the past ten years, there has been a quiet revolution in asthma treatment, with far more people being given preventer inhalers, usually low-dose steroids. The aim is to get the airways in better condition, with the inflammation thoroughly damped down, so that the airway muscles don't go into spasm. The ultimate objective is to make people far less reliant on reliever inhalers, because the potential hazards of over-using them are now realised.

The details of modern asthma management, and the different approaches used, are described on p. 160, following the discussion of the main types of drug used for asthma treatment.

Beta-2 relievers (beta-agonists)

Our airways open up when we produce adrenaline. This is the body's natural response to feeling angry or frightened. The adrenaline widens the airways so that we can run faster or fight more vigorously.

Adrenaline (epinephrine), given as a drug, was among the earliest treatments for asthma. However, it also stimulates the heart to beat faster and raises the blood pressure. While it is useful for emergency treatment (see p. 150) the side effects make it too hazardous for routine use.

The beta-2 relievers work by mimicking adrenaline – they bind to the same receptors in the airways, the beta-2 receptors. Binding to these receptors stimulates the airway muscles to relax, so that the airways open up.

In other respects, the beta-2 relievers are *not* like adrenaline. Clever chemical manipulation has made them sufficiently different from adrenaline to have little effect on the heart and other organs, when taken at normal doses.

Beta-2 relievers are best taken by inhalation. Although tablets and syrup are available these are far more likely to bring on side effects, because the dose needed is so much bigger.

Inhaled beta-2 relievers target the drug directly on the airways, so the dose can be smaller. They also have the great advantage of taking effect soon after being inhaled, and giving full relief from airway narrowing within 10–15 minutes.

There are two different kinds of beta-2 relievers:

- the traditional **short-acting beta-2 relievers** whose effects last for three to six hours (usually about four). The modern consensus is that these should be used only when needed, not taken routinely.

- the newer **long-acting beta-2 relievers**, which last up to twelve hours. These drugs are prescribed for more severe forms of asthma (see p. 154), and are generally used routinely, twice a day.

A key question for asthma sufferers is: How often can short-acting beta-2 relievers be used? Ideas about this have changed considerably over the last twenty years, and no doctor would now want to have patients using a Ventolin inhaler five, six or more times a day – something that was quite common in the past. This level of need for beta-2 relievers indicates that the asthma is poorly controlled and requires treatment with a preventer, to quell the inflammation in the airways.

Detailed policy on beta-2 relievers still varies from one part of the world to another. UK guidelines state that anyone who needs to use a short-acting beta-2 reliever more than once a day, or who suffers from nocturnal asthma, should be given a preventer as well. The international guideline is more stringent: if a short-acting beta-2 reliever is needed more than three times a week, a preventer should also be prescribed.

How safe are these drugs in the long term?

The cause of the big re-think on beta-2 relievers was an epidemic of asthma-related deaths in New Zealand between 1976 and 1988. The death rate from severe asthma attacks was 2–4 times its previous level for a while, and over a thousand New Zealanders died in the epidemic.

There has been a huge controversy over what exactly caused these deaths. Most researchers now agree that the main cause was a new brand of inhaler that delivered a double dose of the drug fenoterol, a short-acting beta-2 reliever with a very powerful effect on the airways and quite high levels of side effects involving the heart. The same brand of inhaler may have been linked to increased death rates in Canada and Germany.

Research suggests that the problem was greatest in New Zealand because sales of the new inhaler were highest there, and because many patients got their inhalers through repeat prescriptions. As a result, people whose asthma was deteriorating badly were not seen by a doctor and were using large amounts of beta-2 reliever, rather than taking preventer drugs. This is now believed to be a major cause of asthma deaths. There are three separate factors involved:

- The beta-2 reliever covers up the effects of the severe inflammation of the airways. People feel reasonably well, because the reliever is opening up their airways, and don't realise just how bad their asthma really is. The untreated inflammation in the airways can eventually lead to a very serious, and potentially fatal, asthma attack.

- The short-acting beta-2 reliever, used regularly, makes the airways more sensitive to exercise, and to allergens such as dust mite or pollen. This means that an asthmatic who is already allergic to these allergens reacts to them at much lower levels in the air.

- The airways become less and less responsive to the beta-2 reliever itself, so that when a serious attack occurs, requiring hospital treatment, huge doses of beta-2 reliever are needed to open up the airways. These massive doses carry a risk of serious side effects involving the heart.

The details of the New Zealand epidemic still evoke controversy. Was fenoterol itself, which is stronger than other beta-2 relievers, the cause of the deaths? Or was it just that the inhaler delivered a double dose – would any short-acting beta-2 reliever be dangerous at twice the normal dose? Or was it over-use of all beta-2 relievers and lack of preventer drugs?

Some common brand names

Common brand names include:

short-acting beta-2 relievers in inhalers – Aerolin, Airomir, Bricanyl, Ventolin

short-acting beta-2 relievers in tablets – Bambec, Bricanyl, Volmax

short-acting beta-2 relievers in syrup – Monovent, Ventolin

long-acting beta-2 relievers in inhalers – Bambec, Foradil, Oxis, Serevent

Until this is resolved, safety-conscious asthmatics may want to assume that any of these possibilities could be correct. An ultra-cautious approach would include:

- Avoiding fenoterol if possible (it is still available in both double-dose and single-dose inhalers – brand name Berotec)
- Not using double-dose inhalers of any beta-2 reliever (i.e. inhalers that deliver 200 mcg/micrograms per puff)
- Not routinely taking two puffs of a single-dose inhaler (check with your doctor if you have been told to take two puffs)
- Using any short-acting beta-2 reliever only 'as needed' – which should be once a day or less according to UK guidelines. Note that, with this level of use, there is absolutely no risk from these drugs: it is only regular over-use that is damaging and dangerous.
- Using a peak-flow meter and ensuring that you are assessed regularly by your doctor
- Always taking your preventer medication as prescribed.

Since about 1990, the death rate from asthma has been falling, particularly in countries with a policy of reducing use of beta-2 relievers, and increasing inhaled steroids. The death rate in New Zealand is now the lowest it has been for 50 years, and at the same level as in other Western countries.

Unnecessary alarm

While investigating the causes of the New Zealand epidemic, medical researchers discovered that patients inhaling a short-acting beta-2 reliever four times a day had more irritable airways after just two weeks. Their airways were also less responsive to the drug, even after this brief period of use.

Some researchers began to ask if the asthma epidemic itself – the increasing number of cases of asthma – *could actually be due to these drugs.* Maybe children with mild wheezing, which might have cleared up if left untreated (and which would have gone untreated in the past) were becoming full-blown asthmatics *because* they were now using beta-2 inhalers?

Many doctors became very concerned about these questions, and a leading medical journal published an article with the provocative title: 'Worldwide worsening wheezing – is the cure the cause?' That was in 1992. Since then, much more research has been done, and it is clear that this particular fear about beta-2 relievers was unfounded.

Unfortunately, there are a few books and other publications around that are spreading unnecessary alarm about these drugs by reporting the debate as it was in 1992. They have taken up that question 'Is the cure the cause?', assumed that the answer is 'yes', and ignored all the subsequent research, which shows the opposite.

Beta-2 relievers in severe asthma

A few patients with severe asthma remain breathless and wheezy, even though they are inhaling moderate doses of a steroid preventer every day. Increasing the dose of inhaled steroids does not make a huge difference to their symptoms, and it substantially raises the risk of steroid side effects.

Taking a **long-acting beta-2 reliever** frequently works wonders for such patients. These relatively new drugs relax the airway muscles, and go on working for 12 hours or more.

There has obviously been concern about long-acting beta-2 relievers having the same sort of insidious side effects as their short-acting colleagues (see p. 153), and so increasing the likelihood of deaths from asthma. However, studies of people taking these drugs suggest that the risks are minimal. Certainly, long-acting drugs taken twice a day are very much safer than short-acting drugs taken four times a day.

Other studies show that the chemical differences of the long-acting drugs, as well as prolonging their effects, also give them a more complex set of actions in the body. For example, they improve the effect of steroids in calming inflammation, and may even have some small anti-inflammatory effect of their own.

Doctors believe that, for patients with troublesome asthma, the benefits of long-acting beta-2 relievers greatly outweigh the risks. But they should only be used in combination with inhaled steroids. Various other options, such as allergen avoidance and the new anti-leukotriene drugs (see p. 159), should probably be investigated as well.

If you are taking long-acting beta-2 relievers, do use them regularly, once every 12 hours – the good effect gradually builds up with consistent use.

Generally speaking, you should not take additional doses in between. These are not intended for use if you have a sudden asthma attack – your doctor will prescribe a short-acting beta-2 reliever for this. This limitation on the use of long-acting beta-2 relievers is certainly appropriate for salmeterol (which was the first of the long-acting beta-2 relievers to be developed) because it is very slow to take effect on the airways. However, one of the newer long-acting beta-2 relievers, called formoterol, begins to work just as quickly as a short-acting beta-2 reliever. Formoterol could, in theory, be used on an 'as-needed' basis to combat asthma attacks. You may want to discuss this possibility with your doctor.

Finally, don't stop taking your preventer drug (e.g. inhaled steroid or cromoglycate), even if you feel a lot better. Long-acting beta-2 relievers are *not* a substitute for preventers.

Some patients with very severe asthma need to take regular doses of short-acting beta-2 relievers *as well as* long-acting beta-2 relievers. You should obviously follow the advice of your asthma specialist closely if you are on this kind of drug regime, and not change anything without approval. However, it might be worth discussing other options, such as anti-leukotriene drugs. In addition, do all you can to combat your asthma in other ways – by reducing allergen exposure, avoiding asthma triggers (see p. 39), and employing various other self-help measures (see p. 41).

Immediate side effects of beta-2 relievers

Minor immediate side effects of these drugs include:

- headache
- nervousness, trembling, restlessness, anxiety; children may become more excitable.
- flushing
- dry mouth
- muscle cramps.

These side effects – all of which are due to the resemblance of beta-2 relievers to adrenaline – usually wear off quite quickly. Some long-acting beta-2 relievers may cause nausea and vomiting.

A pounding heart is usually a relatively minor side effect, but it can be more serious, and should be reported to your doctor.

A few asthmatics find that their airways tighten up when these drugs are inhaled, rather than opening. This is called **paradoxical bronchoconstriction**. If this happens, stop using the inhaler and see your doctor as soon as you can.

Even more rarely, asthmatics can develop allergic reactions to the drugs, or suffer hallucinations or seizures. Obviously you should stop using the inhaler immediately if you experience side effects of this kind, and should see your doctor.

There can be an interaction between beta-2 relievers and other drugs or medical conditions. Should you need a diuretic, tell the doctor or pharmacist that you are also taking a beta-2 reliever, and ask which types of diuretic are safe. If you have high blood pressure, a heart problem, or a thyroid condition, make sure the doctor remembers this when prescribing beta-2 relievers.

Asthma alert

If you ever find that your short-acting beta-2 reliever has no effect within ten minutes, or is needed more than once every four hours, this indicates a serious asthma attack and you need urgent medical help (see p. 100).

During a severe asthma attack, while getting to hospital or waiting for a doctor to arrive, up to 30 puffs of a short-acting beta-2 reliever should be taken as an emergency treatment, to get the airways open. *There is a risk of death if you **don't** use the reliever fully in this situation.* (This emergency dose is safe for almost everyone, but there may be risks if you have a heart condition – get detailed advice from your doctor in advance.)

Ephedrine

Ephedrine and orciprenaline (brand name Alupent) belong to the previous generation of reliever drugs. They are chemically very similar to adrenaline and therefore cause a lot of side effects, especially involving the heart.

These drugs are no longer recommended, and will soon be phased out completely. Some older asthmatics may still be using them, just because they have been on them for years and no one has reviewed their treatment.

If you are taking such drugs, ask your doctor about switching to a newer form of reliever – it will be more effective in treating your asthma, as well as having fewer side effects.

Anti-cholinergics

These drugs, also known as anti-muscarinics, are relievers. However, they work in a completely different way from the beta-2 relievers. They block the action of the **parasympathetic nervous system**, a set of nerves that are the biological equivalent of auto-pilot – working without the intervention of conscious thought. The parasympathetic nervous system has many effects on the body, including keeping the airway muscles nicely toned (see box on p. 235). By blocking the parasympathetic, anti-cholinergics help the airway muscles to relax.

Anti-cholinergics are taken by inhaler, and require 30–90 minutes to achieve their full effects. They should continue working for 3–6 hours.

For most asthmatics, especially those with a strong allergic component to their asthma, anti-cholinergics are generally less effective than beta-2 relievers. But they are useful to children under one year, who may not respond to beta-2 relievers. They

also have a role where asthma is combined with chronic bronchitis – here the anti-cholinergics can sometimes be more effective than beta-2 relievers – and they are particularly useful for asthma with a lot of mucus, because blocking the parasympathetic tends to reduce mucus production. For severe asthmatics, anti-cholergenics may be combined with beta-2 relievers.

Anti-cholinergics should be taken only when needed, not regularly several times a day. If used regularly, they can make the airways more sensitive, just as short-acting beta-2 relievers can (see p. 153).

Side effects

Minor side effects of anti-cholinergics may include a dry mouth, blurred vision, constipation, and irritation of the mouth and throat. A few people suffer nausea or difficulty in passing urine.

Serious side effects are rare. Any increase in the stickiness of the sputum coughed up may be a cause for concern, especially in children. If there is an increase in wheezing or coughing, stop taking the drug and see your doctor.

If you already have glaucoma or prostate problems you should be monitored carefully by your doctor, as these conditions can get worse with anti-cholinergic drugs.

When anti-cholinergics are used in a nebuliser, it is vital that the mask fits well (see p. 163).

Anti-cholinergics for the nose

Another use for anti-cholinergics is in nasal sprays, for the treatment of vasomotor rhinitis, a non-allergic condition that is frequently mistaken for allergic rhinitis (see p. 29). In this disorder, the constant flow of mucus is caused by a malfunction of the parasympathetic nervous system, which is why anti-cholinergics work well.

Steroid inhalers

Most asthmatics nowadays are given a steroid inhaler at some point, as part of their asthma treatment (see p. 160). It will probably be a low-dose inhaler, and the risks of side effects from this are very small. Even at higher doses, inhaled steroids are relatively safe. Many people are unnecessarily afraid of inhaled steroids and refuse to use them until their asthma becomes really incapacitating. It is important not to delay using an inhaled steroid for too long, as this could cause permanent damage to the airways: inflammation eventually thickens the airway wall, leaving it less flexible and therefore less capable of widening.

For side effects of inhaled steroids see p. 145, and for common brand names see p. 147.

Steroid tablets

These are usually a treatment of last resort. But when you need them you need them – and if your asthma has got badly out of control, they can, quite literally, be a life-saver. On the other hand, if there are any other means by which you can tackle your asthma, so that you do not need steroid tablets again in the future – avoiding allergens and irritants, for example, or using other preventer treatments – those means should definitely be taken.

For side effects of steroid tablets see pp. 141–3, and for common brand names see p. 147.

Cromoglycate-type drugs

For asthma, these drugs are taken by inhalation only. They work by blocking the allergic reaction (see p. 148), and are therefore a type of preventer drug.

Cromoglycate-type drugs are usually inhaled four times a day, although your doctor may recommend more frequent inhalations to begin with. Once your asthma is well controlled, you may be able to reduce the dosing regime to three times a day, or possibly twice a day: ask your doctor's advice about this.

Should you decide to stop taking these drugs at some point, talk to your doctor first. It is generally best to reduce the dose gradually, over a period of 7–10 days. Some asthmatics need to introduce (or reintroduce) steroids at this time, to maintain control of the airway inflammation.

Side effects of these drugs

When inhaled, cromoglycate-type drugs can produce short-lived irritation in the throat, which may lead to coughing. This sometimes develops into temporary bronchospasm, causing you to wheeze, but this is really only a minor side effect – it does not indicate that the drug is making your asthma worse.

Asthmatics are sometimes advised to use a short-acting beta-2 reliever (such as Ventolin) before their cromoglycate inhaler, to overcome this problem. However, this would involve using the beta-2 reliever four times a day, which is no longer considered a good idea (see pp. 153–4). Talk to your doctor again if you have been given this advice.

Inhalers that combine sodium cromoglycate with a short-acting beta-2 reliever (e.g. Aerocrom) are not recommended for the same reason.

A better way around the problem of throat irritation may be to switch to an aerosol inhaler because the irritation is much less than with dry-powder inhalers. Using a spacer along with the aerosol inhaler (see p. 162) will help even more.

Serious side effects of these drugs are very rare (see p. 149). For common brand names, see p. 148.

Theophylline

Theophylline-type drugs are also known as **xanthines** or methylxanthines. These drugs are chemically similar to caffeine. They cannot be inhaled, so are taken as tablets or syrup. They start working about 30 minutes after being taken and their effects last for 6–8 hours. Slow-release preparations take 90 minutes to start working, but they last 12–24 hours, and are therefore useful for nocturnal asthma.

In Britain, doctors generally regard theophylline-type drugs as reliever drugs (see p. 152), but rather risky ones whose use is only justified for people with severe asthma. They are given, as an additional treatment, to asthmatics who are not responding well to the usual drug programme (see p. 160). Unfortunately, fairly high doses are needed for theophylline-type drugs to act as relievers i.e. to reverse bronchospasm. There is a very narrow margin between such a dose and one that causes major (and sometimes dangerous) side effects.

Such side effects usually occur when the doctor is still trying to work out the correct dose – this varies from one person to another, so prescribing theophylline-type drugs is no easy matter. Once you are established on a safe dose (and provided your general health and your intake of alcohol, nicotine and medicinal drugs does not vary – see p. 158) you can usually continue taking theophylline without serious side effects.

In the United States, many doctors also give theophylline-type drugs, at much lower doses, to people with mild asthma. At these low doses they do not act as relievers, but they have a slight anti-inflammatory effect and therefore act as preventers. The risk of toxicity is much less. Taking low doses of theophylline allows people with mild asthma to reduce their use of beta-2 relievers. However, inhaled steroids are usually more effective in this role, and are the preferred treatment outside the United States.

Side effects of these drugs

Typical side effects include nausea, vomiting, stomach pains, diarrhoea (sometimes with blood), headache, anxiety, restlessness, insomnia, dizziness, pounding heart or irregular heartbeat.

Any side effect of these drugs should be taken seriously and reported to your doctor as soon as possible. If you cannot get an appointment quickly, it may be best to stop taking the drug before seeing the doctor, as long as you have other drugs to control your asthma. Call your doctor for advice.

It is remarkably easy to overdose when taking these drugs at higher doses (see p. 157). Such overdoses can be fatal. The symptoms include repeated vomiting, shaking, feeling unusually hot, needing to urinate frequently, severe thirst, maniacal behaviour, and irregular heartbeat (palpitations). Delirium and convulsions may occur shortly afterwards, so get hospital treatment *urgently* if you have any of these symptoms.

Unfortunately, a serious overdose can sometimes occur in people who have taken theophylline-type drugs without trouble for many years. There may be no advance warning that anything is wrong – no mild side effects preceding the serious ones. To protect yourself against this, you need regular blood tests from your doctor.

One fundamental problem with theophylline-type drugs is that many different factors – including diet, illnesses other than asthma, and taking other drugs – can alter the way your body deals with the drug. If your liver is breaking the drug down more slowly than usual, the amount in your blood will rapidly increase, and can reach toxic levels.

These are steps that can help prevent an overdose with theophylline-type drugs:

- If you start taking a new drug of any kind, or stop taking a drug (especially the contraceptive pill), or if you change your intake of nicotine or alcohol, ask your doctor – *preferably in advance* – if your dose of theophylline-type drug needs changing.
- A great many drugs interact with theophylline-type drugs, including the new anti-leukotriene drugs. You should always be cautious with any new drug, but take particular care with two antibiotics – ciprofloxacin (brand name Ciproxin) and erythromycin (various brand names) – and with cimetidine (various brand names), used for stomach ulcers and heartburn.
- If you have flu vaccinations, or develop certain illnesses, especially viral infections, heart disease or liver disease, watch for the typical side effects of theophylline-type drugs (see above) and consult your doctor immediately if any occur. These conditions all change the effects of theophylline-type drugs.

- Don't eat meals that are very high in fats or oils. A lot of fatty food causes too much of the drug to be released at once from the slow-release preparations and increases the risk of side effects. Avoid sudden, major, changes to your diet.
- See your doctor regularly for check-ups. Simply getting older changes your reaction to these drugs: your dose may need to change over the years.
- If you are at all forgetful about tablets, keep a careful record of when you have taken your theophylline-type drugs. Be very careful never to take a second dose by mistake.
- Talk to your doctor if you are not taking a slow-release form of theophylline (see box below for brand names). There are usually fewer side effects from these than from the ordinary forms of the drug.
- Wear a Medic Alert bracelet (see box on p. 95) saying that you are taking theophylline-type drugs. If you have a severe asthma attack and are taken to hospital, it is important that medical staff know this, so that they do not give you more drugs of this type.

While pregnant or breast-feeding, it may be advisable to stop taking theophylline-type drugs: discuss this with your doctor. Although the drugs do not affect most unborn or newborn babies, there are occasional reports of toxicity. Less seriously, theophylline-type drugs go through into breast milk, and may make babies irritable and restless. This problem can be solved by always taking the drug just after a feed – this reduces the amount in the milk.

The theophylline-type drugs might produce behavioural problems and learning difficulties in young children although this is unproven. Research shows that there are no problems for children over six.

Some common brand names

Common brand names of theophylline-type drugs include:

slow-release preparations – Lasma, Nuelin SA, Phyllocontin Continus, Slo-Phyllin, Theo-Dur, Uniphyllin Continus

ordinary preparations – Aminophylline, Nuelin

Ketotifen

Ketotifen (brand name Zaditen) is an antihistamine (see p. 138), although it has other effects in addition to those of ordinary anti-histamines. Most significantly, it stabilises mast cells in a similar way to cromoglycate.

One advantage of ketotifen to many people is that it is taken by mouth, in capsule, tablet or syrup form. When it was first introduced, doctors hoped that it would be of particular help in asthma, but it has not lived up to expectations. However, some asthmatics do find it effective. It is worth trying because, if it works, it could permit you to reduce your dose of steroids.

Ketotifen requires up to six weeks to take effect, so continue taking your previous drugs (e.g. steroids) for at least six weeks, or you will risk losing control of your asthma.

Side effects of this drug

Minor side effects from ketotifen include nausea, headache, increased appetite and weight gain, drowsiness, dry mouth and slight dizziness. Do not drive until you are sure that ketotifen does not make you drowsy. Alcohol may pack a more powerful punch than usual, so drink very moderately at first. If drowsiness is a problem, take the drug in the late evening. The sleepy feeling may wear off after a few weeks of taking the drug.

There are no serious side effects from ketotifen, except if taken with drugs for diabetes.

Anti-leukotriene drugs

Leukotrienes are among the messenger chemicals produced by mast cells during an allergic reaction (see box on p. 12). They help to perpetuate the inflammatory process begun by histamine, and they amplify the reaction by attracting more immune cells into the area.

The anti-leukotriene drugs fall into two distinct groups:
- those that bind to the receptors for leukotrienes, called leukotriene-receptor-antagonists. Currently, there are two drugs in this group, montelukast (brand name Singulair) and zafirlukast (brand name Accolate). A third drug, pranlukast, is in the pipeline and currently going through its safety trials.
- those that block the production of the leukotrienes altogether, called 5-lipoxygenase inhibitors. There is only one drug in this group at present, zileuton (brand names Leutrol, Zyflo); it is not yet available in Britain.

As regards tackling inflammation, the anti-leukotriene drugs work in a completely different way from either steroids or cromoglycate. This makes them useful as an add-on treatment, supplementing the effects of existing anti-allergy drugs.

For asthmatics, anti-leukotriene drugs may be particularly good in combination with antihistamines – whereas antihistamines alone are singularly unsuccessful in asthma (see p. 138). Recent research suggests that taking antihistamines together with anti-leukotriene drugs is an effective way to control airway inflammation. However, there have been no large-scale trials of this treatment option yet, and it may be a while before it comes into general use.

In the airways of people with asthma, leukotrienes can directly trigger bronchospasm (contraction of the airway muscles) as well as fostering inflammation and increasing mucus production. This multiple action of leukotrienes makes anti-leukotriene drugs very valuable for asthmatics because they act as both relievers (reversing bronchospasm) and preventers (tackling inflammation).

All the anti-leukotriene drugs are taken in tablet form. If you are trying an anti-leukotriene drug for the first time, don't expect any noticeable effects to occur for about three days. Once you are taking the drug regularly, each dose requires 2–4 hours to have its full effect, but goes on working for 12–24 hours in total.

Although anti-leukotriene drugs have a reliever effect, they cannot give you *immediate* relief from bronchospasm. Asthmatics must therefore carry a short-acting beta-2 reliever (see pp. 152–3) as well, in case of an asthma attack.

For those who dislike inhalers, or tend to forget to use them, the fact that these drugs are taken once a day in tablet form makes them an attractive option. However, they are expensive, and at present doctors prescribe them mainly for young children who have difficulty inhaling their usual drugs.

Side effects of these drugs

The side effects noted in safety trials of these drugs were all minor ones:
- zafirlukast—headache, infection, nausea, diarrhoea, pain
- montelukast—headache, diarrhoea, abdominal pain, cough, and flu-like symptoms
- zileuton—upset stomach

According to the data gathered so far, more serious side effects are unlikely. However, as with all new drugs, **you should report any unusual symptoms to your doctor**, just in case these represent a rare or long-term side effect of the drug (see p. 137).

Very occasionally montelukast causes anaphylaxis, or other allergic reactions, such as itchiness, nettle rash (urticaria) or swelling (angioedema).

Zileuton can cause liver damage, but again this is very rare. Your liver function should be closely monitored by the doctor, by means of regular blood tests, and the drug withdrawn at the first sign of trouble. You should not be given zileuton at all if you have liver disease.

The most worrying development noticed to date is the appearance, in a very few people taking zafirlukast or montelukast, of a disorder called Churg-Strauss Syndrome. The symptoms may include a blotchy purplish rash (due to vasculitis – see second box on p. 73), a flu-like illness, worsening asthma, and numbness or tingling in the limbs. The heart, lungs and nerves are all affected, because eosinophils (see p. 19) are present in large numbers and cause damaging inflammation.

A study of the cases reported so far suggests that this syndrome may not be due to the anti-leukotriene drugs themselves but to other causes, usually (though not always) to a reduction in the dose of steroids. Other patients who are not taking anti-leukotriene drugs, but are reducing or stopping steroids, may also (again, very rarely) develop Churg-Strauss Syndrome. Doctors now suspect that all these patients were already suffering from an underlying eosinophilic disease, which first showed itself simply as asthma, and was quelled by the steroid treatment prescribed for the asthma. The disease was thoroughly masked as long as the patient was using steroids, but when steroids were withdrawn, the underlying disease flared up, producing a wide range of symptoms. In most cases, reintroducing steroids brings these symptoms under control again.

Putting it all together

What is the ideal combination of all these asthma drugs? That is something that your doctor can only work out slowly, because it varies from one individual to another.

The conventional approach to asthma treatment is to start patients on a short-acting beta-2 reliever and then, if the symptoms are not controlled, to add other drugs. This approach is called 'stepping up'. The standard steps, or stages, are as follows:

1. Use a short-acting beta-2 reliever only.

2. Add cromoglycate or low-dose inhaled steroids.

3. Try a higher dose of inhaled steroid or a long-acting beta-2 reliever.

4. Try out each of the following in turn: theophylline, anticholinergic drugs, cromoglycate and higher doses of beta-2 relievers (either inhaled or as tablets/syrup).

5. If there is still no success in controlling symptoms, add regular steroid tablets.

Short courses of steroid tablets may be used at any stage, for the control of sudden, severe, attacks.

Over the last ten years, there has been a change of strategy, and very few people are now kept on Stage 1. Inhaled steroids are now given to most asthmatics, even those with relatively mild asthma. Research from Sweden, where widespread use of inhaled steroids first became general policy, shows considerable benefits to this approach.

If you have gone beyond Stage 2, 'stepping up' is usually followed by 'stepping down'. In other words, when the symptoms have been well controlled for 3–6 months, doses of some drugs are reduced, or certain drugs stopped altogether. If the asthma flares up again, the dose is increased or the drug reinstated. If there are no problems, and symptoms remain stable for a month or two, another reduction is tried.

An entirely different approach to asthma management is now being tried with some patients – starting off with moderate to high doses of inhaled steroids (equivalent to Stage 3) and then 'stepping down'. The idea is to get the inflammation under control promptly and fully at the outset. This often seems to be the best strategy.

A few asthmatics don't get much benefit from steroids. If your dose of steroid needs to be raised repeatedly, or you still need to use your reliever daily in spite of taking steroids, you may have **steroid-resistant asthma**. There are other drugs that can help, including anti-leukotriene drugs and the more powerful anti-allergy drugs (see p. 149).

Alcohol, caffeine and asthma

Some asthmatics experience bronchodilation (opening up of the airways) when they drink alcohol, while others experience bronchospasm (tightening of the airways). For those whose airways open up, there is probably no harm in sometimes having a drink to relieve your asthma symptoms, assuming these are fairly mild. Clearly, it would not be a good idea to make a daily habit of this.

If your airways tighten up with alcohol, you will probably be pleased to hear that it may not be the alcohol itself. Alcoholic drinks contain a great variety of other ingredients, either derived from the original ingredients or generated during the fermentation process. Called 'congeners', these vary from one type of alcoholic drink to another, and they are often the culprits in asthma. So you may well find that, while one kind of alcoholic drink has a bad effect, another is fine.

Caffeine has a far more uniform effect – for most asthmatics it opens up the airways. However, the amount needed to relieve an asthma attack will also produce unpleasant side effects, such as a pounding heart or shaky hands. There are also long-term problems with such high doses of caffeine, including insomnia, headaches, nervousness and 'restless legs'. It is much better to use your reliever inhaler to control an attack: the drug in the inhaler has been chemically tailored to give the maximum therapeutic benefit with the minimum of side effects. Anyone who consumes tea or coffee excessively can make themselves seriously ill, either physically or mentally, and it is not always obvious that caffeine is the cause.

Using inhalers

The value of using an inhaler rather than taking tablets or syrup is explained on p. 141 for steroids. The same principle applies to all drugs.

The oldest type of inhaler is the 'puffer' or aerosol inhaler, properly called a 'pressurised metered-dose inhaler' or MDI. It delivers the drug as a fine, moist, spray. In addition, there are now many devices that deliver drugs in dry-powder form.

If you or your child find the aerosol inhalers difficult, you may do better with a dry-powder inhaler. Your doctor should have several different inhalers available for you to try out, to see which one suits you best.

When you are given an inhaler you must be shown how to use it by a doctor or asthma nurse. A great many asthma patients have a 'poor inhaler technique', and get too little of the drug as a result. This often leads to their asthma getting out of control. The advice given here for using inhalers is no substitute for proper training, and should only be used to supplement what your doctor or asthma nurse has told you.

When using an aerosol inhaler or MDI, remember to shake the inhaler well or you will not get the right dose. Your in-breath must coincide exactly with pressing the canister down: this is the part that many people find difficult. You must breathe in slowly and deeply, otherwise you do not get much of the drug into your airways.

Many asthmatics stop inhaling the moment the spray from the aerosol inhaler hits the back of the throat. The spray contains a **propellant**, which makes it very cold, and there is a natural reflex response to this cold liquid which stops inhalation. This response may be impossible to control. If so, you need a dry-powder inhaler (see right), or a spacer (see p. 162) to use with your aerosol inhaler.

Breath-operated aerosol inhalers such as the Autohaler can be useful for those who find ordinary

Arthritis and inhalers

Those who suffer from arthritis in their hands often find inhalers difficult to use. There are several aids now available to help with this problem – ask your doctor or asthma nurse about these.

aerosol inhalers too hard to use. With these devices, you do not have to push the canister down because your in-breath triggers the release of the drug. Take care not to block the air-intake holes with your hands and don't stop breathing when you hear the inhaler click. (If there is no click, start again and breathe in more forcefully this time.)

One hazard with aerosol inhalers is that, when almost empty, they produce no drug – just the propellant. Although they still 'puff' normally, they are not effective. It may be hard to tell when your inhaler is running low, but you can find out by removing the metal canister and placing it in a bowl of water. It sinks if it's full, and floats horizontally if it's nearly empty. An inhaler that floats vertically, nozzle downwards, is roughly half full.

Many asthmatics find dry-powder inhalers such as the Spinhaler, Rotahaler, Diskhaler, Accuhaler, Clickhaler and Turbohaler are the easiest to use. They have no aerosol device, so none of the problems associated with the coldness of the propellant.

On the other hand, nothing pushes the drug into your mouth and lungs with a dry-powder inhaler: you have to do all the work yourself. This means you have to breathe in quite hard and fast. During a severe asthma attack you may not be able to breathe in hard enough to get a good dose of the drug. Some asthmatics have an aerosol inhaler as well, often combined with a spacer (see p. 162), for use during severe attacks.

For the parents of asthmatics, who want to keep an eye on how much of a drug is being used, most of the dry-powder inhalers allow you to do so.

Do hold your breath

Whichever type of inhaler you use, it is important to give the drugs a chance to do their work. After inhaling, and when your lungs are full, you should hold your breath for at least ten seconds. Then breathe out, but wait at least another 30 seconds before breathing in again.

Side effects from non-drug ingredients

There are other ingredients in inhalers, besides the drug, and they occasionally cause side effects.

Aerosol inhalers are the worst offenders. They can contain up to five non-drug ingredients, such as propellants and surfactants. Some asthmatics are sensitive to one of these, and respond with coughing or bronchospasm when they inhale them.

If inhaled in large amounts, the propellants in aerosol inhalers can give a mild 'high', and asthmatic teenagers and their friends may – *very rarely* – begin abusing inhaled beta-2 relievers. Parents should be alert for the possibility of such problems, but not worry unduly.

Dry-powder inhalers do not need propellants or surfactants, so they are suitable for anyone who develops a sensitivity to these. However, they may contain lactose, or milk sugar, in addition to the drug. Enough lactose is deposited in the mouth and swallowed to provoke symptoms, such as diarrhoea and wind, in people who suffer from severe lactose intolerance (see box on p. 79). Trace amounts of milk proteins in the lactose may be a problem for people with severe milk allergy.

CFCs and inhalers

Aerosol inhalers have long contained CFCs, which are very inert gases (at ground level) and perfectly safe to inhale. Unfortunately, they cause serious damage when they reach the ozone layer high above the earth, so they are being phased out in asthma inhalers, as they are in all aerosols. Other propellants, called hydrofluoroalkanes (HFAs), are being introduced to take their place. The spray from an HFA inhaler may taste and feel different, but it should do exactly the same job as a CFC inhaler: the drug it contains remains the same. Research suggests that these new propellants are very safe, but tell your doctor if your reaction to your inhaler seems to change suddenly.

These new propellants deliver medication more efficiently into the lungs, so that usually only half the previous dose is required. Unlike CFC-type inhalers, they will deliver a constant dose until empty. In addition, they are not affected as much by below-freezing temperatures.

Inhale – then clean your teeth

Asthmatic children are more prone to dental decay than other children, and inhalers are suspected of causing the problem. No one knows, as yet, exactly which ingredient of the inhalers is the culprit – it could be a drug, or a non-drug additive such as a propellant. Alternatively, the fact that the spray from some inhalers is slightly acidic could explain this side effect. Brushing the teeth after using the inhaler, or just rinsing out the mouth with water, is recommended as a preventive measure.

Using spacers

A spacer is a large empty chamber that can be fitted to an aerosol inhaler (a puffer or MDI), to make it more effective and easier to use. The aerosol spray goes into one end of the spacer, and the asthmatic breathes it in from the other end.

When using a spacer, you can breathe normally: you don't have to take all the drug in at once, or hold your breath after you've inhaled. But you should try to breathe as deeply as possible, and hold your breath for up to ten seconds if you can.

Note that spacers are for use with aerosol inhalers only. Spacers allow the aerosol propellant (see p. 161) to evaporate, leaving tiny airborne droplets of the drug to be inhaled. Once the propellant has evaporated, these droplets are no longer cold, so the reflex response that stops inhalation is avoided.

During an asthma attack, spacers are immensely valuable because they allow you to get some of the drug into your airways even though you are unable to take a deep breath. There is a collapsible spacer, called the E-Z Spacer, which folds up into a plastic case small enough to be slipped into a pocket. In a severe asthma attack, having such a spacer could save your life.

In an emergency, if no spacer is available, you can improvise one (see p. 100).

Babies and small children, who cannot yet coordinate the in-breath with pushing the aerosol canister down, need spacers for everyday use. There are spacers designed for children under two years, with masks that fit over the nose and mouth.

When using a spacer, shake the inhaler and then spray it into the spacer once only. Inhale within five seconds. During an asthma attack, you can add another dose from the inhaler every ten seconds, until the attack begins to subside, but keep a count of how many puffs you use (see p. 100).

For a young child, shake the inhaler well, and fit it to the spacer. Put the mouthpiece into the child's mouth, or put the mask on. Tell the child to breathe in and out steadily and listen for the clicking of the valve on the spacer – this shows that it is opening and closing. When the child's breathing is regular, puff a single dose into the spacer. The child should breathe in and out 5–8 times.

Priming a spacer

Prime a new spacer, or one that has been washed, by firing the inhaler into it about five times. Do this before you actually need to use the spacer.

The drug will coat the spacer walls, due to an electrostatic charge on the plastic. You won't be able to see the drug as it forms a very thin coating.

When you come to use the spacer, no more of the drug will stick to the spacer walls, because they are already coated, so the full dose will be available for you or your child to inhale.

Priming new spacers is particularly important when the asthmatic is a young child, because there may be some delay between firing the inhaler and the child actually getting a proper lungful of the drug. The longer the delay, the more chance the drug has to stick to the unprimed spacer walls.

A spacer can be used on a baby while it is asleep, which may make life easier for you both. If you need to use the spacer while the baby or toddler is awake, stroke the mask against the child's cheek first.

Keep smiling and talking so that the situation doesn't seem so frightening. If the baby does start to cry, keep the mask in place: crying will bring on a deep in-breath which is just what is needed.

For an older child, decorating the spacer with coloured stickers can make it appear less daunting. Try to make using the spacer seem like a game. If this fails, don't get into a battle with the child – leave it a while and try again later.

Playing with the spacer when feeling well will help the child to see it as something familiar, not as a frightening piece of equipment associated with asthma attacks.

Nebulisers

A nebuliser delivers high doses of asthma drugs in an easily inhaled form. It is generally used for severe asthma only, or in an emergency to relieve asthma attacks.

A nebuliser can be attached to an oxygen cylinder, which enriches the air–drug mixture with oxygen. This is useful in severe asthma.

The only people who need to have a nebuliser at home for emergencies are those with brittle asthma, whose condition can deteriorate very suddenly and sharply.

For routine use, only a very small minority of asthmatics require a nebuliser. They include:

- Those with such severe asthma that they depend on large doses of drugs to control their symptoms
- Very small children or elderly people with severe asthma, who have difficulty using inhalers. For them, a nebuliser may be the easiest way to take their drugs.

The fact that the hospital's nebuliser is so effective in an emergency gives it a special mystique for many people, who assume that nebulisers are a magical cure for asthma. Nebulisers are widely advertised in specialist publications for asthmatics and, while they are expensive, they can look like the answer to a prayer. Many asthmatics, or their parents, mistakenly believe that owning a nebuliser would be the answer to all their problems. In fact the nebuliser only works so well because it delivers a much higher dose of the reliever drug – a dose which also carries a higher risk of side effects. This high-dose treatment should not be used on a regular basis unless it is absolutely essential. No one should buy a nebuliser without first discussing the matter with their doctor.

Asthmatics who own a nebuliser should have detailed written instructions from a doctor about when and how to use it, and how much of the drug to put in. One hazard of owning a nebuliser is that it may give you a false sense of security during emergencies, and delay you from getting expert medical help when you need it. If the nebuliser is for emergency use you should be told the exact signs that indicate a need to use it and – no less important – the signs that show the attack is out of control and needs hospital treatment.

Take care, when using a nebuliser, not to allow the mist to escape and settle on the face or eyes. Regular exposure to steroid mist can cause cataracts in the eyes, and thinning of the skin on the face. Anti-cholinergics (see p. 156) can cause glaucoma if they come into contact with the eye. The mask must fit very tightly. As an additional precaution, place a scarf around the upper edge of the mask to cover any gaps. Wash the face after using the nebuliser for steroids.

Keep off the cough mixture

Coughing can be a useful reaction in asthma, evicting mucus from the lungs. But in some asthmatics the cough does not produce mucus and seems to be no more than a reflex reaction to the airway inflammation. This type of cough can be debilitating, but it is *not* a good idea to treat it with cough mixture which has no benefit and may mask the seriousness of the asthma. Tackling the airway inflammation with preventer drugs such as steroids is the best course. Simple **expectorants**, which loosen mucus, may be of value – ask your pharmacist about these.

Re-training the immune system

'The summer used to be such a miserable time for me because I'm allergic to grass pollen. For most of my life I have had dreadful hayfever, and my asthma would get worse during the summer as well. Antihistamines knocked me for six, and although there were nose drops that helped a little, they certainly did not resolve the problem completely. Exam time was always a nightmare when I was a student – then, as now, it coincided exactly with the pollen season.'

'Getting a job in Chicago was a turning point in my health. My colleagues were amazed to see me snuffling through the summer and just accepting that nothing could be done to improve matters. The whole approach to treating allergies is different there. Eventually someone marched me off to see her allergist, who said that I should have "allergy shots" and that my health insurance would cover it. The process was very time-consuming at first, and it took a while to work, but the change is remarkable. I've never regretted having the treatment. Summer is a time I can actually enjoy now.'

Not everyone responds this well to immunotherapy, but for those allergy sufferers who do benefit, this is an excellent treatment. It tackles allergies right at their source, by teaching the immune system to react differently to the allergen.

Also known as **Specific Immunotherapy** (**SIT**), **Incremental Immunotherapy** (**IIT**) or simply as **hyposensitisation**, this form of treatment was devised by two English medical researchers, Leonard Noon and John Freeman, who reported their successes with hayfever patients in 1911. Ironically, their treatment is now less readily available in Britain than in any other industrialised nation. Only a small minority of British allergy patients receive immunotherapy. The cause of this strange situation is a ruling made in 1986 by the Committee on the Safety of Medicines (CSM). This states that immunotherapy must only be given where there is resuscitation equipment available, and that all patients must wait for an hour after each injection, in case of side effects. In addition, immunotherapy cannot be used for severe asthma.

The requirement for resuscitation equipment rules out most GP surgeries, and this effectively puts immunotherapy beyond the reach of many allergic individuals in the UK, owing to the extreme shortage of allergists and hospital allergy clinics (see p. 89). (In the past, the lack of allergy specialists meant that most immunotherapy in the UK was given by GPs.)

The CSM ruling was triggered by a number of deaths due to immunotherapy: there were eleven fatalities between 1980 and 1986, with five of these in the eighteen months just before the report. But almost all these deaths were due to very basic errors in the way the injections were given – tragic as the deaths were, the official response to them was inappropriate. Fatal reactions to immunotherapy can be avoided with close attention to ordinary safeguards (see p. 167).

Allergen immunotherapy is still freely available elsewhere in the world, and is regarded as a key part of allergy treatment. The UK is now out of step with all other developed countries, and most doctors feel that the UK restrictions are far too strict.

There are hopes that this situation may change within the next few years, and that more allergy sufferers may be able to take advantage of this valuable treatment. This could be achieved, in part, by investing more National Health Service money in allergy clinics and allergy specialists. In addition, there should be a relaxation of the regulations, so that properly trained GPs can give immunotherapy to patients who are not at high risk of a fatal reaction. For people whose lives are affected by allergies, the reintroduction of this treatment (with appropriate safeguards) would be a huge boon.

The uses of immunotherapy

Immunotherapy is mainly used for airborne allergens such as pollen, house-dust mite and mould spores. Allergies to animals can also be treated with immunotherapy, but the treatment cannot work miracles – if a cat-allergic person decides to keep the cat, the high dose of allergen inhaled every day limits the impact of immunotherapy treatment.

People with straightforward allergic reactions affecting the nose and eyes (allergic rhinitis and conjunctivitis) respond well to immunotherapy. In patients with hayfever, for example, the success rate (patients showing some degree of improvement) is about 80–90%. When nasal allergies are complicated by chronic sinusitis or nasal polyps, the chance of success is a little lower.

Some studies of the long-term effects of immunotherapy suggest that, if it is given to children with hayfever or perennial rhinitis, those children are less likely to develop asthma.

The benefits of using immunotherapy to treat established asthma are less certain. Asthma is a more complex disease than hayfever, and allergies are only one factor among many (see p. 38), which may limit the impact that immunotherapy can make.

Experience suggests that immunotherapy may be a great help for an asthmatic with a strong allergic reaction to a single airborne allergen, such as grass pollen or house-dust mite, but not for other asthmatics. Asthmatics with aspirin sensitivity or chronic sinusitis are unlikely to benefit.

The value of immunotherapy to children with asthma is a subject of great debate among doctors in the United States. Some studies suggest that it is of little real benefit, while others are more positive. One interesting study, that followed asthmatic children for 15 years or more, found that if they were given a full 5-year course of immunotherapy when young, they tended to have fewer asthma symptoms and need less medication in their late teens and early twenties.

Chronic urticaria (nettle rash) is occasionally due to airborne allergens, in which case immunotherapy may help. However, immunotherapy is not recommended for atopic eczema. When people with both eczema and rhinitis try immunotherapy for their nasal allergies, some find that their eczema gets worse.

Insect-sting allergy is a prime candidate for immunotherapy (see pp. 167–8) but food allergy is a different matter, and is not treated with immunotherapy at present (see p. 168).

Who can get immunotherapy?

As a result of the CSM ruling (see p. 164) remarkably few allergy sufferers in Britain receive immunotherapy.

Those with insect-sting allergy, who have suffered anaphylaxis (see p. 58), are the most likely to be offered this treatment. However, even with this frightening and life-threatening problem, which can be treated with almost 100% success by immunotherapy (see p. 168), such treatment is not automatically available.

A few people with severe hayfever that does not respond well to drug treatment may also be given immunotherapy. It is worth asking your doctor about such treatment if you feel you would benefit.

How immunotherapy works

Immunotherapy consists of a series of small injections, just under the skin. The liquid that is injected contains an extract of the offending allergen, for example house-dust mite. The injections are given at regular intervals, usually once a week, although other schedules are possible (see p. 167).

At the outset, a very dilute version of the allergen extract is used, way below the threshold for an allergic reaction. People who seem highly sensitive, on the basis of their skin tests, start on an extract that is even more dilute.

For the next injection, a slightly higher concentration of the allergen extract is used, and the concentration goes on increasing with each successive injection. The idea is to habituate the immune system to the offending allergen, by very gradually raising the dose. Eventually, when the dose reaches a level which generally gives beneficial effects, no further increases are made.

If an allergy sufferer reacts badly to immunotherapy injections (see right) on several successive occasions, the dose may be levelled off before the ideal maximum dose is reached. However, a good allergist will persist for some time in trying to increase the dose because stopping at a lower level often results in the treatment being ineffective.

The first stage of immunotherapy, when the concentration of allergen is being increased week by week, is referred to as the **build-up stage**. The second stage, when the dose is being kept at the same level, is called **maintenance therapy**, and the dose used is the **maintenance dose**.

There is sometimes an obvious improvement by the time the build-up stage is complete, but not always. The benefits of the treatment generally appear within six months of reaching the maintenance dose, but some people have to wait a year or even two before things improve.

As the immunotherapy begins to take effect, symptoms decline and there is often less need for drugs. A great deal of research effort has gone into finding out what lies behind these changes – in other words, what is actually happening to the immune system when immunotherapy is effective.

The answer is that a surprising number of different changes may occur and no two allergy sufferers react to immunotherapy in quite the same way. Frequently there is a shift in the kinds of antibodies the body produces against the offending allergen. Levels of IgG antibodies (which help to block the allergic reaction) go up, while levels of the allergy antibody, IgE, tend to stabilise and eventually

go down. The numbers of mast cells (see box on p. 12) may also decline, and they can become less responsive to the allergen. The balance of power between Th1 cells and Th2 cells may also shift, with the pro-allergy Th2 cells (see p. 11) becoming less influential.

What can go wrong

The secret of safe immunotherapy is to go at exactly the right speed for the immune system of the individual being treated. The doctor should look for feedback from the immune system – signs that show how well it is coping with the steadily increasing dose of allergen – and use these to pace the immunotherapy schedule.

Going too fast – getting ahead of the immune system's ability to cope – is hazardous. A major allergic reaction, called **anaphylaxis** (see p. 58), can occur, and this is the cause of deaths during immunotherapy. However, as long as there is injectable adrenaline (see p. 150) and resuscitation equipment available, even such an extreme crisis can be dealt with safely.

Serious reactions to immunotherapy usually occur:
- during the initial build-up phase; maintenance therapy is much safer
- during the pollen season, for those with pollen allergy
- when a new vial of allergen extract is first being used, because of variations in concentration (see p. 169).

Those most vulnerable to severe reactions are:
- people with asthma, especially severe or unstable asthma
- those who have experienced systemic allergic reactions in the past
- anyone who is extremely allergic, as revealed by skin tests
- anyone taking beta-blockers (see box on p. 150).

With care, these fatalities can be avoided. Patients who are given immunotherapy can ensure their own safety by being well informed about the procedure (see p. 167).

The timing of immunotherapy

There are various different approaches to the timing of immunotherapy. The basic method (which has a good safety record in the US where it is very commonly used) starts with injections once a week. After the maintenance dose has been reached, maintenance injections are given once every 2–4 weeks. The frequency of these may be increased during the pollen season, for people with pollen allergies.

It is the regularity of the injection schedule that gradually creates, and then sustains, immune tolerance, so the treatment is only of value to patients who can reliably keep their appointments.

When immunotherapy is successful, it can eventually be discontinued without any reappearance of the allergic reaction. It usually takes 4–5 years of regular therapy, from the time of the first injection, to get to this point. The benefits then persist for many years, perhaps indefinitely in some people, even without any further injections.

Rush immunotherapy

Trying to speed up the process of immunotherapy greatly increases the risk of a severe reaction (anaphylaxis). However, there are some situations where fast results are needed, and in such cases **rush immunotherapy,** also called **accelerated immunotherapy,** may be used.

During the build-up stage of rush immunotherapy, injections are given every day, or even several times a day. All the usual safety procedures (see below) are observed with particular care, to reduce the chance of a severe reaction.

In **semi-rush immunotherapy**, the build-up injections are given twice a week, and the risks are lower than with daily injections, but still higher than with weekly injections.

Minimising the risks

If you are lucky enough to be offered immunotherapy treatment under the National Health Service, you should not feel concerned about accepting the offer. There is very little risk of a bad reaction because safety procedures are now so stringent.

To minimise the risk of suffering a severe reaction, the doctor will ask you, at each visit, about any reactions that occurred after your previous injection. Reactions might include redness, itching or swelling around the injection site, or (more seriously) symptoms elsewhere on the body, such as nettle rash (urticaria), itchy skin, sneezing, a runny nose, red or itchy eyes, tightness in the throat or chest, coughing or wheezing. Always make a note of such symptoms, so that you don't forget to mention them at the next visit. This is crucially important, as such reactions can indicate that the immune system is being hurried along too fast.

The doctor will also ask if you have an infection of any kind, as this can alter your reaction. You should also tell the doctor about any new medicines being taken, as some, such as beta-blockers (see box on p. 150), can make a bad reaction to the injection more likely to occur.

Asthmatics can expect the doctor to ask about current asthma symptoms, and to check their peak flow both before and after an injection. If there are any symptoms, or if the peak flow is less than 70% of the best-ever value, the injection won't be given.

Severe reactions can sometimes begin several hours after the injection, so stay within reach of a phone for about 24 hours. Among US allergists (who don't require their patients to wait after the injection for more than 20–30 minutes) there are some who believe that everyone undergoing immunotherapy should carry an adrenaline (epinephrine) auto-injector (see p. 150) on the day an injection has been given, for use in the event of a severe reaction. Anyone who has suffered anaphylaxis in response to an insect sting will probably have an adrenaline auto-injector anyway, and this can certainly be used to treat anaphylaxis following immunotherapy. Note, however, that using the adrenaline is just the first step in treating anaphylaxis (see p. 98) and you must then go back to your allergist, or to the nearest hospital emergency department, without any delay.

It is sensible to avoid exercise for two hours after an injection. Be extra-cautious during the pollen season if you are receiving immunotherapy for pollen allergies.

Immunotherapy for insect-sting allergy

'Our daughter has had two really bad reactions from being stung by a wasp. After the second one, the doctor at the accident and emergency department told us that she nearly died. We got so anxious about it that we worried every time we left the house in the summer, and it was even worse if she went out without us. My wife got so upset about it that she wasn't sleeping well. It was affecting the whole family badly.

'Then we heard about desensitisation treatment, and asked our GP, but he said he couldn't do it. According to him, they might be able to do it at the hospital, but it might not work, and it was risky too. We accepted that at first, but then I started doing some research on the Internet, and discovered that in America and Germany this treatment is absolutely standard – someone like our daughter would automatically be given it. 'We felt very angry when we found this out, and went back to the doctor. Eventually Ann was referred to the allergy department at a hospital, and now she is getting this desensitisation treatment. I'm pleased about that, obviously, but I still think it shouldn't have been such a fight to get it.'

Immunotherapy provides highly effective protection for those with insect-sting allergy, and should be given to anyone who has had a severe systemic reaction (see p. 60). Some US allergists also recommend it for adults who have had a cutaneous systemic reaction (see p. 60), on the basis that they may well progress to a severe systemic reaction with the next sting.

Studies of people who have suffered severe systemic reactions, and are then treated with immunotherapy, show that 97% have no systemic reaction to future insect stings. For the 3% who are not fully protected, the severity of the reaction is much reduced and far less likely to be life-threatening. In other words, this is an excellent treatment which can save lives.

Targeting the treatment

Choosing the right venom for immunotherapy can sometimes be difficult. Not everyone with insect-sting allergy sees the insect that caused the reaction. Skin tests may not give the answer either, because there are often positive reactions to several different venoms. Some of these may be false positives (see p. 91) and it is impossible for the allergist to say which one(s) are actually relevant. Most allergists will recommend immunotherapy for all of them, using a mixture of venom extracts.

Where the guilty insect was seen and identified, but other venoms also give positive skin tests, a more difficult decision has to be made. Many allergists carry out immunotherapy for all the venoms that gave a positive skin test, on a 'better safe than sorry' basis. Since there are cross-reactions between venoms (see box on p. 113), there is some sense in this. Other allergists just give immunotherapy for the insect that did the deed.

Will immunotherapy against one insect protect against a related insect? With two closely related insects such as wasps and hornets, which have many allergens in common, it might do – but there is no guarantee. The problem is that, as well as the shared allergens, each venom also has its own unique ingredients. It's impossible to say, with the kind of tests available at present, if an allergic reaction was to shared allergens or unique ones. So immunotherapy against wasp venom *may* give protection against hornet venom, but it will not necessarily do so – and vice versa.

In the case of bumblebee allergy (seen almost exclusively in those, such as horticulturalists, whose work involves handling bumblebees) a more definite answer can be given – honeybee immunotherapy does *not* work. Immunotherapy with bumblebee venom does work, fortunately. The bumblebee extract has to be obtained from specialist sources.

Injections are given weekly during the build-up phase, unless protection is needed urgently, as with work-related sting allergy, in which case rush immunotherapy may be used. Once the maximum dose has been reached, a maintenance injection is needed every 4 weeks. After a year, this maintenance dose can be given every 6–8 weeks.

After 3–5 years of immunotherapy, skin tests with insect venoms are usually tried again. If the results are negative, the immunotherapy will stop. Research now shows that, even if skin tests are still positive when immunotherapy ends, there's an 80–90% chance that no systemic reaction will occur to future stings. Some people are not reassured by this, and prefer to continue with immunotherapy for their own peace of mind. Indeed, research shows that a near-fatal systemic reaction has a long-lasting psychological impact, and that many people continue to feel anxious despite completing immunotherapy *and* reacting negatively to skin tests.

At one time, challenge stings with live insects were given to check whether immunotherapy had actually worked. Few doctors do this now, but your allergist may be prepared to do a challenge test if you ask. Adrenaline and resuscitation equipment would be available if a challenge test were used, so any severe reaction could be dealt with promptly and effectively. The fact that the psychological consequences of insect-sting allergy are so persistent suggests that challenge tests with live insects may have a particular value, in proving incontrovertibly that immunotherapy has worked. Challenge tests are also helpful for those who work with stinging insects, such as honeybees and bumblebees, and who need to be sure that they can go back to work safely.

Immunotherapy for food allergy?

The hope that immunotherapy might help people with food allergy has not, as yet, been realised. What doctors are aiming for here is simply to protect against the effects of accidentally eating a tiny amount of the food – no one is expecting that a child with peanut allergy will ever be able to eat peanut butter sandwiches.

Even this rather limited ambition still seems like a distant dream. The process of giving the injections is nerve-racking because of the constant risk of a severe reaction. The risks prevent the dose of allergen being increased very much, so the beneficial effects are small. While there may be some reduction in sensitivity, it is not enough – or not reliable enough – to be of any practical value.

Research is now focused on developing modified forms of the food allergens (allergoids). The idea is that they should induce tolerance without any risk of a bad reaction. Peanuts are currently at the centre of this research, and modified peanut allergen could become available in the next few years. Even if it works, it is unlikely to allow patients to eat without restriction.

The future of immunotherapy

It is not just those with food allergy (see p. 168) who might benefit from the use of **allergoids** – modified allergens that induce immune tolerance without provoking severe reactions. Researchers are currently tinkering with a great variety of allergens in the hope of producing allergoids, so that immunotherapy can become a safer and more streamlined procedure. Already, researchers in Germany have made an allergoid from birch pollen that can reduce hayfever symptoms with a series of just seven injections given before the pollen season.

Researchers are also working hard to produce standardised versions of ordinary allergens – in other words, allergen extracts that always contain a standard amount of the allergen. The aim is not only to reduce the number of treatment failures (which can occur if the extract does not contain enough allergen) but also to avoid mishaps when a new vial of allergen extract is used (differences in strength between one vial and another are one cause of anaphylactic reactions).

Standardisation is difficult, because the starting materials – skin particles from horses, for example, or dust-mite droppings – are natural materials and therefore variable. Some samples contain far more of a particular allergenic ingredient than others.

One way around this problem is to develop accurate methods of measuring the amount of allergen in the extract. Another approach is to abandon the whole business of making extracts, and produce allergens artificially, in a laboratory. This is done by inserting the gene for the allergen – the gene for the Der p1 allergen of house-dust mite, for example – into bacteria. These bacteria then act as production units, manufacturing large amounts of the allergen every day. With this high-tech approach, the exact content of the allergen preparations can be controlled.

These high-tech allergen preparations are extremely pure, and therefore very effective – as long as the person receiving immunotherapy really is sensitised to the particular allergen that is included. Unfortunately, most natural allergenic materials contain two, three or even more separate allergens. In house-dust mite droppings, for example, while Der p1 is the allergen that affects most people, there is also an allergen called Der p2, and a few people are more sensitive to this than to Der p1.

Artificially produced allergen preparations usually include the main allergen only. For the minority of people who are more severely allergic to one of the other allergens, this extract will not work. Eventually this problem will no doubt be circumvented by means of more precise skin testing before immunotherapy begins – skin tests with individual allergens, rather than with allergen extract containing a mix of allergens.

A far more radical approach to immunotherapy is now the focus of attention for some medical researchers. They are hoping to devise preventive treatments which can stop allergies before they start, for use by children from atopic families (see p. 8). The underlying idea here is to reverse the basic shift in the immune response, from Th1 cells to Th2 cells. It is this shift to Th2 cells which produces the allergic tendency (see pp. 11–13).

Some interesting findings have already been made in this area, including the surprising discovery that the balance of Th1 cells and Th2 cells can be adjusted even in people with long-standing allergies. Inspired by discoveries about hygiene and allergy (see p. 21), British researchers have made a vaccine from extracts of African soil bacteria, and used it to treat patients with asthma. The results are promising, with at least one-third of the asthmatics tested showing far less reaction to inhaled allergen after they had been injected with the vaccine. This was just a pilot study, but a full scientific trial is planned and, if the treatment proves as useful as the preliminary studies suggest, this could be a common treatment in a few years' time.

Chapter 6

diets for allergy and intolerance

This chapter covers two main types of diet: avoidance diets and diagnostic diets. Both are intended for people with sensitivity to food.

An **avoidance diet** is for people who already know what food or foods affect them, and simply need to avoid those foods. A **diagnostic diet** is for those whose symptoms suggest that they might be suffering from food sensitivity of some kind, and who cannot be diagnosed by indirect methods such as skin tests, because true food allergy is not involved. A diagnostic diet is intended primarily to show whether or not food is causing the symptoms.

The diagnostic diets themselves fall into two basic categories. Firstly, there are diets that, by a process of elimination, identify a particular food (or foods) as a cause of symptoms. Called **elimination diets**, these are used to diagnose idiopathic food intolerance (see p. 74) and certain other kinds of sensitivity reactions to particular foods. An elimination diet is *purely* diagnostic – simply a means to establish which foods are at fault. To this end, all commonly eaten foods are avoided at the outset, and each food is then tested individually. Once an elimination diet is complete, the information gathered is used to establish a suitable avoidance diet. For example, if milk, wheat and oranges caused symptoms during the testing phase of the elimination diet, those foods are all avoided in future.

Secondly, there are **specific diagnostic diets**, which are a great deal simpler to carry out than elimination diets. A specific diagnostic diet aims to reduce the intake of a particular substance that is found in certain foods. The substances concerned – histamine or nickel, for example – are known to cause particular symptoms in susceptible people.

A specific diagnostic diet simply cuts out all the foods that contain large amounts of the substance under suspicion. If this diet alleviates the symptoms, and does so consistently, it is plausible that the substance concerned is indeed the culprit. However, the diet should be stopped and then started again, preferably several times, to check the response. Once the sensitivity is confirmed in this way, the avoidance diet which follows is basically the same as the diet used for diagnosis.

Note that there is no agreed terminology for these different kinds of diet, and the definitions given above will not necessarily be followed in other publications. You may even come across 'elimination diet' being used to mean 'avoidance diet', which is particularly confusing. If you are consulting other sources of information, check the context carefully to see what meaning is intended.

There is one odd man out in this chapter – the diet to protect against asthma, described on pp. 206–7. It is neither an avoidance diet nor a diagnostic diet, but a health-promoting diet of the kind commonly advocated to combat other widespread conditions, such as cancer and heart disease. In fact, it has a remarkable number of similarities to diets that reduce the risk of these other diseases.

The anti-asthma diet is immensely healthy, whereas many avoidance diets carry a risk of malnourishment. An allergic individual following any kind of restrictive diet – especially a child – should be medically assessed for the possible risks. That is why it is important to talk to your doctor before starting any dietary treatment or investigation. A referral to a dietician or nutritionist may be necessary, and your doctor can arrange this.

When malnutrition does occur as a result of self-treatment, there are often very complex factors at work. One potential hazard with dietary treatment is that psychological problems can easily become

entwined with obsessions about food. Eating can be a potent form of self-expression, or a way of exerting control over oneself and others. Many doctors have seen patients who are mistakenly convinced that food sensitivity is at the root of their health problems, or those of their children. In some cases, no amount of objective evidence to the contrary will deflect people from such beliefs.

A few people with mistaken beliefs of this kind impose very restrictive diets on themselves – or sometimes on the whole family. The food rules that they establish may be a way of limiting contact with the outside world, avoiding other problems and issues by making diet the central focus, or simply making demands on other people's time and attention.

The current fad for identifying 'food allergy' using very dubious diagnostic tests (see p. 93) will probably send many more psychologically vulnerable people down this route.

Another unhelpful trend in the dietary field is the wholesale (and usually ineffective) use of vitamins, minerals and other supplements for a great variety of diseases, including allergy and other forms of sensitivity. It is important to realise that none of the sensitivity diseases described in this book has nutritional deficiency as its primary cause, so supplements are not a major part of treatment in most cases. For the majority of people with some kind of sensitivity disease, a supplement will make only a small difference, if any. However, it is true that, with *some* sensitivity problems, certain supplements may be helpful to certain individuals. The use of Vitamin C in asthma (see p. 207) is one example of this, and there are some other instances mentioned in Chapter 2.

Generally speaking, it is better to get the vitamins, minerals and other nutrients you need (such as antioxidants) from food, not from tablets. Studies of adult-onset asthma have shown that only natural Vitamin E protects against the disease: supplements have no effect.

Many vitamins and minerals, along with various plant and animal extracts, are now referred to as **nutriceuticals** – in other words, substances that are classed as nutritional supplements for legal purposes, but are being marketed as if they were medicinal drugs (pharmaceuticals). Many doctors are concerned about this, if only because of the duplicity involved. These substances can be sold freely to the public only because they are, in theory, nutritional supplements, yet they are actively promoted to the public as if they were drugs.

The marketing is usually indirect, to avoid falling foul of the law, but very effective nonetheless. Advertisements for the product avoid making any medicinal claims, since these would be unlawful, and just speak vaguely of 'health-giving properties'. The specific medicinal claims are made in magazine articles (which often appear right beside the advertisement), penned by journalists who have been supplied with a great many 'facts' – actually unsubstantiated claims – by the manufacturer of the supplement. These claims are reproduced uncritically, so the journalists are simply acting as mouthpieces for the manufacturer. There is no law preventing this.

This is a ruse that circumvents important laws intended to protect consumers from misleading advertising. Few of these products are likely to be damaging – although there are concerns about some, especially beta-carotene supplements (see p. 207). What matters here are the large amounts of money being made from products that frequently have few benefits for those who take them.

Reading food labels

What exactly is in ready-made food? People with food sensitivity, especially those with severe food allergy or coeliac disease, need a simple answer to this question, but frequently they don't get one. Research among food-allergy sufferers has found that, in the course of a year, half of them inadvertently eat the food they are trying to avoid, owing to a lack of information about ingredients. Restaurants and canteens are responsible for many of these accidents, and most of the fatalities (see p. 111), but packaged food also plays a part.

Unfortunately, many food ingredients that are potentially allergenic, such as milk and eggs, appear in packaged food without this being stated on the label in everyday language. The information is usually there somewhere, however – you just need to know what words to look for.

Decoding food labels

The problems with food labels fall into two general categories:
- some of the ingredients are described using technical terms. These are usually specific constituents of the original foodstuff e.g. lactalbumin, one of the proteins found in milk.
- some manufactured ingredients can be made from different starting materials. So an item such as 'edible starch' could be made from either wheat or maize (corn), while 'hydrolysed protein' could be made from soya, maize or yeast, sometimes with wheat added.

One day, no doubt, manufacturers will realise what a burden this type of obscure labelling imposes on their allergic customers and will start using plain language. In the meantime, food-allergy sufferers just have to learn all the terms that may be used for their culprit food or foods.

Labels used in health-food shops and delicatessens are another matter altogether. Here the problem is with exotic-sounding items, such as kamut, which is actually an allergenic food (wheat).

Maize (Corn)
Items always made from maize: dextrose, cornflour, cornmeal, cornstarch, polenta

Items sometimes made from maize: baking powder, cereal starch, edible starch, food starch, glucose syrup, hydrolysed protein, hydrolysed vegetable protein, malt, malt flavouring, modified starch, modified food starch, starch, textured vegetable protein, vegetable gum, vegetable protein, vegetable starch

Note that the gum on envelopes and stamps is sometimes made from maize, and that many medicines contain cornstarch.

Eggs
Items always made from eggs: ovalbumin

Items sometimes made from eggs: lecithin (In fact this is rare in foods – lecithin is usually derived from soya. Only in pharmaceuticals is lecithin likely to be derived from egg.)

Terms used for egg on cosmetics and toiletries: Ovum

Fish
Be very cautious when travelling. The use of fish meal as an ingredient of spicy sauces is common in Southeast Asia, and in some

parts of Africa. The strength of the spices may make the flavour of the fish undetectable.

Milk

Items always made from milk: casein, caseinate, lactalbumin, whey

Terms used for milk on cosmetics and toiletries: Lac

If you see the term 'dairy-free' on standard packaged foods, you can safely assume that the contents are free from goat's and sheep's milk, as well as cow's milk. But be more wary with home-made or locally produced foods labelled 'dairy-free' – some people think that 'dairy' refers only to cow's milk.

Parev or pareve is a term used for kosher (Jewish) food that contains neither milk nor meat. However, there can be contamination with traces of milk.

Lactose is a sugar produced from milk, and while it is not allergenic itself, it may contain a trace of allergenic milk proteins. The amounts involved are tiny, and will only affect the most sensitive individuals.

The label 'non-milk fat' sometimes misleads people if they just glance quickly at labels. The fact that a product contains non-milk fat does not, of course, mean that it is entirely milk-free – remember to look for all the synonyms of milk (see above).

Nuts

Items always made from nuts: frangipane, marzipan, praline

Standard packaged food will almost always include the nuts by name, but if you are buying other food (e.g. from a stall selling home-made food) watch out for the above names.

Be very cautious about unrefined nut oils (see p. 110). Almond essence may be produced chemically, in which case it is safe, but some is made from real almonds and could be allergenic.

Terms used for nuts on cosmetics and toiletries: Prunus, Juglans, Bertholletia, Corylus

Peanuts

Items always made from peanuts: arachis oil, groundnut oil, satay sauce

Unrefined peanut oil should be avoided. This is not much used, and unlikely to be encountered except in Indian and Oriental cooking. Most groundnut oil sold in Britain and Europe, or used in packaged foods, is refined and considered safe (see p. 110).

Alternative names: arachide, beer nuts, cacahuete, earth nuts, goobernuts, groundnuts, monkey nuts

You are only likely to encounter these names on imported food, or when travelling. Always be very careful with Indian or Southeast Asian food, where the use of peanuts is very common and often not at all obvious. Avoid chocolate from Poland, which often contains peanuts that are not declared on the label.

Items sometimes made from peanuts: hydrolysed vegetable protein (The usual source is soya or wheat, but some is derived from peanuts.)

Terms used for peanut on cosmetics and toiletries: Arachis hypogea, Arachis oil

Sesame

Items always made from sesame or containing some sesame: gomashio, halva, hummus (houmus), tahini

Standard packaged food will almost always use the term 'sesame' on the label, but if you are buying other food (e.g. from a health-food shop or a stall selling home-made food) watch out for the above names.

Check carefully for sesame in any Chinese packaged food (e.g. stir-fry oils) and in the drink Aqua Libra. Sesame oil is usually unrefined and therefore allergenic (see p. 110). Watch out for contamination by traces of sesame in bakeries and delicatessens where goods are sold unwrapped.

Term used for sesame on cosmetics and toiletries: Sesamum indicum

Shellfish

Items sometimes containing shellfish: curry paste, fish sauce and other sauces/pastes used in Southeast Asian cooking

Standard packaged food should mention shellfish specifically, but you may need to read the label carefully. Be cautious about bottles of imported sauce, and home-made or takeaway food.

Soya

Items always or usually made from soya: miso, soy sauce, tofu, textured vegetable protein, vegetable protein

Items sometimes made from soya: hydrolysed protein, hydrolysed vegetable protein, lecithin, vegetable gum, vegetable starch

Changes in ingredients

Unfortunately, the ingredients of a product can change without any obvious warning on the label, or any change in the packaging. You should always check the label in detail, every time – even on foods that you have eaten before without any trouble.

Wheat

Items always made from wheat: bran, flour, graham flour, hard flour, strong flour, wholemeal flour (there are non-wheat brans and flours, of course, but the words 'bran' or 'flour', without any qualification, usually mean wheat)

Regional names for particular types of wheat: bulgur or bulgar wheat, chilton, couscous, dinkel, durum, einkorn, farro, fu, kamut, semolina, spelt, triticum, triticale (a hybrid of wheat and rye)

Items sometimes made from wheat: baking powder, cereal binder, cereal filler, cereal protein, cereal starch, edible starch, food starch, hydrolysed protein, hydrolysed vegetable protein, modified starch, modified food starch, starch, textured vegetable protein, vegetable protein, vegetable starch.

Assume that bread, crispbread, pastry, pasta and noodles are made from wheat, unless definitely labelled otherwise (and read the label in detail too, because a little wheat is often added to items such as rye bread and rye crackers).

Note that buckwheat is not wheat at all – it is not even a cereal. Nor does it commonly affect coeliacs, as is sometimes claimed, though a few coeliacs may develop an intolerance reaction to it, through eating it very regularly.

For more information on avoiding gluten, see p. 177.

Yeast

Items usually made from yeast: leavening

Items sometimes made from yeast: hydrolysed protein, hydrolysed vegetable protein

Labelling loopholes

Manufacturers do not have to include on the label:
- Any ingredients used in an earlier manufacturing process e.g. yeast used to make bread for breadcrumbs, wheat flour added to spices or mustard powder during the grinding process, or bread used to innoculate blue cheeses with mould – this can leave minute traces of gluten in the cheese

- Residues left by substances used during processing, such as wheat flour used to dust processing lines or prevent dried fruits from sticking together. Manufacturers do not need to declare these residues on the label because the substance serves no function in the final product and is present in amounts that are considered insignificant. The vast majority of those with coeliac disease or food allergy will tolerate such microscopic traces, but the most sensitive individuals may not. Some coeliacs are even affected by food additives manufactured from cereals (see p. 177).
- The individual constituents of a composite ingredient (such as breadcrumbs on a fish fillet, or slices of salami or sausage on a pizza), if that composite ingredient makes up less than 25% of the finished product. This is called the 25% rule. Taking sausages as an example, these can contain quite a few allergenic foods including soya, milk powder or wheat. These offending ingredients could make up 5%, 10% or even more of the finished product, so you need to be vigilant when reading labels. An amendment to this rule is now being debated by the European Parliament. The 25% rule would no longer apply to the major allergenic foods – milk, eggs, tree nuts, peanuts, sesame, fish, crustacean shellfish (shrimps, prawns, etc.), soya, wheat and all other cereals that contain gluten. Sulphite additives (see box on p. 207) are also on the list. Under the proposed new rules, which are expected to come into force in December 2001, if a composite food contains one of these ingredients, that ingredient must be declared on the label.

'May contain' labels

Labels reading 'May contain nut traces' are springing up like weeds on packaged food. Similar labels relating to sesame, milk and eggs are also starting to appear.

Allergy sufferers, suddenly unable to eat foods that they formerly enjoyed, feel very frustrated about this development. Many suspect that these labels are often just a defensive tactic – warning off consumers with food sensitivity when the chance of the food containing the allergen is actually very small. The danger is that some allergy sufferers may stop taking the labels seriously. Teenagers, in particular, are increasingly dismissive of 'May contain' labels, and this is a huge worry for parents.

Could the need for 'May contain' labels be eliminated altogether with more careful factory procedures? The problem here is that, with nuts, perfect cleaning of production machinery is extremely difficult. Most machines have nooks and crannies in which a nut from one production process can become lodged, only to free itself later during the making of a non-nut product. It is quite possible that someone could encounter a whole nut, or substantial pieces of nut, in a non-nut product. That is why no one with nut allergy, even if it is relatively mild, should disregard 'May contain nut traces' labels.

Some makers of confectionery and biscuits have now set up dedicated nut-free production lines, with stringent precautions to avoid any possibility of contamination. This allows them to market products that are guaranteed nut-free. If you cannot purchase these locally, you may be able to order them by mail or over the Internet (see p. 255).

Note that packaged foods that have been produced on nut-free production lines in the past can be switched to different production lines, that necessitate a 'May contain nut traces' label.

In some cases, a product is manufactured in two separate places, one of which is nut-free, while the other is not. Consequently, the same product may sometimes be sold with a 'May contain' label and sometimes without. Don't disregard these labels, however illogical they might seem.

Packaging errors

As most people with food allergy are now aware, ready-made foods sometimes go out in the wrong packaging. Alarming cases that have occurred in recent years include hazelnut yoghurts labelled Toffee Yoghurt, and Vegetable Bake (containing nuts) sold in packets intended for Vegetable Lasagne (no nuts).

Manufacturers are increasingly aware of the hazards and when mistakes are discovered, allergy information web-sites and organisations such as the Anaphylaxis Campaign are quickly informed, so that they can alert allergy sufferers.

Belonging to such an organisation (see p. 255), and/or checking web-sites regularly, is definitely recommended for anyone with food allergy. However, you should bear in mind that no information service can protect you completely from this hazard. The odds against it are high, but one day you might just be the unlucky person who first discovers a packaging error by suffering an allergic reaction. To protect yourself as far as possible:

When is a nut not a nut?

Those with nut allergies often worry about eating nutmeg and coconut. In fact, allergic reactions to these are rare. People with nut allergy are no more likely to react to nutmeg or coconut than anyone else.

Tiger nuts or chufa nuts are not nuts at all, but the roots of a sedge plant – they are most unlikely to cross-react with true nuts.

Peanuts, botanically speaking, are not true nuts at all. They are legumes (pulses). There can be cross-reactions with soya and/or lupin (proceed very carefully with this novel food ingredient) but reactions with other pulses are rare. Cross-reactions with tree nuts such as almonds and Brazils, are quite common however (see p. 15). Many people with peanut allergy can in fact eat tree nuts, but they should be aware that a cross-reaction could develop at some stage.

Because cross-reactions between tree nuts are so common, doctors tend to speak simply of 'nut allergy'. However, it is possible to be allergic to one type of tree nut, without being allergic to others.

- always check that the food in the packet looks like the photograph on the packet
- double-check, when you serve the food, by noting the conspicuous ingredients of the meal (carrots, for example), and ensuring that they are indeed on the list of ingredients – any discrepancy should make you suspicious
- note the smell and appearance of any ready-made food, before you taste it. Do this even for very simple things such as flavoured yoghurts
- only have a very tiny mouthful at first, and if you have any tingling of the lips or other symptoms, however mild, stop eating immediately (this is helpful for true food allergy only, not for coeliac disease)
- be especially cautious about vegetarian food if you are allergic to nuts or soya.

Latex in food

Those with latex allergy may react to very small traces of it in food. This sometimes occurs with packaged food or restaurant food that has been prepared by workers wearing latex gloves. On one occasion a highly allergic individual reacted to a water glass that had been handled by someone wearing latex gloves. The amounts of latex involved are minuscule, and only affect those with severe latex allergy. However, there is a strong case for workers handling food to wear non-latex gloves, especially with the rise in cases of latex allergy.

There are also reports of people with latex allergy reacting (usually very mildly) to cold-seal adhesives in food wrappers, such as those used for ice cream. The reaction only occurs if the wrapper actually touches the lips or mouth.

Gluten-free and wheat-free diets

Apricot and apple Eve's pudding

When it comes to making bread and cakes, wheat has some remarkable cooking properties that nothing else can match. Its characteristic proteins, called **gluten**, form very strong elastic threads. These make a stringy dough that can be stretched and stretched as the bread rises. As a result, the bubbles of gas given off by the yeast or baking powder are all embraced by the dough, giving an open, airy consistency to the finished product.

Have no illusions – without wheat flour you cannot make a crispy baguette or a well-risen cottage loaf. If you are able to eat rye, then rye flour makes a pretty good substitute, because it also contains gluten, though not as much as wheat flour. But a gluten-free diet excludes rye too (see p. 177), and then baking definitely becomes a challenge.

Even on a gluten-free diet, however, you can still make several perfectly edible, even delicious, types of bread and cake. The secret, especially with bread, is to accept that the texture is going to be different from wheat-based bread, but to add enough interesting flavours to give the finished product its own special character. The gluten-free bread you make at home will taste vastly better than the pale and pappy commercial substitutes – and at a fraction of the price.

Wheat-free and gluten-free bread tends not to keep as well as ordinary bread, so make a batch of small loaves and freeze some of them. You can slice them before freezing, then extract and defrost a few slices at a time, as needed. Bread that is not frozen should be kept in a plastic bag in the refrigerator. Even when kept in this way, the bread gets rather dry and tough after a few days, and will benefit from being toasted. Try spreading it with butter, margarine or solidified olive oil (see page 183) *before* putting it under the grill – this revives bread far better than ordinary toasting.

Pastry-making without wheat is also a challenge (see p. 180) but cakes, biscuits and other sweet items are much less of a problem. As long as you accept the limitations of non-wheat flours, cakes can be made perfectly well using gluten-free flours. With the right culinary tricks, you can even make a light fluffy sponge (see pp. 180-81).

To thicken sauces and gravy, you can use cornflour or any other non-wheat flour.

If you have an allergy or intolerance to other foods, besides wheat, the recipes here can be adapted accordingly. For example, commercial egg replacers (see p. 186) can be used in place of eggs, and milk substitutes (see p. 183) can replace cow's milk.

Wheat-free diets

This section is for people with an allergy or intolerance reaction to wheat. Those with coeliac disease should read the section on gluten-free diets.

In devising a successful diet for yourself, you need to take account of two factors:

1 How sensitive are you? If you have a true allergy (see p. 62) to wheat, you may be very sensitive and need to avoid even the tiniest amount of wheat. But if you are just intolerant of wheat (see pp. 74–6), you probably won't react to such small amounts, so you don't need to be so careful.

2 Are you sensitive only to wheat, or do you also react to related cereals, namely rye, barley and oats? Some people have to avoid these as well, because of cross-reactions (see p. 14).

Those who are highly sensitive to wheat *and* have cross-reactions to related cereals, need to follow the same kind of diet as the most sensitive coeliacs (see Gluten-free diets). Ready-made gluten-free foods (such as bread and biscuits) can be useful, and they should be safe for you, unless you are ultra-sensitive.

Those who don't have any cross-reactions to related cereals can tolerate the following:

- rye bread and rye crackers, as long as they are 100% rye – always double-check. If you buy rye bread from a local bakery, and it is unlabelled, make sure the staff understand that you must always have 100% rye bread. Ask them to tell you if they ever change the recipe – and jog their memories about this from time to time.
- beer – as long as it is brewed using barley. Most beer is, but watch out for German Weissbier, which is made from wheat.
- oatcakes, as long as they don't contain wheat flour or bran. Check the label carefully.

Gluten-free diets

A gluten-free diet is more restrictive than a wheat-free diet, since gluten is also found in rye, barley, triticale and spelt. All these must be carefully avoided.

At one time, this list would have included oats as well, but new research suggests that the proteins found in oats, called **avenin**, are sufficiently unlike gluten to be safe for many coeliacs. If you have coeliac disease, you *must* have medical approval before eating oats. Only those who are healthy and doing well on a gluten-free diet should try oats, and they should not eat more than one small serving (less than 50g) per day. It is vital that the oats are grown, harvested, transported, milled and packaged separately from all wheat to avoid contamination.

Various flours are used to make gluten-free breads, including flours derived from rice, potatoes, soya beans and buckwheat (not a true wheat). These special flours are sold in health-food shops, and can also be bought by mail order. For gram flour, try Indian groceries. There are also special gluten-free bread mixes available in both health-food shops and pharmacies, but these almost always contain soya, and it is best to avoid eating too much soya (see page 71).

Coeliacs who are extremely sensitive to gluten, and have to avoid all trace of it, should be very careful about ready-made food.

These are just some of the unexpected sources of gluten:

- Thickeners and stabilisers sometimes contain traces of gluten. These additives are very widely used in ready-made foods.
- A number of food additives (including caramel, citric acid, dextrin, mono- and di-glycerides, gum base, malt, malt flavouring, maltodextrin, maltose, MSG and vegetable gum) are manufactured from wheat, barley or oats. Although the amount of gluten/avenin they contain is extremely small, it can affect a few coeliacs.
- Barley enzymes, used to make rice milk, some brands of soya milk, soy sauce and miso, can leave minute traces of gluten in the finished product. Blue cheese can also contain minute traces of gluten (see p. 174).
- Whisky and gin – both grain-based spirits – can contain gluten. So may distilled white vinegar. These will only affect the most sensitive coeliacs, whereas beer must be avoided by all coeliacs, since it is made from barley.
- Composite ingredients in ready-made food are covered by the 25% rule (see p. 174), and frequently contain wheat.
- Wheat flour may be used as an aid to food preparation, leaving tiny residues in the food (see p. 174).
- Non-wheat flour may be delivered to the factories, or transferred from one area to another, through hoppers or vacuum tubes that have previously been used for wheat flour. Very low levels of contamination can occur in this way, sufficient to affect those coeliacs who are extremely sensitive. This is one problem with gluten-free foods (see below), unless they are made in dedicated gluten-free factories.
- Products labelled 'gluten-free' may not be suitable for the most sensitive coeliacs. Testing for very small amounts of gluten is difficult, and the international standard set by the FAO/WHO (not more than 200 parts per million) is dictated by what can be accurately measured, and therefore policed. Many countries (e.g. Sweden and the US) feel that the permitted level of gluten should be lower, and have set their own standards. These higher standards can be achieved by careful control of the production methods.

There is a great deal of useful detailed information about gluten in food on the Internet, but there is also some very misleading information on one particular web-site. It is advisable to consult several different sites.

Wheat-free baking powder

Some brands of baking powder contain a little wheat flour. You can make a wheat-free version by mixing 60g (2oz) sodium bicarbonate with 130g (4½oz) cream of tartar and 60g (2oz) of a non-wheat flour. Sieve together very thoroughly.

Brown bread

This mixture of buckwheat and potato flour makes a light-textured loaf that also toasts well.

PREPARATION TIME: 15 minutes, plus about 1 hour rising time
COOKING TIME: about 35 minutes
MAKES: 1 large loaf

250g (9oz) buckwheat flour
250g (9oz) potato flour
1 tsp salt
1 sachet easy-blend yeast
1 tbsp black treacle
25g (1oz) butter
1 large egg, beaten

Mix the flours, salt and yeast in a large bowl and rub in the butter. Dissolve the treacle in 225ml (8fl oz) hand-hot water. Add this and the egg to the flour, and mix to a soft dough. Transfer to a buttered 900g (2lb) loaf tin, wrap in a polythene bag and leave in a warm place for about 1 hour – or until the mixture has risen to the top of the tin.

Bake in a preheated oven at 220°C/ 425°F/gas mark 7 for about 35 minutes until risen and firm to the touch. Remove from the tin and tap the base – it should sound hollow. If not, return to the oven for a further 5 minutes. Cool in the tin for 10–15 minutes.

Variations: many different kinds of flavourings can be added to this bread. Try seeds such as poppy seeds, mustard seeds, caraway seeds and onion seeds (Indian stores usually stock these with their spices). Sunflower seeds and sesame seeds – either plain or lightly toasted – are also good. A combination of black olives, sun-dried tomatoes and a pinch of mixed herbs makes a Mediterranean-style bread.

Seeded rice bread

This makes a delicious, 'nutty', textured loaf that is yeast-free as well as wheat-free. It toasts quite well.

PREPARATION TIME: 30 minutes
COOKING TIME: 40 minutes
MAKES: 1 small loaf

150g (5½oz) brown rice, well rinsed
100g (3½oz) rice flour
100g (3½oz) fine oatmeal
1 tsp wheat-free baking powder
1 tsp salt
50g (1¾oz) sunflower seeds
25g (1oz) linseed
1 large, slightly under-ripe pear, peeled, cored and coarsely grated
2 large eggs, beaten
2 tbsp vegetable oil
4 tbsp buttermilk, live natural yogurt, milk or milk substitute

Cook the rice in plenty of boiling water for 15–20 minutes until tender. Drain thoroughly and cool slightly.

Preheat the oven to 200°C/400°F/gas mark 6.

Combine all the ingredients in a large bowl, then transfer to a well-oiled 450g (1lb) loaf tin and bake for about 40 minutes, until slightly risen and golden, and firm to the touch. Cool slightly, then turn out onto a wire rack and leave until completely cold. Serve cut into thick slices.

Banana loaf

This semi-sweet bread is yeast-free as well as gluten-free. It is good for packed lunches – and it toasts well.

PREPARATION TIME: 10 minutes
COOKING TIME: about 1 hour
MAKES: 1 large loaf

4 medium ripe or under-ripe bananas
300g (10½oz) brown rice flour, sieved
100g (3½oz) butter, softened
2 tbsp wheat-free baking powder
2 large eggs
225ml (8 fl oz) milk or soya milk

Butter and line the base of a 900g (2lb) loaf tin. Peel and cut up the bananas and place in a food processor with the remaining ingredients. Blend thoroughly, then transfer the mixture to the prepared tin. Bake in a preheated oven at 180°C/ 350°F/gas mark 4 for about 1 hour until risen and firm to the touch. Cool in the tin then turn out onto a wire rack and leave to cool completely.

Rich herb bread

This is useful for those who have to avoid yeast as well as wheat/gluten.

PREPARATION TIME: 20 minutes
COOKING TIME: 30–40 minutes
MAKES: 1 small loaf

110g (4oz) gram or chickpea flour
1 tsp syrup or honey
2 tbsp olive oil
1 tsp salt
1 unripe pear, peeled and grated
200ml (7fl oz) boiling water
2 eggs
½ onion, finely chopped
fresh herbs (thyme, tarragon or marjoram)

Mix the first five ingredients, then pour on the boiling water. Separate the eggs, beat the yolks thoroughly and add to the flour mixture when it has cooled, along with the onion and herbs. This mixture should now be the consistency of double cream. If too thick, add a little more water.

Whisk the egg whites until they will stand in soft peaks. Carefully fold them into the flour mixture. Pour into a well-greased loaf tin and cook at 180°C/ 350°F/gas mark 4 for 30–40 minutes.

Crispy millet baps

Tasty and filling, these are popular with children. They make no pretence to be bread but are an excellent substitute for breakfast toast or a lunchtime sandwich. They are free from yeast, milk and eggs, as well as wheat.

PREPARATION TIME: 30 minutes
COOKING TIME: about 20 minutes
MAKES: about 20 small baps

225g (8oz) millet seeds
1 tsp salt
150g (5½oz) peanut butter (or cashew, pecan or another nut butter)
1 tsp sesame seeds, toasted until golden
oil for frying

Wash the millet and soak overnight. Wash again to remove the starch, drain and add 600ml (1 pt) of water plus the salt. Boil over a low heat for 20 minutes, or until the water is absorbed.

While still hot add the nut butter and sesame seeds. Mix together well using a potato masher to break up the millet. Take egg-sized lumps of the mixture, roll into a ball between the palms of your hands, then squash into a flattish shape. It is vital to do this while the mixture is still warm.

Fry the baps in oil over a low heat, for about 20 minutes, or until the outside is golden and crunchy. (They can also be frozen, and then fried from frozen, for a quick meal.) Serve with fruit or a salad.

Savoury spiced pancakes

This variation on a traditional drop scone makes a good substitute for bread. The pancakes are delicious served warm from the pan. When cold, they may be reheated in a moderate oven.

PREPARATION TIME: 25 minutes
MAKES: about 27

Seeded rice bread

100g (3½oz) gram flour
100g (3½oz) rice flour
1 tsp wheat-free baking powder
1 tbsp ground cumin
large pinch of salt
1 large egg
300ml (½ pt) coconut milk
vegetable oil for frying
To serve:
Skinned and chopped fresh tomato mixed with a little freshly chopped coriander, or fried mushrooms with chopped spring onion and parsley moistened with a little crème fraîche.

Mix the dry ingredients together in a bowl then beat in the egg and coconut milk to give a thick batter. Set a large non-stick frying pan or griddle over medium heat. Generously oil the surface of the pan then drop well-spaced tablespoons of the mixture into the pan.

Cook until the edges of the drop scones start to form bubbles and the base of each is golden, then carefully turn and cook on the second side until golden. Keep warm, covered with a clean tea towel, while you make the rest.

Serve warm, spread with butter or topped with one of the savoury mixtures.

Pressed prune and walnut bread

Variations: for sweet drop scones omit the cumin and add 30g (1oz) caster sugar and either a sweet spice such as cinnamon, or the finely grated zest of 1 lemon or orange.

Pressed prune and walnut bread

Based on a traditional Spanish recipe, this is delicious served with cheese, or as a snack on its own.

PREPARATION TIME: 10 minutes, plus overnight
COOKING TIME: 45 minutes
MAKES: 1 x 18cm (7in) loaf

500g (1lb 2oz) ready-to-eat pitted prunes
100g (3½oz) walnut or pecan halves
50g (1¾oz) brown rice flour
1 large egg, beaten

Place all the ingredients in a bowl and mix together. Press into an oiled 18cm (7in) sandwich tin, cover with oiled foil and cook in a preheated oven at 170°C/ 325°F/gas mark 3 for 45 minutes. Place a heavy weight on top and leave until completely cold before unmoulding. Serve cut into thick slices using a serrated knife.

Walnut macaroons

Lemon surprise pudding

Rich cheese biscuits

These crisp biscuits are good to serve with drinks. Store them in an airtight tin.

PREPARATION TIME: 20 minutes
COOKING TIME: about 25 minutes
MAKES: 20 biscuits

55g (2oz) soya flour
40g (1½oz) potato flour
40g (1½oz) rice flour
115g (4oz) butter, softened
115g (4oz) Cheddar cheese, grated
1 large egg, separated
2 tbsp seeds such as celery or poppy

Mix the flours together in a bowl, then work in the butter, cheese and egg yolk to give a firm dough. Roll into 20 balls. Lightly whisk the egg white and turn the balls in it until lightly coated, then dip in the seeds to lightly coat.

Space the balls well apart on baking trays and press down firmly to flatten. Bake in a preheated oven at 200°C/400 °F/ gas mark 6 for about 25 minutes until golden. Cool slightly then transfer to a wire rack. Leave until cold and crisp.

Whisked sponge cake

This cake's lightness lies in the whisking. A trail of the mixture, falling from the whisks, should remain visible for at least 30 seconds. Then it's time to add the flour.

PREPARATION TIME: 25 minutes
COOKING TIME: 25–30 minutes
MAKES: 1 x 23cm (9in) cake

75 g (2¾oz) gram flour
50g (1¾oz) cornflour
4 large eggs
125g (4½oz) caster sugar
50g (1¾oz) butter, melted
To serve:
jam or lemon curd
whipped cream (optional)
caster sugar

Millet tabbouleh

Tabbouleh is a salad from the Middle East that is traditionally made with cracked wheat. Millet makes a very tasty wheat-free alternative. This dish can be useful for packed lunches.

PREPARATION TIME: about 40 minutes
MAKES: 4–6 servings

175g (6oz) millet
7 tbsp olive oil
3 tbsp lemon juice
3 tbsp each freshly chopped mint and
  flat-leaf parsley
2 spring onions, finely chopped
salt and pepper

Place the millet in a saucepan with 1 tbsp oil and cook over medium heat, stirring, for 2–3 minutes until lightly toasted. Stir in 350ml (12fl oz) boiling water and simmer uncovered for about 20 minutes until the water is absorbed and the millet seeds are just cooked. Transfer to a bowl, stir in the rest of the oil and season generously. Stir in the lemon juice and fork it through the mixture. Leave to cool, then add the herbs and spring onion and stir well.

Variations: add other finely chopped ingredients such as tomato, red pepper or dried apricots.

Wheat-free flan pastry

Make a flan as suggested below, or chill the pastry then grate it roughly over a savoury or sweet pie filling. For a savoury pie, the grated pastry can be mixed with grated cheese.

PREPARATION TIME: 15 minutes, plus 30
  minutes freezing
COOKING TIME: about 20 minutes
MAKES: 1 x 20cm (8in) flan case

125g (4½oz) fine cornmeal (maize flour)
50g (1¾oz) gram flour
25g (1oz) arrowroot powder
25g (1oz) ground almonds
75g (2¾oz) butter or baking margarine
1 egg white

Mix the dry ingredients together in a bowl then rub in the butter. Mix to a soft dough with the egg white. Press the pastry evenly into a 20cm (8in) fluted flan tin and set in the freezer for a minimum of 30 minutes.

Preheat the oven to 200°C/400°F/ gas mark 6 and cook the flan case towards the top of the oven for about 20 minutes, until lightly golden.

Variation: for sweet pastry, add 25g (1oz) caster sugar

Sift the flours together. Butter a 23cm (9in) spring-release tin and line the base with greaseproof paper. Using a hand-held electric whisk, whisk the eggs and sugar in a heatproof glass bowl over a saucepan of simmering water for about 10 minutes until thick and mousse-like.

Fold the flour into the egg mixture in 2–3 batches until completely incorporated, then fold in the butter.

Transfer to the prepared tin and cook in a preheated oven at 190°C/375°F/gas mark 5 for about 25 minutes until risen and golden. Cool slightly then remove from the tin and cool on a wire rack. When cold, split and fill with jam or lemon curd, and whipped cream if wished. Dust with caster sugar.

Walnut macaroons

These biscuits are good with coffee. Store in an airtight container. If you want, only decorate half of them with walnut halves, then sandwich together with the other halves using coffee-, chocolate- or orange-butter cream, or whipped cream. Do this just before serving.

PREPARATION TIME: 15 minutes
COOKING TIME: about 45 minutes
MAKES: 24

rice paper
2 egg whites
100g (3½oz) golden icing sugar
100g (3½oz) walnut pieces, finely chopped
grated zest and juice of ½ small unwaxed lemon (if waxed, wash thoroughly in hot water)
24 walnut halves

Line a large baking tray with rice paper. Whisk the egg whites in a heatproof glass bowl until stiff. Stir in the icing sugar, chopped walnuts, lemon zest and juice, and stir over a saucepan of simmering water for about 10 minutes until the mixture is slightly stiffened. Drop well-spaced spoonfuls of the mixture onto the rice paper and top each with a walnut half.

Bake in a preheated oven at 150°C/300°F/gas mark 2 for about 45 minutes. They should be risen but still slightly chewy. Cool on the tray, then trim away the excess rice paper.

Lemon surprise pudding

The surprise is in the two layers. You end up with a creamy lemon sauce topped with a delicate sponge.

PREPARATION TIME: 20 minutes
COOKING TIME: about 45 minutes
MAKES: 4–6 servings

50g (1¾oz) butter
125g (4½oz) caster sugar
2 large eggs, separated
25g (1oz) cornflour, sieved
25g (1oz) fine cornmeal (maize flour), sieved
finely grated zest and juice of 2 unwaxed lemons (if using waxed lemons, wash thoroughly in hot water)
250ml (9fl oz) milk
To serve:
icing sugar

Cream the butter and sugar with 1 tbsp hot water until pale and fluffy. Beat in the egg yolks followed by the flours. Slowly stir in the lemon zest and juice, and then the milk. The mixture may appear to have curdled but this is normal.

Whisk the egg whites to form soft peaks, then fold into the lemon mixture. Transfer to a 1litre (1¾pt) ovenproof dish and set in a roasting tin. Pour hot water from a kettle around the dish and cook in a preheated oven at 180°C/350°F/gas mark 4 for about 45 minutes, until risen and just firm to the touch. Dust with icing sugar and serve immediately.

Apricot and apple Eve's pudding

This wheat-free Eve's pudding can be varied by changing the fruit. Try peaches, strawberries or blackberries instead of the apricots.

PREPARATION TIME: 30 minutes
COOKING TIME: about 1 hour
MAKES: 4–6 servings

411g can of apricot halves in juice
2 medium cooking apples, peeled and thickly sliced
50g (1¾oz) caster sugar
Topping:
125g (4½oz) butter, softened
125g (4½oz) caster sugar
2 large eggs
125g (4½oz) ground almonds mixed with 1 tsp wheat-free baking powder
50g (1¾oz) flaked almonds
To serve:
pouring cream or whipped cream

Pour the juice from the can of apricots into a saucepan, add the apple and sugar and cook gently for about 5 minutes, until the apple is softened. Remove from the heat and stir in the apricots. Transfer to a 1litre (1¾pt) ovenproof dish.

In a separate bowl, cream the butter and sugar together until pale and fluffy then beat in the eggs one at a time. Fold in the ground almonds and baking powder. Spread the almond mixture over the fruit and sprinkle with flaked almonds. Cook in a preheated oven at 180°C/350°F/gas mark 4 for about 1 hour until risen and golden and just firm to the touch. Serve with pouring cream or whipped cream.

Fruit lassi

Avoiding milk and lactose

There are two quite distinct reasons for avoiding milk: either to avoid **milk proteins** or to avoid **lactose**, the sugar found in milk. It is important not to confuse these two because the details of the avoidance diet required are different. Only a few people need to avoid both milk proteins *and* lactose.

Diarrhoea and wind in response to drinking milk, but few other symptoms, usually indicates a reaction to lactose – but a reaction to milk proteins could be an alternative explanation. If it is a reaction to lactose, this may be due to either primary lactase deficiency or secondary lactase deficiency – your doctor can order tests to make an exact diagnosis (see p. 79). Note that a bout of diarrhoea, however caused, often produces a temporary lactose intolerance (secondary lactase deficiency).

Any symptoms other than (or in addition to) diarrhoea and wind strongly suggest a reaction to milk proteins. This might be a true allergy, another type of immune reaction to milk (see pp. 72–3), or an idiopathic intolerance reaction (see pp. 76–7). In theory, skin tests should identify true allergic reactions to milk proteins. Unfortunately, skin tests are not infallible, and it is possible to have a genuine allergy or other immune reaction to milk proteins, but give negative skin tests. This is especially common with babies (see p. 65 and p. 69). There are no accurate tests that can confirm intolerance reactions to milk proteins.

It is possible to have sensitivity to both milk proteins *and* lactose.

If tests do not give you a definitive answer, you may have to try both types of diet and see which one works. Remember that lactose intolerance may be only temporary.

Avoiding milk proteins

If you have a sensitivity reaction to cow's milk proteins, then you need to avoid:

- milk and all milk-based drinks, including lactose-reduced milk; drops and tablets to reduce lactose (see Using lactase replacers, p. 183) are safe and could be used with a tolerated milk (e.g. goat's milk)
- cream, yoghurt, crème fraîche
- all kinds of cheese, cottage cheese and cream cheese (some people may be able to tolerate Norwegian brown cheese, called Gjetøst, which is made with milk whey)
- white sauce, béchamel sauce and other creamy sauces
- custard, rice pudding and other milk-based puddings
- almost all home-made cakes, biscuits, cookies, pancakes and pastry
- some bread, rolls, waffles
- almost all chocolate
- casein, caseinate, and lactalbumin in packaged foods (see p. 173); you may be able to tolerate whey but experiment cautiously.

Unless your sensitivity is fairly mild, you will also need to avoid:

- butter, except clarified butter (ghee)
- most kinds of margarine (they generally contain milk derivatives, but some are milk-free – health-food shops are a good source of these).

As long as you do not have a severe allergy to milk, you should be able to tolerate clarified butter. Make this by melting butter over a low heat, pouring it into a glass jar, and leaving it to cool in the refrigerator. The milk proteins will settle to the bottom, and be visible as whitish granules – only eat the clear butter above this level.

Alternatively, put olive oil into a wide-necked container and place in the freezer. It will solidify, and can be used as a spread in place of butter.

A few of those with cow's-milk allergy can tolerate sheep's milk, and possibly (but less commonly) goat's milk. However, most people must avoid these as well. (There are also rare individuals who are allergic to goat's and sheep's milk but not to cow's milk.) Ass's milk, if you can get it, is tolerated by most with cow's-milk allergy. There are many substitutes for cow's milk now available, such as soya milk, almond milk, rice milk and hazelnut milk. Try a health-food shop for these. All can be used in place of ordinary milk when cooking.

Margarine or clarified butter can be used in recipes that call for butter. Soya yoghurt and cream make reasonable substitutes for ordinary yoghurt and cream.

Avoiding lactose

If you have lactose intolerance, you must avoid:
- milk and all milk-based drinks, unless lactose-reduced
- cream, crème fraîche
- most kinds of yoghurt, especially mild yoghurt. A very strong, acidic yoghurt may contain little lactose. The bacteria that make yoghurt turn lactose into lactic acid, so the more acidic it is, the less lactose it contains.
- cottage cheese and Norwegian brown cheese, or Gjetøst. Other kinds of cheese are usually so low in lactose that they are tolerated. Only those people with extreme lactose intolerance need to avoid all cheeses.
- white sauce, béchamel sauce, custard, rice pudding and other milk-based puddings
- almost all home-made cakes, since milk is generally used for baking. Items cooked with butter but not milk, such as biscuits, cookies and pastry, are usually tolerated, as is butter itself, and all margarine.
- lactose in medicines. Lactose powder is used in many tablets and capsules, just to bulk out the drugs. The amount used can be sufficient to evoke symptoms in some people with lactase deficiency. Certain asthma inhalers also contain lactose (see p. 162), and a small amount may be swallowed. The lactose from inhalers will affect you only if you have *severe* lactase deficiency.

Soy-based products, and all other milk substitutes are lactose-free. Sheep's milk, goat's milk and other milks (including human breast milk) all contain lactose.

Using lactase replacers

Many people with lactose intolerance are able to eat a more varied diet by using **lactase replacers**. These provide a temporary supply of the missing enzyme, lactase (see p. 79), which helps out by digesting the lactose in milky foods. Lactase replacers must be taken at the same time as the milky food, and are only effective for that one meal. The more lactose there is in the meal or snack, the more of the lactase replacer you need – trial and error is the only way of working out how much you need for a particular food. There are a number of different brands of lactase replacer now available, and it is worth trying out several. Some people find that they are sensitive to an added ingredient in some brands. Sources of lactase replacers include health-food shops and specialist suppliers – these can be located through the Internet (see p. 255).

Savoury white sauce

Savoury white sauce is the base of many dishes. Here the flavour of the wine and stock goes well with chicken, vegetables or fish.

PREPARATION TIME: 7–8 minutes
MAKES: approx. 600ml (1pt)

50g (1¾oz) milk-free baking margarine
50g (1¾oz) plain flour
200ml (7fl oz) dry cider or dry white wine
400ml (14fl oz) vegetable or chicken stock
1 bay leaf, salt and pepper

Melt the margarine in a small saucepan and stir in the flour. Cook, stirring, over a low heat for 1 minute then stir in the cider or wine, followed by the stock. Add the bay leaf and simmer, stirring occasionally, for 5 minutes until thickened. Season to taste.

Variations: add approx. 6 tbsp finely chopped herbs, e.g. parsley, chives, tarragon or chervil; or add English or French mustard; or add lemon juice.

Sweet white sauce

PREPARATION TIME: 5 minutes
MAKES: approx. 300ml (½ pt)

2 tbsp cornflour
25g (1oz) caster sugar
300ml (½pt) apple or white grape juice
4 tbsp soya cream
25g (1oz) milk-free margarine

In a saucepan, mix the cornflour and sugar with a little of the juice to give a smooth paste then gradually stir in the rest of the juice and bring to a simmer over a low heat. Simmer for 1–2 minutes until thickened, stirring all the time. Finally, add the soya cream and margarine.

Variations: melt in 100g (3½oz) or more of milk-free chocolate; or add rum or brandy to taste; or add 4–6 pieces finely chopped stem ginger together with 1–2 tbsp of their syrup.

Pancakes

Soya milk has a slightly thicker consistency than cow's milk and therefore more is used in this pancake recipe than would be needed in a traditional one.

PREPARATION TIME: 25 minutes

MAKES: approx. 16 small pancakes

150g (5½oz) plain flour, sieved
2 large eggs
pinch salt
450ml (16fl oz) soya milk
oil or milk-free margarine for frying
To serve:
lemon juice and caster sugar or golden
    syrup

Combine the flour, eggs, salt and soya milk in a liquidiser until smooth. Alternatively place the flour, eggs and salt in a bowl and slowly whisk in the soya milk to form a thin batter.

Heat approx.1 tsp oil or margarine in an 18cm (7in) non-stick frying pan and swirl until hot. Pour in sufficient batter to just cover the base of the pan and cook until golden. Turn and cook on the other side until golden.

Serve with lemon juice and caster sugar or with golden syrup.

Apple and frangipane tart

An alternative to a milk-based custard tart. The combination of apple and almond is delicious. Serve freshly baked. It can also be eaten cold, but if possible, warm it a little before serving.

PREPARATION TIME: 30 minutes

COOKING TIME: 1–1¼ hours

MAKES: 8 servings

Pastry:
175g (6oz) plain flour, sieved
100g (3½oz) milk-free baking margarine,
    softened
25g (1oz) caster sugar

Filling:
50g (1¾oz) milk-free sunflower margarine
100g (3½oz) ground almonds
100g (3½oz) plus 1 tbsp caster sugar
2 egg yolks
2 tbsp dark rum, brandy or orange juice
2 large dessert apples
4 tbsp apricot jam

Work the flour, margarine and sugar together with 1 tbsp cold water to make a soft dough. Roll out and use to line a deep 20cm (8in) fluted flan tin. Chill this while you prepare the filling.

Preheat the oven to 190°C/375°F/ gas mark 5. Beat together the margarine, ground almonds, 100g (3½oz) caster sugar, egg yolks and rum. Peel, core and roughly chop one apple and stir into the mixture. Spread this in the pastry case. Core and thinly slice the remaining apple and arrange the slices on top. Sprinkle with the remaining sugar and bake for 1–1¼ hours until risen and golden. Cool slightly then brush the surface with the apricot jam (warm this gently in a saucepan first).

Coconut rice pudding with mango

This pudding is based on a Thai recipe. The rice pudding will become thicker the longer it cooks and also as it cools. Make sure the mango is ripe.

PREPARATION TIME: 45 minutes

COOKING TIME: 30–40 minutes

MAKES: 6 servings

175g (6oz) pudding rice, rinsed
50–75g (1¾–2¾oz) sugar
1 litre (1¾ pt) carton rice milk
400ml (14fl oz) coconut milk
To serve:
1 extra large ripe mango, peeled
    and diced
toasted coconut shreds

Place the rice in a large saucepan with 50g (2oz) of the sugar and the rice milk and coconut milk. Bring to a simmer, stirring. Simmer gently for 30–40 minutes, stirring occasionally, until the rice is cooked and the milk absorbed. Add the extra sugar if wished. Serve warm or cold, topped with mango and toasted coconut.

Baked strawberry creams with strawberry sauce

The riper the strawberries the better, to give intensity to both the creams and the sauce.

PREPARATION TIME: 30 minutes

COOKING TIME: 20–25 minutes

MAKES: 6

100g (3½oz) caster sugar
4 tbsp Muscat wine
1 tsp lemon juice
350g (12oz) strawberries, hulled and
    sliced
4 large eggs, beaten
Sauce:
225g (8oz) strawberries, hulled and
    chopped
2 tbsp icing sugar
2 tbsp Muscat wine
To serve:
a few whole strawberries

Preheat the oven to 170°C/325°F/gas mark 3. Set six 150ml (¼pt) ramekins in a small roasting tin. If you plan to unmould the creams, oil the ramekins lightly.

Place the sugar, wine, lemon juice and strawberries in a saucepan and heat gently to dissolve the sugar. Bring to the boil and cook, uncovered, for 5 minutes. Cool slightly then purée in a liquidiser and whisk into the beaten eggs. Pass through a sieve then pour into the ramekin dishes.

Pour hot water from a kettle around the ramekins and cook in the centre of the oven for 20–25 minutes until lightly set.

Remove the dishes from the tin and allow to cool. Chill, if wished.

Combine all the sauce ingredients and liquidise until smooth. Pass through a fine sieve.

Serve the creams in the ramekins with a little sauce poured on top and decorated with a whole strawberry, or carefully unmould, pour a little sauce over, then decorate with a whole strawberry.

Variation: oil the ramekins. Dissolve 100g (3½oz) caster sugar in 4 tbsp water in a small saucepan over gentle heat, then cook to a rich caramel without stirring. Pour a little caramel into each oiled ramekin then continue as above. Pour the wine for the sauce into the pan used to make the caramel and warm gently to dissolve any leftover caramel, then continue with the sauce as above.

Frozen vanilla dessert

This is a cross between a sorbet and an ice cream.

PREPARATION TIME: 30 minutes, plus freezing
MAKES: 4–6 servings

1 vanilla pod, split
150g (5½oz) caster sugar
500g carton soya yoghurt

Place the vanilla pod and sugar in a saucepan with 300ml (½pint) water. Dissolve over gentle heat then bring to a simmer and simmer for 20 minutes. Leave to cool then remove the pod, scraping all the seeds from it and returning them to the syrup. Beat in the soya yoghurt and freeze.

You will get the best texture by using an ice-cream machine. Alternatively, freeze in a plastic container then remove from the freezer and beat the mixture well until smooth (you can do this in a food processor). Return to the freezer. Repeat this process once or twice.

Baked strawberry cream with strawberry sauce

Frozen vanilla desert

Variations: add 100g (3½oz) melted plain chocolate; or add 2 tbsp instant espresso coffee dissolved in 2 tbsp hot water. Alternatively, dissolve 100g (3½oz) caster sugar over a gentle heat in a small saucepan until it turns to a rich caramel; then add 100g (3½oz) unblanched almonds and stir with a metal spoon until they start to pop. Transfer to an oiled tray and leave to set. Crush roughly and add to the basic mixture.

Fruit lassi

This refreshing Indian drink can also be made with frozen fruit, in which case don't use iced water – cold will do.

PREPARATION TIME: 10 minutes
MAKES: approx. 1.35 litre (2¼pt)

500g carton soya yoghurt
50–75g (1¾–2¾oz) sugar
225g (8oz) berries such as raspberries, strawberries, blackberries or blueberries or the equivalent weight of chopped fruit such as mango, peach or papaya
600ml (1pt) iced water

Place all the ingredients in a liquidiser and blend until smooth.

Banana and strawberry shake

A special treat for a child who cannot have milk.

PREPARATION TIME: 5 minutes
MAKES: 600 ml (1 pt)

2 large, very ripe bananas
150g (5½oz) strawberries
1½ tbsp olive oil
a little nutmeg or other spice, if liked
200ml (7fl oz) water

Peel the bananas and roughly chop the fruit. Combine all the ingredients in a blender until very smooth. Serve immediately, or cover tightly and store in the refrigerator.

Variations: use a nectarine or a skinned peach instead of strawberries; use coconut milk (available in tins) instead of olive oil, and the flesh of a small mango, or half a large mango, instead of strawberries.

Egg-free diets

Tempura-style vegetables

There is nothing quite like an egg, especially when it comes to baking. Egg protein is the magical ingredient that holds together a pancake, and creates the light and delicate structure of sponge cakes, batter, soufflés, mousses and meringues.

Unfortunately, egg protein is also a potent allergen for some people, and a source of intolerance reactions for others.

Egg replacers, designed mainly for cake making, are one answer. They can be purchased from specialist suppliers (see p. 255) or ordered via your local health-food shop. These are protein-rich mixes which aim to simulate the structural properties of eggs, not the flavour. Recipes are usually supplied with the replacer, and it is best to follow these recipes at first, for guaranteed results. Once you have got the feel of using the egg replacer, you can experiment with substituting it for eggs in other cake recipes.

Note that these egg replacers make no attempt to simulate the richness and characteristic taste of eggs. You may need to add extra butter or other fats to your cake mix if using egg replacers. Vanilla extract can also improve the flavour of an egg-free cake.

Can cooking make eggs safe?

Cooking changes proteins, as eggs illustrate vividly. When a hot oven turns liquid egg white into a hard meringue, or a sloppy cake mix into a firm sponge, the visible effect is due to the egg protein being fundamentally changed.

Heating changes the basic molecular structure of the egg protein, in a process called **denaturing.** Whereas natural egg protein is liquid, denatured egg protein is solid.

Denaturing egg protein has subtle effects, as well as these obvious ones. When the structure of the molecule changes, *some* of the epitopes (the key features recognised by allergy antibodies – see box on p. 15) are obliterated. For a few allergy sufferers – those who react only to the epitopes affected by denaturing – thorough heating can therefore turn the egg allergen into a harmless substance.

If eggs are hard-boiled, the denaturing process occurs to the fullest possible extent. Consequently, some people with egg allergy can eat hard-boiled eggs without ill-effects. However, the same people still react badly to lightly cooked eggs, such as those in a soufflé or omelette because, with partial cooking, the denaturing process is incomplete.

Cakes made with eggs pose an interesting question – given that the cooking process for cakes is prolonged and at a high temperature, could they too be safe? This is something that allergists have not so far investigated.

If you want to test your response to hard-boiled eggs, you must do so under full medical supervision with resuscitation equipment available. Those who find that they can tolerate hard-boiled eggs might then want to test their reaction to cakes made with eggs. Again, there must be medical supervision for the test, in case of severe life-threatening reactions. You will, of course, have to convince your allergist that such a test is worthwhile.

Egg protein is not unique in being susceptible to denaturing – most proteins can be denatured, some by heat, some by other means. But only in a few cases (tuna fish, and fresh fruits and vegetables – see p. 110) does denaturing tend to destroy the allergenic epitopes.

Very rarely, changing the structure of a protein by cooking may actually *create* an allergenic epitope where none exists in the raw protein. There have been cases of individuals with an allergy to cooked fish but not raw fish, and to pecan nuts in biscuits but not uncooked pecans. Roasting peanuts makes them much more allergenic.

Tempura-style vegetables

Beer is a good alternative to eggs for making a batter and gives this Japanese batter a wonderfully light crisp texture. Have all the vegetables ready prepared so you can cook and eat the tempura as quickly as possible.

PREPARATION TIME: about 45 minutes

MAKES: 4–6 servings

400–500g (14oz–1lb 2oz) prepared vegetables cut into bite-sized pieces – choose from red pepper, asparagus, broccoli, spring onion or red onion, carrot, courgette, baby corn, button mushrooms, aubergine
150g (5½oz) self-raising flour, sieved, plus extra for coating vegetables
1 tsp salt
2 tbsp sesame seeds
250ml (9fl oz) lager or Japanese beer
vegetable oil for deep-frying
To serve:
equal quantities soy sauce and dry sherry mixed together, or sweet chilli sauce

Toss the prepared vegetables in flour until lightly coated then shake off the excess. Heat the oil in a large saucepan over medium heat until a cube of bread dropped in turns brown in 30 seconds.

Mix the measured flour, salt and sesame seeds and quickly stir in the beer – don't worry if the mixture is slightly lumpy. Dip the vegetables in the batter, a few pieces at a time, and then immediately into the hot oil. Cook until crisp and golden.

Drain on kitchen paper and keep warm in a hot oven. Continue in the same way until all the vegetables are cooked.

Serve with a dipping sauce made of soy sauce and dry sherry, or dip in sweet chilli sauce.

Caramelised onion tart

Feta in a crisp polenta jacket

Caramelised onion tart

This makes a good substitute for quiche and other egg-based flans. The long, slow cooking of the onions is important to bring out their natural sweetness.

PREPARATION TIME: 45 minutes

COOKING TIME: 30 minutes

MAKES: 6–8 servings

1kg (2lb 4oz) onions, halved then thinly sliced
4 tbsp olive oil
125g (4½oz) streaky bacon, finely chopped
1 tsp caraway seeds
salt and freshly ground black pepper
350g (12oz) bread dough or puff pastry

Place the onions in a very large saucepan with the oil, bacon and caraway seeds and cook over medium heat, stirring occasionally, for about 30 minutes until the onions are softened and lightly caramelised. Season generously.

Roll out the dough thinly and use to line a deep 24cm (9½in) fluted flan tin. Prick the base with a fork then fill with the onion mixture. Cook on a baking sheet in a preheated oven at 230°C/450°F/gas mark 8 for 30 minutes until the dough or pastry is crisp and golden.

Variations: replace the bacon with 125–175g (4½–6oz) crumbled goat's cheese or 125–175g (4½–6oz) diced smoked tofu, for a vegetarian version; or add a handful of pitted olives.

Feta in a crisp polenta jacket

The oil must be really hot to ensure a crisp crust for these delicious cheese croquettes.

PREPARATION TIME: 15 minutes

MAKES: 4 servings

vegetable oil
200g (7oz) feta cheese, cut in 8 fingers
40g (1½oz) cornmeal
To serve:
salad of your choice, e.g. tomato, cucumber, red onion and flat-leaf parsley, or skinned and charred red peppers with rocket

Pour the oil into a saucepan and set over a high heat. Meanwhile, dip the cheese fingers in iced water for about 1 minute then roll in the cornmeal until evenly coated. Deep-fry for 1–2 minutes until crisp and golden. Drain on kitchen paper and serve at once on top of the salad.

Egg-free pancakes

Lemon cake

Tofu filling for a savoury flan

This very simple savoury flan filling makes an egg-free, milk-free substitute for quiche. This recipe makes enough filling for a 20cm (8in) pastry case.

PREPARATION TIME: 5 minutes
COOKING TIME: about 25 minutes

250g (9oz) tofu, natural or smoked
1 tbsp wine vinegar or lemon juice
1 tbsp dried mixed herbs
200ml (7fl oz) soya milk

Combine all the ingredients in a blender and pour into a pre-baked flan case. Cook in a preheated oven at 190 °C/375 °F/gas mark 5 for about 25 mins until set.

Variations: add either sautéed chopped onion; chopped cooked ham with spring onion; roasted vegetables, such as carrot, peppers and tomatoes; or cooked spinach, beetroot or broccoli.

Tofu mayonnaise

This mayonnaise can be flavoured with chopped herbs, roasted garlic purée or tomato purée. It will keep, covered, in the fridge for 3–4 days.

PREPARATION TIME: 5 minutes
MAKES: approx. 250ml (9 fl oz)

100g (3½oz) soft tofu
100g (3½oz) Greek yoghurt
1 tsp English mustard
1 tbsp Dijon or wholegrain mustard
iced water
salt and pepper

Blend all the ingredients except the water, salt and pepper in a liquidiser. Season to taste and thin as required with iced water.

Avocado dressing

This dressing is delicious with tomato salads, prawns or grilled steak. Keep it tightly covered otherwise it will discolour quickly.

PREPARATION TIME: 5 minutes
MAKES: approx. 250ml (9 fl oz)

1 medium-sized ripe avocado
4 tbsp vegetable oil
2 tbsp white wine vinegar or lemon or
*   lime juice*
iced water
salt and pepper

Halve, stone, peel and chop the avocado and blend in a liquidiser with all the remaining ingredients except the water, salt and pepper until smooth. Season to taste and thin as required with iced water.

Egg-free pancakes

These pancakes can be served with either savoury or sweet fillings.

PREPARATION TIME: 25 minutes
MAKES: 10 x 18cm (7in) pancakes

100g (3½oz) plain flour
2 tbsp arrowroot powder
300ml (½pt) milk
vegetable oil or melted butter for
*   frying*
To serve:
golden syrup, jam or lemon juice and
*   caster sugar*

Mix the flour and arrowroot, then stir in the milk to give a smooth batter. Leave to rest, ideally for 20 minutes.

Heat 1 tsp oil in an 18cm (7in) non-stick frying pan and pour in 2–3 tbsp batter, enough to just cover the base of the pan, swirling it as it falls into the pan to give a thin layer. Cook until golden on one side then carefully turn and cook the other side. Repeat until all the batter is used up. To ensure a crisp result every time, make sure the fat is hot.

For a sweet pancake, serve with golden syrup, jam, or lemon juice and caster sugar.

For savoury pancakes, fill with a white sauce flavoured with smoked fish and prawns, or ham and parsley, or ratatouille and cheese.

Raspberry and sherry syllabub trifle

Syllabub makes an unusual topping for this trifle with its egg-free shortbread base, but if you prefer, make a custard with custard powder and top with whipped cream. Vary the fruit with the seasons – poached pears, fresh orange, and cooked cranberries are all suitable.

PREPARATION TIME: 15 minutes
MAKES: 6–8 servings

175g (6oz) butter shortbread

6 tbsp medium or sweet sherry

225g (8oz) fresh or frozen raspberries

284ml carton whipping cream

50g (1¾oz) caster sugar

To serve:

25g (1oz) toasted flaked almonds

Roughly break the shortbread and put in the bottom of a trifle bowl or any decorative serving bowl. Sprinkle with 2 tbsp sherry then top with the raspberries. Whip the cream and sugar with the remaining sherry until it holds its shape, then pile on top of the raspberries. Chill until required, then, just before serving, sprinkle the top with flaked almonds.

Lemon cake

This cake has a tangy lemon flavour and a slightly dense texture. Serve it plain or with fresh berries and whipped cream or crème fraîche. Try replacing the lemon with orange.

PREPARATION TIME: 15 minutes

COOKING TIME: about 1 hour

MAKES: 1 x 19–20cm (7½–8in) cake

100g (3½oz) butter, melted

200g (7oz) caster sugar

250g (9oz) self-raising flour, sieved

1 tbsp baking powder

250g (9oz) natural yoghurt

finely grated zest and juice 1 small

unwaxed lemon

1–2 tbsp milk (optional)

To serve:

icing sugar

Butter a 19–20cm (7½–8in) spring-release tin and line the base with greaseproof paper. Place all the ingredients in a large bowl and beat well to a firm dropping consistency. You may need to add 1–2 tbsp milk, depending on the type of yoghurt you have used. Transfer to the prepared tin, level the surface then bake in a pre-

heated oven at 180°C/350°F/gas mark 4 for 50–60 minutes until risen and just firm to the touch. Cool in the tin for about 30 minutes, then transfer to a cooling rack until completely cold. Dust with icing sugar.

Fig, orange and pear shortcake

PREPARATION TIME: 20 minutes

COOKING TIME: 45 minutes

MAKES: 8–10 servings

250g (9oz) chopped dried figs

finely grated zest and juice 1 medium

unwaxed orange

1 ripe pear, chopped

250g (9oz) plain flour, sieved

175g (6oz) butter

100g (3½oz) light muscovado or soft

brown sugar

1 tsp ground cinnamon

To serve:

icing sugar (optional)

Place the figs, orange zest and juice and the chopped pear in a saucepan and cook over medium heat until the figs and pear are soft and all the juice has been absorbed. Place the flour, butter, sugar and spice in a food processor and blend. Alternatively, rub in by hand until the mixture resembles fine crumbs. Add 1 tbsp cold water and stir until the mixture forms rough lumps. Press half the cake mixture onto the oiled base of a 19cm (7½in) spring-release tin. Spread the fruit mixture on top, then finish with the remaining cake mixture, pressing it down lightly.

Cook in a preheated oven at 180°C/350°F/gas mark 4 for 45 minutes. Cool in the tin. Dust with icing sugar, if wished, and serve in wedges.

Variations: replace the figs and pear with dried apricots and an apple; or replace the figs with prunes, dried pineapple or dried mango.

Date and walnut loaf

Dates give this egg-free cake a wonderfully moist texture that is even better after a day or two. Store in a cool place in an airtight container.

PREPARATION TIME: 15 minutes

COOKING TIME: about 45 minutes

MAKES: 1 large loaf

250g (9oz) chopped dried dates

100g (3½oz) light muscovado or soft

brown sugar

25g (1oz) butter

2 tsp ground mixed spice

1 tsp bicarbonate of soda

275g (9¾oz) self-raising flour, sieved

100g (3½oz) walnut pieces

To serve:

butter (optional)

Place the dates in a large bowl with the sugar, butter, spice and bicarbonate of soda. Mix well, then pour on 250ml (9fl oz) boiling water. Leave to cool slightly then beat in the flour followed by the walnuts. Transfer the mixture to an oiled and base-lined 900g (2lb) loaf tin. Level the surface and cook in a preheated oven at 180°C/350°F/gas mark 4 for about 45 minutes, until risen and just firm to the touch.

Cool in the tin for about 30 minutes, then transfer to a wire rack to cool completely. Serve in slices, with or without butter.

Yeast-free diets

Sultana, hazelnut and rosemary bread

In terms of its traditional use, yeast is not really a food – it is a microscopic but hard-working domesticated creature that has helped us with the business of food preparation for many thousands of years. The ability of yeast to turn sugar into alcohol and carbon dioxide gas has long made it a valuable ally in the manufacture of both bread and alcoholic drinks.

In addition to this traditional use, yeast has, in the past 50 years, found a role as a true foodstuff in the form of yeast extract. This derivative of yeast, with its strong flavour, has also become an ingredient of stock cubes and 'meat extracts'.

These are the most concentrated sources of yeast – foods to which yeast has been deliberately added (such as bread and wine), plus the modern extracts of yeast.

People with an intolerance reaction to yeast usually need to avoid only these concentrated sources of yeast.

In addition to foods containing domesticated yeasts, there are many foods which become naturally colonised by wild yeasts, invisible scavengers whose spores are in the air all around us, like microscopic wasps, just waiting for a pot of jam to be opened.

Wild yeasts quickly multiply on fruit, fruit juice, jam or any other sweet food, but unless the food is obviously fermenting (i.e. it smells 'yeasty') the levels of yeast it contains are relatively low. However, there are also some foods that contain wild yeasts in quite significant numbers even before you buy them. They include dried fruits, such as raisins and sultanas,

and manufactured foods that are fermented or which take a while to mature, such as soy sauce, yoghurt and cheese. In all cases, the slow production process inadvertently encourages the growth of wild yeasts. Again, the amount of yeast in the food is far less than that in bread, wine or yeast extract.

Do these wild yeasts matter? For people with yeast intolerance, probably not. In the case of true allergies to yeast, however, wild yeasts might be sufficiently numerous in some foods to evoke a reaction from the most highly sensitive individuals.

Wild yeasts may also be significant for anyone with the controversial condition known as yeast overgrowth (see p. 82). Some of those suffering symptoms which suggest this condition, and who are following a no-yeast-no-sugar diet (see p. 205), may need to avoid all sources of yeast for a while, including foods containing wild yeast.

Concentrated sources of yeast include:
- beer, wine, cider and vinegar
- Marmite, Vegemite, or any other brand of yeast extract
- yeast-based vitamin tablets; also most B-complex vitamin tablets unless specified as 'yeast-free'
- stock cubes, gravy powder, Oxo, Bovril and other 'meat extracts'
- bread (except unleavened breads such as soda bread, matzos, pitta bread and chappatis),
- all other forms of leavened dough, including breadsticks, pizza, bread rolls, croissants, teacakes, doughnuts, Danish pastries and Chelsea buns
- some packaged food labelled with synonyms for yeast. (see p. 174)

Low-level sources of yeast include:
- distilled drinks such as whisky, gin, brandy and vodka
- spirit (distilled) vinegar
- yoghurt, sour cream, buttermilk, cheeses
- dried fruits and vegetables
- sauerkraut (pickled cabbage) and possibly other pickled vegetables
- soy sauce, miso, tofu
- tea (but not green tea, jasmine tea etc.)
- any fruit if unpeeled; very ripe fruit even though peeled
- jam, fruit juice or wine that has been open for a while; many commercial fruit juices also contain a significant amount of yeast – dead but still allergenic – at time of purchase
- leftovers that have been in the refrigerator for more than two days.

Note that some of the ingredients in the recipes that follow, such as raisins, yoghurt and sun-dried tomatoes, may contain wild yeasts and therefore not be suitable for those on a strict yeast-avoidance diet. You should adjust the recipes to suit the kind of diet you are following.

Home-made stock

A good stock is essential for many recipes. As well as being yeast-free, this home-made stock tastes a great deal better than most ready-made stock cubes.

PREPARATION TIME: 10 minutes
COOKING TIME: about 2 hours (or 45 minutes in a pressure cooker)
MAKES: 850ml (1½ pints)

1 carrot
1 onion
1 stick of celery
fresh thyme or other herbs, or a bouquet garni of dried herbs
the remains of a carved roast chicken
1.5 litres (2¾ pints) water
salt and pepper
dry sherry (optional)

Peel and slice the vegetables. Tie the fresh herbs together with fine string. Put the chicken into a large saucepan, cover with the water, and add the other ingredients.

Bring to the boil, cover and simmer for 2 hours. Or cook in a pressure cooker, at high pressure for 45 minutes; in this case, use only 1 litre (1⅔ pints) water.

Allow to cool a little, then pass through a coarse sieve and discard everything except the liquid. When cold, skim off the fat from the surface. Heat through until liquid again, then add salt and pepper to taste, and a dash of sherry.

This stock will keep in the refrigerator for 2–3 days, or in the freezer for 3 months. When freezing, allow room in the container for expansion. If space is limited in the freezer, simmer the stock further until very concentrated, then freeze in an ice-cube tray, to make frozen stock cubes. Enclose in a plastic bag once frozen.

Easy brown bread

This yeast-free brown bread is based on a traditional Irish soda bread recipe.

PREPARATION TIME: 10 minutes
COOKING TIME: about 45 minutes
MAKES: 2 small loaves

450g (1lb) 100% wholemeal bread flour
225g (8oz) white bread flour
2 tsp bicarbonate of soda
1 tsp salt
2 x 284ml cartons buttermilk, or natural yoghurt, thinned with a little milk, to make the same quantity

Place the wholemeal flour in a large bowl. Sift the white flour, bicarbonate of soda and salt over it and mix well. Stir in the buttermilk and enough cold water to make a fairly soft dough. Divide the mixture between two 450g (1lb) buttered loaf tins and cook in a preheated oven at 200°C/400°F/gas mark 6 for about 45 minutes until risen and firm to the touch.

Remove from the tins and check that the loaves sound hollow when tapped on the base – if not, put back into the tins and return to the oven for 5–10 minutes more. When ready, cool on a wire rack.

Corn bread with chillies

Seeded muffins

Layered potato pizza

Corn bread with chillies

If you need to avoid wheat as well as yeast, try replacing the wheat flour with rice flour or soya flour – or use all cornmeal.

PREPARATION TIME: 20 minutes
COOKING TIME: 45 minutes
MAKES: 1 large loaf

150g (5½oz) plain flour, sieved
150g (5½oz) fine cornmeal (maize flour), sieved
40g (1½oz) sugar
½ tsp salt
4 tsp baking powder
2 large mild fresh chillies (red or green), de-seeded and finely chopped, or one dried chilli
4 tbsp olive oil
1 large egg, beaten
150ml (¼ pt) natural yoghurt
150ml (¼ pt) milk
25g (1oz) Cheddar cheese, grated (optional)

Mix all the dry ingredients in a large bowl then stir in the chillies and remaining ingredients and mix to a soft dough. Transfer the mixture to a buttered 20cm (8in) round cake tin, sprinkle with cheese if desired, and cook in a preheated oven at 200°C/400°F/gas mark 6 for about 45 minutes until risen, golden and firm to the touch.

Leave in the tin for 15–20 minutes, then turn out onto a wire rack to cool completely.

Variations: add 100g (3½oz) sautéed chopped bacon; or 100g (3½oz) sweetcorn kernels; or 4 finely chopped spring onions.

Sultana, hazelnut and rosemary bread

This bread is delicious with cheese. It is best eaten within a day or two of making. Store in a cool place.

PREPARATION TIME: 1 hour soaking time, plus 15 minutes
COOKING TIME: about 45 minutes
MAKES: 1 large loaf

100g (3½oz) sultanas
150ml (¼ pt) hot tea
approx. 175ml (6fl oz) natural yoghurt
50g (1¾oz) skinned hazelnuts
250g (9oz) plain flour, sieved
250g (9oz) wholemeal flour, sieved
40g (1½oz) sugar
2 tsp baking powder
1 tsp bicarbonate of soda
1 tsp salt
1 large egg, beaten
4 tsp freshly chopped rosemary

Soak the sultanas in the hot tea for about 1 hour then drain, reserve the tea and make up to 300ml (½pt) with the yoghurt. Roughly chop the hazelnuts and toast in a dry frying pan. Mix the dry ingredients together in a large bowl then stir in the egg, yoghurt mixture, sultanas and rosemary, and work to a firm dough. Knead lightly and shape into a long loaf. Cut slashes in the top of the loaf and transfer to an oiled baking tray.

Cook in a preheated oven at 200°C/400°F/gas mark 6 for about 45 minutes until risen and firm to the touch. Cool on a wire rack.

Mediterranean scones

Serve fresh with butter or cream cheese.

PREPARATION TIME: 15 minutes
COOKING TIME: 15 minutes
MAKES: 9

250g (9oz) self-raising flour, sieved
1 tsp baking powder
¼ tsp ground black pepper
50g (1¾oz) butter
50g (1¾oz) sun-dried tomatoes, chopped
50g (1¾oz) pitted green olives, chopped
1 tbsp freshly chopped basil or 1 tsp dried basil, or other herbs to taste

1 large egg beaten with 5 tbsp milk
milk for brushing (optional)
3 tbsp grated cheese – Parmesan or any
   other hard cheese (optional)

Sift the flour and baking powder together then add the pepper and rub in the butter until the mixture resembles fine crumbs. Stir in the tomatoes, olives and herbs and mix to a fairly soft dough with the egg and milk mixture.

Roll out to about 2.5cm (1in) thickness on a lightly floured surface and stamp out 6cm (2½in) rounds. If wished, brush the top of each scone with milk and sprinkle with 1 tsp grated cheese before baking.

Place on a baking tray and cook in a preheated oven at 220°C/425°F/gas mark 7 for about 15 minutes until risen, golden and firm to the touch. Cool on a wire rack.

Seeded muffins
These seeded American-style muffins make an excellent breakfast.

PREPARATION TIME: 15 minutes
COOKING TIME: 20 minutes
MAKES: 12

300g (10½oz) self-raising flour, sieved
2 tsp baking powder
pinch salt
100g (3½oz) soft brown sugar
50g (1¾oz) pumpkin seeds
50g (1¾oz)) sunflower seeds
25g (1oz) each sesame seeds and linseed
4 tbsp vegetable oil or 50g (1¾oz) butter,
*   melted*
2 large eggs beaten with 200ml (7fl oz)
*   milk*
To serve:
marmalade or jam

Place all the ingredients in a large bowl and beat well until evenly mixed. Spoon into a muffin tray lined with paper cases, or use paper cases on their own. Cook in

a preheated oven at 200°C/400°F/gas mark 6 for about 20 minutes until risen and just firm to the touch. Serve warm – not hot – with marmalade or jam.

Spinach and cheese polenta
Polenta can be served warm with a 'sloppy' consistency to go with stewed meat or vegetables, or left to set firm – as here – then sliced and fried. Delicious served with cooked ham, bacon or tomatoes.

PREPARATION TIME: 30 minutes
MAKES: 10–12 slices

250g (9oz) fresh spinach
25g (1oz) butter
1 small onion, finely chopped
175g (6oz) cornmeal, sieved
1 tsp salt
½ tsp ground nutmeg
2 egg yolks
40g (1½oz) each freshly grated Parmesan
*   and mature Cheddar cheeses*

Wash the spinach, remove the stalks squeeze out the excess water and shred. Melt the butter and cook the onion over medium heat for 5 minutes to soften. Increase the heat, add the spinach and cook until wilted and there is no free liquid. Add 850ml (1½pints) boiling water then slowly stir in the cornmeal, salt and nutmeg. Cook over a low heat for 10 minutes, stirring frequently until thickened. Remove from the heat and stir in the egg yolks and cheeses. Allow to cool slightly then transfer to a cling-film-lined 450g (1lb) loaf tin. There should be sufficient cling film for it to be folded over the top of the tin. Shape the mixture and cover with the cling film. Leave until cold, then slice, and fry or grill.

Layered potato pizza
Layered sliced potatoes form the base for this 'pizza'.

PREPARATION TIME: 40 minutes
COOKING TIME: 25 minutes
MAKES: 3–4 servings

1kg (2lb 4oz) waxy potatoes, peeled and
*   thinly sliced*
2 cloves garlic, crushed (optional)
1 tsp finely chopped fresh rosemary or
*   thyme*
3 tbsp olive oil
400g can chopped tomatoes
125g pack mozzarella cheese, thinly
*   sliced*
salt and freshly ground black pepper
To serve:
fresh basil or rocket leaves

Toss the potatoes with the garlic and herbs, and season very generously with salt and pepper. Pour 2 tbsp of the oil into a 30cm (12in) non-stick frying pan and arrange the potatoes in overlapping slices. Set over medium heat for 10 minutes until lightly browned. Do not move the potatoes around, but allow them to stick together into a big circular 'pizza' base. Brush the remaining oil on a baking tray. Place the pizza base on this and cook in a preheated oven at 230°C/450°F/gas mark 8 for 15 minutes until tender.

Meanwhile, cook the tomatoes over medium heat until all the liquid has evaporated. Season generously then spread over the potato base. Top with the mozzarella and return to the oven for about 10 minutes. Serve sprinkled with fresh basil or rocket leaves.

Variations: after adding the mozzarella, top with classic pizza combinations, e.g. anchovies and olives, or pepperoni, or mushrooms and ham.

Elimination diet

An elimination diet is a method of diagnosing idiopathic food intolerance (see p. 74) and certain other forms of food sensitivity where indirect tests, such as skin tests, are unhelpful. The principle of the elimination diet is very simple. It begins by removing from the body every food that could possibly cause a reaction, and seeing if this produces a symptom-free state. If it does, the elimination diet then presents the body with different foods, each in its pure form, to see which ones cause symptoms.

While the principle is simple, the practicalities of the elimination diet can be much more complex, and it is vital to understand the details fully before you start. There is absolutely no room for 'cheating' with this diet – one mouthful of cake is enough to ruin the whole thing. You need forward planning and a lot of self-discipline, backed up by a good stock of the permitted foods for moments when hunger overcomes you. Some cooked foods, stored in the freezer in individual portions for quick defrosting, are a great help.

Doing an elimination diet incorrectly is not just a waste of time. Some people acquire new sensitivities during the diet, which may make it very much more difficult to do a second elimination diet. So plan ahead and get it right first time.

The planning stage

First of all, start an accurate symptom diary. This will give you a precise picture of how bad things are now, before you try any dietary measures. A detailed daily symptom record, covering a period of about two weeks, can be very useful, whether or not you actually do an elimination diet. It can serve as a baseline against which to judge the effects of any future treatment.

Before you begin an elimination diet, you must see your doctor and ask if it is safe for you to do the diet. Read through the next four pages first – the more you know about elimination diets, before talking to your doctor, the better.

There are some conditions where, although an elimination diet can be very helpful, it should not be attempted without full medical supervision. Two main causes for concern exist:

- For people who are undernourished to start with, the elimination diet may be too demanding – it is difficult to eat enough calories during the first few weeks of the diet, unless an elemental diet is used as a supplement (see box on p. 196). If you are underweight, or have rheumatoid arthritis or Crohn's disease, the possible use of elemental diets is something you should discuss with your doctor.
- With certain diseases (see list that follows), *the testing stage may induce severe symptoms*. Sometimes these can be life-threatening and need immediate medical attention.

Medical supervision during food testing is recommended for anyone with these conditions:

- Crohn's disease – testing can bring on a prolonged relapse. Very small amounts of food should be tested initially, and the quantity slowly increased.
- Brittle asthma – after a period of avoidance, a culprit food can bring on a severe and possibly life-threatening asthma attack.
- Atopic eczema – the risk of reactions is higher if skin tests are positive (see p. 198).
- Chronic urticaria – occasionally there is an immediate reaction to an offending food. It is advisable to test foods in very small portions (just a mouthful) at first. If there is no reaction whatever after four hours, a normal portion can be tested.

Note that an elimination diet is not suitable for anyone with true food allergy (see p. 62). If you have ever had an immediate reaction to any food, or any symptoms in the lips or mouth, testing foods can be dangerous. Caution is also necessary if you have ever reacted to a food with violent vomiting and/or diarrhoea some hours after eating. This could be due to an infection, of course, but such symptoms can also, very rarely, result from true food allergy (see p. 64). Finally, if you have ever suffered anaphylaxis from any cause – not just food – the testing phase of an elimination diet might be risky. Ask your doctor's advice.

Once you have your doctor's permission to try the diet, work out how the stages of the diet will fit in with your life over the weeks or months ahead. Until it is over, eating food made by other people is virtually out of the question. When eating away from home, you must either take prepared food with you, or just eat very simple foods – such as permitted fruits or nuts. Think about the practicalities of carrying food for meals away from home.

Finally, devise the diet you will follow during the exclusion phase (see right), locate shops that sell the more unusual foods, and stock up on everything required.

You will continue to eat a lot of these foods for the first few weeks of the testing stage, so you may want to buy extra stocks and refrigerate them for longer storage, especially if the sources of supply are some distance from your home.

Note that food ingredients in medication could interfere with the results of the elimination diet. For example, if you are very sensitive to maize (corn), the cornflour that is added to many antihistamines and other drugs could create much confusion. Food-free medicines are available – talk to your pharmacist about this initially, then to your doctor if you need a different prescription.

The exclusion phase

During the first part of an elimination diet, you exclude all the foods that you normally eat, plus any closely related foods. For example, if you normally eat oranges, you should avoid all other citrus fruits, including lemon, limes and grapefruit, even though you do not normally eat these. If you normally eat plenty of broccoli, you should omit all its relatives, such as cabbage, kale, spring greens and cress.

The best way to conduct the exclusion phase is not to follow a set menu, such as the well-known 'lamb-and-pears' diet, but to draw up your own list of permitted foods. This can include foods that you have never eaten before, and those you eat rarely.

The list should run to at least ten items. One problem with an exclusion phase that consists of only two foods (as in the 'lamb-and-pears' diet) is that you are bound to eat a huge amount of these foods. This is asking for trouble if you have a tendency to food intolerance, because you can quite quickly become sensitive to new foods if eating them in large amounts.

Your list of permitted foods should include:

Some starchy items. These are essential for keeping hunger at bay: try some of the more exotic root crops, such as sweet potatoes, yams, dasheen and cassava. These are available in large supermarkets and in small shops catering to Indian, African, Chinese and Caribbean communities. (Cook them as you would potatoes. In the case of cassava, it must be boiled, not baked.) You can also eat parsnips, turnips, chestnuts and pumpkin. Tapioca, sago, buckwheat, millet, quinoa and sorghum are other possibilities: a health-food shop is a good source of some of these. Use rice if it is not normally part of your diet. Do not include sweetcorn or maize meal, even though you do not normally eat these – corn products are very widely used in packaged food, and sensitivity to corn is not uncommon.

Several fruits and vegetables that you don't normally eat. Exotic produce such as mangoes and okra can help a lot in keeping the diet tasty. Avocados, which are very rich and nutritious, can be included if you don't eat them often.

Some protein items. For carnivores, this is the easy part – any meat that you don't normally eat is suitable. Consider turkey, rabbit, pigeon or game, for example. (Soak rabbit meat in salt water overnight to get rid of the strong taste, if you dislike this.) Strict vegetarians have more problems here, since goat's milk, sheep's milk and all birds' eggs are disallowed – their proteins are much too similar to those of normal milk and eggs. Soya products such as tofu should definitely be avoided, as should other pulses initially, because sensitivity to these is a possibility among vegetarians. Quorn, or mycoprotein, could affect anyone sensitised to yeast, and should not be included. Fortunately the exclusion phase is fairly brief, so a low intake of protein will not be disastrous. Including some nuts on your list of permitted foods will help, as these contain protein. If nuts are part of your normal diet, you may have to resort to rarely eaten kinds such as macadamias, cashews or pistachios.

Elemental diets

An elemental diet is a powder that contains all the nutrients the human body needs but is free from the substances in food that provoke allergic and intolerance reactions. It is mixed with water to create a complete substitute for food. Originally designed for space travel, this totally synthetic form of sustenance is also known as 'the astronaut's diet'.

Used alone during the exclusion phase, elemental diets are the basis for the ultimate – and theoretically foolproof – elimination diet. They sustain you through the exclusion phase, and continue to provide your basic diet during the testing phase.

For anyone with multiple food sensitivity, using an elemental diet circumvents the problem of finding ten or more safe foods with which the elimination diet can begin.

Those who are underweight can also benefit from using an elemental diet, simply as a calorie-boosting supplement during the exclusion phase and testing phase.

Unfortunately, elemental diets taste fairly unpleasant and are quite expensive. You may need a prescription, so talk to your doctor. Ideally you should get an elemental diet that does not contain sucrose (sugar).

Some items that make good snacks. Nuts, pumpkin seeds, sunflower seeds, fresh fruit and dried fruit are all useful for times when you are away from home, or feel hungry between meals. At the outset of the diet, use only unsulphured dried fruit – available from health-food shops. At a later stage, you can test ordinary dried fruit (all of which is treated with sulphur preservatives – see box on p. 207).

A cooking oil, preferably one that you have not used much in the past. Use this fairly liberally, to keep the calorie content of your diet at a reasonable level.

Note that this is a very plain diet – you eat the permitted foods and absolutely nothing else. You cannot use spices, herbs or other flavourings. Salt is allowed, but sugar is out, as are tea, coffee, alcohol and all soft drinks. You must drink only mineral water and *pure* juices from permitted fruits.

Don't use canned or packaged versions of the permitted foods. Buy raw food and cook it yourself. The idea is to avoid food additives and other contaminants, such as those from the linings of cans.

Throughout this phase, and the next, you must be very careful not to eat too much of any one food. Never eat any food every day, and stay away from any food that you begin to develop a real passion for – this is always a bad sign in people with food intolerance. It is better to go a little hungry (assuming you are not underweight to start with) rather than binge on any of the permitted foods. Acquiring new sensitivities is all too easy.

Assuming you do have food intolerance, and you have excluded all the foods that affect you, there should be a complete clearance of symptoms within 7–10 days. The response is usually unmistakable. A partial or slight response is probably just a coincidence, and should be discounted, except for those with rheumatoid arthritis (see below).

Be warned that you may feel a great deal worse before you get better. For those who do have idiopathic food intolerance, the first 5–6 days of the diet can be very unpleasant – usually they suffer the same symptoms as before the diet, but far more severe.

Some conditions, such as Crohn's disease and rheumatoid arthritis, may require a longer exclusion phase, but there is no point in continuing beyond three weeks. Bear in mind that long-term structural damage to arthritic joints may prevent a complete recovery. A partial but sustained improvement in the joints, accompanied by a distinct improvement in general health, suggests that food could well be playing a part in causing the disease, and that it is worth going on to the testing phase.

Symptoms that are only intermittent, such as chronic urticaria or migraine, pose a special problem. You need to decide, before starting the diet, how long the exclusion phase should continue in order to give you a clear sign that your state of health is improved. A symptom diary is vital here. If, for example, your symptom diary shows that you sometimes have a week that is symptom-free but you never get through two weeks without an attack, then your exclusion phase should continue for two weeks.

You should only go on to the testing phase if you improve during the exclusion phase. If you do not improve, you have excluded the possibility of food intolerance, and can give up the diet.

The testing phase

This part of the diet, which is sometimes called the reintroduction phase, takes about 8 weeks. It requires careful observation of your symptoms, and constant self-discipline about everything you eat. You should not stop or delay the testing unless you are ill – it is vitally important to complete it as quickly as possible.

Foods have to be reintroduced one at a time, with a space between in which symptoms can be observed. It sounds simple, but this is where errors can easily occur.

During this phase, as well as noting your symptoms daily, you should also record absolutely everything you eat.

For the first 2–3 weeks you should test foods that are unlikely to cause symptoms. Start by testing fruits, vegetables and meats that you do not eat very often normally, but which you do like. If they pass the test, you can use them to vary your diet. This will make life much easier and reduce the risk of developing new sensitivities.

Next test foods that you do eat reasonably often, but not every day. Leave the most likely culprits – the foods you eat very regularly, such as wheat and milk products – until you have established a safe diet that contains at least 25 different foods. This safe and relatively varied diet should be the backdrop against which you test staple foods.

The testing procedure changes over time, because your sensitivity may decline as the diet progresses. During the first 8 weeks, you should test one food each day, eating a normal-sized portion for lunch or supper. A reaction to the food might occur quite soon after the meal, or some hours later. Any symptoms that occur within the following 24 hours should be provisionally attributed to that food.

Unfortunately, bowel symptoms can sometimes take longer to develop – up to 48 hours. This can confuse things when a new food is being tested every day.

There may also be uncertainty about intermittent conditions such as chronic urticaria. You may not be absolutely sure that the problem really responded to the exclusion phase. If so, when the symptoms recur during the testing phase, this may be due to a food, or it may just be coincidence.

Should there be any doubt about which food caused a particular set of symptoms, cut out all the suspect foods for now, and retest them after a couple of weeks, using a three-day testing procedure (see below).

When a reaction does occur to a food, stop all testing and go back to the safe diet until you feel completely better. But don't wait too long before resuming testing. You need to get through most of the testing within 8 weeks because, for some people, intolerance to the foods begins to fade after that.

This does not mean that the intolerance has been 'cured', unfortunately. A period of eating the food regularly will soon bring the problem back.

If you are still testing foods after 8 weeks, you must change to **three-day testing** – eat a normal portion of the food every day for three days, stopping only if you get symptoms. Should you have no reaction to the food by the end of the fourth day, you can consider it safe. (But leave it out of your diet for at least another four days.)

There are some special procedures for testing certain foods:

- When you test wheat, even if it is quite early on, use the three-day test procedure (see above). Reactions to wheat can be very slow. (If you have rheumatoid arthritis, you should spend a full five days testing wheat, and eat it at least twice a day.) Don't use bread to test wheat because this also contains yeast and other ingredients. Use a pure wheat cereal such as Shredded Wheat – moisten it with fruit juice if you cannot have milk. Note that some people who react to whole-wheat are sensitive to the wheat germ, and can tolerate refined wheat, as in white bread and flour. For others only white flour is a problem – they are usually reacting to additives in the white flour. Careful testing will sort out these issues.
- Test milk before cheese and butter. You may react to one but not the others. If you react to fresh milk, wait a few weeks, then test evaporated milk. Later, you can test goat's milk and then sheep's milk. Some people can tolerate these, but must be very careful not to consume too much of them.
- You can test yeast using Marmite or yeast-based B-vitamin tablets. Do this before you test mushrooms.

- At some point, test a canned food. This is to check for reactions to the lining material used on cans. Choose something that contains no other ingredients or additives, such as carrots. Test it first in a frozen or fresh form, so that you are sure you don't have a reaction to the food itself.
- Throughout the testing period, continue with cooking all your own food from scratch. At a fairly late stage in the testing, when you have tested most foods, spend three days eating packaged food. The idea is to eat a wide range of different food additives all at once. Read the labels carefully (see p. 172) to check that all the food ingredients are ones which you have already tested and found safe. You are unlikely to react to these packaged foods, but if you do, you should then conduct tests with all the individual food additives. You may need some help from a dietitian for this (see p. 201).

Testing becomes more and more uncertain after twelve weeks. If you have not completed it by then, reintroduce all the untested foods. Should your symptoms come back, cut all those foods out again, then test them individually.

What next?

For anyone who recovers during an elimination diet, and successfully identifies their problem foods, a period of complete abstinence from those foods follows. After about a year, it is worth testing the foods again, as the sensitivity may have subsided.

If, after a year or two, you find that a food no longer makes you ill, don't go back to your old ways – remember that you must only eat the food occasionally. Once every three or four days is a good rule of thumb for a food to which you were previously intolerant. You might get away with having it slightly more often than this, but never go back to eating it daily. If it starts to become your 'favourite food' again – the thing you fancy more often than anything else – watch out.

Good nutrition is an important issue for anyone avoiding certain key foods. If you have cut out all milk products, for example, you should probably be taking a calcium supplement, unless you eat a lot of other calcium-rich foods. Ask your doctor to refer you to a dietician or nutritionist if you are on a restrictive diet and feel you need help.

An elimination diet for children with eczema

Before putting your child on any kind of restrictive diet, it is vital that you talk to your doctor. The risks of malnutrition are far higher for children, and there can be serious long-term consequences, such as stunted growth or impaired intelligence. You must therefore have medical consent and supervision for an elimination diet.

For young children with atopic eczema, there is rarely any need for a stringent elimination diet, such as that described on pp. 194–7. Children are usually sensitised to only one or two commonly eaten foods.

In the case of recently weaned infants, it is enough to simply cut out individual foods, one at a time. Avoid each food for two weeks, while observing symptoms carefully.

For older children a simple elimination diet, with an exclusion phase which just avoids the most likely culprits, works well. The foods that you should exclude at the outset are:
- any food which has given a positive skin-prick test (see p. 69)
- any food which you think may have caused digestive symptoms, such as diarrhoea, either now or in the past
- eggs, milk and all milk products
- beef and chicken
- citrus fruits (oranges, lemons etc.)
- food additives.

If the child's skin is no better after a week of this diet, cut out the following foods as well:
- peanuts and other nuts
- soya
- fish
- wheat and maize (corn)
- tomatoes
- lamb

If there is no response after another week, food is unlikely to be contributing to the eczema.

For the testing phase, use three-day testing, as described on p. 197, if you have fewer than ten foods to test. Use one-day testing if you have more than ten foods to test.

You should begin by testing a very small amount of the food. Wait ten minutes for any symptoms (not just skin symptoms – the mouth or stomach may also be affected) then give a little more if nothing has happened. Build up gradually to testing a normal portion of the food.

A more cautious approach is required for children who give positive skin-prick tests to foods, or have a history of symptoms in the mouth or digestive tract. They are more likely to suffer severe symptoms in the lips, mouth and throat – the type of reaction associated with food allergy. *Emergency medical treatment may be needed*. You can see if there is any likelihood of a severe immediate reaction to foods by starting with a test on the face, and then the outer lip (see box on p. 23). If nothing happens, it is probably safe to go on to the next stage – giving the child a very small amount of the food to eat. However, you should have medical supervision for

Rare reactions

Very occasionally, atopic eczema sufferers on milk-avoidance diets develop a sensitivity reaction to calcium supplements. There is no scientific explanation for this, but it has been very well documented in two children. Should you encounter this problem, the answer may be some alternative natural source of calcium: sardines or other small fish, eaten whole, are one possibility, assuming your child will eat fish. A dietician can advise on how much is needed per day.

There has also been one well-documented report of a child reacting to mineral water. When the water she usually drank was changed to another brand, her eczema cleared up. This is very unlikely to be a common problem.

this procedure in the case of foods that gave positive skin tests. If your child has both *severe* eczema and additional symptoms (such as nettle rash, or symptoms in the mouth or digestive tract) it may be advisable to have medical supervision when testing **all** foods.

Bear in mind that atopic eczema naturally fluctuates a great deal. To observe the effects of trying out a food, you need the child's skin to be in a steady state. That means being absolutely consistent about applying steroids and moisturisers, avoiding (for the period of testing) any stressful situations that could provoke a flare-up, not exposing the skin to sudden doses of irritants or air-borne allergens, and keeping scratching under control. Be aware of other factors that could muddy the waters by provoking a flare-up of eczema – such as teething, or a cold (see p. 44).

If certain foods are identified as provoking eczema symptoms, and you decide to cut the food from your child's diet, a nutritional supplement may well be needed. Ask your doctor to refer you to a nutritionist or dietician.

Other diagnostic diets

These diets are not used by (or even known to) the majority of doctors. While some, such as the low-nickel diet, have been subjected to rigorous scientific testing and have shown their worth, others have not been tested scientifically. The evidence in favour of them is purely anecdotal – in other words, doctors have used these treatments repeatedly and observed good results with some of their patients. That is not hard science, but it is how innovations in medicine often begin.

There are few risks with any of these diets – the number of foods to be avoided is small, and you are most unlikely to become malnourished. Your doctor should not object to you trying any of these diets, however sceptical he or she may be about its possible benefits.

Low-nickel diet

This diet is sometimes of benefit to adults with eczema. There are various pointers which indicate that the diet may help, as described on pp. 55–6.

Make sure that you have absolutely no contact with any nickel (e.g. in jewellery, jeans studs, watches or hair clips) throughout this diet, and for at least two weeks before starting it.

Ideally you should also stop treatment with steroids or anti-histamines a week or so before starting the diet. This allows any improvement to be easily observed. Obviously you should get your doctor's permission to do this.

The diet could take anything from six weeks to six months to take full effect. Some people have a complete clearance of their eczema, while for others there is a partial but distinct improvement.

The foods with a high nickel content, which should be avoided as far as possible, are:

- shellfish
- green beans and peas
- beansprouts and lucerne sprouts
- dry beans and lentils (pulses) of all kinds; soya protein and products containing it (e.g. vegetarian sausages and burgers)
- spinach and kale
- lettuce, leeks
- wheat bran (avoid bran cereals and other products; replace wholemeal bread with white bread, or eat it in moderation only – you can get plenty of fibre from fruits and vegetables; do not eat multi-grain breads at all)
- oatmeal, millet and buckwheat
- raspberries, prunes, pineapple, figs
- chocolate and cocoa
- tea from drinks dispensers (restrict intake of other tea and coffee, and don't make them too strong)
- peanuts, hazelnuts, almonds and marzipan
- liquorice
- sunflower seeds, linseed
- baking powder, in large amounts
- vitamin or mineral preparations that contain nickel (check the label carefully)

Nickel is also found in drinking water, and absorbed from certain cooking utensils, so:

- Do not use items plated with nickel (e.g. tea balls, some tea strainers, egg beaters). The extremely shiny appearance of nickel makes these easy to recognise.
- Do not cook acid fruits in stainless steel pans, since the acid leaches some nickel out of the stainless steel. An enamel cooking pot is safe.
- Minimise the amount of tinned food that you eat.
- In the morning, run off the first litre of water from the tap, as this may contain nickel released from the tap itself.

Several other foods and drinks seem to aggravate the skin of nickel-sensitive people, even though the foods are not rich in nickel. These foods should also be avoided:

- beer, wine
- herring, mackerel, tuna
- tomatoes, carrots, onions, apples; oranges and other citrus fruits, including their juices.

Low-chromium and low-cobalt diets

Skin sensitivity to chromium or cobalt can, very occasionally, result in a tendency to react to these same metals when consumed in food or drink (see pp. 55–6).

Unfortunately, both chromium and cobalt are essential for good nutrition, so avoiding them is fraught with problems. You would need the help of a really good dietician, or a doctor with a particular interest in nutritional problems, to guide you through a diet of this kind.

The only measure you can safely take at home is to cut down on excessive consumption of these metals, for three weeks only, to see if this produces any improvement in your symptoms. If it does, that should encourage you to seek expert help for a more thorough avoidance diet.

In the case of cobalt sensitivity avoid:

- all canned and bottled beer.

In the case of chromium sensitivity avoid:

- beer, wine and cider
- yeast extract and yeast tablets
- black pepper
- calf's liver
- wheatgerm and wholemeal bread
- cheese.

If you also have nickel sensitivity, avoid nickel-rich foods (see p. 199) at the same time.

Low-histamine diet

Histamine in food is mostly produced by bacterial action. The majority of people can break down any histamine they eat, as long as the amount is not excessive (see box on p. 67).

Temporary susceptibility to histamine may accompany viral hepatitis or other liver conditions.

A permanently impaired ability to detoxify histamine is relatively unusual. When it does occur it can result in symptoms such as chronic urticaria, migraine or recurrent headaches. A low-histamine diet may help in these cases. All of the following should be avoided:

Very high histamine content:

- red wine, champagne
- tuna, sardines
- Emmenthal and Camembert cheeses.

High histamine content:

- beer, white wine
- anchovies
- Gouda, Roquefort, Stilton and all other well-matured cheeses
- salami and other well-matured sausages, Westphalian ham
- sauerkraut
- spinach
- tomato ketchup.

If you improve only partially on this diet, this may indicate that you are on the right track (histamine is indeed the problem) but that the bacteria in your gut are undermining your efforts with the additional histamine which they generate. You can investigate this possibility by trying a low-carbohydrate diet, as described on p. 53.

Low-amine diet

Naturally occurring substances called amines, found in many different foods, can have a drug-like effect on the blood vessels making them open up a little and so increasing the blood flow. The effect is usually small, but some people are more susceptible than others. A low-amine diet is worth trying if you have chronic urticaria or migraines, and have not improved with other treatments. A low-amine diet can also be useful in atopic eczema: amines in food are not a basic cause of eczema, but they can aggravate the rash by increasing blood flow to the skin. To begin with, cut out all foods listed below:

Very high amine content:

- all cheeses except cottage cheese
- dark or plain chocolate
- yeast extract (Marmite etc.), miso, tempeh, tomato paste, tandoori spice mix, stock cubes, ready-made sauces

- cola drinks, orange juice, tomato juice
- any dried, pickled or smoked fish
- sausages, pies and smoked meats, beef liver, chicken skin
- broad beans, spinach
- sauerkraut
- almonds.

High or moderate amine content:
- milk chocolate
- soy sauce
- beer, wine and cider
- pork, including bacon and ham, salami, chicken liver, offal
- all fresh or tinned fish, except white fish
- all nuts except chestnuts and cashews
- sesame seeds, sunflower seeds
- avocados, aubergines, mushrooms, tomatoes, broccoli, cauliflower
- olives and olive oil
- oranges, lemons and other citrus fruits
- pineapples, bananas, raspberries, strawberries, pineapples, plums, grapes, dates, figs, kiwi fruit, passion fruit.

Continue for at least three weeks, and longer if your symptoms are normally intermittent. If you improve, you can then experiment with reintroducing small portions of foods from the second list, three or four times a week. Gradually build up to a higher intake, but cut back if your symptoms return.

Organic diet

The objective here is to avoid pesticides, i.e. chemical sprays applied to kill fungi and insect pests. This may be helpful for people with chemical intolerance (see p. 84).

'Chemical-free' or 'unsprayed' food (crops grown without pesticides) will do just as well as 100% organic food (which is grown without either pesticides or artificial fertilisers).

The highest intake of pesticides is from fresh fruit and vegetables, so if your budget is tight, concentrate on buying organic or chemical-free versions of these. If you have a garden, growing some of your own food will reduce the cost.

You can also reduce the pesticide content of ordinary fruits and vegetables by:
- Storing them for as long as possible before using them, because the pesticides break down quite quickly
- Always peeling them. With difficult-to-peel items such as peaches and tomatoes, pour boiling water over them and leave them to stand for a few minutes first, as this loosens the skin. Rinse in cold water, then peel.

- If peeling is not possible, washing them very well with soap or detergent, then rinsing them thoroughly
- Cooking them, as this drives off some of the pesticides; avoid inhaling the steam and ventilate the kitchen well while doing this.

You should drink mineral water from a reputable source, or use a very high-quality water filter (not a jug filter).

Additive-free diet

Food additives are occasionally the culprit in chronic urticaria (see p. 53). At the same time as avoiding additives, people with chronic urticaria should cut out other potential culprits – alcohol, spices and all aspirin-like drugs (see box on p. 151).

An additive-free diet may also be of value for some people with chemical intolerance (see p. 84).

In the case of children with Attention Deficit Disorder (ADD), also called Hyperkinetic Syndrome, the role of additive-free diets is a contentious issue (see p. 81).

An additive-free diet is very healthy but quite hard work. It means making all your own food from 100% fresh, unmodified produce (you cannot have bacon or ham, and even things like cooked chicken and ready-to-eat salad can contain some additives; so does most restaurant food). Note that wines, beers and other alcoholic drinks can contain many additives without declaring them on the label. (German bottled beer is an exception here.) Baked goods sold unwrapped can also contain many additives without declaring them.

Stop using toothpaste unless it is an additive-free brand. You can buy such toothpaste from a health-food shop – or use sodium bicarbonate powder instead. Drink mineral water or filtered water (you need a good-quality filter for this, not a jug filter).

Medicinal drugs can contain colourings and other additives, so you should try to get additive-free versions. Talk to your pharmacist about this initially.

Assuming the symptoms clear up, testing can begin, but you will probably need medical help to work out exactly which additives are at fault. It is difficult to organise these tests at home, because most foods contain such a mixture of additives.

With chronic urticaria, there is the possibility of quite severe reactions on testing, so medical supervision is desirable. You can undertake cautious testing with **small** amounts of tap water, spices and alcohol at home, but make sure you are in a position to get emergency medical help if you need it. ***Aspirin or aspirin-like drugs should not be tested at home***. Life-threatening reactions are common in sensitive individuals, and temporary avoidance can heighten your reaction.

Investigating food intolerance
IN COLICKY BABIES

If you have followed the measures described on pp. 78–9 but have had little or no success in reducing colic symptoms so far, it makes sense to look into the possibility of a food sensitivity reaction (either intolerance or a mild allergy) to food *proteins*. This is a very different problem from lactose intolerance (an inability to digest the milk *sugar*, called lactose due to a shortage of lactase – see p. 79), although the two can get entangled, creating a complex and confusing set of responses.

The complications arise because, when there is diarrhoea as a result of allergy or intolerance (or from any other cause, including infections) it temporarily strips the gut of its lactose-digesting capacity. This problem is called **secondary lactase deficiency**, and it will correct itself quite quickly once the real cause of the diarrhoea is eliminated.

Unfortunately, the routine medical tests for lactase deficiency do not distinguish between this temporary problem and the much rarer **primary lactase deficiency**, which is inherited and life-long.

So if your child has had these routine tests, and you have been told that they show primary lactase deficiency, it remains possible that the real problem is a reaction to milk proteins (or proteins from other foods), and that the lactose intolerance is an *effect* of this, which adds to the diarrhoea, but is not the root cause of it. If so, eliminating the offending food from the baby's diet (or the mother's) will produce impressive results, whereas reducing or eliminating lactose only helps a little.

The purpose of the dietary investigations described here is to discover which foods are causing problems for your baby. In the case of bottle-fed babies, the answer is usually cow's milk – and this is often the culprit for breast-fed babies too – but not necessarily.

For a breast-fed baby it can be any food that the mother is eating. A tiny proportion of what the mother consumes goes through into the breast milk, and these few molecules of food are enough to provoke a reaction in the child.

Bottle-fed babies

For bottle-fed babies, proceed as follows:

- Change to an alternative milk-free formula (see box on p. 66). Wait two weeks before concluding there is no improvement – recovery can take time – and try another type of formula before you decide this is not the answer.
- If there is no joy with alternative infant formula, consider the possibility of relactation: stimulating the flow of your own breast milk once again. Breast-feeding support groups (see page 255) can give you advice. Avoid all dairy products while breast-feeding and take a calcium supplement.

For babies who are old enough, and who have severe symptoms, early weaning is one option, but this must be done very carefully:

- Keep all dairy products out of the baby's diet – read labels carefully on prepared foods and know all the different names used for milk (see page 173). Test beef cautiously as it shares some proteins with milk.
- To avoid new food sensitivities developing, keep eggs, fish, wheat, chocolate and oranges off the menu until the child's first birthday, then introduce them gradually. Avoid peanuts and other nuts for three years if possible.
- Keep maize (corn) out of the diet for the first six months, because it is a common ingredient in formula feeds, and the child may have become sensitive to it. Note that some medicines contain corn syrup, but this will only affect those

who are very sensitive. A pharmacist can check the full list of ingredients in medicines, and suggest alternatives.

• No food should be given to the baby every day, or in large amounts. You can use unusual starchy foods, such as sweet potatoes, yams, quinoa and millet (see p. 195), to ring the changes. These all make excellent baby foods.

• Never force a child to eat any food that is disliked. Try serving it again, once or twice, but give up if there are still fierce objections to the smell or taste – these are often a sign of intolerance or allergy.

• Ask your doctor to refer you to a paediatric nutritionist so that the diet can be checked. A calcium supplement will probably be needed. Other vitamins or minerals may also be lacking.

Breast-fed babies

For breast-fed babies, the approach is quite different – the main focus here is on what you, the mother, eat and drink.

Firstly, start keeping a food diary, and a record of the baby's symptoms. Are there any detectable patterns? Does the colic get worse if you drank red wine on the previous day, for example? Note that sometimes the time-gap is more than a day, but it should be reasonably consistent for any one food.

At the same time, eliminate all items other than breast milk from the baby's diet, including:

• any solids (e.g. baby foods)
• fruit juice
• medicines or vitamin drops that contain other ingredients (e.g. colouring or corn syrup)
• nipple creams containing arachis oil (peanut oil).

Ask your doctor or pharmacist for alternative versions of medicines or vitamins, without added ingredients. Give boiled water to make up for fruit juice. Wait a week or so to see if things improve.

For the next stage, cut out coffee, tea and all alcoholic drinks. Allow a week for this, and continue with the food/symptom diary meanwhile. If there is no improvement, go on to the next stage, while still avoiding coffee, tea and alcohol.

For the next stage, compile a list of suspect foods, based on your food diary. Add to this list:

• cow's milk and all milk products
• any foods that you craved when pregnant
• any foods that you normally eat in large amounts
• anything you dislike but have been eating because it's 'good for you' or 'good for the baby'
• any of the following foods if you eat them regularly: eggs, wheat, oranges and other citrus fruits (lemons, grapefruit etc.), tree nuts, peanuts, fish, chocolate, chicken and beef.

Once you have your list prepared, talk to your doctor. Say that you would like to try eliminating cow's milk for two weeks to start with, and then – if the colic has not cleared up – all the other foods on your list as well (again, for two weeks). You will need to take a calcium supplement. If there is strong opposition to your plans, based on a fear that your diet will be inadequate, ask for a referral to a nutritionist. Obviously this needs to be arranged promptly. The fear of under-nutrition, which is dangerous for both yourself and the baby, is a very reasonable one, but with sensible precautions any mother can safely carry out this investigation.

Eat at home during this time, as you cannot possibly know all the ingredients in café or restaurant meals. Read the labels on packaged meals and watch out for synonyms (see pp. 172–4).

If your baby recovers, and you want to pinpoint the problem food so that your diet becomes less restricted, you can test foods individually. Wait until there has been no sign of colic for a week. Choose one food and eat a portion every day for a week. If the colic does not reappear, cut this food out again and choose a second food to test – again, eat this daily for a week. Stop eating the food sooner if the colic returns. (Foods that proved safe can be reintroduced again later, but you need a break after the testing week.) Test cow's milk last.

Some babies get better during the exclusion phase but do not respond to any of the foods when tested. The temporary break from the problem food seems to be all they need to lose their sensitivity. In such cases, the mother can go back to an unrestricted diet, but not to exactly the kind of diet she ate before – no food should be eaten every day, nor in large quantities, or the colic may return.

Many babies get over their sensitivity after one or two months without the problem food, so it is worth testing again after a while, especially if you are eating a very restricted diet.

Where cow's milk turns out to be the offender, goat's milk or sheep's milk might be tolerated, but wait until the baby is completely free of symptoms and experiment cautiously. Alternatively, drink one of the new milk substitutes now available (see p. 183).

If the baby clearly responds to a food in the mother's diet (for example, cow's milk or peanuts), this food should be given cautiously when first introduced to the child after weaning, in case he or she has a true allergy to it. An allergy test may be helpful in deciding whether to introduce the food, at all.

Re-balancing the gut flora

The **gut flora** are a large collection of bacteria and yeasts living, usually without harmful effects, in our intestines. Some of these microbes are acquired by a baby during birth – several of the most useful kinds live in the vagina too, and the baby swallows them *en route* to the outside world. Recent research shows that babies delivered by Caesarean section take much longer to acquire the normal gut flora. However, they catch up eventually because, like other babies, they pick up bacteria in the months immediately after birth, mainly from the mother.

There are hundreds of different kinds (species) of microbe in the gut flora, with the exact mix varying from one person to another. They eat the remains of our meals, and provide certain benefits in return:

- they make some useful vitamins that we can then absorb
- they keep disease-causing bacteria at bay simply by being there, taking up all the potential 'parking spaces' on the lining of the gut so that alien bacteria can't find a foothold
- they may also aid digestion in some way, although this is less certain.

On the downside, the gut flora also produce toxins, but we have had aeons of evolution to get used to these, and the liver normally breaks them down quite happily. Only if the liver is badly diseased (as in cirrhosis) do these toxins become a problem.

The immune system is familiar with these fellow-travellers and tolerates them, while ensuring that they do not invade the body any further. However, a loss of immune competence, as in AIDS, can allow them to become invasive and cause disease.

Research into the gut flora is a relatively new field of medicine, and most of the studies have been published in rather obscure medical journals. So the majority of doctors are unaware that abnormalities of the gut flora – the increase of some species at the expense of others – have been found in patients with rheumatoid arthritis, atopic eczema, irritable bowel syndrome and Crohn's disease. The relationship between these abnormalities and the disease process is unclear at present: it is not necessarily a cause-and-effect relationship. The implications, as far as treatment is concerned, are far from clear as yet.

The controversial condition known as 'candidiasis' appears to be a particular form of gut-flora imbalance, in which yeasts are overly successful. It is called **yeast overgrowth** in this book (see p. 82).

Among the factors that can cause an imbalance in the gut flora are:

- prolonged or repeated treatment with antibiotics; also a single high-dose treatment, as may be given before a hysterectomy operation (see p. 76). These seem to kill off the beneficial bacteria in the gut flora, allowing others to flourish.
- severe diarrhoea, which can deplete the normal community of bacteria. Usually the effect on the gut flora is temporary, but it can sometimes be long-lasting and may lead to food intolerance (see p. 76).

Additional factors that might contribute to a disturbed gut flora are:

- a diet that is high in sugar and refined carbohydrates; this is thought to give yeasts an unfair advantage over other members of the gut flora, by providing yeasts with their preferred food
- taking the contraceptive pill; this is very controversial, but some doctors believe there is a link between the widespread use of the contraceptive pill and the number of cases of suspected yeast overgrowth in young women.

Bacterial replacers

Bacterial replacers, also known as **probiotics**, supply live bacteria to replenish the gut flora with favourable species.

Experimental trials suggest that taking bacterial replacers may be a useful treatment for irritable bowel syndrome and atopic eczema. This approach may also be of value in yeast overgrowth, when combined with dietary treatment (see below). There have been no trials of bacterial replacers in other diseases.

All bacterial replacers have to be taken every day: the bacteria do not seem to establish themselves permanently in the gut flora. And any benefits from taking them vanish within a few days of stopping the treatment – so this is quite an expensive option.

Unless the bacteria in the product are alive – and alive in considerable numbers – the bacterial replacer is of no value. Refrigeration is the key to keeping the bacteria alive since, after three days at room temperature, their numbers start to decline steeply. Bacterial replacers purchased from a health-food shop may have been stored at room temperature for some time and so contain very few live bacteria. Buying by mail, directly from the supplier, is a good plan: ask how long the delivery usually takes.

Many different brands of bacterial replacer are now available. To locate companies selling by mail order, see p. 255.

The no-yeast-no-sugar diet

Although this diet has not been tested scientifically, it is widely used by doctors who are interested in gut-flora disturbances, and often produces strikingly good results with people who had previously intractable health problems. This is not hard scientific data, but the impressive results with certain patients (see p. 82) suggest that the diet is sometimes worth trying. Those with symptoms ascribed to yeast overgrowth or 'candidiasis', especially bowel problems and an itchy anus (see p. 82), most frequently benefit.

The best way to do this diet is to start with a relatively low-key approach (Stage 1). Only progress to more stringent dietary measures if you don't improve adequately. If there is no improvement at all, even on the Stage 4 diet, then you can be reasonably sure that yeast overgrowth is not the cause of your problems.

Stage 1

If you are taking the contraceptive pill, talk to your doctor about changing to another form of contraception. Although the link between yeast overgrowth and the pill is not in any way established, stopping the pill often seems to be beneficial.

Cut out sugar and all sweet foods, including honey, syrup, jam, chutney, pickles, cakes and biscuits, soft drinks and fruit squash. Note that 'no-added-sugar' jam should also be excluded – it is very rich in fruit sugars. Also avoid dried fruits, and change any medicines taken as syrups to tablet form. Do not eat peanut butter, tinned sweetcorn or baked beans, except sugar-free brands. Avoid sweet potatoes, and any vegetables that become sweet when cooked e.g. baked parsnips, caramelised onions. Your 'sweet-tooth' should be your guide – if it tastes sweet, it's off the menu. Only artificial sweeteners are allowed.

Not eating sugar is thought to deprive the yeast of much of its food supply. Persist with this diet for 4–6 weeks. If you are no better, or only partially better, go on to Stage 2.

Stage 2

In addition to the restrictions of Stage 1, cut all fruit out of your diet, except for pure, unsweetened lemon juice and lime juice. These juices, plus salads and lightly cooked vegetables, should give you enough Vitamin C – or you could take a supplement.

Cut out white bread and anything made with white flour (e.g. pancakes, pastry, noodles and other pasta). Small servings of wholemeal bread, potatoes and unpolished rice ('brown rice') are allowed. Your staple diet should be vegetables and high-protein foods such as meat, fish and eggs.

Do eat herbs, spinach and fresh garlic, as these may help to curb the growth of yeast. Don't eat cheese or anything fermented.

Stick with this diet for at least four weeks, and longer if you begin to feel partially better. If you feel a lot better, continue for several weeks, then gradually reintroduce fruits and other excluded foods – but not sugar, honey, jam, syrup or any other very sweet foods.

Stage 3

In addition to all the restrictions of Stages 1 and 2, cut out any foods containing yeast (see p. 190). Why this should work is not entirely understood (see p. 83).

A response to this diet, even a partial response, is a good sign. Consider going on to Stage 4.

Stage 4

Your doctor must agree to you trying this diet, as it may not be safe for everyone.

Avoid all starchy foods including bread, flour, potatoes, rice, pasta, cornmeal, parsnips, beans, lentils etc. Nuts can be eaten in small quantities, but not cashew nuts. This is an extreme diet which gives the yeast almost nothing to live on. No one should stay on this diet for more than a few weeks: it is only used to confirm the diagnosis, or to get the problem under control before tackling it with other treatments.

If there is any improvement with the Stage 4 diet, talk to your doctor about anti-fungal drugs (see p. 83).

A DIET TO PROTECT
against asthma

There is growing evidence that several aspects of the modern Western diet make asthma more likely to develop. Parts of this evidence are very convincing, while other findings are less conclusive as yet. Some people might argue that, until all the facts about diet and asthma are firmly established, no dietary changes should be recommended. However, all the dietary changes that might protect against asthma are also very valuable for general health.

This diet is potentially useful for:
- Atopic families who wish to reduce the chance of their children developing asthma. Other preventive measures, such as allergen avoidance and exercise (see Chapter 8), are obviously important as well.
- Anyone who already suffers from asthma – with this diet, their symptoms may diminish.

The main elements of the anti-asthma diet are:
- A high intake of **fresh fruit**. Researchers in Britain and the Netherlands have shown that people who eat more fruit have better lung function, and are less likely to develop asthma or bronchitis. Apples have a particularly good effect on the airways, according to one recent study. Many other studies show a link between **Vitamin C** – the major vitamin in fruit – and asthma prevention. This makes sense because Vitamin C is an **antioxidant** which inactivates the pro-inflammatory substances (called oxidants) that are found in cigarette smoke and other polluted air. In addition to Vitamin C, many fruits contain beta-carotene (see below) – mangoes and apricots are the richest sources.
- Regular helpings of **carrots**, which contain the orange pigment **beta-carotene**. This is another antioxidant that can help prevent inflammation in the airways. It should be obtained from food, not supplements (see p. 207).

- A high intake of **fresh green vegetables**, especially broccoli, spring greens, dark green cabbage, peas, parsley and courgettes. One Australian study has shown that children who eat fewer vegetables are more likely to wheeze. The benefits of vegetables may be partly due to the fact that they contain beta-carotene and (if eaten raw or only lightly cooked) Vitamin C. Dark green vegetables are also a good source of **magnesium**, and researchers find that people with a higher magnesium intake have healthier airways. Magnesium is believed to protect against asthma by helping the muscles of the airways to relax.
- Plenty of **tomatoes and tomato products**, such as tomato juice, tomato sauce, ketchup and paste. The special protective effect of tomatoes is not entirely explained by their Vitamin C or beta-carotene content – another antioxidant, called lycopene, may be the crucial ingredient here. Good news for fast-food fans – the benefits of tomato paste are even seen among pizza eaters who are significantly less vulnerable to asthma.
- Daily intake of **sunflower seeds**, or sunflower oil and margarine. These are by far the best natural source of **Vitamin E**, another antioxidant (see left) which helps to reduce the risk of becoming asthmatic. Vitamin E taken in supplements seems to have much less beneficial effect than natural Vitamin E from food.

• A good intake of the minerals **zinc**, **manganese** and **selenium**, as well as **magnesium** (see p. 206). Shortage of any of these minerals may be linked with asthma. It is important not to eat too much wheat bran or unyeasted wholemeal bread, especially with main meals, as these block the absorption of several minerals.

Good sources of zinc include meat, shrimps, clams and oysters, with smaller amounts in cheese and egg yolks. Nuts, lentils and beans are fairly good sources of zinc, while soya protein blocks its absorption.

As well as being found in dark green vegetables, magnesium is plentiful in sardines, peanuts, hazelnuts, walnuts and lentils. Other fish, lean meat, milk, cheese and bananas contain smaller amounts.

Manganese is found in eggs and milk, and though the amounts are small, these are good sources because the mineral in them can easily be absorbed. While green leafy vegetables, whole grains and tea apparently contain more manganese – and are frequently recommended as a source of this mineral – in fact very little can be absorbed from those foods. Lentils are a moderately good source of manganese.

Selenium is most plentiful in fish and meat. It may be scarce in home-grown plant foods in areas of the world (notably Finland and parts of New Zealand) where selenium is lacking in the soil.

• A limited intake of **meat**, especially red meat, plus a complete avoidance of kidney, liver and other offal meats. An entirely vegetarian diet incurs a risk of mineral deficiencies however (see above). On balance, it is probably best to eat meat once a week or less.

• A low intake of **salt**. Researchers in Kenya found that children eating a high salt diet (which equals the *average* salt intake in Britain and other parts of the developed world) were at greater risk of becoming asthmatic. For existing asthmatics, increasing the amount of salt eaten can make asthma worse, while reducing salt can lessen symptoms. Male asthmatics seem to be more vulnerable than females. Salt probably affects the muscles of the airways, making them more likely to contract

The role of supplements

You should try to get all the nutrients you need from food rather than supplements. However, there are times when a supplement can be useful. Any asthmatic who has to cope with the effects of high air pollution, especially ozone and sulphur dioxide (see pp. 130–31), may find a supplement of Vitamin C beneficial. However, you should avoid very high doses of Vitamin C (e.g. 1 gm/day) as they can cause disturbed sleep. Use natural sources for Vitamin E (see p. 206) if you can, but taking a supplement is better than nothing.

Vegans should think about taking a multi-mineral supplement, given the difficulties of ensuring an adequate intake of zinc, manganese and selenium from vegetable food (see left). Vegetarians may also benefit from a mineral supplement.

Some supplements, in certain circumstances, can do more harm than good. **Omega-3 oils** (also called w-3 oils, concentrated fish oils, or EPA and DHA) may make asthma worse for some people (see box on p. 221). **Beta-carotene** (sold alone and as part of mixed antioxidant supplements) may, according to some studies, promote cancer at the high doses used in many supplements. It should only be obtained from food.

Foods and drinks that bring on asthma attacks

The anti-asthma diet tackles the inflammation of the airways and the underlying tendency of the airway muscles to go into spasm – in other words, it is concerned with the *long-term* treatment or prevention of asthma. In addition, you should obviously avoid any foods which aggravate asthma *in the short term*. Various foods and drinks can bring on an asthma attack:

• Foods and drinks containing sulphur-based preservatives tend to give off the irritant gas **sulphur dioxide** while being chewed or swallowed. Some asthmatics are more sensitive to sulphur dioxide than others. The foods that most commonly cause problems are dried apricots and other dried fruit (except those labelled 'unsulphured'), shellfish, french fries, ready-made salads and fruit salads. Sulphur-based preservatives are used widely in the catering industry. On packaged food, look for 'sulphite' and 'metabisulphite' or E numbers 220–227. Soft drinks, wine, beer and cider almost always contain sulphur-based preservatives.

• Foods that cause heartburn (GER – see p.38) can aggravate asthma for some people.

• Alcoholic drinks may make the airways contract for some asthmatics (see box on p. 160).

• Some asthmatics need to avoid foods containing histamine (see box on p. 67).

• A few asthmatics respond badly to the smell of food cooking. The most severely affected can suffer an asthma attack from *any* food aroma. Cromoglycate-type drugs (see p. 148) or anti-cholinergics (see p. 156) may block this reaction.

Needless to say, if you have a sensitivity reaction to any food listed for the anti-asthma diet you should not eat this food.

'I always wanted to be a doctor, and I enjoyed medical school immensely, but once I became a GP, I no longer felt quite so sure about what I was doing. It seemed clear to me that there were a lot of people coming to my surgery who I couldn't do much for. And there were others who, while I could treat their obvious medical problems with some success, remained distressed and were not coping well with life. Once I became a senior partner in this practice, I experimented with having a counsellor come in for one session a week, and then an osteopath for the bad backs. It was popular with the patients, and I saw some people improve enormously. Now we have stress-management classes too, and one of my colleagues has trained in acupuncture, which he uses for selected patients. We also use elimination diets for patients with a lot of long-term problems like migraine. Overall, I think of it in terms of having more tools at our disposal – being able to tackle things from a different angle when standard medicine isn't hitting the spot.'

Geoffrey, a GP in the north of England, is typical of the reconciliation that is now beginning to occur between conventional medicine and alternative medicine. But he also has plenty of criticisms to make of the alternative scene. 'The idea that alternative medicine is "holistic" while conventional medicine isn't, really raises my hackles. Most GPs could be magnificently holistic if they had an hour with each patient as alternative therapists usually do. We have just fifteen minutes, on average, and we have to pack a lot into that – including our basic duty to eliminate the possibility of serious organic disease such as cancer. Time pressure is everything now, and it has squeezed the humanity out of medicine, to a very large extent. But the potential for a holistic approach is there – most doctors have a tremendous store of wisdom and life experience at their disposal, which could form the basis of a holistic approach to treatment if only there were more time to spend with each patient.'

It is in search of a more unhurried and all-embracing approach to treatment that many people turn to alternative medicine. Frequently, what they get out of the therapy has less to do with the actual methods used, and still less with the theories behind those methods, but everything to do with spending a quiet hour with someone supportive and caring who listens to all the complex concerns that surround any illness, gives reassurance or advice, or just offers a 'safe space' in which to talk about life's difficulties.

Other people turn to alternative therapies due to a more serious disillusionment with orthodox medicine. When patients with inscrutable medical problems – such as persistent unexplained diarrhoea, joint pain or chronic urticaria – are given a succession of different diagnoses by different doctors, they often lose faith entirely in modern medicine and reject orthodox treatment in favour of alternatives. This is a great mistake. Modern medicine isn't perfect, but that is only to be expected, because it is not a fixed body of knowledge but a *process* – a continuing journey of questioning, investigation, discovery and improvement. Scientific medicine has come a tremendously long way from the state of ignorance that prevailed two centuries ago, and it will undoubtedly go farther.

Conventional medicine has a great deal going for it – ask anyone over 50, with severe lifelong asthma, what they think of treatment now compared to treatment in the 1950s or early 1960s. You will hear a hymn of praise to the improvements in both drugs and drug delivery systems. Asthma is just one example – conventional medicine has a lot to offer for all the classical allergic diseases. Alternative medicine should

always be regarded as an adjunct to conventional treatment, not a replacement. That is why many doctors prefer the term **complementary medicine**.

A third reason for using alternative medicine is a more philosophical one, a need to understand illness in some larger sense, often part of a general search for meaning in life. Some types of alternative treatment attempt to offer metaphysical reasons for allergy – rather than the mundane explanations of antibodies and immune cells that are given in this book – and this can be attractive to some people. There is no harm in this approach, which can prompt you to make a critical review of your life, look at unresolved emotional issues, or reassess choices that are making you unhappy.

But not all illness, or worsening symptoms, can be explained by emotional causes, and the rigid belief that every illness must have a meaning can be damaging. It easily degenerates into the wholesale psychologisation of illness, the kind of blame-the-victim mentality which can attribute hayfever to 'Emotional congestion; fear of the calendar; a belief in persecution; guilt' and asthma in babies to 'Fear of life; not wanting to be here'. Both these diagnoses are taken from the best-selling *You can Heal your Life* by Louise Hay, which is very influential among some alternative therapists. This compulsive psychologisation of illness can be profoundly damaging, and if your complementary therapist is preoccupied by ideas of this kind, you could find yourself on a very long guilt trip indeed.

Apart from the psychological aspects of alternative medicine, there is the question of whether it actually works in a practical sense – whether it provides more than just emotional support and placebo effect (the benefit that comes from any treatment which you believe in). This is always the central question for scientific medicine in relation to its own treatments,

and conventional doctors naturally apply the same criteria to alternative medicine. Most of this chapter is concerned with trying to answer that question.

Unfortunately, there are so many different kinds of alternative therapy available today that it is impossible to cover all of them in this book. To complicate matters further, many complementary therapists now practise two or more different techniques, mixing them to produce their own unique cocktail of diagnosis and treatment. This eclectic approach can span a remarkable range – you may find a therapist doing distinctly whacky stuff such as iridology (looking at the eye to diagnose all illness – it has been tested and definitely doesn't work), combined with something perfectly rational such as an elimination diet. (The elimination diet might be presented as a 'detox diet', but it is actually being used to detect food intolerances.)

With new forms of therapy springing up all over the place, a healthy scepticism is a distinct asset for the consumer. Be sceptical about any diagnostic test or treatment that is only being practised by one person in the country, or in the world – when doctors hit on something that works, they want other doctors to try it out. World exclusives in medicine are usually suspect.

Avoid any practitioner who tells you to stop using your drugs without your doctor's consent. Likewise, avoid those with a messianic gleam in their eye, an evident disregard for logic or reasonable discussion, or an amazing cure that fixes everything from acne to AIDS. Very few of those who sell bogus cures and phoney diagnostic tests are complete rogues. Most are nice people who are quite genuinely convinced that they have indeed found the answer to people's problems. The powers of placebo effect (see p. 233) can sustain such a conviction for a very long time.

ALTERNATIVE FORMS OF
desensitisation

When Leonard Noon reported his first tentative experiments with immunotherapy for hayfever, in 1911 (see p. 164), he believed that pollen contained a toxin. Most people were 'immune' to this toxin, he said, in the same way that people might be immune to measles or diphtheria, but hayfever sufferers lacked this immunity. Noon thought that his steadily increasing doses of pollen, injected just under the skin, were inducing immunity to the pollen toxin, in the same way that a smallpox vaccine could induce immunity to smallpox.

Noon's theory was all wrong, as we now know, but the important thing was that the treatment seemed to work. In fact it transformed the lives of some patients, especially those who were very severely affected by hayfever. One spoke of a 'marvellous cure', another of 'going for walks to kick my old enemy the hay'.

So doctors kept using Noon's treatment, and in time – when it became clear that Noon's theory was flawed — medical researchers began trying to figure out how the injections *really* worked.

Surprisingly, they have still not succeeded, even though a great deal is now known about the changes that can occur in people undergoing immunotherapy. Despite a wealth of detailed knowledge (see p. 166), it remains impossible to say exactly how conventional immunotherapy reduces allergic reactions. Surprising discoveries about the effects of conventional immunotherapy are being made all the time.

New methods of immunotherapy are still being devised today, and there are three different approaches being taken.

Firstly, there are doctors experimenting with modifications of the technique devised by Noon. For example, instead of injecting the allergen extract, some doctors are giving it to their patients in capsule form, to be swallowed. Others are giving it as a liquid, to be placed under the tongue and held there for a few minutes, then spat out. Sound scientific trials show that both these methods work well, at least with some allergens. Surprisingly, some trials show that certain allergens, when held under the tongue, are not absorbed into the bloodstream, but simply stay stuck to the surface of the mouth – somehow exerting an effect on the immune system from this vantage point.

There are also experiments with speeded-up immunotherapy (see p. 167), called **ultrarush** techniques – at the outset, injections are given at hourly intervals, or even more frequently (in hospital, of course, where severe reactions can be dealt with immediately). Doctors have found that they can induce a remarkably rapid tolerance of the allergen in this way.

The second approach is to apply modern medical knowledge about allergic reactions and so develop entirely new methods of immunotherapy (see p. 169). Such research involves working out, from first principles, novel ways of modifying the immune response in general, or the reaction to one allergen in particular.

This theory-led approach is certainly successful for classical allergies such as hayfever and perennial allergic rhinitis, where there is a good understanding of the basic mechanism (i.e. the malfunctions of the immune system that produce the disease). But for those diseases where the underlying mechanism is only partially understood, such as atopic eczema, this approach is not necessarily the best one. And for diseases such as food intolerance, where the cause of the illness remains largely unknown, it is a complete non-starter.

The third type of approach is to devise a technique by trial and error, and then puzzle out the 'how' question later. This is the same sort of path as Noon originally took, and some believe that this kind of pragmatic experimental approach – practising a method which seems to be effective, even though it's a mystery how it works — is as valid now as it was in 1911. Others disagree.

The two most widely used methods that have been developed in this way are Provocation-Neutralisation and Enzyme-Potentiated Desensitisation. Although these techniques are practised by doctors with a conventional medical training, they remain 'outside the pale' as far as orthodox medicine is concerned. The controversies that surround them are discussed below.

Enzyme-Potentiated Desensitisation (EPD)

This technique has been developed by a British doctor, Dr Len McEwen, who began work on it in the 1960s. It is now practised in many parts of the world, including the US, Germany and Italy.

EPD is used for a far wider range of problems than conventional immunotherapy, being given to people with food intolerance and chemical intolerance, as well as to those with true allergies. This — along with the fact that it is unclear how it works — contributes to the controversies that surround it, because these conditions do not have the same basic causes.

Dr McEwen began with the observation that, when immune cells are aroused during inflammation – whether caused by allergy or some other stimulus – they release large amounts of an enzyme called beta-glucuronidase. This enzyme increases the immune response to the allergen or antigen that provoked the inflammation.

Dr McEwen experimented with injecting beta-glucuronidase into the skin, along with very small amounts of allergen, believing that in such circumstances the enzyme might have the opposite effect, and reduce the immune reaction to the allergen. Eventually he discovered a combination of enzyme and allergen which seemed to have the desired effect.

EPD has been tested, in a rigorous scientific manner, and the results suggest that it can work for hayfever and asthma, as well as for childhood migraine and hyperactivity in children when these are triggered by foods.

In one trial with hayfever patients, researchers measured the levels of anti-pollen IgE following EPD treatment, and it did not rise during the pollen season as it normally does in those with hayfever. This kind of finding is impressive because it is unlikely to be due to placebo effect.

In addition, doctors using EPD claim that it is very effective for patients with allergies who have not done well on the standard course of immunotherapy injections (see p. 164), and for those suffering from atopic eczema — a condition that rarely responds well to conventional immunotherapy. This fits in with other studies suggesting that the immune changes brought about by EPD are fundamentally different from those induced by traditional immunotherapy.

Patients with true food allergy have been given EPD, and while it does not enable them to eat their culprit food, it does seem to reduce their reaction to accidental exposures.

Doctors in the Netherlands are using EPD as a treatment for people with Chronic Fatigue Syndrome (CFS), and report that it helps about 50% of patients.

Unfortunately, the number of good scientific trials that have been carried out for EPD is relatively small (thorough and convincing scientific trials cost a lot of money, and this is not easy to obtain in the case of non-drug treatments, especially speculative ones). It would require a great deal more evidence to convince the majority of doctors that EPD works and, despite the evidence in its favour, there is a great deal of prejudice against it among orthodox allergists.

One point in favour of EPD is that it uses very small amounts of allergen, and is therefore very safe – anaphylaxis has never occurred with this technique.

Provocation-Neutralisation

'After following conventional methods [of immunotherapy] for thirteen years, I heard Carleton H. Lee deliver a paper on provocative testing in 1965, at a meeting of the American College of Allergists in Chicago. I was naturally sceptical, but tried his suggestions when I returned to my office. The results can only be described as astounding. Many patients with unresolved allergic problems responded markedly and rapidly. Many with resistant asthma or perennial allergic rhinitis improved greatly or cleared completely when food injection therapy was added to their inhalant injection therapy.' So wrote Dr Joseph B. Miller — a distinguished allergist and paediatrician, and a Professor of Medicine at the University of Alabama, in 1972.

The technique which he learned from Carleton H. Lee was controversial then and, although Miller developed it with great care and precision during the years that followed, it remains controversial now.

There are two elements in provocation-neutralisation: testing and treatment. Both are used for a wide range of problems – not just classical allergic diseases, but also food intolerance and chemical intolerance. As with EPD (see left), this is one of the controversial aspects of the technique.

Although provocation-neutralisation involves an injection technique that looks, superficially, very much like conventional immunotherapy (see p. 164), there are several important differences. Firstly, the allergen extract used (in the case of true allergies) is a very dilute extract, so that far less of the allergen is injected than in conventional immunotherapy. Likewise, in the case of food intolerance and chemical intolerance, the extracts of the offending substance are used in highly dilute form.

Secondly, the idea of the **neutralising dose** – which is the central plank of provocation-neutralisation — is quite different from anything in conventional immunotherapy. Broadly speaking, the conventional technique (see pp.165–6) works by slowly re-educating the immune system with a gradually increasing dose of the allergen. Only after a succession of injections does the immune system start to behave differently on encountering the allergen. By contrast, in provocation-neutralisation treatment, the neutralising dose is claimed to have an instantaneous and direct effect on the body, 'turning off' symptoms that have already begun. This is the **neutralisation** aspect of the technique. The doctors who practise this technique do not claim to know how the neutralising dose might work.

According to the theory of provocation-neutralisation, the strength of the extract that acts as a neutralising dose is specific for a particular allergen and a particular person. It can only be worked out by a rather slow procedure involving a series of injections. These are **intradermal injections** – they place the allergen extract in the skin, at a slightly deeper level than a skin-prick test. (For treatment, rather than testing, **subcutaneous injections** are used – these go deeper than intradermal injections, placing the allergen extract just underneath the skin. Neither hurts very much.)

Ideally, the neutralising dose should be decided on by measuring the size of the **wheal** (a raised area of skin around the injection site), and whether it grows, stays the same size, or disappears. The doctor or nurse carrying out the procedure can, in theory, work out the neutralising dose just by careful examination of the skin wheals.

However, it is part of the tradition of provocation-neutralisation techniques that verbal feedback from the patient is also taken into account – so if the patient says that an injection has turned off the symptoms, that reinforces the belief that the neutralising dose has been found.

The problem with this aspect of provocation-neutralisation is that expectations, and the power of suggestion, can become involved. So if the doctor or nurse says 'you may find that this next injection makes the symptoms go away', that is often exactly what happens – because the forces of placebo effect (see p. 233) come into play. Unfortunately, verbal interactions such as this are a key aspect of the provocation-neutralisation procedure in many clinics.

Just the same hazard besets provocation-neutralisation if it is used to *test* for the existence of allergy or intolerance, because it is quite common for practitioners to tell patients which allergen (or other offending substance) is being injected and to ask if any symptoms are provoked by the injection. This is not good practice – if someone expects to react to a particular substance, they are quite likely to produce symptoms through purely psychological mechanisms (see pp. 232–3).

Quite apart from this, the question of allergy testing with provocation-neutralisation techniques is contentious, because the pioneers of the technique, such as Professor Miller, never advocated using provocation-neutralisation in this way. Using it as a routine test for sensitivity reactions was a later development, and there are many doctors today who, while they practise provocation-neutralisation as a treatment, say that it does not work well as a test for sensitivity reactions. While they agree that injecting a dose which is either stronger or weaker than the neutralising dose may provoke actual symptoms (this is the **provocation** aspect of the technique) they don't think the reaction is reliable enough to form the basis of a test for allergies. Nor do they think that using skin-wheal measurements alone (i.e. silent testing) turns the technique into an accurate test for allergies. That is not what the provocation-neutralisation technique was designed for – it is about treatment, not testing.

The evidence from research

Recent research from the Nova Scotia Environmental Health Centre in Canada confirms that testing by provocation injections is not reliable. The subjects in this study were all suffering from multiple chemical intolerance, a condition which – for one reason or another – makes patients liable to develop symptoms at any time. No less than 70% of these patients experienced symptoms in response to a dummy injection which contained none of the offending substance. Indeed, 15% of patients also produced a skin wheal in response to some of the dummy injections, confirming that even this reaction may be subject to the power of suggestion (see pp. 232–3).

Looking just at the patients who did *not* react to the placebo injection (i.e. those least susceptible to suggestion) the test still did not yield any reliable result – a person might react to one injection with a particular substance, but fail to react to a subsequent injection with the same substance. The authors concluded that their patients were 'in a state of heightened sensitivity as the result of the chronic irritation by various environmental components and other external and internal stressors'. In this state of sensitivity, patients are so close to the brink all the time that the smallest thing can trigger symptoms. So the apparent reactions to the test injections were actually determined by other factors – some psychological factors (including a psychological response to the prick of the needle) and some external ones, such as exposure to smells or very small amounts of airborne chemicals.

Another recent research study, carried out by scientists at the University of California, confirmed the finding of the Nova Scotia team as regards testing. Although this study did not set out to look at the use of the neutralising dose for treatment, some of the patients were given neutralising doses during the testing process and the researchers observed that 'in most cases a single neutralising injection relieved the symptoms'. This casual observation clearly needs to be confirmed by more rigorous testing. Oddly enough, despite this positive observation about the neutralising doses, the overall conclusion of the researchers was to completely dismiss *all* aspects of provocation-neutralisation as 'the result of suggestion and chance'. This conclusion has been very widely publicised in the US as part of a general campaign against provocation-neutralisation and doctors who practise it.

Other researchers have looked at treatment with neutralising doses, using stringent scientific methods (a double-blind placebo-controlled trial — see p. 90), and found that they *do* work. In one such trial, patients with asthma, and allergies to dogs or cats, were treated with injections of the neutralising dose. They showed a reduction in the sensitivity of their airways, as measured by objective tests. In another experiment, patients with perennial allergic rhinitis and an allergy to house-dust mite were studied, and the neutralising dose was given as drops of allergen extract placed under the tongue (**sublingual drops**) – an alternative to injections. The blockage of the nose, as measured by scientific tests, was reduced by the neutralising dose.

A great many more trials of this kind would be required to convince most doctors that provocation-neutralisation works.

Furthermore, the recent study from California – which observed a number of practitioners of provocation-neutralisation at work with their patients — showed that these practitioners need to be a lot more rigorous and objective in their approach. However, the fact that provocation-neutralisation is often practised badly does not necessarily mean that the basic technique is without any value. There are a great many level-headed doctors and patients who, while initially very sceptical about provocation-neutralisation, have found it surprisingly effective – just as Professor Miller did back in 1965.

Deciding for yourself

So is provocation-neutralisation an option that is worth trying for your condition?

As regards *testing*, the answer is probably 'no'. The most reliable tests are skin-prick tests or RAST blood tests for true allergies (see pp. 91–2), an elimination diet for food intolerance (see p. 194), and avoidance followed by re-exposure (a challenge test) for chemical intolerance.

As regards *treatment* for true allergies, conventional immunotherapy has been far more thoroughly tested and, if you can get it (not easy in Britain — see p. 164), is probably a better bet. It is definitely the best treatment for allergy to insect stings.

The major advantage that provocation-neutralisation has over conventional immunotherapy, in the case of true allergies, is that it is far safer. Because such small amounts of allergen are used, anaphylactic reactions (see p. 58) don't occur.

When it comes to treatment for food intolerance, complete avoidance of the problem food(s), for a period of a year or two, is usually a very effective treatment (see p. 77). Other forms of treatment are only needed for people who find that they have intolerance to a great many different foods (*on the basis of an elimination diet*, not hair tests, blood tests and the like — see p. 93) and cannot devise an adequate diet from the foods they are able to eat. For such people, provocation-neutralisation may be worth a try. Many patients feel that they have gained considerable help from this treatment. They report suffering fewer symptoms and being able to return to a more nutritionally balanced diet.

In the case of chemical intolerance, the first line of treatment should be to avoid the substances concerned as far as possible, eat a good balanced diet, and take a vitamin and mineral supplement if nutritional deficiencies are suspected. Treating any underlying hyperventilation (see pp. 226–9) can also help considerably. Only if there are persistent symptoms, and you are sure these are not due to psychological causes, might provocation-neutralisation be worth a try. Some people with chemical intolerance do find it is helpful, but whether this is a real effect, or simply placebo, remains uncertain.

If you decide to give provocation-neutralisation a try, find a practitioner who has good medical qualifications, who seems objective and sensible in their approach, and who doesn't make implausible claims for the technique. Take note of what other treatments the practitioner offers, and whether these seem rational or not – this is often a good guide to the care and objectivity with which provocation-neutralisation is carried out.

Ask the doctor how he or she assesses the neutralising dose, and avoid anyone who does not use the traditional method of a series of injections combined with wheal measurement. When the neutralising dose is being assessed, say that you would like it to be done 'single-blind' – that is, you don't want to be told anything about what is being injected. Reporting how you feel to the doctor or nurse during the assessment is fine, but only mention really significant symptoms, or a very definite clearance of the symptoms, if this occurs. These precautions will help you to be sure that you are getting something which is of genuine benefit, rather than just a very expensive form of placebo treatment.

Acupuncture

Acupuncture shot to fame in the West in 1972, when James Reston, a correspondent for the *New York Times*, fell ill with appendicitis while covering President Nixon's historic trip to China. Following the removal of his appendix, he received acupuncture treatment for pain, and was highly impressed with its effects.

His Chinese doctor invited Reston to witness the use of acupuncture in anaesthesia, and he reported the remarkable fact that patients undergoing surgery could be free from pain with just a few tiny needles inserted into carefully chosen points on the body. They remained alert and talkative throughout the operation.

Traditional Chinese medicine has enjoyed a good reputation in the West ever since, but what few people realise is that acupuncture anaesthesia is a very new invention. Surgery was not traditionally practised in China and it was only in the 1950s, after Chairman Mao had urged Chinese doctors to unify Western and Chinese medicine, that the anaesthetic potential of acupuncture was discovered.

The remarkable effects of acupuncture anaesthesia made a huge impression on doctors in the West – a high-profile success that has had both good and bad results. On the positive side, conventional medicine has been prepared to take acupuncture seriously, and to undertake some research into its effects. On the negative side, most

of that research has concerned pain control – the effects of acupuncture on the **endorphins**. These are natural painkilling compounds produced by the body (their effects are mimicked by opiate drugs such as morphine and heroin).

Western researchers have paid little attention to how acupuncture affects most other aspects of health, including the immune system and allergic diseases. One exception to this is asthma, where certain nerves do play a large part in producing the symptoms (see box on p. 235).

Treating the person

Diagnosis and treatment are far more orientated towards the individual patient in traditional Chinese medicine, and diagnostic labels such as 'allergy' or 'hayfever' are less important than the particular character of a person's *Qi* (see box on p. 215), as detected by the acupuncturist. A traditional Chinese acupuncturist pays great attention to the quality of the different pulses and takes them at the start of every appointment, and at intervals during treatment, to check how the *Qi* flow has changed. Each treatment session is unique and tailored to the individual's condition at that particular moment.

This makes it very difficult to carry out conventional scientific research into traditional acupuncture.

In an effort to make acupuncture accessible to research, a more Westernised and formulaic approach has been developed, using orthodox medical diagnosis and needling a set of acupuncture points that are prescribed for that medical condition. Experts in traditional acupuncture feel that this approach – first name the disease, then apply a standard remedy – will often fail, and is missing the whole point of acupuncture.

That is not the only problem with Westernised acupuncture, as Dr David Eisenberg of Harvard University, a leading expert on acupuncture, points out. He describes a typical acupuncture session in China: 'Each time the acupuncturist inserts a needle, he or she asks the patient, "Do you have it or not?" referring to the patient's "obtaining the *Qi*" (*de Qi*). The question asks whether the patient has felt a sensation of fullness, distension, pins and needles, or the like, from the insertion of the needle in the spot being used... Most Chinese have experienced acupuncture and they understand the phenomenon of *de Qi*... By contrast, most Western patients seeking acupuncture therapy know nothing of the phenomenon of *de Qi*. Not knowing what sensations they should anticipate, they cannot tell the acupuncturist whether a needle is in the right place. When both therapist and patient know little about *de Qi*, as frequently occurs in Western acupuncture clinics, the result is bound to be disappointing.' Fortunately it *is* possible to find acupuncturists who have been properly trained, and the sensation of 'obtaining the *Qi*' is perfectly detectable, even to a sceptical Westerner, so look for someone who pays attention to this.

There can be emotional and psychological reactions to acupuncture, so make sure that you also feel relaxed with your acupuncturist and that there is a certain empathy between you.

Does acupuncture work for allergies?

According to Chinese theories, acupuncture can have some benefits in any illness – if you are ill, your flow of *Qi* must be disturbed, and it will help to put that right. Indeed, most people do feel a sense of well-being after an acupuncture session.

To look at this from a Western scientific perspective, acupuncture can stimulate your body to increase its production of endorphins (see p. 214). This gives you a mild high, similar to that you'd get from running for a couple of hours. Feeling relaxed and confident helps most people to cope better, and gives them a new perspective on life's problems. Since the mind plays some part in almost all illness (if only to aggravate the effects of an underlying physical problem), inducing a more positive state of mind can be of benefit.

If you are looking for a more specific effect on your allergies, then it is hard to say what acupuncture can give you – there is little evidence simply because Western researchers have not investigated this area, except in the case of asthma.

Several studies show that acupuncture can have a small but detectable short-term effect in opening up the airways of asthmatics. This is not surprising because acupuncture affects the autonomic nervous system, the 'auto-pilot' section of the nervous system (see box on p. 235). As well as controlling heart-rate and breathing, the autonomic nervous system can tighten or relax the muscles around the airways.

A short-term effect is just that – it doesn't treat the real problem. What matters more in asthma is the long-term impact of any treatment on the underlying inflammation of the airways (see p. 36). Although some studies of acupuncture treatment have found a general improvement in the state of the airways, and a reduction in inflammation, other studies have not. However, only one study to date used an individualised approach to acupuncture, as opposed to a same-for-everyone formula. It is interesting that this study *did* find good long-term effects on airway inflammation.

The larger picture

Acupuncture is just one element of Chinese medicine, which has several other techniques available. In China (and in some Chinese clinics in the West) these techniques are used together, as different ways of tackling the same problem. No traditional Chinese doctor would dream of trying to treat every patient with acupuncture alone and, in the case of a patient with allergies, herbal remedies would usually be a central part of the treatment. Eczema, in particular, may respond well to traditional Chinese herbal treatment, taken by mouth – but be very cautious about using Chinese herbal creams (see pp. 220–21).

The flow of energy

Acupuncture is rooted in ancient Chinese ideas of the human body, which are radically different from those of Western medicine:

- Vital energy, called *Qi* or *Chi* (and always pronounced 'chee'), is what distinguishes living bodies from dead ones. It should flow easily and harmoniously throughout the body, nourishing and protecting the organs. When the flow of *Qi* is blocked, or becomes unbalanced, then illness develops.
- Channels called meridians are the conduits for *Qi* in the body. They mostly run vertically (i.e. from head to toe) and the points where acupuncture needles are inserted all lie on these meridians.
- The flow of *Qi* can be measured by carefully taking pulses – not just one pulse as in Western medicine, but several different kinds of pulse.
- By detecting disturbances in the flow of *Qi*, and correcting them, existing illness can be cured, and incipient illness prevented, before there are any obvious symptoms.

The nature of the meridians and the acupuncture points remains a mystery to Western doctors. Some parts of the meridians run roughly along the lines of certain nerves or blood vessels, but they do not follow them exactly. The acupuncture points have no anatomical reality – there is nothing to see either on the surface or under the skin. However, many are located near major nerve endings or over deep pressure receptors.

Homeopathy

'We believe that a serious effort to research homeopathy is clearly warranted despite its implausibility.' That was the conclusion of a group of German and American scientific researchers who, in 1997, looked at every study of homeopathy they could find. This prestigious trans-Atlantic team carefully assessed the scientific validity of each study, and then considered the data from studies that were of reasonably good quality.

This kind of study, in which all the available research data on a topic are combined, is called a **meta-analysis**. There were 119 research studies which were good enough to be included in this meta-analysis and, taken together, these studies suggested that homeopathy does indeed have some real effects. In other words, it produces significantly more benefits than simple placebo effect – the psychosomatic improvement which tends to occur with any treatment, even a dummy pill (see p. 233).

Some of the most convincing scientific studies included in the meta-analysis were those relating to homeopathic remedies for allergic conditions (see p. 217). But what exactly does this mean for allergy sufferers? Is homeopathy a treatment that is worth a try? Unfortunately, it is difficult to say.

Firstly, the evidence from the homeopathy meta-analysis is far from overwhelming, as the researchers themselves point out. The observed improvements – the overall differences between the placebo and the homeopathic remedy – are not huge. Secondly, even if there are *some* homeopathic treatments that have real effects, it does not mean that *every* kind of homeopathic treatment works. Homeopathy is a very broad field, with a multitude of different approaches. The types of homeopathy that have been tested, and appear to help, may bear little or no relation to the homeopathic remedies that are generally available (see p. 217).

'Let like cure like'

The central idea in homeopathy – often known as the principle of **similars –** is that a substance which causes a particular set of symptoms can also, if handled in the right way, cure symptoms of a similar kind. In the words of Samuel Hahnemann, the German doctor who invented homeopathy at the beginning of the 19th century, 'Let like cure like.'

The natural substances that form the basis for homeopathic remedies are mostly derived from toxic plants or minerals. (Sometimes extracts from diseased tissue – called **nosodes** – are used instead, but this is a relatively recent development. So is the use of allergen extracts, such as pollen, described on p. 217.) Hahnemann himself began with the standard drugs of his own day, such as belladonna and arsenic compounds. His innovation was to use them in very much smaller doses than his fellow physicians, and to apply them to entirely different diseases.

Hahnemann worked by first discovering what the effects of the drugs were, when taken by a healthy person (he experimented on himself and his family for this). Then he tried to match the symptom pattern produced by the drug with the symptoms of a particular disease. For example, he observed that belladonna produces hallucinations and a hot, dry skin – symptoms that were also seen in children with scarlet fever. He claimed that, by giving belladonna *in very small doses*, much less than was normally used, he could stimulate the body to heal itself of scarlet fever.

Hahnemann, unlike his medical contemporaries, also advocated a good diet, fresh air and exercise. And he was heartily opposed to the conventional medicine of his day, a brutal business that involved a great deal of blood-letting and large doses of very toxic medicines. Considering how useless, and indeed dangerous, the orthodox medicine of the time frequently was, Hahnemann's successes were not really surprising.

'Less is more'

Homeopathy today is the ultimate version of the 'less is more' philosophy. A homeopathic remedy is prepared by taking the basic ingredient, dissolving it in water, and then diluting that solution over and over again. Imagine pouring a bottle of wine into the Pacific Ocean, and you have a rough idea of how dilute homeopathic remedies are. Making extreme dilutions was an idea introduced by some of Hahnemann's followers, after his death.

Dilution is only part of the story, however. With each dilution, homeopaths apply a special shaking-and-tapping technique known as **percussing.** This was originally done by hand, but now is often done mechanically. Homeopaths believe that percussing makes the active substance *more* powerful, despite the dilution. The term used by homeopaths is **potency**, and a homeopathic remedy of the highest potency is the one that has been most thoroughly diluted and percussed.

In fact, a simple calculation, using the basic laws of physics, shows that there is nothing there at all but water – many homeopathic remedies are watered down so thoroughly that not one single molecule of the active substance is likely to remain. It is this which leads medical researchers to use words such as 'implausibility' (see p. 216) when talking about homeopathy.

What homeopaths do

A homeopath starts by considering all your symptoms (not just allergies, but any other symptoms as well) and various other characteristics that conventional doctors do not usually consider, including physical appearance and psychological traits. The homeopath then chooses a substance which, if taken at full strength, would produce a comparable set of symptoms and characteristics. This approach is called **classical homeopathy.**

In addition, homeopaths often give advice on diet, sleep, exercise and allergen avoidance. As in the early days of homeopathy, this may be the most important part of the treatment.

Like many other complementary therapists, homeopaths will listen if you need to talk about personal problems and emotional difficulties, and will offer reassurance or advice. This can be valuable, though not everyone would agree that a homeopath is the best source for such help. There are two distinct traditions within homeopathy – a scientifically inclined tradition (represented today by experiments with homeopathic immunotherapy – see right) and a highly metaphysical tradition. Among the many ideas floating about within the metaphysical tradition is the notion that all illness is a result of psychological or moral failings. Attitudes of this kind, which are quite common among complementary therapists, can be very damaging (see p. 209).

Sometimes homeopaths recommend avoiding certain foods, on the assumption that the patient suffers from food intolerance, though they rarely use an elimination diet (see p. 194), the only way to achieve accurate diagnosis.

In addition to all this, some homeopaths also give herbal remedies where they think it will help. This approach is called **complex homeopathy.**

A much more recent development within homeopathy is **homeopathic immunotherapy** or **HIT**, which uses an extreme dilution of an allergen (such as pollen or dustmite) to treat people who are allergic to that substance. While homeopathic immunotherapy was inspired by conventional immunotherapy, the relationship between the two is a very distant one indeed. The extensive dilution process means that the liquid used for homeopathic immunotherapy is unlikely to contain even one molecule of the allergen. This puts it in a completely separate realm from conventional immunotherapy, where the presence of the allergen, and the steadily increasing dose with successive injections, is what produces the beneficial effect (see p. 166).

Does it work for allergy?

Two scientific trials suggest that HIT makes a difference, albeit a small one, for hayfever and pollen asthma. In the meta-analysis described on p. 216, one of these trials was given a good rating for scientific reliability, and the other was considered fairly good.

Another type of homeopathic treatment that appeared to be effective for patients with allergic asthma was one using a **nosode** – an extract of the asthmatic airway itself. A small sample of the airway was taken from each asthmatic patient, diluted and percussed, then given to the patient as a treatment. It seemed to work, and the scientific rating of this trial was very high.

The third homeopathic treatment that appeared to have an effect in valid scientific studies was Galphimia, used for symptoms in the eye caused by pollen allergy.

If you go to a local homeopath, it is very unlikely that you will be given either of the first two treatments – these are only used experimentally, in large research centres.

The Galphimia treatment might be available from a local homeopath, but it will not necessarily be in the same form as the treatment used in the scientific trial.

Herbal remedies
WESTERN AND EASTERN

Plants make a great many different chemical substances, mostly for the purposes of dissuading other living beings – fungi, insects and grazing animals – from consuming their leaves, roots and fruits. These chemical substances are extraordinarily potent and diverse. Many taste disgusting, some are virulent poisons, and many will induce vomiting or diarrhoea. None of these effects are surprising, given that substances such as these are produced to defend the plant. However, some of the chemical substances produced by plants happen to have a beneficial drug-like action for people suffering from certain diseases. This is the basis of **herbalism**, sometimes known as **botanical medicine**.

Over the millennia, herbalists have, through trial and error, tried to discover which plants have worthwhile effects. Indeed, this process probably began with our ape ancestors – chimpanzees have been observed, when they are ill with parasitic infections, for example, to carefully select and eat particular leaves that have therapeutic effects. If chimpanzees do this, it is a fair guess that the ape-like ancestors of human beings also did so.

At some point in human history – or prehistory – this use of wild plants became a systematic and specialised activity, now known as herbalism. No doubt the patients who went to see herbalists (like patients visiting their doctors today) expected a cure for every ill, and no doubt herbalists felt bad about telling anyone that the problem was incurable. At this point, quite a bit of wishful thinking and placebo effect (see p. 233) probably found its way into herbalism. The outcome was a mixed bag of herbal remedies – some that worked, some that had no effect at all (apart from placebo effect), and a few that were positively toxic but whose bad effects escaped notice because of the seriousness of the diseases being treated.

In recent times, a few herbal remedies have been put through rigorous scientific tests. As one might expect, some work and some don't. More details of those that have been shown to work for allergies are given on p. 221. First, however, it is important to consider some of the misconceptions that surround herbal medicine, especially those relating to side effects. These misconceptions are rooted in the basic philosophy of herbalism, so it is also important to look at this – and at other points of view about herbal treatment.

The 'Mother Nature' viewpoint

Some modern herbalists maintain that, for every human ill, nature has created a complete cure somewhere in the plant world – the job of herbalists is simply to identify that cure. This belief is essentially religious and anthropocentric – that is, it assumes that the welfare of human beings is the central focus of the plant world. This goes against common sense, because it suggests that plants produce a complex array of chemical components, not for their own benefit, but for ours. Falling into a bed of stinging nettles should be enough to cure most people of such views.

A related idea, and one that is far more widely accepted, is that anything 'natural' must automatically be either harmless or positively beneficial to human beings. This view is regularly promoted by advertisers of all kinds, whether they are selling face cream, shampoo or breakfast cereal.

When the word 'natural' is used as an endorsement of herbal remedies, it is generally understood to mean 'therefore totally harmless'. Nothing could be farther from the truth, as a quick survey of the plant world shows: hemlock is natural, belladonna is natural, and ricin – the most deadly poison known – is natural. All come from plants. Indeed, many wild plants are either poisonous to humans, or produce very unpleasant effects if eaten.

Belladonna, of course, while being deadly poisonous in sufficient quantities, is also a medicinal plant. Its most significant ingredient, atropine, is a useful drug-like substance in small amounts, and a poison in larger amounts. There is no sharp dividing line between these positive and negative aspects – even a small beneficial dose will have some undesirable effects too.

In other words, herbs produce **side effects**, in just the same way that medicinal drugs do. This is almost inevitable – anything that alters body functions enough to act as a drug will usually have some other unwanted effects.

In the case of herbal medicines, there is an added complication. Plants contain dozens, even hundreds, of different chemical substances, many of which have no benefits for humans at all – they are just plain toxic. These plant toxins can produce various unpleasant effects of their own, to add to the side effects of the useful ingredients. So the possibility of side effects is actually *higher* with herbal medicines than with medicinal drugs.

The side effects that occur with herbal treatment are sometimes very serious. Deaths have occurred in some cases, and in others, irreversible damage has been done.

The 'pure-is-best' viewpoint

Many modern anti-allergy drugs were first obtained from plants – cromoglycate (see p. 148), for example, was originally extracted from the roots of an Egyptian plant called ammivisnaga. The ground-up roots of this plant contain a great many other things besides cromoglycate, whereas the pharmaceutical preparations of cromoglycate are pure and of known strength. This pure form of the drug has also been tested very thoroughly by pharmaceutical companies, in order to demonstrate its effectiveness to identify the correct dose, and to look for any serious side effects.

As modern science sees it, herbalism is just a very crude and primitive form of pharmacology (the study and use of medicinal drugs). Much of pharmacology originally developed out of herbalism and other folk cures, by analysing the remedies used, identifying the active substances in them, then purifying these and – if possible – puzzling out how they work.

An advocate of scientific pharmacology would maintain that, with modern drugs, the patient is just taking the substance that works, not a mysterious cocktail of unknown plant chemicals. In other words, you know what you are getting with a drug. You also know it has a good chance of working, and a relatively small chance of causing serious side effects. With a herbal remedy, you are, to some extent, taking a leap in the dark.

Ephedra sinica, the herb known to the Chinese as Ma-huang, illustrates this point well. It contains a mixture of substances, including the powerful drug called ephedrine – it was named after the plant. Ephedrine (see p. 156) can relieve the narrowing of the airways that occurs during an asthma attack. The presence of ephedrine gives Ma-huang the ability to ease asthma, although it is more often recommended to help with weight loss. Unfortunately, over-use of Ma-huang can cause a spasmodic contraction of the blood vessels in the brain, which can result in injury or death. Liver toxicity has also been recorded (see p. 220).

As for its anti-asthma ingredient, ephedrine, although this drug was once important in conventional asthma treatment, it is rarely prescribed now. Ephedrine has long been superseded by asthma-relievers that have a more precise effect on the airway muscles, and so produce fewer side effects.

The multiple-action viewpoint

Practitioners of Chinese herbal medicine, in preparing a treatment for atopic eczema, combine ten or more different herbs. There are some conditions, they say, that can be treated with a single plant, but atopic eczema is not one of those. It requires a mixture – and none of the ingredients of that mixture, taken alone, has any effect. What they are claiming is that the different drug-like substances in the herb mixture have a **synergistic action,** working together to treat the disease.

This same idea is sometimes applied to the many different chemical substances found in a single plant. Some herbalists argue that a herbal remedy is better than a modern drug precisely because it contains a cocktail of different drug-like substances, the effect of one augmenting or balancing that of another.

There is no actual evidence to support this claim, but the fact that Chinese herbal mixtures have some success in treating difficult cases of atopic eczema (see p. 221) demands that Western doctors at least take the possibility of synergistic action seriously.

It might seem that this multiple-action viewpoint goes against the whole grain of Western scientific pharmacology – the 'pure-is-best' approach. However, Western medicine frequently treats certain allergic diseases, such as asthma and chronic sinusitis, with a mixture of drugs. The difference is that each of these modern drugs also works when taken alone, and each has a clearly defined and well-documented action.

The Chinese approach

One fundamental concept of Chinese medicine is that, rather than just matching the remedy to the disease, the treatment should also be based on the particular characteristics of the patient concerned. This idea is shared by some other Eastern systems, such as Ayurvedic medicine.

Whereas a Western doctor might see you as a person with atopic eczema, a traditional Chinese doctor sees you as a person with a certain constitution which has got out of balance and so produced symptoms in the skin. The constitution is usually the main focus of treatment, not the eczema. This approach means that different eczema patients get different herb mixtures, and the same is true for other allergic diseases.

A traditional Chinese doctor will assess your constitution by taking your pulses (there are several in Chinese medicine, not just one), asking various questions, and studying the appearance of your tongue – the same sort of diagnostic process that is used prior to acupuncture.

For the purposes of scientific investigations, where a uniform treatment is necessary, this traditional approach has been modified. A single standardised treatment is applied to a particular disease – and the disease itself is diagnosed by Western medical criteria. Whether this is really comparable with traditional Chinese herbal medicine is open to question. The same caveat applies to any off-the-peg Chinese herbal formula that is sold direct to the public, rather than being prescribed for an individual patient by a trained practitioner.

The traditional philosophy of Chinese medicine makes for a lot of variability in herbal preparations. That is why categorical statements about side effects cannot be made – while one mixture used for atopic eczema may contain a potentially toxic ingredient, another mixture may not.

Using herbal remedies safely

Always talk to your doctor before taking any herbal medicine, because of the risk of side effects, or interactions with any conventional drugs that you may be using.

If possible, get herbal treatment from someone who is also a doctor qualified in conventional medicine. Ideally, your herbalist should have access to laboratory facilities and should order blood tests to monitor your reaction to the herb(s). Monitoring every 1–3 months is necessary with some herbs, to check for serious side effects such as toxicity to the kidneys or liver (see below).

Before buying herbal remedies from a health-food shop or via the Internet, contact the manufacturer and ask to see detailed reports of trials showing that the product is safe.

Think very carefully before taking a herb that has not undergone full safety trials. Find out all you can about the herb and discuss the matter with your doctor. Don't fall for the 'it must be safe – people have been taking it for centuries' argument. If a herb is only toxic to a minority of people, and its bad effects are slow to emerge (so people don't get ill or die immediately after taking it for the first time), its deadliness can escape notice for a very long time, perhaps indefinitely. In the case of pharmaceutical drugs, highly sophisticated information-gathering systems are needed to ensure that such rare-and-slow effects are noticed (see p. 137) but nothing of the kind exists for herbal medicines.

Above all, do not neglect vital medical treatment (e.g. inhaled steroids for asthma) while trying out herbal remedies, as this can be dangerous. Always follow your doctor's advice about your drug treatment.

Risks to the liver

Among the side effects recorded for herbal treatment, liver damage is especially alarming. Deaths from liver failure have occurred with both Western and Chinese herbal treatment. Liver toxicity has been recorded with the following herbal remedies:

- chaparral
- germander
- skullcap
- mistletoe
- senna
- valerian root
- Chinese herbal teas prescribed for atopic eczema, but this is not true of all eczema preparations – several of the most widely used ones appear to be relatively safe.
- jin bu huan
- ma-huang or ephedra (*Ephedra sinica*).

Should you feel ill while taking a herbal remedy, stop taking it immediately and see your doctor. The early symptoms of liver toxicity, which you should watch out for, include jaundice (yellow skin, and a yellowish tint to the whites of the eyes), pale faeces, dark urine, nausea and pain (usually in the region of the stomach).

Illicit steroids

Be very cautious indeed about pots of Chinese herbal cream sold for atopic eczema. Analysis of a selection of such creams found that two-thirds illicitly contained powerful steroids – the very drugs that the people buying the creams were anxious to avoid. The dose of steroid in these herbal creams was alarmingly high, considering the purposes for which some of them had been pre-scribed – such as use on the face of a baby. A substantial risk of serious side effects existed with these adulterated creams.

Sensitivity reactions to herbs

Like other natural products, herbs can provoke a true allergic reaction, and anyone with a tendency to allergies is at particular risk. Although any herb could, in theory, cause such a reaction, some seem especially likely to do so:

• The popular herb echinacea, which is said to promote heal-ing and have antibiotic properties (an unproven claim) quite often causes allergic reactions. It is a member of the daisy family (Compositae) so reactions are particularly likely in those with allergy to ragweed or mugwort.

• Preparations containing royal jelly (obtained from honey-bees) have sometimes caused near-fatal anaphylaxis in those allergic to pollen. Propolis, obtained from bees, should also be treated with caution.

Contact dermatitis often occurs with tea-tree oil and some other plant-derived substances applied to the skin (see p. 55).

Herb–drug interactions

Using herbal remedies and taking medicinal drugs at the same time can be hazardous. These are the herbs that interact with anti-allergy drugs:

• aloe vera, buckthorn, cascara sagrada bark, ginseng, and senna pod or leaf can all interact with steroid tablets

• squill, lily of the valley and pheasant's eye can increase the action and side effects of betamethasone (a steroid); rhubarb root also interacts with this drug

• kava-kava, if taken with cetirizine (an antihistamine) can increase side effects such as drowsiness and poor coordina-tion; it may have the same effect with other antihistamines

Note that many drugs prescribed for conditions other than allergies may interact with herbs. Some of these interactions can be seri-ous, so check with your doctor before taking any herbal medicine.

Herbs that may work for allergies

Of the herbal treatments that have been tested, the following appear to have potential benefits for people with allergies:

• **Chinese herbal teas** for atopic eczema have shown sub-stantial good effects in scientific trials with both adults and children. Patients with widespread and persistent eczema – the kind that is particularly difficult to treat – were chosen for these trials, which were all carried out in London. The puz-zling thing is that when exactly the same herbal treatment was studied in Hong Kong, with Chinese youngsters suffer-ing from eczema, there was no improvement. The reasons for this are unclear as yet.

If you are interested in trying Chinese herbal medicine for eczema, it is advisable to be monitored properly, as liver tox-icity has sometimes occurred (see p. 220). Be warned that the stuff tastes vile, and you have the daily chore of boiling it up for 90 minutes before taking it. It can have a very mild lax-ative effect at first. Don't use Chinese herbal creams unless they are guaranteed steroid-free (see p. 220).

• *Euphorbia acaulis* has shown good effects with atopic eczema. Liquorice root may also help, but can have serious side effects if taken in large amounts.

• **Evening primrose oil** taken in capsule form, is known to calm inflammation, and might be helpful for atopic eczema. Don't chew the capsules, as irritation of the throat can occur. Epileptics should not take this oil.

• *Ginkgo biloba* seems to reduce the reaction to allergens. For those with asthma it may also calm inflammation in the airways.

• **Ayurvedic medicine** utilises two herbs, *Coleus forskohlii* and *Tylophora asthmatica,* in the treatment of asthma. The former relaxes the airway muscles, in much the same way as beta-2 reliever drugs, making the airways open up. The latter has more general benefits in asthma, but also some unpleasant side effects: it can cause nausea and soreness in the mouth.

• **Saiboku-to** is a Japanese herbal treatment for asthma. Studies suggest that it may have beneficial effects on airway inflamma-tion and may allow a reduction in the dose of steroids needed. However, the scientific quality of these studies is poor.

Omega-3 oils

These oils are derived from certain types of fish. They are obviously not herbs, but they are often sold alongside herbal remedies in health-food shops, which is why they are included here. Generally speaking, omega-3 oils have a calming effect on inflammation, but asthmatics who are sensitive to aspirin may find that they gradually get worse if they take omega-3 oils. This is probably due to problems with the production of messenger chemicals called prostaglandins in people with aspirin sensitivity (see box on p. 151). The connection is that omega-3 oils can act as raw materials for the manufacture of prostaglandins and leukotrienes. The details of how omega-3 oils cause trouble for aspirin-sensitive people are not yet understood.

Therapies
THAT PROMOTE RELAXATION

Controversy abounds in medicine, especially when it comes to alternative forms of treatment, but there is one thing that almost everyone agrees on: feeling calmer and more relaxed is good for your health. There are many ways in which a person's mental and emotional state can affect their allergies or other sensitivity reactions (see pp. 232–7), and these help to explain the beneficial effects of relaxation.

There are several different types of approach that can help in the quest for a calmer state of mind and a more relaxed state of body:

• Straightforward relaxation techniques which you learn and then practise for yourself, either on a daily basis, or whenever you need them, or both. Examples include relaxation exercises of various kinds, biofeedback, autogenic training and self-hypnosis.

• Relaxation techniques that are rooted in spiritual practice, such as meditation, yoga, t'ai chi or chi kung (qi gong). Some other martial arts, in addition to t'ai chi, also have a strong element of spiritual practice.

• Treatment techniques such as massage, aromatherapy, reflexology and short courses of hypnotherapy, that are intended to help you feel more relaxed. Acupuncture (see p. 214) can also have this effect. Some therapists providing this type of treatment will also teach you simple relaxation exercises to use at home.

• Investigative approaches that look into the fundamental causes of tension, and attempt to deal with deep-seated emotional problems: psychotherapy (in its many different forms), psychoanalysis, long-term hypnotherapy when this has psychotherapeutic aims, and biodynamic massage.

In the long run, approaches that make you dependent on another person (an aromatherapist or reflexologist, for example), in order to feel relaxed, are usually less helpful than those that give you an active role. If you are learning and practising a technique, as with relaxation exercises or yoga, this puts you in charge of your state of mind.

The techniques that are rooted in spiritual practice, especially meditation and yoga, are particularly helpful because they invite you to take a very broad view of the problems that face you, and the situations that cause you stress. Firstly, rather than focusing very narrowly on your own tense muscles and recurring difficulties, they look at the human situation as a whole – at the basic causes of tension and unhappiness in human beings. Secondly, rather than trying to graft a relaxed viewpoint onto a horribly unrelaxed daily existence (which is what most of us now endure) a regular meditation practice can result in a fundamental and long-lasting change in outlook, with a greater sense of wholeness, direction and stability. This is something that happens naturally within the stillness of meditation practice, and it should be very much an individual process of change, not something imposed from outside. At a purely practical level, a spiritual practice tends to improve relationships with other people, and since a great deal of our stress is caused by the people around us, any improvement in our social interactions can reduce stress enormously.

Some kind of psychotherapeutic approach may be the best choice for those who have tried and failed with other techniques, or achieved only a temporary reduction in stress levels. By tackling the problems at a deeper level, it is often possible to achieve a more profound and long-lasting solution.

Many people discover that, whenever they try to relax or to meditate, they feel even more agitated and anxious. Others begin to cry, or show other signs of distress. Not surprisingly, people who react in this way quickly give up their attempts to unwind, because their responses are so disturbing. Underlying these reactions to relaxation exercises there may be deep-seated problems, usually going back to childhood, that can only be held at arm's length with the help of a tense and always-busy approach to life.

Constant mental activity is part of this defensive strategy, which is why relaxing or meditating is such a frightening experience. Although it is tempting to run away from the problem, by plunging back into a life of frenetic activity, mental and physical, this is ultimately no solution. Some form of psychotherapy is usually needed to deal with these long-standing problems.

Whatever you decide to try, make sure that the teacher or therapist seems like a calm and relaxed person. You should also look for someone who is sympathetic and supportive about your illness. Avoid like the plague those who attribute all allergies and other physical symptoms to mental or emotional problems. Such people can cause immense psychological damage – if you don't get 100% better it will, of course, be your fault.

Hypnotherapy

Hypnosis has a distinctly shady reputation, because of its use – or misuse – in stage and television performances. If hypnosis were not so valuable medically, it would probably be rejected entirely by conventional medicine, on the strength of this reputation. The fact that hypnotherapy is used by some entirely mainstream doctors, as a legitimate treatment for conditions such as atopic eczema, is a great testament to its effectiveness.

Hypnosis is certainly a mysterious phenomenon, and it is difficult to say exactly what happens when a person is hypnotised. Dr Ruth Lever, a qualified doctor who combines hypnotherapy with conventional medical practice, describes the hypnotic state as 'not a form of unconsciousness but rather an altered form of consciousness, in which the patient is more open to suggestion than he would normally be, and in which a corridor is opened between the conscious and the subconscious mind'.

It is certainly *not* true that the hypnotised person is under the control of the hypnotist or hypnotherapist. Autonomy is retained, and no one under hypnosis can be forced to do anything that is really against his or her will. While the person may experience a different state of mind, he or she remains aware of what is going on in the room and anything that is said.

The exact change in mental state during hypnosis varies greatly from one person to another. Some people respond far more readily than others, and go into a deeper hypnotic state. (These same people are more susceptible to placebo effect, a psychological response to drugs or other forms of treatment – see p. 233.)

At one time, it was thought that only adults could be hypnotised. Children seemed to be immune to hypnosis, but in fact they are just immune to the particular hypnotic techniques used for adults. With the right techniques, children can also be hypnotised.

Hypnotherapy treatment can be quite brief, taking only a few sessions. This approach relies on suggestions from the therapist to achieve relaxation, a change in perceptions (e.g. that the skin feels cool and smooth, for someone with atopic eczema) and a change in habits (e.g. stopping scratching).

Another approach is to use hypnosis as a means towards achieving personal insight into emotional problems by accessing suppressed memories. This is a long-term treatment, which has much in common with psychotherapy. It should only be practised by those who have full psychotherapy training.

Scientific studies show that hypnotherapy can be of benefit in both asthma and atopic eczema. Make sure you get a really well-qualified hypnotherapist – preferably someone who also has conventional medical training, or psychotherapy training, and plenty of experience.

You may be given exercises in self-hypnosis to do at home, or tapes, possibly music tapes to be played at bedtime for children with eczema. These can be very useful in reinforcing the messages from the hypnotherapy sessions about sleeping deeply and not scratching.

Relaxation exercises

Acquiring the knack of relaxing is a very personal thing – what works for one person will be useless for another. You may have to try several different techniques before you find one that is right for you.

Guided imagery is often an effective method, and increasingly popular with the widespread availability of relaxation tapes. The tape will ask you to sit in an armchair, or lie down, and picture the scenes described ('waves are lapping gently on the golden sand…' etc.). If you are able to visualise the scene, this should induce a more relaxed state of mind – rather like the relaxation you get from watching a good film.

There are also tapes of special music, or music combined with natural sounds (waves, seagulls etc.) that are intended to produce a relaxed state of mind. Much of this music is incredibly banal, and it may irritate you more than relax you! However, there are also some excellent tapes available, so shop around.

One time-honoured method of relaxing is to sequentially contract, and then release, muscles in each part of the body, beginning with the hands or feet. This is known as Jacobsonian systematic relaxation training or progressive muscle relaxation. A study of children suffering from asthma found that this training increased the peak flow by an impressive 32% for some children, although others did not do quite so well.

Autogenic training

Based loosely on self-hypnosis, autogenic training is a very down-to-earth approach to relaxation which may be useful for anyone who is wary of things esoteric. You are taught to concentrate on different parts of your body in turn and imagine them growing warm and heavy. Beginning with 'my right arm is heavy and warm…' (repeated three times, either out loud or in your head) you work your way through the rest of the body: 'my left arm…' , 'both my arms…' , 'my right leg…' etc.

You could, in theory, teach autogenic training to yourself, using a book, but it is helpful to have to go to a class. The teacher can encourage you to persist when you feel discouraged by your slow progress, and can help with any problems that arise.

Teachers of autogenic training often add more specific lines at the end of the exercise, such as 'my breathing is calm and regular' for asthmatics, or 'my skin is soft and cool' for someone with eczema. A study of asthmatics found that they performed better in basic lung-function tests after eight months of regular autogenic training.

Autogenic training can sometimes evoke strong reactions if there are long-standing problems or suppressed feelings and memories. In these situations, the training sessions may need to incorporate some elements of psychotherapy. Teachers vary in the extent to which they can offer this.

Yoga

Yoga, in its original form, provides a complex religious philosophy of life. If followed with dedication, it affects the whole person – physical, mental, emotional and spiritual. Those who have practised yoga seriously for many years achieve a great deal of mental focus and calmness, plus a surprising level of control over bodily functions such as blood pressure and heart rate. These profound changes are achieved through a combination of breathing exercises (*pranayama*), yoga postures (*asanas*), meditation, cleansing practices and careful attention to diet and way of life.

Yoga has now been practised in the West for over a century, and during that time it has been watered down and very thoroughly Westernised. There are now forms of 'yoga' that consist of little more than stretching and relaxation.

For the greatest benefits from yoga, look for classes with a more rigorous approach. If the particular kind of yoga is specified e.g. Hatha yoga or Kundalini yoga, the chances are that you'll be getting something more authentic.

Iyengar yoga is the most common form taught in the West, but it is rather narrow, concentrating almost entirely on postures. A form of yoga that includes breathing exercises is probably more useful, especially if you have asthma.

Before you sign up for a class, talk to the teacher and find out what it includes. If you are asthmatic, make sure the teacher is really experienced in working with asthmatics. It is all too easy to get the yoga breathing exercises wrong, making the breaths too deep. This can turn into a form of hyperventilation (see p. 226).

Approaching the breathing exercises with a 'got to get this right' attitude is another pitfall for Westerners doing yoga. Most of us have the unfortunate habit – acquired in early childhood – of tensing up and 'really trying' when we are taught anything. This is a major obstacle to doing yoga breathing correctly. Eastern attitudes are much more easy-going and this helps asthmatics much more, because relaxing as you breathe is the key to it all.

Meditation

Basic meditation involves stilling the mind – either emptying it of all thoughts, or focusing it on one very simple object. This is fantastically difficult for most people at first, but with time, and regular daily meditation, it gradually becomes easier.

Many different forms of meditation exist. Most are part of a spiritual tradition such as Hinduism, Sri Lankan Buddhism, Tibetan Buddhism, Zen Buddhism, or Taoism (Daoism). Meditation also forms part of yoga, and it is a cornerstone of most martial arts, though this tends to be played down when these are taught in the West. In each case, meditation takes a slightly different form and has different psychological effects.

A practice known as transcendental meditation (TM), is one of the most widely available – the teaching is arranged by a large international organisation, and can prove expensive. It is cheaper, and probably better in the long run, to go to classes in a local Buddhist centre or consult one of the many books and tapes on this subject.

Biofeedback

This is the most thoroughly scientific, rational and high-tech of alternative treatments. Biofeedback uses technology to measure the state of some part of your body – a part that is usually under automatic control, such as the electrical activity in your brain – and relays this information back to you (hence bio-feedback) .

The feedback is shown by means of swinging needles on dials, flashing lights or bleeping sounds. The idea is that you gradually learn to influence the signal, by noticing that it has changed very slightly in the desired direction, and then re-running (in your head) the thoughts or feelings which apparently led to that change.

In quite a short space of time, you can, with this method, alter bodily states that are beyond voluntary control in most people. Scientific studies show that biofeedback can teach people to regulate their heartbeat, for example, or reduce the amount of acid produced by the stomach. Although yoga practitioners have long claimed to be able to influence such bodily functions, it was only with the invention of biofeedback that scientists accepted this was possible.

Biofeedback can also teach asthmatics to relax tight airway muscles, something that has been demonstrated convincingly in scientific trials. Unfortunately, the specialised equipment needed for this particular form of training is not generally available.

If you sign up for biofeedback, you will probably be trained with equipment that measures the electrical resistance of the skin (this varies with how tense you are) or the electrical activity of the brain. This kind of equipment can help you learn to relax at will.

Massage and aromatherapy

There are many different varieties of massage, and most are relaxing to some extent. Regular massage treatments may improve your general sense of calmness and your ability to cope with life's stresses and problems. In the case of long-standing asthma, massage may also help with tension in the muscles of the chest, back and neck, which frequently develop during asthma attacks.

Aromatherapy is really a form of massage, with the use of scented oils. Bear in mind that the strong smell of some oils can provoke asthma attacks (see p. 39), while other oils can irritate the skin of people with atopic eczema or contact dermatitis.

Biodynamic massage involves a much more subtle touch than other forms of massage and it has different aims. The central objective is to identify bodily tensions that are a result of repressed memories or blocked impulses, and to rebalance the energies of the body. Think of this more as psychotherapy than as massage. It can be very helpful.

Reflexology and zero balancing

Reflexology is based on the belief that specific zones on the soles of the feet correspond to particular parts of the body, and that stimulating those zones on the feet (by gentle pressure) can induce a healing process at distant points in the body. It may or may not be true – certainly, having your feet massaged is immensely pleasurable and can induce a profound relaxation.

Zero balancing is a sequence of static touch, gentle holding and light pressure, applied to specific parts of the body. It can induce a state of great well-being and calmness.

Psychotherapy

The basic tenet of psychotherapy is that it is much more painful and exhausting to keep on repressing bad memories than it is to bring them out into the open, in a safe therapeutic situation, which allows you to process them and move on. Dealing with deep-seated problems lets you relax and live life more fully. In some cases it may help with physical symptoms, such as allergies.

There is a bewildering choice here, with so many different varieties of therapy on offer. Fortunately, according to recent research, they *all* work to about the same extent, as long as you have a good rapport with the therapist. But if you *don't* click, the therapy doesn't usually work, however expert the therapist might be. So make sure you have an introductory meeting before committing yourself to a course of therapy, and don't be afraid to say 'no' and try someone else, if you don't feel quite right with the therapist.

Counselling can also be valuable, and again you will do much better with someone you feel at home with, but who is not afraid to challenge you when necessary.

Breathing exercises

Breathing is a delicate art, and it is possible to get it wrong, in a variety of ways and for a variety of reasons. A poor breathing pattern can gradually become habitual, without the person concerned being aware that his or her breathing is at all abnormal.

Allergy and sensitivity reactions sometimes play a part in causing abnormal breathing, and the symptoms produced by a poor breathing pattern may then augment the symptoms of sensitivity, creating a vicious circle. Correcting an abnormal breathing pattern, by means of breathing exercises and re-training, can produce remarkable improvements in health for some people.

Breathing too much

Taking in too much air, often called over-breathing or **hyperventilation,** is the most common breathing disorder. It can produce a variety of rather strange symptoms (see p. 227) that are sometimes diagnosed correctly, and treated appropriately, but often get overlooked or misdiagnosed.

The primary purpose of breathing is to obtain **oxygen** from the air and absorb it into the blood. The lungs are a crucial interface here, a trading post for gases that are exchanged between the bloodstream and the external air. The delicate, moist membranes that cover the inner surface of the lungs are accessed by millions of tiny thread-like blood vessels known as capillaries. Oxygen from the air seeps into the blood through the thin walls of these capillaries. At the same time, the lungs clean the blood of **carbon dioxide**, a waste gas produced by the body's metabolism. As oxygen seeps into the blood, carbon dioxide seeps out.

That is the school-textbook view of breathing, and it is correct up to a point. But it is over-simplified and misleading if it simply portrays oxygen as totally good and carbon dioxide as totally bad. In fact, there is a correct level in the blood for both gases, and too little or too much of either can cause problems.

Carbon dioxide plays an important role in the equilibrium of the blood because, when dissolved in any liquid, carbon dioxide makes a weak acid. So the amount of carbon dioxide present is crucial in deciding the acidity of the blood. Given that the blood reaches every part of the body, it is not surprising that any changes from its normal composition have far-reaching effects.

Normally, blood is very slightly acidic, and that is what the body is accustomed to. While some body parts can cope with small changes in the acidity of the blood, other parts respond very badly. The nerve cells are particularly vulnerable to changes in acidity.

Hyperventilation, or over-breathing, has relatively little effect on the level of oxygen in the blood, which is carefully controlled, but it can lower the level of carbon dioxide in the blood, thus making it less acid. More commonly, hyperventilation just makes the level of carbon dioxide vary a great deal.

When the carbon dioxide levels in the blood yo-yo about all the time, this has some unpleasant effects. In particular, it disrupts the smooth running of the nerve cells, which is why many of the symptoms of hyperventilation involve the senses, feelings or behaviour.

The symptoms of hyperventilation can include:
• numbness or pins-and-needles in the hands and feet, occasionally affecting the lips and tongue as well
• difficulty in swallowing
• aching muscles, cramps, tremors and twitches
• sudden loss of strength in the muscles
• dizziness, confusion, unreal or spaced-out-feelings
• blurred vision, ringing in the ears
• headache, migraine
• breathlessness
• aching in the chest
• abnormal heart rhythm
• sensitivity to bright lights and loud noises.

There may also be some severe psychological symptoms:
• panic – a brief but intense state of anxiety
• prolonged anxiety or depression
• hallucinations, although this is rare
• mood swings and phobias, most frequently a fear of dying. The irrational conviction that death is imminent can be overwhelming, even in someone who is young and apparently in good health.

Each of these symptoms can, of course, be caused in several other ways, but when this whole cluster of symptoms – or a large number of them – occurs together in an individual, that person is very likely to be a hyperventilator.

When there are short self-contained bursts of hyperventilation, the effects are often described as a **panic attack.** Doctors usually have no trouble recognising this problem, but – not surprisingly – are often misled by the sustained psychological symptoms of chronic (long-term) hyperventilation. Many people with chronic hyperventilation are diagnosed as having some kind of mental illness, and they may go for years without getting the right diagnosis.

Hyperventilation and sensitivity reactions

The link between sensitivity reactions and hyperventilation seems to be a complex one. Unfortunately, very little research has been done in this area, so what follows is based on the case histories of patients, and the collective experience of doctors, not on hard scientific data.

In some cases, a sensitivity reaction may directly provoke a change in breathing pattern. This is what appears to happen for some people with **caffeine sensitivity**. Cutting out all caffeine-containing drinks (coffee, tea and colas) seems to put a stop to the hyperventilation symptoms, because the multiple symptoms promptly disappear.

In other cases, a severe sensitivity problem such as **multiple chemical intolerance** results in an anxious state of mind, and the anxiety leads to hyperventilation. Hyperventilation, pure and simple, may also masquerade as chemical intolerance (see p. 236).

Wheezy as a mountain breeze

Ionisers – devices that supposedly turn indoor urban air into a fresh mountain breeze – are often promoted as alternative devices that can clear allergens from the air. In the case of asthma, however, research shows that some ionisers can actually make symptoms *worse* by generating ozone, which irritates the airways. It is usually the cheaper ionisers that do this. More expensive models are less likely to produce ozone, but they are unlikely to help either. Several scientific trials show that ionisers have no significant benefits when used by asthmatics.

Hyperventilation and asthma

While hyperventilation can develop in anyone, asthmatics are particularly vulnerable. During an asthma attack, especially a severe one, developing an abnormal breathing pattern is an entirely understandable reaction. In an attempt to get more air, you may start breathing more rapidly and taking air into the upper chest, using the accessory muscles of breathing (see p. 230). These muscles should not normally be used when you are at rest – they exist to give you extra breathing capacity when running fast.

As long as the asthma attack lasts, this forced breathing does no harm, because its effects are cancelled out by the narrowing of the airways. But if this over-breathing persists after the attack has ended, then too much air is going in and out of the lungs, so carbon dioxide levels in the blood begin to fall.

Simply feeling anxious can also trigger off rapid upper-chest breathing. If you get very worried when an asthma attack starts, you may begin hyperventilating just out of anxiety.

For asthmatics, in addition to the usual symptoms of hyperventilation (see p. 227) there are some subtle effects of hyperventilation that can make asthma worse:

- The airway muscles (and all other muscles that are not under voluntary control) contract slightly when carbon dioxide levels in the blood fall.
- Mast cells are quicker to degranulate (see box on p.12) when there is less carbon dioxide, and this triggers allergic symptoms.

Just to complicate matters, one of the symptoms of hyperventilation is breathlessness. Sometimes this is the most prominent symptom in non-asthmatic hyperventilators, and the doctor overlooks the other symptoms and gives a diagnosis of asthma. In such cases, people are told they have asthma when they are actually suffering from hyperventilation alone.

Testing for hyperventilation

You can do two simple tests for hyperventilation at home, if you think that it could be playing a part in your symptoms. (If you are asthmatic, only do these tests when you have no asthma symptoms and your peak-flow reading is good. Make sure your reliever inhaler is nearby, in case of a bad reaction to the test.)

The first test should be done when you have some symptoms that might indicate hyperventilation (see p. 227).

Find a clean paper bag and hold it over your nose and mouth while breathing normally. Any symptoms that are due to hyperventilation should clear up, because, by re-inhaling the air that you have just breathed out, you will increase the level of carbon dioxide in your blood.

The second test is done when you *don't* have any of the symptoms listed for hyperventilation.

Speed up your breathing, and inflate your upper chest with each breath. Do this for a few minutes. Do any of your usual symptoms appear? If they do, this suggests that they may be caused by hyperventilation.

If either of these tests indicates hyperventilation, make an appointment to see your doctor. It is important that you should have a proper medical diagnosis, so that you get the right professional treatment.

Treating hyperventilation

If you hyperventilate, you could be taught a more healthy breathing pattern by a physiotherapist – ask your doctor for a referral. Certain complementary therapists, such as osteopaths and Feldenkrais practitioners, can also teach good breathing patterns, and so can experienced yoga teachers (see p. 224). A teacher or therapist who works at a relaxed pace, is not too dogmatic, and helps you to find your own way to healthy breathing, is preferable to one who tries to impose a regimented breathing pattern on you.

On the assumption that most hyperventilators don't just over-breathe, but also breathe with their upper chest and under-use the diaphragm (see pp. 229–230), all these different practitioners will take a combined approach – tackling both sides of the problem at once. This represents an important difference from the Buteyko method (see below).

The Buteyko method

The stated aim of the Buteyko method (also called the Buteyko treatment) is to stop people from hyperventilating. However, Buteyko practitioners do not work with people who have the symptoms of hyperventilation, as recognised by conventional medicine (see p. 227). Instead they work with asthmatics – *any* asthmatics, not just those whose symptoms suggest that they might be hyperventilators.

The rationale for this is the claim, by the originator of the exercises, Professor Konstantin Buteyko, that asthma is actually *caused* by hyperventilation. (What is more, Professor Buteyko cites hyperventilation as the cause of no fewer than 150 different diseases, including allergies, eczema, migraines, insomnia, bronchitis, high blood pressure and haemorrhoids. However, his treatment is only marketed for asthma.)

The claims made for the success of the Buteyko method in treating asthma are startling. According to one training centre, it can get 97% of asthmatics off most of their drugs and able to control attacks within a week of starting.

Not surprisingly, this is a bit of an exaggeration. But the real achievements of the Buteyko method are still quite impressive: an

Australian research study showed that during the course of Buteyko lessons, the overall use of reliever inhalers (e. g. Ventolin) fell substantially and remained relatively low 3 months later. However, the patients' average peak flow stayed the same, and 15% of those studied were admitted to hospital with a severe asthma attack during the trial. In the 8 months that followed, 30% needed a course of steroid tablets – indicating a substantial worsening in their condition. In other words, the Buteyko method can give some help to many asthmatics, but the claim that it can get almost everyone off asthma drugs and free of asthma is just hype.

Professor Buteyko's claim to have discovered the *fundamental cause* of asthma is clearly untrue. What he seems to have discovered is that there are many more hyperventilators among asthmatics than was widely realised, and that they generally show no obvious symptoms of hyperventilation. His other important contribution is to suggest that mouth-breathing may create a lot more problems for asthmatics than previously recognised.

The Buteyko method has three aspects:
- unblocking the nose
- training to breathe through the nose, not the mouth
- training to take fewer breaths and pause between breaths.

Unlike other treatments for hyperventilation (both conventional and alternative), the original Buteyko method pays no attention to teaching asthmatics to breathe with the diaphragm. However, a few Buteyko practitioners are now beginning to incorporate this aspect of treatment.

If you decide you would like to try the Buteyko method, there are several different options. Classes are the most expensive route, with very high fees being charged. There are video cassettes you can buy, which are less expensive. Alternatively, there are various books, which are much less costly, and which explain how to do the exercises (see p. 255).

Whichever option you choose, it is vital that you get your doctor's permission before starting. Ensure that your reliever inhaler is in your pocket while doing the exercises, because they could provoke an asthma attack. Keep taking your preventer drugs regularly throughout the treatment. If you start to feel much better and want to reduce your dose of preventer, you must talk to your doctor first.

Don't follow the Buteyko method blindly, because some of the advice given is dangerous. For example, some Buteyko publications advise you to refuse oxygen if you are taken to hospital with a severe asthma attack. They claim that oxygen levels in the blood are not reduced during a severe asthma attack, but this is just not true. Measurements clearly show that the level of oxygen gets very low, **and this is frequently the cause of death**.

Another very peculiar Buteyko idea is that you should not try to shift mucus from your airways because mucus 'protects you' against losing too much carbon dioxide. This too is dangerous advice. Accumulated mucus narrows the airways, adding to your asthma symptoms, and it can even block a small airway completely. The part of the lung served by that airway then collapses – a serious complication that no asthmatic would want.

Using the right muscles

Hyperventilation is often linked with an abnormal way of breathing, in which the wrong muscles are used. This is one common pattern that conventional doctors recognise for hyperventilators:
- The main muscle of breathing – the diaphragm (see below) – is not used fully
- The muscles of the upper chest become involved in breathing, even at rest, when they should not be needed
- There are lots of rapid, shallow breaths
- The breathing is quite irregular, with deep, sighing breaths from time to time, or frequent yawning.

Even in those who do not hyperventilate, breathing with the upper chest, and/or neglecting the diaphragm, can become a problem. This pattern of breathing is sometimes linked to anxiety and emotional problems (see p. 230).

To understand what goes wrong, you need first to know about the healthy way to breathe.

The **rib-cage** and the **diaphragm** are the work-horses of breathing. You can feel your rib-cage through your skin, and feel its movements, but the diaphragm is far more inaccessible. It lies below the lungs, but above the stomach and intestines.

In its contracted state, the diaphragm becomes a thick slab of muscle, with a slight curve, like an inverted saucer. When it relaxes, it becomes far more curvaceous, changing to a shape like an inverted bell. In this shape, there is less space for the lungs above the diaphragm.

If you are breathing correctly, the diaphragm contracts when you breathe in and relaxes when you breathe out. The contraction lowers the dome of the diaphragm, pulling the base of the lungs downwards and so making them expand.

Breathing out requires no muscular force whatever, as long as you are just sitting or walking about (and therefore not breathing hard). The lungs are naturally elastic, like balloons, so they automatically contract and force out the air, once the diaphragm relaxes into its bell-like shape and stops pulling them downwards.

While you cannot feel the diaphragm itself, you can feel the effect of its in-breath contraction. As it contracts, the diaphragm pushes down on the stomach and intestines, so that your abdomen bulges out a little with each breath. Western women, conditioned to admire an unnatural flat-bellied body shape (unnatural for a woman, that is), often breathe badly because they are trying to 'hold the tummy in'. This steely tightening of the muscles across the front of the abdomen opposes the contraction of the diaphragm, and prevents a natural and relaxed in-breath.

The diaphragm should do virtually all the work of breathing in, when you are not exerting yourself much. The upper part of the rib-cage should hardly expand at all and the muscles that run between the ribs, the **intercostal muscles**, should not be working.

When you become more active, and therefore need more oxygen, the upper chest automatically starts to expand with each in-breath. At this point the intercostal muscles become involved, along with a whole team of other muscles in the chest region – these are known as the **accessory muscles of breathing**.

The effects of an asthma attack

In the grip of a severe asthma attack, you may well start using the accessory muscles of breathing to try to take in more air. If you have frequent attacks, or if this way of breathing gets to be a habit and goes on between attacks, then the chest may be distorted by the constant use of the accessory muscles, plus the over-inflation of the lungs. Severe asthmatics often have high shoulders and a 'barrel-chested' look as a result of this. Hyperventilation may also start in this way.

Observing how you breathe

To discover whether you are breathing with your diaphragm or your upper chest, lie on your back with your left hand on your belly, and your right hand on your upper chest. Just lie still for a few minutes, let your arms relax, then start to pay attention to your hands. When you breathe in, which hand rises? It should be the left hand, with little or no movement in the right.

Alternatively, bend over and hold the back of a chair with your hands. Your back, head and arms should form a straight horizontal line, at right angles to your legs. Just stay quietly in this position for a while. It is very difficult to breathe with the upper chest in this pose, whereas breathing with the diaphragm is easy. If you feel fine in this position, then you are probably breathing well normally.

Correcting upper-chest breathing

Learning to breathe with the diaphragm is often an important part of correcting hyperventilation (see p. 228). It should also be taught to anyone who has the kind of chest deformities that develop in severe asthma (see above).

Diaphragmatic breathing, or **abdominal breathing** as it is sometimes called, should help make you feel more relaxed because the in-breath can disperse tensions in your abdomen. This is where many people 'hold on to' their fears, with chronically tense abdominal muscles. When you start breathing into this area of tension, it is important to take things gently and not force the breath downwards. Be aware of any resistance to the in-breath in the abdomen, and of any emotional reactions that occur when you challenge this resistance.

Sometimes breathing in this way for the first time can bring up emotional difficulties that may need careful handling. That is why it may be better to learn abdominal breathing from someone who has time to deal with such issues, and with whom you feel very comfortable and relaxed – for example, a yoga teacher or an alternative therapist who you like and trust. Physiotherapists tend to take a very brisk and practical approach to breathing, which may not be entirely appropriate or helpful when habitual ways of breathing are tied up with emotional problems.

When learning to breathe with the diaphragm, be careful not to get carried away and become a 'belly breather', whose every in-breath sends the abdomen bulging out like a mainsail. The abdominal muscles should oppose the downward movement of the diaphragm to some extent, without being too tense.

Clearing the nose

Breathing through the nose, rather than the mouth, is beneficial for asthmatics, because it cleans and warms the air. It can also help those with chronic sinusitis because it oxygenates the air in the sinuses, which discourages some of the more troublesome microbes responsible for sinus infections.

This technique for clearing a blocked nose, part of a set of breathing exercises for opera singers, is based on a time-honoured yoga exercise called **alternate nostril breathing**:
- Sit with your mouth closed.
- Press your right nostril against your nose to close it, using the thumb of your right hand.
- Breathe out through your left nostril.
- Press your left nostril against your nose with the index finger of your right hand, to close it. (The hand makes only a very small movement from side to side.)
- Breathe in through your right nostril.
- Repeat the sequence.

Once you have got the hang of this, do ten fairly rapid breaths, with no pause between out-breath and in-breath. Pause and rest.

Repeat using your left hand, and reversing the flow of the breath: out through the right nostril and in through the left. Again, do ten breaths and then rest.

Alternatively, try the following exercise, which is recommend by Buteyko practitioners for unblocking the nose. This technique has not been tested scientifically, but the reports of asthmatics who have used it suggest that it often works wonders, even with children who could never breathe through their noses previously:

- Have your reliever inhaler to hand, just in case the exercise brings on an asthma attack.
- Breathe as you do normally, and at the end of a normal out-breath, close your mouth and hold your nose
- Stay like this, without inhaling, for as long as you can without discomfort. Walk around the room while you are doing this or, if you are young and fit, do something more strenuous – either walk upstairs or squat-then-stand several times.
- When you need to breathe in, keep your mouth shut but release your nose
- Breathe in slowly through the nose
- Repeat the exercise if your nose becomes blocked again.

Special exercises for asthma

In addition to tackling the problem of hyperventilation, if one exists, asthmatics can use other breathing exercises to tackle specific aspects of their asthma.

Clearing mucus from the lungs A physiotherapist can teach methods of clearing mucus from the airways which are suitable for asthmatics. Ask your doctor for a referral. You could also try the following exercises:

Huffing Take an in-breath, then tighten your abdominal muscles very sharply, to push the air out. Imagine there is a candle in front of you, and you are trying to extinguish it, but using your belly muscles only. Your out-breath should make a short soft 'huff' sound – if it is more of a loud 'wooosh', you are contracting the muscles in your chest as well as those in the belly. Try again, and focus your attention on your belly as you make the out-breath.

The in-breath should be effortless with this exercise – it just bounces back in. Do as many huffs as you can without feeling breathless. Rest and repeat. The aim is to build up stamina until you can do thirty or more huffs in succession.

Pursed-lips breathing Take a fairly deep in-breath, then purse your lips together. As with huffing, your belly muscles have to do all the work of the out-breath, but in this exercise they are working against the muscles of the lips. The aim is to divide the out-breath into as many fragments as possible – to push the air out through the lips in a succession of tiny, forceful blasts.

One objective of these exercises is to encourage mucus to start moving up to the top of the airways. From there, it can be cleared with a little throat-clearing cough. Note that the mucus will probably take a while to reach the throat – this may happen some time after you do the exercise. For maximum effect, repeat these exercises several times each day.

Coping with asthma attacks

The crucial thing during an asthma attack is to focus on your out-breath, not your in-breath. Of course this goes against the grain, because you feel so desperate for air, but remember that the central problem is stale air from your last in-breath, now trapped in your lungs by the narrow airways. If you can focus on exhaling this used air, you will have more space for fresh air to come in with the next in-breath.

At times when you are *not* suffering from an asthma attack, it is worth doing some exercises that improve the strength of your out-breath. The key problem during an asthma attack is that the natural elasticity of the lungs, which should power the out-breath, is not equal to the challenge of pushing out all that air through narrowed airways in a short space of time. In this situation, contracting your abdominal muscles so that they push upwards and assist in emptying the lungs is helpful.

The two exercises described above for clearing mucus – huffing and pursed lips breathing – also strengthen those abdominal muscles which can assist you with your out-breath during asthma attacks.

Strengthening exercises

Several different exercises or pursuits that strengthen the breathing muscles seem to produce an improvement in asthma. The reasons for this are not understood.

Asthmatics who take up a wind instrument, such as the flute, often report that their asthma improves considerably. The same effect has regularly occurred with asthmatics who undertake classical training in singing. One set of exercises, taught to aspiring opera singers and designed specifically to strengthen the diaphragm, has been scientifically tested and shown to improve asthma and reduce the need for drugs. These exercises can be learned at home (see p. 255). There are also some mechanical devices which can strengthen the breathing muscles (see p. 255).

The role of the mind
IN ALLERGY AND INTOLERANCE

'I get ill if I do a long coach journey – six or seven hours say. I usually feel sick by the end of the journey, and have a headache. The funny thing is, if I'm walking along the street and I happen to see a coach of the kind that I do long trips on, I feel a bit sick then too, just for a short while. It seems crazy, but I get ill just from *seeing* the coach.'

What Jake is observing is the powerful effect of the mind on the body, in the reaction known as **conditioning**. Some people are more susceptible to it than others, but no one is completely immune.

The Russian scientist Ivan Petrovich Pavlov first demonstrated conditioning in 1889, with his famous dog-and-dinner-bell experiment. Pavlov rang a bell every time he fed the dog, and eventually the dog would salivate each time it heard the bell, whether dinner was being served or not. Its stomach would also begin to secrete acid, in anticipation of the meal, simply on hearing the bell.

Modern-day experiments have shown that conditioning works with immune reactions too. For example, rats can be conditioned by repeatedly giving them an immunosuppressive drug and always adding saccharin to their drinking water on the day the drug is given. Subsequently, just the taste of saccharin in the water is enough to suppress their immune responses.

This surprising discovery is partially explained by the finding that there are nerves running to the lymph nodes – key areas where the immune responses are coordinated. In other words, the immune system and the nervous system, once thought of as completely separate domains, are in conversation with each other. In fact this is a three-way discussion, because the hormones are also involved. The study of these complex interactions, which we are only just beginning to understand, is known as **psychoneuroimmunology.**

Even before Pavlov carried out his classic experiment, Dr John MacKenzie of Baltimore had discovered that an artificial rose, in the vase on his desk, would bring on an attack of rhinitis and asthma in one of his patients who believed that she was allergic to roses. (In fact such an allergy is unlikely – see box on p. 127. It is usually the strong scent that triggers symptoms, the allergy being to something else, often grass pollen, which is in the air when roses flower.)

Much more recently, something similar happened – this time unintentionally – when a boy with severe hayfever and pollen asthma was undergoing hypnosis aimed at helping him relax. Part of the hypnotist's standard technique was to describe an idyllic scene in an alpine meadow, and ask the subject to imagine being there. For this boy, it worked all too well – the thought of the grass pollen in the meadow brought on a severe asthma attack. The hypnotist, with great presence of mind, asked him to imagine a helicopter suddenly appearing in the sky and rescuing him from the meadow – and the asthma attack subsided.

Scientific tests, carried out in a laboratory, back up these casual observations. For example, many people who are allergic to grass pollen will suffer an asthma attack if the experimenter says they are inhaling grass pollen through a mouthpiece – even though they are actually inhaling fresh air.

It can work the other way as well. Telling the same asthmatics that they are now inhaling a reliever drug will stop the attack, even though they are still breathing the same air as before. This is the basis of **placebo effect**, the benefit that tends to occur with any treatment, even a dummy pill, as long as patients believe that the treatment will work.

Note that it is not necessarily the immune system producing all these reactions. There are also direct effects of the mind on the skin, in atopic eczema, on the airway muscles, in the case of asthma, and on the nose in rhinitis. Some of these are due to the autonomic nervous system (see box on p. 235) while others are much less well understood.

The findings described above should be reassuring for anyone who has noticed that their allergy or asthma symptoms are sometimes affected by their thoughts and feelings. There is no need to feel bad about this, and it certainly doesn't mean that your allergies are 'all in the mind'. Conditioning, and other psychological responses, are an entirely natural reaction to a very real illness.

However, if you suspect that psychological reactions are making a big contribution to your symptoms, you could try to address the problem directly. Hypnotherapy (see p. 223) can be particularly useful in this regard, because those who are most susceptible to conditioning are also very responsive to hypnotic suggestion – which can counteract the conditioning messages. Hypnotherapy can also help those asthmatics who become psychologically dependent on their inhalers – something that happens quite often, especially in people with severe asthma. In the words of one asthmatic 'If I found that I'd left my Ventolin at home, that would sometimes start me off wheezing straight away. I was so afraid of being without it.' Of course, it is important to carry your reliever inhaler with you at all times, but this kind of excessive psychological dependence is distinctly unhealthy. At worst, it can lead you to over-use your reliever inhaler, which can increase your risk of a life-threatening asthma attack (see pp. 153–4).

Sometimes the psychological effects involved in allergies and asthma are far more complex and deep-rooted than this, not just a matter of simple conditioning. It is not uncommon for asthma attacks, in particular, to be provoked by family tensions and anxieties, or by suppressed memories from childhood. This can occur even though the asthma also has a clear-cut physical cause, such as an allergy to house-dust mite. Some people find that their asthma always gets worse when they are in a certain place, with a certain person, or in a particular situation. These problems are usually helped by psychotherapy (see p. 225).

While hypnotherapy and psychological treatments can sometimes be valuable, it is vital to remember that the mental factors in allergic reactions are always operating in combination with purely physical responses – such as the triggering of mast cells by allergen (see box on p. 12). Using psychological treatments alone is as much of a mistake as ignoring the mental and emotional dimension of ill-health completely. The two aspects of treatment – physical and psychological – should always go hand in hand. Be very wary of alternative therapists who over-emphasise the psychological aspects (see p. 209).

Under the skin

To see a baby with severe eczema is heart-breaking for any parent – tormented by something it cannot understand, the child often experiences touch, not as a comforting and pleasurable contact, but as a further irritation. According to some psychologists who have studied eczema in depth, suffering from severely itchy skin in the early years of life may create long-lasting psychological problems. They believe that the discomfort associated with the skin, and especially with being touched, interferes with normal processes of relating to the world and developing loving relationships with others. That is why it is so important to get the skin symptoms under control, with the proper use of steroid creams, skin care, dietary changes if appropriate, and an anti-scratching programme (see p. 46).

How allergies affect the mind

In studying the psychological aspects of allergy, researchers have discovered that some patients frequently have thoughts that catastrophise the situation. In the case of atopic eczema, these thoughts might go along the lines of 'this terrible itching will never end' or 'none of the treatment really makes much difference'.

Such thoughts may be just below the surface of the conscious mind most of the time, and it is only by developing the ability to notice what is going on internally that the allergy sufferer can become aware of them.

Researchers have also found that, when negative thoughts such as these arise, eczema sufferers are far more likely to scratch their skin and so make the eczema worse. Thus the thought becomes a reality – a self-fulfilling prophecy.

The tendency to catastrophise difficult situations is something that most people develop (or acquire from others) at a very young age, and it may take some effort to even become aware of this mental habit, let alone change it. Yet it is possible to start thinking about illness, and about life in general, in a different way – for example, as a difficult challenge but one that can usually be overcome.

Allergies are in no sense unique. Any long-term disease that causes intense discomfort, makes life unpredictable or limits your activities, is bound to have profound effects on the personality. However strong a person you are, it affects your life, and influences you in a very deep way – shaping you as a thinking and feeling individual. This is especially true if illness begins at an early age, becoming part of your formative interactions with your parents (see box on p. 233) or marking you out as different from other children.

This shaping can have both positive and negative aspects, and it is important to recognise that there is a choice about which aspect you emphasise. It is never too late to try to change the emphasis. Counselling or psychotherapy (see p. 225) may help with this, especially if the counter-productive attitudes to the illness are deeply rooted in family experiences.

The role of the mind in asthma

The diagnosis of **intrinsic asthma** has long since been abandoned. This diagnosis, which was commonplace in the 1950s and 1960s, technically meant 'asthma with no external cause'. But the widespread assumption was that the cause was psychological. As older asthmatics will tell you, this made their lives particularly miserable, because they were held responsible for their disease. Families were often ashamed of having an asthmatic child.

The injustice of this sweeping assumption is clear today. Modern research shows that an external stimulus which initiated the asthma, such as an allergen, can usually be found. Among asthmatic children, an allergic cause exists in 80–90% of cases. Even where no specific stimulus can be found, there is still a clear-cut state of inflammation in the airways. No one with any knowledge of asthma would now claim that it is an entirely psychosomatic disease, nor even that it is predominantly psychosomatic.

Nevertheless, once asthma has begun, the mind may play an important role in bringing on attacks, or making them worse, as many asthmatics know from their own experience. This is entirely understandable when you think how closely breathing is tied up with our emotional lives – fear, sadness, excitement and anger all alter the usual breathing pattern in different ways, and any of these reactions may trigger an asthma attack.

The interactions between the mind and the airways are complex in the extreme, and vary from one person to another. Anxiety and tension can make asthma a great deal worse for some people, while others only suffer an asthma attack when the stress is over. A few people actually have *less* trouble with their asthma when under stress and, oddly enough, this is the reaction that is easiest to explain. Stress activates the sympathetic nervous system (see box on p.235), which produces adrenaline, and the adrenaline opens up the airways.

For stress to make asthma worse, as it frequently does, there must be some other reaction going on which overrides the effect of the adrenaline. Doctors don't know exactly what this is, but asthmatics who get worse when stressed could be hyperventilating (see p. 226) just a little – not enough for it to be obvious, but enough to make their airway muscles contract.

Breathing through the mouth, rather than the nose, can also occur under intense stress, and this is bad for the airways because the air they receive tends to be drier, dustier and possibly colder, for not having passed through the nose first. This raw air may irritate the sensitive airway linings of an asthmatic, and so make the airway muscles tighten. Small local nerves, that run directly from the airway linings to the airway muscles, could cause this reaction.

Psychological symptoms from sensitivity reactions

'People thought that because the hospital couldn't find anything wrong with me, and because I wasn't terminally ill, there was nothing wrong with me at all. No one could understand how I was feeling, or even believed me. My friends and family lost patience with me. I overheard one member of my family saying they thought I was just attention-seeking. This hurt me so much. I hated being ill all the time. I wanted to go out and enjoy myself and do the things I'd always done, but I couldn't because I felt so bad.'

Josey, who is now 27, was ill in this way for seven years, and her symptoms were so incapacitating that she had to give up work and abandon any sort of social life. Now, as she puts it, 'I have my life back again.'

The cause of her symptoms – dizziness, confusion, panic attacks, depression, shortness of breath, and a conviction that she was dying – turned out to be a sensitivity to caffeine which was inducing hyperventilation (see p. 226). Giving up tea, coffee and cola drinks restored her to normality very promptly, and she has not relapsed since, except on one occasion, when she unwittingly took a headache remedy that contained caffeine.

What is clear from Josey's story is how much the disbelief of those around her added to her problems. She felt trapped by her symptoms, which she could not overcome, while everyone around her assumed that the whole problem was in her head, and that she could 'snap out of it' if she chose to.

The suffering of patients like Josey could easily be avoided if more GPs knew how to recognise hyperventilation. This is one of those conditions that is well described in the medical literature, but does not always get onto the curriculum in medical schools. As a result, many hyperventilating patients go through a lot of expensive and time-wasting investigations, and may not get a proper diagnosis even then. This is especially sad when hyperventilation is so easy to diagnose and treat (see p. 228).

While the symptoms of hyperventilation are easy to spot, once you know what to look for, this is certainly not true of all

The autonomic nervous system

The autonomic nervous system is a kind of 'autopilot' – a set of controls that generally keeps you well adjusted to your external circumstances without you having to think consciously about the situation at all.

The autonomic nervous system controls all the involuntary muscles – those in the heart, around the digestive system, and around the airways. It also controls the state of the blood vessels, including those in the skin. The autonomic nervous system does its work by issuing two different sets of signals – one set that gears the body up for action and one set that calms the body down.

Two completely separate nerve networks, the sympathetic nervous system and the parasympathetic nervous system, issue these different signals. The target organs – the airways, heart, skin, and so on – all receive input from both networks.

The 'get active' signals are issued by the **sympathetic nervous system,** which comes into play at times of stress, excitement, fear or anger. When you can hear your heart pounding or feel your pulse race, that is your sympathetic nervous system at work. It also makes your nasal passages and airways open up, because extra oxygen is needed for intense physical activity, and it tightens the muscles around the blood vessels, which raises your blood pressure.

'Chill out' messages are delivered by the **parasympathetic nervous system**. This network comes on-stream when you know you can afford to relax. It slows down the heart, lowers the blood pressure, encourages the digestive system to do its work, and makes the airways grow narrower because less air is needed when you are less active.

Adrenaline (epinephrine) is the messenger substance released by the sympathetic nervous system. Its action in tightening the muscles around the blood vessels allows adrenaline to be employed as a drug, which saves the lives of people affected by anaphylaxis (see p. 150). During anaphylaxis, there is a massive fall in blood pressure produced by histamine (see box on p. 12), but an injection of adrenaline can reverse this.

Both adrenaline and its derivatives, the beta-2 relievers such as Ventolin (see p. 152), also help in asthma attacks. They do this by making the muscles around the airways relax.

The messenger substance of the parasympathetic nervous system is **acetylcholine**. Drugs which *oppose* its action – the anti-cholinergics – can also help relieve an asthma attack (see p. 156) by blocking the airway-narrowing action of the parasympathetic.

One of the ways in which acupuncture appears to work is by adjusting the activity of the autonomic nervous system. When acupuncture is used to deal with the immediate symptoms of an asthma attack, this is probably how it makes the airways open up.

sensitivity reactions. Food sensitivity can occasionally cause some unexpected psychological symptoms, such as bouts of hysterical crying (see p. 80) that no conventional doctor would ever associate with food.

Inevitably, patients with sensitivity problems such as these will initially be diagnosed as having a psychological illness rather than a physical one. It may be a very long time before the correct diagnosis is established.

Even if the patient works out the link between eating the food and experiencing the psychological response, the doctor may well remain unconvinced. What complicates matters for doctors is that quite a few people with genuine psychological problems would prefer to think that these have a non-psychological cause, such as a sensitivity to food. (In the opinion of most doctors, patients of this kind are far more common than patients with psychological problems that are genuinely caused by food or chemical intolerance.) For such patients, accepting that their problems have a psychological cause means thinking about what that cause might be – and it is often something deeply distressing which the person would rather forget.

Unfortunately, for people who get into this situation, the phoney explanation doesn't actually help at all, though it can provide a temporary distraction. Ignoring unpleasant hidden memories is not the answer – the problem does not go away, it just festers. Facing up to the real underlying problem is the only way to get rid of the distress (see p. 225).

If you have psychological symptoms of any kind, bear in mind that psychological causes are by far the most likely. Such causes can include difficult life circumstances, damaging experiences during childhood, loss of close relationships, or extremely traumatic incidents in the more recent past. Where there are long-standing problems, neurological factors (damage to the nerves or brain) or metabolic factors (something affecting the balance of chemicals in the brain), might also play a part, or sometimes be the sole cause.

For a busy doctor, without much time to spare, it is immensely difficult to distinguish patients who really do have psychological symptoms due to food or chemical intolerance, from patients with psychological problems that they have mistakenly attributed to an intolerance reaction.

What adds to the difficulty is that, with time, psychological causes can sometimes be grafted onto a straightforward intolerance problem. This occurs because illness of any kind can produce some psychological problems of its own, especially if the person affected cannot lead a normal life. The psychological effects of the illness invariably get worse if the person concerned has been treated with disbelief by doctors, family or friends – as is frequently the case when a person has indefinite long-term symptoms that are due to food or chemical intolerance. Separating the secondary psychological reactions to the illness (or to the scepticism of others), from the primary psychological symptoms that are genuinely produced by the intolerance reactions, is far from easy.

Hyperventilation and chemical intolerance

Hyperventilation (see pp. 226–9) and chemical intolerance (see p. 84) often go hand in hand. A person who is sensitive to airborne items which they cannot avoid inhaling, such as perfume or petrol fumes, may well feel apprehensive when they catch a whiff of these, and unconsciously alter their breathing in response. They may hyperventilate.

If they do, this can both aggravate the sensitivity symptoms, and increase their anxious feelings – because one key symptom of hyperventilation is anxiety (see p. 227). In this way the problem begins to feed upon itself, and can spiral out of control.

Hyperventilation, pure and simple, may also *masquerade as* chemical intolerance. In these cases, a deep underlying anxiety probably exists in the person concerned, and one way in which this expresses itself is as a fear of synthetic chemicals. The person's fear triggers hyperventilation, which is the initial cause of symptoms. That is not how the person interprets those symptoms however – because the person was anticipating a reaction to synthetic chemicals, the symptoms seem to confirm that a reaction has occurred. Again, a vicious circle has been started which is hard to break.

Another possible scenario is that someone with a few sensitivity reactions – for example, a reaction to perfume and cigarette smoke – starts to feel concerned about other chemical substances, and to suspect that these might also cause problems. If an anxious reaction to the presence of these substances develops into hyperventilation, symptoms will ensue from the hyperventilation. These symptoms will appear to confirm the person's fears about yet more sensitivity reactions. In this way, people with relatively mild chemical intolerance can begin to believe that their chemical intolerance reactions are far more extensive and disabling than they actually are.

Where the symptoms of hyperventilation are all tangled up with symptoms due to genuine chemical intolerance, opinions tend to split. Some doctors will interpret all the symptoms as psychological, while other doctors will attribute them all to the intolerance. Both are over-simplifying the problem, and missing a crucial ingredient – hyperventilation. Recognising and treating hyperventilation (see p. 228) can help a great deal to alleviate the illness.

The psychologisation of illness

'From the moment Joanna was born, she was never hungry.' Sandra recalls. 'It took all day to force an ounce of milk down, and she seemed to have terrible stomach pains. At six months old, after countless trips to the doctor, she was admitted to hospital. The hospital doctors couldn't work out what was wrong, and in the end they said that she was just very independent and that she wouldn't eat until she could feed herself. I couldn't believe my ears – what a thing to say about a six-month-old baby!' But as far as the doctors were concerned, that was that.

As Joanna got older, the symptoms got worse. She developed severe constipation, opening her bowels only once every four weeks. Because her over-full bowel put so much pressure on her bladder, she wet herself several times a day. 'She hated school, because the other children teased her, saying she smelled. And she had such awful stomach pains that she couldn't bend down to tie her shoelaces. When she was six she was admitted to hospital for a second time.

'Again they said there was nothing physically wrong with her and it was all in her head, and this time they decided that it must be because something traumatic had happened at home. They wanted her to see a psychiatrist. It was terrible. I knew nothing like that had happened to her at home, but it was impossible to convince them.' There was talk of Joanna being taken away from her parents, because of suspicions about child abuse.

Two weeks before seeing the psychiatrist, something happened to change Joanna's life. Sandra saw an item on television about a book on food allergies. She bought the book and, remembering how fiercely Joanna had rejected milk as a baby, she hazarded a guess that milk was the problem. She immediately took all dairy products out of Joanna's diet.

The effect was astonishing. 'Within twelve hours her tummy ache had gone, and after six weeks she began opening her bowels almost every day. She stopped wetting herself, and was so much happier and healthier.' In fact, all of Joanna's symptoms went away, and she has remained well on a milk-free diet.

Psychologisation is most frequently encountered by patients with medical problems that are unrecognised by conventional medicine – Joanna is a typical example of such a patient. Occasionally, however, those with true allergies find themselves in the same situation. Take, for example, someone who has collapsed after being stung by a wasp but gives a negative skin-test result to wasp venom. In the case of insect-sting allergy, skin-tests are supposed to give very few false negatives – so the doctor may be sceptical about the patient's observation of what happened. A RAST test (see p. 92) may be ordered, but sometimes this too gives a false negative.

Doctors are – not unreasonably – more inclined to believe that the patient is an unreliable witness (there was never any insect involved), or that the patient has a psychological problem that has led to this consultation, than that both these tests gave a false-negative result. A patient in this position may need to be quite persistent to get proper treatment. The same goes for anyone else with unusual allergic reactions who is initially labelled 'psychological' by their doctor. In such cases, good communication is everything.

Good communication with your doctor

Given the intense pressure under which they work, doctors often react badly to symptoms that don't fit into a neat diagnostic pigeonhole, or don't respond to standard treatment. They simply do not have the time for unravelling complex problems and there is a common tendency to automatically 'psychologise' such symptoms. This often does great damage to the patients concerned, boxing them into a corner from which it is impossible to escape – the more they try to convince the doctor their symptoms are genuine, and request further tests or treatment, the more the doctor views them as difficult, demanding patients with psychological problems. Unfortunately, it is part of the dogma about psychosomatic illness that patients affected by it will object vehemently to such a diagnosis. So the more you insist that the symptoms are not psychological, the more this confirms the diagnosis as far as many doctors are concerned.

The psychologisation of illness becomes a real nightmare where the patient is a child, and parents are accused of actually causing the symptoms in some way (see Joanna's story, left). This has happened more than once to children with unusual sensitivity reactions.

Good communication skills may stop you from sliding into this situation with your doctor. Firstly, whatever else you do, stay very very calm. Getting emotional, agitated or angry always causes doctors to suspect a psychological cause for your symptoms.

Secondly, be very open with the doctor, and don't conceal anything. Be clear about describing symptoms, and accurate about times, the intensity of the reaction and any other details. Never, ever exaggerate. If you are given to describing things quite colourfully in everyday life, tone it down as much as possible for your doctor's benefit.

Thirdly, don't make your own diagnosis – doctors are taught to believe that patients who diagnose themselves may well be suffering from hypochondria. Present any medical knowledge you have acquired from books or the Internet as tactfully as possible. Finally, it will probably help a lot to use the appropriate words to describe your illness when talking with the doctor (see pp. 6–7).

Chapter 8

protecting children from allergies

'Good health is one of the most important things we can give our kids,' says Martha, now in her sixties with two grown-up children.

'When I see how bad my daughter's asthma is, and how hard her life is sometimes because of it, I do feel bad about the fact that I smoked when I was pregnant. But we just didn't know in those days. Even my doctor smoked. No one thought anything of it.

'I stopped when she was little, because it seemed to me that her wheezing got worse whenever I lit up. I'm sure that stopping then was better than nothing. It must have helped.

'In any case, there's no point feeling guilty about things now – that won't change anything. But if I'd known what damage it could do, I would have stopped sooner.' Martha's regrets stem from the discoveries made in the past decade about the effects of smoking on allergies. We now know that smoking during pregnancy increases the amount of IgE (the allergy antibody) in the blood of a newborn baby – an indication that he or she is at an increased risk of developing allergies. After the birth, exposing a child to cigarette smoke continues to encourage high levels of IgE in the blood, as well as irritating the airways and making asthma more likely to develop.

The research on smoking is just one part of a worldwide research effort, during the past 20–30 years, into the possible causes of the allergy epidemic. That research can help parents who are themselves atopic (allergy-prone) to reduce the risk of passing their allergy problems on to their children.

Who should be implementing these preventive measures? Firstly, any prospective parents who have allergies themselves, or had them as children. They are at higher risk (compared to a non-allergic parent) of producing a child who is susceptible to allergies. The risk is especially high if both parents have or have had them at some point in their lives.

Secondly, these preventive measures could be worthwhile for parents who don't have allergies themselves, but who come from atopic families (families with a tendency to allergy). If you or your partner have brothers, sisters or parents with allergies, you are more likely than the average person to produce allergic children.

Finally, if you already have one allergic child – even though you and your partner don't have allergies yourselves, and no one else in the family does – there is a higher-than-average chance that subsequent children will have allergies. Your allergic child is a sign that the genes for allergy are there.

Given the important role that genes play in allergy (see p. 8), preventive strategies make a lot of sense for parents-to-be with allergies in the family.

Unfortunately, this is a topic which often generates confusion – some people assume that if a trait is genetic, it will inevitably come out in the child, and that nothing can be done to prevent this happening. Although that is true for some inherited traits, such as metabolic abnormalities (see box on p. 75), it is not at all the case for allergy.

Developing allergic disease is not inevitable unless a child has a very big dose of the genes that favour

allergy. Only a few children – generally those whose mother and father are both badly affected by allergies – will come into this category. Even with these very high-risk children, following the measures described here will probably help to reduce the severity of their allergic problems.

For most children at risk of allergies, even though they have some pro-allergy genes, there has to be an unfavourable environment to actually produce allergic disease. 'Environment' here means *everything* external that affects the child, including diet, air quality, allergens, diseases and medical treatment. Factors occurring before birth, such as the mother's lifestyle during pregnancy, are also part of the child's environment. It is the interplay between genes and environment that will decide whether your child develops allergies or escapes them.

This interaction is not a simple one, however, and different aspects of the environment operate in different ways. Firstly, there are some environmental factors that work at the most fundamental level – conspiring with the pro-allergy genes to make the overall tendency to allergy far stronger. These are factors such as cigarette smoking by the mother during pregnancy, or excessive hygiene during childhood, which influence the fundamental make-up of the child's immune system. Secondly, there are environmental factors, such as early exposure to house-dust mite or grass pollen, which can cause trouble by provoking specific allergic reactions. Note that factors like these will not become important unless the allergic tendency is already there.

Efforts to reduce the risk of allergy operate on both types of factor.

On the one hand, there are measures such as quitting smoking or easing up on hygiene, which tackle the allergic predisposition itself. These measures are, in effect, trying to make a Western child's immune system more like the immune system of a child from a poor rural village in the developing world, whose chance of developing allergy is very low indeed.

On the other hand, there are measures such as reducing dust-mite levels, that try to stop the development of particular allergic reactions.

Obviously, if measures of the first kind could be truly successful, there would be little or no need for measures of the second kind. But this kind of success is very difficult to achieve in modern Western society. Although we can certainly improve matters a great deal, and lessen the tendency to allergy, the conditions that would completely reverse it are beyond our reach at present. So both kinds of preventive measure remain necessary.

In reading the pages that follow, it is important to keep things in perspective, and not feel excessively anxious about your child. Do what you can, but don't feel guilty if you can't manage everything that is suggested here. And if you already have a child with allergies, please *don't* feel guilty about things that might have contributed to this. Only hindsight is perfect, and you no doubt did the best you could, given the information you had at the time, and the many other constraints and difficulties that you faced. That is the best that any of us can do.

Pregnancy,
BREAST-FEEDING
AND WEANING

Having a baby should, first and foremost, be a positive and enjoyable experience. Inevitably, there are also anxieties involved, and the huge amount of advice you receive while pregnant – from doctors, midwives, friends, relatives, and even well-meaning strangers – can add to these anxieties. You may feel that the last thing you need is any more advice. But if you are susceptible to allergies yourself, taking steps to avoid allergies developing in your baby could, in the long run, save you a great deal of time, worry and expense – quite apart from the benefits for the child.

Most of the measures described here are based on strong scientific evidence, or on the long-term experience of doctors and midwives, so you can feel sure the effort is worthwhile. While taking these measures cannot absolutely guarantee that your child will grow up allergy-free, it will shift the odds in the right direction. And even if your child does not escape allergies entirely, you can feel confident that these protective measures will have made the child's problems less severe than they would otherwise have been.

Planning the pregnancy

As far as developing allergies is concerned, a baby is most vulnerable during the first year of life – and especially the first few months. This is because the newborn's immune system is geared towards making the allergy antibody, IgE (see box on p. 12).

If a baby is exposed to a large dose of powerful airborne allergens during this first phase of life, he or she is at risk of making IgE to those allergens. (The same is true of food allergens – these are dealt with on pp. 241–3.) Although there will probably be no symptoms at the time, these can develop later, in the form of hayfever, perennial rhinitis (a year-round nasal allergy – see p. 28) or asthma.

As a parent, you should be focusing your efforts on reducing the allergen load for your baby during the first year, and especially during the first 4– 6 months.

Timing the birth

In the case of pollen, the best approach – if you can manage it – is to plan conception so that the birth occurs shortly after the season for the most troublesome allergenic pollen in your region. That way the baby will be over 6 months old by the time the next pollen season comes around.

Studies of birth month and allergy show that British children run the greatest risk of hayfever if they are born during April or May – just in time for the grass-pollen season in early June. In Scandinavia, those born in early spring, shortly before the birch-pollen season, are the most vulnerable.

Allergens in the home

In the case of household allergens such as house-dust mite and moulds, the sooner you can begin work to reduce the level in your house (see pp. 244–5) the better. Recent research shows that a foetus may have its first encounter with the allergens of the house-dust mite as early as 16 or 17 weeks of age. By then, the foetus is already swallowing a little of the fluid that surrounds it in the womb – the amniotic fluid. This normal activity introduces any substances found in the amniotic fluid to the baby's immune system, via specialised areas of immune recognition in the gut. During the sixteenth or seventeenth week of pregnancy, the powerful allergens produced by dust mites begin to show up in the amniotic fluid.

How do these allergens get there? The dust-mite allergen was originally inhaled by the mother, then absorbed from her lungs into her bloodstream, and then passed from there into the amniotic fluid.

This is a controversial area, but some medical researchers believe that this early contact with allergen could explain why a few newborns are already capable of mounting an allergic reaction to dust mite. Actual symptoms of allergy may not appear for several months or years, but the essential first step – making the allergy antibody, IgE (see box on p. 12) – seems to have occurred already for some babies.

In situations where IgE does the job it is supposed to do – protecting against worms and other parasites (see p. 13) – this advance programming of the immune system before birth has definite advantages. A child whose mother is infected with parasites is born with the ability to make IgE against those parasites, even though he or she has had no direct contact with them before birth. The baby's immune system has been forewarned of the likely hazards of life in the outside world, and is already armed to tackle them.

While this is obviously valuable in conditions where parasitic infections are rife, emerging into a carpeted and well-upholstered world with IgE against dust mite already in the bloodstream is a serious disadvantage, because it can pave the way for perennial allergic rhinitis and asthma.

Given the trouble caused by dust-mite allergen, some doctors think that women should try to reduce their exposure to it during the second half of pregnancy, so that little or none reaches the unborn child. At present it is not known for sure if this can make a difference to the risk of allergies developing in a child, but it seems plausible.

What is absolutely clear, from several previous studies, is that the level of house-dust mite in the home immediately after birth does make a distinct difference as regards the chance of allergy developing. Minimising a newborn baby's exposure to dust mite is definitely worthwhile, and the measures needed to achieve this are described on pp. 244–5.

Carrying out these measures will raise the level of dust-mite allergen in the air temporarily, so it makes sense to do the work in the early stages of pregnancy (or – even better – before conception), rather than expose yourself and the foetus to a tremendous burst of allergen later on in pregnancy.

There may be other potential allergens which you should try to eliminate from your home before the baby arrives, such as pet allergens (see p. 245).

Pregnancy

First and foremost – don't smoke while you are pregnant, or afterwards (see box on p. 107). Any other smokers in the household should smoke outdoors.

What about your diet during pregnancy? Should you be careful about this? Food allergens, such as those from cow's milk, do reach the foetus, passed from the mother's blood to the baby's blood via the placenta. And a few babies are born already capable of making IgE against food allergens. On the basis of these findings, some doctors have suggested that avoiding potentially allergenic foods (such as eggs, cow's milk and peanuts) during pregnancy might help to reduce the risk of food allergy. However, evidence from research trials in which pregnant women followed a restricted diet, and their children were later studied for allergies, does not show any convincing benefit. And in some studies, the women on restricted diets have not gained as much weight as they should, and the babies have been slightly below average weight at birth. Most doctors now think that dietary restrictions during pregnancy are not worthwhile – it is more important to eat well and get enough nutrients.

It does seem sensible not to overeat any particular food during pregnancy, although there is no scientific evidence on this point (simply because researchers have not yet looked for such evidence). In particular, don't overdo it with milk and milk products. Make sure you get enough calcium, obviously, but don't force yourself to drink huge amounts of milk, especially if you have any distaste for it. Talk to your doctor, midwife or health visitor about the possibility of a calcium supplement, if you dislike milk.

Breast-feeding

'The cornerstone of allergy prevention is breast-feeding,' according to Dr Erika Isolauri of Tampere University Hospital in Finland.

At one time, this would have been a controversial statement, but there is now a substantial body of scientific evidence to support the 'breast-is-best' idea in relation to allergy prevention. A number of different studies have shown that exclusive breast-feeding, up to at least four months of age, reduces the risk of developing food allergy or atopic eczema (or both) in the early years of life.

Exclusive means exactly that – no solids at all until after four months, and no supplementary feeds with infant formula (which is made from cow's milk, and therefore contains cow's milk allergens). Unfortunately, it is sometimes far from easy to ensure that formula feeds are not given just after birth, by well-intentioned nurses on the maternity ward. Given what we now know about the immune system of the newborn, this is the worst possible time to be delivering an onslaught of potentially allergenic cow's milk proteins.

Quite apart from the immediate effect of introducing cow's milk allergens to the baby, a bottle can disrupt the development of a good breast-feeding relationship between mother and child, and may lead to the early abandonment of breast-feeding.

Why should this happen? Firstly the baby does not have to suck as hard on a bottle teat as on a real nipple, and he or she may never develop the knack if given bottles at an early stage. Secondly, allaying the baby's hunger with a bottle can also mean that he or she demands less at the next breast-feed – and since the mother's milk supply is partly influenced by the level of demand, this can be detrimental. Some experts believe that occasional bottle-feeds can start a downward spiral of ever-diminishing supply from the mother.

Dr Arne Høst of the Department of Paediatrics at Odense University Hospital in Denmark, who has made a special study of breast-feeding, recommends giving boiled water as a supplement during the first three to four days of life, if the breast milk supply is inadequate. After that time, the mother's own supply should increase to meet the needs of her baby. Introducing bottle-feeds at an early stage can prevent this delicate balance of supply-and-demand from ever being achieved.

Sometimes, despite everything being done just right, a mother's supply of milk never quite matches her infant's appetite. When this happens, and the child concerned is from an allergy-prone family, the breast milk should be supplemented with an ultra-safe formula feed called a hydrolysate (see box on p. 66).

Hydrolysates should also be used for infants at high risk of allergy who, for whatever reason, cannot be breast-fed. Note that there are two categories of hydrolysate – **extensively hydrolysed formula** and **partially hydrolysed formula**. For the purposes of allergy prevention, an extensively hydrolysed formula should always be used because it has the lowest risk of causing food allergies.

Preparing to breast-feed

Because breast-feeding is natural, many first-time mothers just assume it will come naturally. Sadly, it often doesn't.

Cracked nipples are a major obstacle. They are the equivalent of chapped hands, caused by the prolonged wetness and chafing on the nipple during breast-feeding. Because cracked nipples are so sore, breast-feeding can then become a major ordeal rather than a pleasurable experience as it should be.

What is more, infectious bacteria can enter the breast through the cracks in the skin, causing mastitis, which is painful and may require antibiotic treatment. Some of the antibiotic may go through into the milk, and this is not necessarily a good thing for the baby (see p. 247).

Fortunately, cracked nipples can easily be avoided. The trick is to make the skin on the nipples tougher and more resilient, so that it does not crack. Start during pregnancy, in about your fourth month. When you have a bath or shower, rub your nipples vigorously with your flannel for a few minutes. After three weeks of this, graduate to a soft toothbrush, and brush them gently, then more firmly when they feel ready. Progress to a medium, and then a hard toothbrush. By your seventh month of pregnancy, you should be on to a nailbrush. 'I followed this programme, with my first baby,' reports Jane, a mother of two, 'and I was the only mother in my post-natal group who didn't get cracked nipples.'

Breast-feeding support groups can be enormously helpful, when you start breast-feeding, or when you feel things are not going right. Some groups have local advisers, all mothers themselves with first-hand experience of breast-feeding. Having such an adviser with you, watching you breast-feed your new baby and making suggestions, or pointing out where you are going wrong, can make all the difference. Look for such a group locally, and establish contact with them well before your due date. You may be able to talk with an adviser before the birth, which can be useful.

Having prepared yourself, you then have to prepare the nursing staff in the hospital where you will give birth, for the fact that you want to breast-feed exclusively. That means no supplementary feeds from the staff – not even one bottle. The risks of this practice, in sensitising vulnerable babies to cow's milk, are still not widely known, so you will probably need to be persistent and make your feelings very clear. Talk to your midwife about this well before your expected delivery date, and find out what policy the hospital has about supplementary feeds. Then see the relevant staff at the hospital.

The nurses are most likely to give the baby a bottle because he or she is crying while you are asleep, and they don't want to wake you. Staff change all the time, so you will probably need to put a notice on the crib or cot, to be certain that the baby is never bottle-fed while you are sleeping. If this seems 'over-the-top', consider the experience of British researchers investigating allergy prevention who wanted to ensure that a group of newborns were never given supplementary feeds. They put warning stickers on both the babies' cots and the mothers' beds, as well as asking the midwives and mothers to be very vigilant. Despite this effort, several of the babies being studied were given bottles.

Sometimes nurses give a bottle because they believe that the baby is not getting enough milk from the breast. It is entirely possible that your milk supply will not be quite adequate in the first few days, but it should increase rapidly. The best thing, if breast-milk supply is inadequate, is to give boiled water as a supplement during the first 3–4 days of life (see left).

Diet during breast-feeding

'When I was nursing Toby, if I had red wine with dinner, he would cry and cry the next day. At first I thought maybe it was just coincidence, but then I kept a careful note of when he had bad days, and what I'd had the night before, and the pattern was so clear – it was the wine sure enough.'

Judy is not the only mother to have noticed the effects of red wine on a breast-fed baby, but it comes as a surprise to most women to learn that pretty much *everything* they eat works its way into breast milk, though in very tiny amounts.

The food molecules that get through into breast milk can certainly affect babies who are already sensitised to a food. Cow's milk is the classic example – cow's milk proteins get into human milk if the mother consumes any milk, cheese, yoghurt or other milk products. Babies who have already been sensitised to cow's milk (by a supplementary bottle-feed, for example, or even in the womb – see p. 241) react badly to the breast milk, unless the mother avoids all dairy products.

What is less certain is whether the traces of allergen in breast milk – cow's milk allergen or that from any other food – might be capable of *starting off* allergy or sensitivity. Are these minute traces enough to sensitise babies with a strong tendency to allergy? If they are, then mothers of high-risk infants might be well advised to avoid certain allergenic foods while breast-feeding. Some studies do suggest that there is a reduction in food allergy if breast-feeding mothers avoid cow's milk, eggs, nuts, fish and soya. But if this restrictive diet makes your life impossible, then it is better to breast-feed your baby and eat what you like, than to not breast-feed at all.

Unfortunately, some babies do get eczema, in spite of being exclusively breast-fed. If this happens with your child, there are various steps you can take to deal with the problem (see box on p. 248).

Weaning – when and how

The key to reducing the allergy risk for babies is to turn that old political jibe 'too little, too late' on its head. Research shows that, as far as weaning is concerned, it is 'too much, too early' that increases the chance of allergic reactions developing. Suddenly presenting an infant of three months with a great variety of solid foods, including potent allergens such as eggs, peanuts and fish, can increase the likelihood of food allergy and/or eczema developing. Weaning late, with a limited number of safe foods, should be your goal.

At least four months of exclusive breast-feeding is now the standard recommendation for allergy prevention, and it is well supported by scientific evidence. Weaning should begin some time between four and six months of age.

But how long should breast-feeding continue after weaning begins? There is little concrete evidence here, but there is a strong belief in the medical community that breast-feeding should go on for several more months if possible, allowing the weaning process to be very gradual. The idea is to introduce new foods one at a time, alongside breast milk.

As well as allowing the immune system lots of time to adjust to each new food, prolonged breast-feeding may help in another way as well. Recent research suggests that breast milk contains substances which influence the baby's immune system, nudging it in the right direction – away from any tendency to allergies.

Avoid those expensive little jars of ready-made baby food. Most contain potent allergens such as cow's milk, wheat or soya. Making your own baby foods is not difficult, and is the best way to ensure that your child gets only low-risk foods.

Nipple cream – with peanuts

If your nipples begin to feel sore during breast-feeding, and you need a nipple cream, check very carefully that the product you buy doesn't contain peanut oil (arachis oil). This very early exposure is believed to be responsible for sensitising some allergy-prone children to peanuts.

When children react to peanuts the very first time they eat them – as sometimes happens – this shows that some earlier exposure to peanut allergens must have occurred, to produce the allergic sensitisation. It is possible that sensitisation occurred because peanut allergens from the mother reached the baby in the bloodstream before birth, or later via breast milk. But many doctors think that nipple cream containing peanut oil is the most likely culprit.

Other measures

TO PROTECT AGAINST ALLERGY

No single factor lies behind the allergy epidemic – the causes are many and various (see p. 20). What this means for parents interested in allergy prevention is that there is no single measure which will ensure that your children do not develop allergies. Instead there are a great many different things that can be done, each of which reduces the risk to some extent. The more of these you do, the lower the risk becomes.

Avoiding allergens

Starting before the birth is best, if you want to reduce allergen exposure for your child (see p. 240). But if you have missed the boat with that one, don't despair – there is still a lot to be gained by reducing allergen exposure at a later stage.

If you are ridding your home of allergens after the child's birth, bear in mind that things will get worse before they get better– there will be a temporary surge in airborne allergen as a result of the clean-up operation, and you will need to protect the child from this. The best strategy is for the child to be away for a few days while the work is done, especially if you are taking out carpets, furniture or mattresses. Remember to protect yourself as well, if you are allergy-prone (see p. 109).

One of the most important steps you can take to reduce allergen levels is improve the natural ventilation of your home. This lowers the humidity (assuming you don't live in an extremely humid climate), which helps combat both moulds and dust mites. Ventilation also flushes out allergens in the air, especially cat, dog and mould allergens. Half the problem with modern houses is that the airtight seals around doors and windows, introduced to conserve heat and save energy, turn the indoor air into a rich stew of allergens and irritants.

House-dust mite

Avoiding high levels of house-dust mite in the home is one of the most valuable things you can do to reduce the risk of allergies in your child. Not only is house-dust mite a powerful allergen in its own right, it may also act as an *agent provocateur* as far as the immune system is concerned (see p. 12), and may help to initiate allergic reactions to *other* potential allergens – such as those from pets or indoor moulds.

Even if you do nothing else to protect your new baby from mite allergen, at least buy a new mattress and pillow for the cot, with ready-fitted allergen-proof covers. Do the same for the portable crib, if you have one. Choose anti-mite products that are designed for babies and are guaranteed safe – there is a risk of suffocation with some loose covers sold for older children and adults (see p. 245).

You may want to eliminate house-dust mite from your own bed as well as the baby's, because there will probably be times when you take the baby into bed with you for a feed or a cuddle – and times when, as a toddler, he or she just barges in! It is good to know that your child is still breathing air free from dust-mite allergen in these circumstances.

Deal with your own bed as soon as you can. Some doctors believe that lowering your exposure to dust mite during pregnancy may reduce the risk of sensitising your baby before birth (see p. 241).

When taking anti-mite measures with your own bed, make sure that there is no risk of suffocation to the baby from the allergen-proof materials used. Microporous membranes based on plastic could, if sucked onto the baby's face during sleep, cause suffocation. Loose covers on duvets are worrying in this respect. Buy a new duvet with a built-in allergen-proof cover, for preference, or a duvet that can be laundered at 60°C or above.

All the other measures for combating dust mites, described on pp. 114–17, will help to protect your child. Buy a good anti-allergen vacuum cleaner if you possibly can, and keep your baby out of the room while vacuuming if you can't (open the windows too). Make sure the baby only has new soft toys, preferably washable ones (see p. 116).

It is also an excellent idea to reduce dust-mite levels in the carpets and soft furnishings (see p. 117), because children tend to have very close contact with these in their early years. A crawling baby, motoring enthusiastically around the sitting room floor, is stirring up the stockpile of dust-mite allergen that is found in any carpet, and inhaling it in full measure. An adult walking around the same room has a far lower exposure, because dust-mite allergen, being relatively heavy, stays near the ground.

The best possible option is to go for non-carpet flooring, which doesn't encourage dust mites. Parents tend to worry about the hardness of this, for a baby or toddler. In fact babies are far more robust than we generally believe, and a hard floor is actually no problem for a small child who has never known the luxury of carpeting.

If you really hate the idea of your baby having anything other than carpet to play on, the next best option is to get new carpet, so that you start with zero dust mites. You must then prevent dust-mite numbers from building up too much, by means of good ventilation, or with the use of a powerful dehumidifier (see p. 117).

Although the first year is the most vulnerable time for your baby, you mustn't let your guard drop too much as time passes. The moment when a toddler moves from a cot to a 'big bed' is sometimes the beginning of allergy symptoms because, after carefully protecting their child from dust mites in infancy, parents then put him or her into a bed with a used mattress. This sudden exposure to a high dose of dust-mite allergen can be the start of asthma. Get a new mattress if you can, and put allergen-proof covers on it. Alternatively, put allergen-proof covers on the existing mattress.

Moulds

Mould spores are another potent allergen, and you should avoid bringing up a vulnerable child in a damp house if you can, because moulds will be growing there in abundance. Even in a house that is not obviously damp, it is a good plan to reduce indoor humidity (see p. 119). Carpets and furnishings that are full of mould spores (see p. 122) should be replaced.

Pets

What about pet allergens – should you find another home for your cat or dog when you are expecting a baby? This is a difficult question because the latest research shows that pets are a double-edged sword as far as allergies are concerned.

As you might expect, a baby with allergic tendencies who is born into a house with a resident cat or dog is more likely to show allergic reactions to cats or dogs some years later. On the other hand, there is now research showing that having an animal in the house *reduces the risk of allergies overall*, especially for a child with no brothers or sisters. This is probably because the pet makes the environment less hygienic for the child, fulfilling the same anti-allergy role as brothers and sisters would in the early life of a child (see p. 246).

If you are planning to give your child the kind of grubby childhood that seems to protect against allergy (see p.246) the additional protection provided by a pet is probably unnecessary. On the other hand, you could view your pet as having both pros and cons, and decide to keep it, while implementing all the other anti-allergy measures described here. If you do this, ensure that the house is well ventilated (so pet allergens don't build up to very high levels indoors) and keep the pet out of the child's bedroom so that he or she is not breathing huge amounts of pet allergen while asleep. You could also wash the pet regularly (see p. 125) to reduce allergen levels in the air.

If your child begins to show any signs of allergy to the pet, you must then find it another home.

Avoiding irritants

As well as increasing ventilation and eliminating cigarette smoke from the home completely, it may be worth evicting certain specific items that produce irritant gases.

The main ones are:

- gas cookers (if you can't afford to switch to an electric cooker, at least improve the ventilation in your kitchen as much as possible)
- easy-clean plastic wall coverings and flooring
- materials such as chipboard and MDF, which give off formaldehyde.

The evidence regarding the possible role of these in increasing the risk of allergies and asthma is described on pp. 128–9. In addition, although there is no evidence on this point, common sense would suggest getting rid of any plastic or lacquered items that have a powerful smell.

Generally speaking, although traffic pollution can act as an irritant, it seems to play a lesser role in *causing* allergies and asthma than most people imagine. However, it may sometimes play a part, especially if there are high levels of diesel fumes in the air (see p. 131).

Infections – friend or foe?

A large group of Italian military cadets were recently studied by doctors interested in the causes of allergy. By taking blood samples and testing them for antibodies to common infections, the doctors could see what diseases the men had been exposed to early in life. At the same time, the young conscripts were assessed for allergies.

Allergies were least frequent among the young men with antibodies against three common infections that are dispersed via food and faeces – Hepatitis A, *Toxoplasma gondii* and *Helicobacter pylori*. Only one in twelve of the cadets in this group had allergies.

Among the men with no antibodies against any of these infections, the rate of allergy was nearly three times as high – one in five of these cadets had allergies.

The doctors carrying out this experiment believe that these three infections are not necessarily important in themselves, but that they identify individuals who were 'reared in an environment that provides a higher exposure to many other orofecal or food-borne microbes'. In other words, they grew up in the kind of household where washing your hands before meals wasn't considered too important.

This study adds to the growing body of evidence (see p. 21) which shows that an over-clean environment during childhood encourages the development of an allergic disposition.

Those with lower rates of allergy include:

- children raised on farms with livestock. The more exposure the children have to farm animals, the less the likelihood of them developing allergies.
- children from homes with high levels of bacterial toxins in the household dust (see p. 21)
- children who have fewer baths, and wash their hands less often (see p. 21)
- children with brothers and sisters, especially those with older siblings. One study showed that having brothers provided more protection against allergies than having sisters, which makes sense when you think how much dirtier little boys get.
- children who go into kindergarten, nursery school or day care with other children at an early age – this is only valuable for children without brothers and sisters
- children with pets at home – the benefits are much more pronounced for children without brothers and sisters.

The Italian study is especially important because, for the first time, it gives detailed information about *the kinds of* infections that make a difference in allergy prevention. The military cadets were also checked out for antibodies to measles, mumps, rubella, chickenpox and herpes. None of these infections gives protection against allergies – only infections carried in food and faeces do.

Exactly what practical use you make of these discoveries is up to you. For most of us, the importance of hygiene was so firmly instilled during our own childhood that it is quite hard to suddenly become more relaxed about it. But do let your children play in the garden, if you have one, and don't worry so much about how dirty they get. Encourage them to do some gardening – medical researchers believe that harmless bacteria in the soil may be particularly important in educating the immune system away from allergies (see p. 21). Let them play with pets, as long as the animals are not carrying harmful parasitic worms (talk to your vet about whether pets should be treated for parasites). Ease up on hand-washing and, if this is your first baby, make sure he or she plays with other children as early in life as possible.

A few chest infections do seem to increase the risk of asthma, notably Respiratory Syncytial Virus (RSV). If this infects babies, it provokes an IgE-reaction (see box on p. 12) which may encourage the development of allergies. Unfortunately, there is very little you can do to protect your child from this common virus, but it makes sense not to take the baby to a hospital for unnecessary trips (visiting relatives, for example) because RSV infections are often picked up in hospital.

Taking care with antibiotics

The possible role of antibiotics in making allergies more likely to develop is an exceedingly controversial topic. Before making any practical decisions in this respect, you must consult your doctor. Never go against your doctor's advice, if he or she thinks that antibiotics are necessary.

Several different studies have now produced evidence of a link between antibiotic use before the age of one or two, and the later development of allergies, asthma or both. The best of these studies was carried out by doctors in Oxford, who followed 1900 children up to the age of sixteen. Among children at risk of allergy (because their mothers had allergies) taking antibiotics before the age of two was linked with an increase in the rate of allergy from 32% to 54%. The more courses of antibiotics a child received, the greater the risk.

The type of infection for which the drugs were prescribed was not important, as far as the risk of allergy was concerned, but the type of antibiotic did make a difference. Broad-spectrum antibiotics, which kill a wide range of bacteria, were more risky – suggesting that the depletion of friendly bacteria in the gut (see p. 204) could be responsible for increasing the allergy risk. Penicillins seemed less likely to promote allergies than erythromycin or cephalosporins.

This research is not widely known, as yet. And because there is a widespread assumption that giving an antibiotic can do no harm, even if it is unnecessary, antibiotics are sometimes prescribed when they serve no purpose. In particular, antibiotics are often given for virus infections, especially in childhood, despite the fact that antibiotics are of no value whatever against viruses. Research shows that doctors are sometimes responding to pressure from anxious parents when they prescribe antibiotics – it is difficult for some parents to accept that a virus infection cannot easily be treated and just has to 'run its course'. (Although there are drugs that combat viruses, these are expensive and produce unpleasant side effects – they are reserved for very serious virus infections such as hepatitis.)

Obviously, when a child needs antibiotics to deal with a serious infection there can be no question about giving them. This is why you should always follow your doctor's advice. But it is also worth asking the doctor the following questions before giving antibiotics to your child:

- are you sure that this is a bacterial infection, and not a virus infection?
- would it be possible to do tests and check that it is a bacterial infection, before prescribing antibiotics?
- what is the chance of the child overcoming the infection without antibiotics?
- would it be dangerous to wait and see if the infection clears up naturally?

Vaccination

The same Oxford research team that investigated antibiotics (see left) also looked at the question of vaccination and allergy. They found a link between vaccination for pertussis (whooping cough) and increases in asthma, eczema and hayfever. However the increases were not large, and a study from Sweden found that whooping cough vaccination did not have any effect on rates of allergy and asthma. And researchers in Ethiopia have found that whooping cough vaccination actually *reduces* the risk of allergy in their country.

This is clearly a complex issue. The contradictory results from different parts of the world suggest that the 'big picture' is what counts here – the overall combination of childhood infections, antibiotic treatment and exposure to harmless bacteria such as those in the soil or from animals. Depending on this big picture, vaccination against whooping cough may push the allergy risk one way or the other.

There are many other arguments both for and against vaccination and, given our current state of ignorance about the possible effect on allergy, these other considerations are probably more relevant. Discuss the matter in detail with your doctor before making a decision.

Protecting children

WHO ALREADY HAVE ALLERGIES

Doctors in Japan recently tried a very simple experiment in allergy prevention. They chose babies suffering from atopic eczema who were allergic to foods, but not allergic to house-dust mite. Dividing the babies into two groups, the doctors put special allergen-proof covers, designed to protect against house-dust mite (see p. 115), on the mattresses of all the babies in the first group. Babies in the second group were given ordinary cotton covers.

When the babies were one year old, they were tested again for allergy to house-dust mite. Two out of three children in the second group now gave a positive skin test to house-dust mite.

By comparison, only one in three of the children from the first group gave a positive skin test. In other words, using the anti-allergy covers for these high-risk children had cut by half the number who developed an allergic reaction to dust mite.

As this experiment shows, even if a child has already developed allergies, it is not too late to bring protective measures into play. Indeed, an allergy problem in infancy, such as atopic eczema, can be seen as a warning sign to parents, telling them that they should reduce the child's exposure to allergens as much as possible.

As well as reducing dust-mite levels, you should minimise your child's exposure to moulds at home by limiting indoor humidity (see p. 119) and cleaning up any existing mould growth (see pp. 122–3). This will lessen the chance of mould allergy developing.

Try to avoid staying, even temporarily, in any house that is damp or has old carpets and mattresses. When you are moving house, or carrying out any kind of renovation work, remember that this will stir up a lot of dust-mite and mould allergens. Protect your child by arranging for a stay away from home.

This pro-active approach should not just apply to airborne allergens, but also to food, in the opinion of some experts. They suggest that any child with a true allergy to cow's milk or egg should not be given peanuts, tree nuts, fish or shellfish until three years of age, to avoid sensitisation to these potent food allergens.

Pets are a more difficult issue, with both pros and cons as regards allergy-prone children (see p. 245). If you decide to keep your cat or dog, always ventilate the house well, and wash the animal regularly if you can (see p. 125). Be alert for your child developing an allergic reaction to your pet – don't turn a blind eye to the symptoms, as parents sometimes do because they are reluctant to accept that the child has become allergic to the family's much-loved pet. If your child does develop an allergy to the pet, the best option is to find the animal another home as quickly as possible (see p. 124).

Breast-fed babies with atopic eczema

Although breast-feeding is a good way of protecting children against atopic eczema, it is no guarantee. Sometimes babies become sensitised to food, in spite of being breast-fed, and then they may react to traces of that same food, eaten by the mother and coming through in her breast milk.

Skin-prick tests (see p. 91) may help to identify the foods responsible for the eczema. Otherwise, a simple elimination diet by the mother, as used for colic (see p. 203), may pinpoint the offending food. Keeping that food out of the mother's diet will often clear the baby's eczema.

Sometimes a breast-fed child's eczema remains severe, despite the elimination of suspect foods from the mother's diet. In this case, what should be done? New research from Dr Erika Isolauri – a staunch advocate of breast-feeding – suggests that the best option at this point is to stop breast-feeding. Her research team found that breast-fed children with persistent eczema had a slower growth rate, either due to the disease itself, or to the restricted diet followed by their mothers. When these babies were switched to an artificial amino-acid formula (see box on p.66), their eczema symptoms subsided, and their growth picked up.

Is vaccination safe for children with egg allergy?

The influenza vaccine and a few others (e.g. yellow fever) are grown in eggs and can contain egg allergen. These are not usually given to people with egg allergy. The measles vaccine is grown in cells taken from eggs, and may contain a minute trace of egg allergen. Allergic reactions to measles vaccine have been reported among individuals with egg allergy – but only those who are extremely sensitive. New studies suggest that the risk from measles vaccine is very small, and children with egg allergy can be safely immunised. However, there should be resuscitation equipment available when the vaccine is given to children who have suffered a severe anaphylactic reaction to egg in the past, and those with severe asthma as well as egg allergy.

Never too late?

The role of modern ultra-clean lifestyles in promoting allergies is now well established (see p. 21). If your child already has allergies, it may seem as if these discoveries have come too late to help – but that is not the case. Some research suggests that the battle for supremacy between Th1 and Th2 cells (see p. 11) – the unseen power struggle which decides whether a child will be allergy-prone – is not really settled until some time between the ages of 5 and 7 years. So there is still some potential for intervening up to this age. Some studies suggest that the immune system can be pushed away from an allergic disposition at an even later age, right up to adolescence.

Several research groups are working on vaccination strategies (for example, using extracts of soil bacteria) that might be able to achieve this. The initial results are promising and suggest that these vaccines can even help adults with allergies. Unfortunately, such treatments will not be available for many years. In the meantime, you can probably reduce your child's chance of developing new allergies, and perhaps make the existing ones less severe, by easing up on hygiene (see p. 246).

Fresh air and exercise

With the boom in watching TV and videos, and playing on computer games, some modern children hardly go outdoors at all. As far as allergies and asthma are concerned, there are two big disadvantages to being a juvenile couch potato. For a start, the couch is also home to dust mites in their millions, and the child who spends most of the day slumped on it is breathing in more than his or her fair share of mite allergens.

The other drawback is that the child is not running about and using his or her lungs to the full. Airways that are never stretched (because the child never gets out of breath) lose their youthful flexibility in time. Once this has happened, the airways can never be stretched to their full capacity. Some doctors believe that this may make asthma more likely to develop, or help to make it more severe once it has developed. Inactivity also encourages obesity, which increases the risk of asthma developing.

Getting outside and running around, or engaging in other vigorous exercise, should be encouraged for any child with allergies. Obviously, you should balance this against the need to protect the child from pollution peaks and (if your child has hayfever) pollen peaks. Children with exercise-induced asthma should use their reliever inhalers to allow them to take exercise (see p. 41).

Keep the air at home free from irritants such as nitrogen dioxide (see p. 128) which may encourage new allergies to develop, and can make existing asthma worse.

Medical treatments

Antihistamines may have a preventive role in very young children with allergies. A study of 1–2 year-olds with atopic eczema found that the antihistamine cetirizine, taken daily for 18 months, halved the chances of the children developing asthma later.

The children who benefited in this study were those with several risk factors for becoming asthmatic. They had moderate to severe atopic eczema, at least one close relative with allergies, and allergic sensitisation to pollen or house-dust mite, as shown by skin-prick tests (see p. 91).

The cetirizine was taken at fairly low doses and had no bad effects on the children in this study. What is more, it benefited their skin as well as reducing the risk of asthma: those taking the drug had less need of high-strength steroid creams. Unfortunately, these excellent results have not yet become widely known among doctors, so few children with atopic eczema are receiving antihistamines at present.

No one yet knows if other antihistamines have the same effect as cetirizine. Only ketotifen, which is an atypical anti-histamine (see p. 159) has been studied. It too protected some children with allergies from developing asthma.

Immunotherapy may also have a protective effect. One study, involving children suffering from nasal allergies, found that those given immunotherapy were less likely to develop asthma (see p. 165). Another study shows that immunotherapy for children with mite allergy halves the risk of their developing new allergic reactions to other allergens.

Index

Numbers shown in **bold type** indicate either definitions of technical terms or the main entry on a topic

Useful addresses

SUPPORT ORGANISATIONS

United Kingdom

The British Allergy Foundation
Deepdene House
30 Bellgrove Rd
Welling
Kent DA16 3PY

Tel: 020 8303 8525

Runs a telephone helpline, where callers can obtain immediate advice from an experienced allergy nurse. The helpline is open from 9am– 5pm, Monday to Friday, on 020 8303 8583. There are also support groups throughout the UK, which organise regular meetings and can give advice. You need to join BAF to be part of a local group.

BAF was founded by a group of medical specialists with the aim of improving awareness, prevention and treatment of allergy. It is therefore very orthodox in its approach, and in the advice given.

The Anaphylaxis Campaign
PO Box 149
Fleet
Hampshire GU13 0FA

Tel: 01252 542029
Fax: 01252 377140
Website: www.anaphylaxis.org.uk

An excellent campaigning organisation that must have saved many lives through its hard work in making caterers and food manufacturers aware of the risks of food allergy. The newsletter will keep you up to date with potential new hazards. Runs awareness workshops for teenagers with anaphylaxis, and publishes useful material for younger children.

National Asthma Campaign
Providence House
Providence Place
London N1 0NT

Tel: 020 7 226 2260
Helpline: 0845 7 010203
Fax: 020 7704 0740
Website: www.asthma.org.uk

This is staffed from 9am–7 pm, by trained asthma nurses who can answer queries about asthma. Calls are charged at local rates.

National Eczema Society
163 Eversholt Street
London NW1 1BU

Tel: 020 7388 4097

Republic of Ireland

Asthma Society of Ireland
Eden House
15-17 Eden Quay
Dublin 1

Tel: 1 878 8511
E-mail: asthma@indigo.ie

Australia

Allergy and Environment Sensitivity Support and Research Association
PO Box 298
Ringwood
Victoria 3134
Australia

Tel: 03 9888 1382

National Asthma Campaign
(Australia)
1 Palmerston Crescent
South Melbourne
Victoria 3205

Tel: 03 9214 1476
Fax: 03 9214 1400
Hotline: 1800 032 495 (for ordering publications)
E-mail: nac@netlink.com.au

Asthma Foundation of Western Australia
61 Heytesbury Rd
Subiaco
Western Australia 6008

Tel: 08 9481 1234
Fax: 08 9481 1292

Asthma Victoria
69 Flemington Rd
North Melbourne
Victoria 3051
Tel: 03 9326 7088
Fax: 03 9326 7055

New Zealand

Allergy Awareness Association
PO Box 120701
Penrose
Auckland 6
New Zealand

Tel: 09 303 2024

The Asthma and Respiratory Foundation of New Zealand
PO Box 1459
Wellington
New Zealand

Tel: 04 499 4592 (subject to change in 2001)
Fax: 04 499 4594 (subject to change in 2001)
Website: www.asthmanz.co.nz
E-mail: arf@asthmanz.co.nz

Produces various useful leaflets and a newsletter. There are also local asthma associations throughout New Zealand; this central organisation can put you in touch with these.

Asthma New Zealand
581 Mt Eden Road
Auckland
P O Box 67 066
Mt Eden

Tel: 09 623 0236
Fax: 09 623 0774
E-mail: aas@asthma-nz.org.nz

OCCUPATIONAL ALLERGIES

If you are concerned about occupational allergies and asthma, try the excellent website maintained by the Department of Public Health Sciences at Edinburgh University:

www.med.ed.ac.uk

This includes a Directory of Internet Sites in Occupational and Environmental Health, which you can use to pursue your particular query or concern.

Australian readers may also like to try the site maintained by the National Occupational Health and Safety Commission of Australia: www.worksafe.gov.au

EMERGENCY ALERT BRACELETS

Anyone who suffers from anaphylactic shock (see p. 58) should wear an emergency alert bracelet or pendant. Key medical information is engraved on the bracelet, and there is also a telephone number which gives medical staff access to a computer database where essential medical data about you is available. These useful items are sold by a non-profit-making company:

MedicAlert Foundation
2323 Colorado Avenue
Turlock, California 95382-2018

Consult their web page for national organisations: www.medicalert.org

ANTI-ALLERGY PRODUCTS AND FURTHER INFORMATION

For sources of the anti-allergy products mentioned in this book, a comprehensive list of suppliers, and consumer information about anti-allergy products, log on to the Allergy-Intolerance website at:

www.allergy-intolerance.com

From there, you can go direct to the websites of support organizations, suppliers, etc. Alternatively, if you only have limited access to the Internet (e.g. in a public library), you can print out the details found there and contact the groups that interest you by post or telephone.

Allergy news updates, and articles by medical specialists on particular topics, are also available on the Allergy-Intolerance website, plus details of all patient support organizations, medical associations, sources of recipes, and other information resources. You can pose questions there on any of the subjects covered by this book. You can also comment on anything in this book, and share your personal experiences of allergy and intolerance with others via this website.

ACKNOWLEDGEMENTS

Linda Gamlin would like to thank Professor Jonathan Brostoff and Dr Anthony Ham Pong for their many helpful comments on the text, Dr Michael Tettenborn for his advice about atopic eczema, and Dr Michel Joffres and Brenda Sabo for their observations on provocation-neutralisation. Thanks also to Professor John Warner for some very useful discussions, to David Reading of the Anaphylaxis Campaign for answering innumerable queries about food allergy and food labelling, and to Dr Hedda Kraker von Schwarzenfeld, Dr David Stern, Scott Adams of Celiac Support, and Dr Maurice Smith of Unilever for help with specific questions. All the other doctors, medical researchers and other health professionals whose work is described here, either directly or indirectly, are also gratefully acknowledged. Thanks are also due to Chris Allan, Denise Curwen, Janet Davies, Dee Gill, Ruth Simmons, Vicki Young and the many other allergy sufferers whose stories are told in these pages, and to Hilary Mandleberg, Charlotte Harvey and Elizabeth Stubbs for sharing their experiences as parents. Finally, special thanks are due to Dr John Hart for his immense help during the final stages of the book.

PICTURE CREDITS

2 left Bubbles/Anthony Dawton; 2 centre & right Patrick McLeavey; 3 robertharding.com/N A Callow; 4 NHPA/ Stephen Dalton; 6 left Gettyone Stone/Peter Cade; 6 centre The Image Bank/Joe Devenney; 6 right Gettyone Stone/Laurence Monneret; 8 The Image Bank; 10 Science Photo Library; 14 Anthony Blake Photo Library/Maximilian Stock Ltd; 16 Gettyone Stone/Laurence Monneret; 20 The Image Bank/Joe Devenney; 22 Gettyone Stone/Peter Cade; 24 left Bubbles/Loisjoy Thurston; 24 centre Gettyone Stone/James Darrell; 24 right Anthony Blake Photo Library/Maximilian Stock Ltd; 26 NHPA/Stephen Dalton; 28 Gettyone Stone/James Darrell; 30 robertharding.com /Ydav Levy; 33 Bubbles/Loisjoy Thurston; 36 Gettyone Stone/Ralph H Wetmore; 41 The Image Bank/Paola Curto; 42 Bubbles/Loisjoy Thurston; 47 Collections/Sandra Lousada; 50 Elizabeth Whiting & Associates/Midgley; 54 The Stock Market/Mauro Panci; 58 robertharding.com/Mitch Diamond; 60 Science Photo Library/Claude Nuridsany; 62 Anthony Blake Photo Library/Martin Brigdale; 64 Anthony Blake Photo Library/Kieran Scott; 67 Anthony Blake Photo Library/Tim Hill; 68 Gettyone Stone/Jon Gray; 70 Anthony Blake Photo Library/Maximilian Stock Ltd; 72 Gettyone Stone/ Laurence Monneret; 74 Anthony Blake Photo Library; 76 robertharding.com/John Miller; 80 Gettyone Stone/P Cade; 82 Science Photo Library; 84 Gettyone Stone/Roy Botterell; 86 left Gettyone Stone/Tony Latham; 86 centre Science Photo Library/BSIP, Jolyot; 86 right The Image Bank/Ross Whitaker; 88 Gettyone Stone/Tony Latham; 90 Science Photo Library/BSIP, Taulin; 94 Science Photo Library/BSIP, Jolyot; 98 Linda Gamlin; 102 The Image Bank/Ross Whitaker; 106 Bubbles/Loisjoy Thurston; 108 left Bubbles/Jennie Woodcock; 108 centre robertharding.com/Nelly Boyd; 108 right The Image Bank/Stephen Wilkes; 110 Anthony Blake Photo Library; 112 robertharding.com/N A Callow; 114 Gettyone Stone/Ian Shaw; 120 Gettyone Stone/Pal Hermansen; 124 Bubbles/Jennie Woodcock; 126 The Image Bank/Stephen Wilkes; 128 robertharding.com/Nelly Boyd; 132 DIAF/J C Gerard; 136 left Patrick McLeavey; 136 centre Bubbles/Ian West; 136 right Linda Gamlin; 138 Patrick McLeavey; 140 Linda Gamlin; 148 John Walmsley; 152 Bubbles/Ian West; 164 The Image Bank/Noah Cross; 170 Patrick McLeavey; 172 Gettyone Stone/Joe Polillio; 176–192 Patrick McLeavey; 194 Bubbles/Loisjoy Thurston; 202 Gettyone Stone/ Laurence Monneret; 204 Patrick McLeavey; 206 Katz Pictures/Adrian Kool; 208 Gettyone Stone/Andy Whale; 208 left robertharding.com/Scott Campbell; 208 centre John Walmsley; 208 right Rex Features; 210 Retna/Philip Reeson; 214 Gettyone Stone/Andy Whale; 216 Rex Features; 218 John Walmsley; 222 robertharding.com /Scott Campbell; 226 Gettyone Stone/Zugy Kaluzny; 232 Gettyone Stone/Jon Bradley; 240 Bubbles/Anthony Dawton; 244 Linda Gamlin; 248 Powerstock Zefa.